On the Subject of Citizenship

On the Subject of Citizenship

Late Colonialism in the World Today

Edited by
Suren Pillay

BLOOMSBURY ACADEMIC
LONDON • NEW YORK • OXFORD • NEW DELHI • SYDNEY

BLOOMSBURY ACADEMIC
Bloomsbury Publishing Plc
50 Bedford Square, London, WC1B 3DP, UK
1385 Broadway, New York, NY 10018, USA
29 Earlsfort Terrace, Dublin 2, Ireland

BLOOMSBURY, BLOOMSBURY ACADEMIC, and the Diana logo are trademarks
of Bloomsbury Publishing Plc

First published in Great Britain 2023

Cover design by Charlotte Daniels

A catalogue record for this book is available from the British Library.

A catalog record for this book is available from the Library of Congress.

ISBN: HB: 978-1-3502-2895-5
PB: 978-1-3502-2899-3
ePDF: 978-1-3502-2897-9
eBook: 978-1-3502-2896-2

Typeset by Deanta Global Publishing Services, Chennai, India

To find out more about our authors and books visit www.bloomsbury.com and
sign up for our newsletters.

For Thandika Mkandawire and Sam Moyo

I dedicate this volume to the memory of two of Africa's finest intellectuals and raconteurs, the late Thandika Mkandawire (1940–2020) and Sam Moyo (1954–2015). In conversations, both strongly encouraged me to commemorate the book's significance with an event and a publication. Sam Moyo was supposed to join us as a contributor to this volume but tragically passed away in a car accident in Delhi a few months before the colloquium. Mkandawire and Moyo were exemplars of a combative criticism conducted in solidarity and friendship with Mahmood Mamdani, where ideas were forged, and arguments sharpened, often in the trenches of that insurgent intellectual community headquartered in Dakar, Senegal, the Council for the Development of Social Science Research in Africa (CODESRIA).

Contents

Acknowledgments   viii

List of Contributors   ix

Introduction: On the Subject of Citizenship—Theorizing Postcolonial
Predicaments with Mahmood Mamdani *Suren Pillay*   1

1   Decolonizing the World: On Mamdani's Thought *Kuan-Hsing Chen*   9

2   Of Citizen(s) and Subject(s): Mamdani on Research, Methods, and
Commitments in Postcolonial Africa *Siba N'Zatioula Grovogui*   27

3   Thinking with Citizen and Subject *Talal Asad*   45

4   Beyond the Custom/Market Dichotomy: Women's Rights to Land and
the Challenge of the Commons *Nivedita Menon*   61

5   Empire in the Era of DIY Colonialism: Barbarism or Slavery in the
(Post)Colonial Context? *Abdelwahab El-Affendi*   85

6   The Contemporary Challenge of Citizenship in Ethiopia and the Role of
Empire in the Making of Subject Populations *Namhla Thando Matshanda*   103

7   Political Identity and Postcolonial Democracy *Karuna Mantena*   123

8   Colonial Legacies of Ethnicized Violence, Gendered Subjectivity, and
Feminist Emancipatory Politics *Lyn Ossome*   141

9   The Bifurcated Society: Citizen and Subject in Contemporary South
Africa *Steven Friedman*   155

10   Predicaments of the Colonized: Being Coloured, Indian, and Free after
Apartheid *Suren Pillay*   173

11   The Legacy of Bandung *Partha Chatterjee*   189

12   Looking Back, Looking Forward *Mahmood Mamdani*   209

Index   221

Acknowledgments

The first and obvious debt of gratitude for this volume goes to a book, *Citizen and Subject: Contemporary Africa and the Legacy of Late Colonialism* (1996) and its author. It was Mahmood Mamdani's attempt to make sense of political violence through a reflection on the colonial legacy of citizenship that sparked debate and new directions of scholarship, like few books coming from the African continent did, in the 1990s. And continues to do so. The gathering of interlocutors who assembled in 2016, along with Mahmood Mamdani, at the University of the Western Cape in Cape Town to mark the twentieth-anniversary commemoration of the book, brought with them a generosity of spirit that deserves the second debt of gratitude. Most of those reflections have found their way into this volume. I would like to thank the presenters and those who contributed as discussants and chairs to that event. The colloquium itself was made possible through a generous grant from the Andrew W. Mellon Foundation, and I wish to thank Saleem Badat for his support. The event was hosted by the Centre for Humanities Research, and I thank the then director, Premesh Lalu. My colleagues Heidi Grunebaum, Patricia Hayes, Leslie Witz, Ciraj Rassool, Lameez Lalkhen, and Michelle Smith provided additional support, both intellectual and logistical. Ruchi Chaturvedi offered constant guidance and assistance. In shepherding the articles toward publication, I would like to especially thank Ursula Arends for her professionalism as copyeditor. My first contact with Bloomsbury Press was with Tomasz Hoskins, who welcomed the idea of the volume with enthusiasm. I then had the good fortune to work with Nayiri Kendir as editorial assistant and Atifa Jiwa as commissioning editor. I wish to thank them, as well as the contributors, for their patience and continuous support.

Thank you to the publishers for permission to reprint the following articles:

Chatterjee, P. (2017), 'The Legacy of Bandung' in Eslava, M. Fakhri, & V. Nesiah (Eds.), Bandung, Global History, and International Law: Critical Pasts and Pending Futures Cambridge: Cambridge University Press.

Chen, K. H. (2017), 'Review essay: on Mamdani's mode of thought' in Cultural Studies, 31:4, 580–601.

Friedman, S. (2021), 'The Bifurcated Society: Mahmood Mamdani, Rural Power and State Capture' in Prisoners of the Past: South African Democracy and the Legacy of Minority Rule. Wits University Press: Johannesburg.

Mamdani, M. (2018) 'Preface' in Citizen and Subject: the Legacy of Late Colonialism, Princeton University Press: New Jersey.

Contributors

Talal Asad is Distinguished Emeritus Professor of Anthropology, City University of New York, United States. His research interests include religion and secularism, Islamic traditions, political theories, and the Middle East. His most recent publications include *On Suicide Bombing* (2017).

Partha Chatterjee is Professor Emeritus of Anthropology and of Middle Eastern, South Asian, and African Studies, Columbia University, United States. His research interests include slavery, colonialism, race, racial capitalism, war, nationalism, displacement, trauma, institutions, law, governmentality, empires, states, and sovereignties. His most recent publications include *I Am the People: Reflections on Popular Sovereignty Today* (2020).

Kuan-Hsing Chen is Professor, Institute for Social Research and Cultural Studies, Chiao Tung University, Taiwan. His research interests include inter-Asian cultural studies. Among his most influential publications is *Asia as Method: Toward Deimperialization* (2010).

Abdelwahab El-Affendi is Provost and Acting President, Doha Institute for Graduate Studies, Qatar. His research interests include political science, mass violence, democracy and democratization, and Middle East politics. He is the author of a number of books, including *For a State of Peace: Conflict and the Future of Democracy in Sudan* (2002).

Steven Friedman is Research Professor, Politics Department, University of Johannesburg, South Africa. His research interests include the study of democracy. His most recent publications include *Prisoners of the Past: South African Democracy and the Legacy of Minority Rule* (2021).

Siba N'Zatioula Grovogui is Professor of International Relations Theory and African Political Thought, Cornell University, United States. His research interests include international relations theory, political theory, and African thought. He is currently in the final phase of completion of a manuscript titled *The Gaze of Copernicus: Postcolonialism, Serendipity, and the Making of the World* (forthcoming).

Karuna Mantena is Professor of Political Science, Columbia University, United States. Her research interests include modern political thought, modern social theory, the theory and history of empire, and South Asian politics and history. Mantena's recent publications include *Mass Satyagraha and the Problem of Collective Power* (2022).

Namhla Thando Matshanda is Senior Lecturer in Political Studies, University of the Western Cape, South Africa. Her research interests include international relations, African politics, and postcolonial processes of state formation in Africa; she is especially interested in local conceptions and articulations of statehood in the Horn of Africa. Her most recent publications include *Ethiopian Reforms and the Resolution of Uncertainty in the Horn of Africa State System* (2020).

Nivedita Menon is Professor of Political Thought, Centre for Comparative Politics and Political Theory, Jawaharlal Nehru University, India. Her research interests include political theory, feminist theory, and Indian politics. Her most recent publications include *Hindu Rashtra and Bollywood: A New Front in the Battle for Cultural Hegemony* (2021).

Lyn Ossome is Senior Research Associate at the University of Johannesburg, South Africa. She specializes in feminist political theory and feminist political economics. She is the author of *Gender, Ethnicity and Violence in Kenya's Transitions to Democracy: States of Violence* (2018).

Suren Pillay is Associate Professor, Center for Humanities Research, and Deputy Dean of Research and Postgraduate Studies, Faculty of Arts and Humanities, University of the Western Cape, South Africa. He has published on political violence, citizenship, and political and epistemic decolonization. His most recent publications include *The Problem of Colonialism: Assimilation, Difference, and Decolonial Theory in Africa* (2021).

Introduction

On the Subject of Citizenship—Theorizing Postcolonial Predicaments with Mahmood Mamdani

Suren Pillay

This book originates from a colloquium held to engage with the prominent Ugandan political theorist, Mahmood Mamdani's most influential text, *Citizen and Subject: Contemporary Africa and the Legacy of Late Colonialism* (1996). For more than four decades now Mamdani has been a prolific and influential scholar, at first primarily in the study of Africa but also of the postcolonial world and global politics. His work continues to illuminate our understanding of conflicts of belonging and citizenship through their fine-grained historical interpretation.

In a broader sense, the collection explores the relationship between the colonial past, the postcolonial present, and how we might imagine a future politics differently. It is concerned with two central questions: first, how does the politics of naming that colonialism has put into play continue to shape the polarizations of violence we see in postcolonial democracies, from South Africa to Sudan, from India to Ethiopia, to the fates of global emancipatory visions that once were, such as Bandung? And second, how might we best decolonize knowledge if we wish to decolonize the legacy of citizenship?

This is the first book-length volume that takes an influential text of Mamdani as an argument about how to theorize the world today. Critical engagements with his texts are numerous, but specific—they have debated his study on the Rwandan genocide (Mamdani, 2002), his take on the "war on terror" after 9/11 (Mamdani, 2004), or his critique of liberal humanitarianism in Darfur (Mamdani, 2009). But none have treated a text of his from a range of geographical and historical vantage points, as a work of political theory that extends beyond case studies, into a method for theorizing contemporary predicaments of postcolonial freedom from the vantage point of the South. In this volume, scholars engage with Mamdani as a critical thinker who does not just tell us specific things about specific places at specific times. As some of chapters here argue, embedded in his writing is an important method for understanding political predicaments shared in common.

When Mamdani posed the question in *Citizen and Subject* of the problem of postcolonial Africa as the question of not only how Europe underdeveloped Africa but also how "Europe ruled Africa," it broke new ground in contemporary scholarship on violence in post-independence Africa (Ogot, 2009). It turned our attention to the *political* question of citizenship and belonging as central to making sense of seemingly intractable conflicts. If we were to move toward emancipative, less violent, and more democratic societies in Africa, *Citizen and Subject* argued that we would have to reimagine political community as grounded in the particular histories that colonial rule had bequeathed us. In the more than twenty years since the publication of *Citizen and Subject*, the arguments in the book have been taken up in a range of different ways in Africa, and across the previously colonized world (see Austen, 1996; Carbone, 1996; Lonsdale, 1996; Cooper, 1997; Tignor, 1997; Youé, 2000; De Goede, 2017).

To the despair of a number of scholars, many political elites, and modernizing nationalists alike, contemporary political violence across the globe remains significantly expressed in terms of identity—all the particular attachments—like race, ethnicity, religion, and patriarchy—that colonial secular modernity promised to emancipate the colonized from (see Jackson and Rosberg, 1982; Bates, 1983; Huntington, 1993; Hoffmann and Ignatieff, 1994; Easterly and Ross, 1997; Appiah, 2001; Bikhu, 2008; Castells, 2010; Hall, 2012). The promise and hope of liberal political modernity, in particular, was that it would offer a political form—the nation-state; a political value—that of universal equality; and that it would cultivate freedom as individualized, with minimal external impediments (Mason, 1999; Kennedy, 2000; Abizadeh, 2002; Benhabib, 2002; Sen, 2008). Of course, the threshold of achieving these was constantly to be renegotiated if you were a colonized subject under tutelage. The abstract story of liberal freedom is also then the concrete history of imperial and colonial conquest. The teleological assumption of this modernity was that freedom, equality, and modernity would result in the dissolution and loosening of the hold of particular attachments, whether these be religious, ethnic, or racial, on the individual, other than the national. Attachments were consigned to the sphere of "culture," while freedom was designated as that which flourished in the sphere of individualized civic life. If the former was static, fixed, regressive, conservative, and traditional, the latter was dynamic, changing, emancipative, modern, and progressive. The grounds of a modern political community, coupled with its complementary economic form—a market economy—offered liberals the promise of a peaceful future best suited to the flourishing of human freedom. In Africa, in particular, the trouble in realizing this image of the good society has been defined as the cultural problem of the persistence of tribalism (Bates, 1974; Jackson and Rosberg, 1982; Ndegwa, 1997; Herbst, 2000; Ranger, 2012).

We might add now more prominently religion and race to that persistence of particulars. These are said to work against the aspiration toward abstract equality and citizenship. While most liberals concurred that these would evaporate over time, many on the left shared this modernist assumption as well, even though critical of the usefulness of political instability for the interests of global capital. Recall the famous slogan of the late Mozambican leader, Samora Machel: "For the nation to live, the tribe must die" (Darch and Hedges, 1975). To make sense of the persistence of particulars, many on the left theorized identity as the strategic invention and deployment of premodern categories now mobilized to secure economic interests, particularly the control of the natural resources that made neocolonies useful only for their primary commodities (Amin, 1972; Rodney, 1973). The insights of political economy were remarkable, but by the 1990s, in the wake of the end of the Cold War, and the resurgence of identity politics, they were increasingly found to be wanting in explanatory valence by some scholars (e.g., key interventions here were Chatterjee, 1986; Anderson, 2006; Hall, 2012).

It was in this political-conceptual conjuncture that *Citizen and Subject*'s stakes were mapped.[1] If we are to think our way out of these postcolonial predicaments, we would have to theorize the question of "the political," as Hannah Arendt might say (Wolin, 1983), or seek a practice of political reform, as Mamdani argued, in an autonomous sphere that needed to be theorized on its own terms. Not that it was a sphere not shaped in relation to other domains of power—the economy, culture, and society. But political identity needed historicizing as a discreet object, not collapsible into cultural identity, nor overdetermined by economic logics. It was a reminder of a Fanonian political injunction: the horizon of anti-colonial freedom should not require reproducing the legacies of colonial rule, but transcending it. If emancipation was to decolonize the political sphere, it would be necessary to decolonize citizenship.

Even more acute expressions of political violence articulated in identitarian forms define our political present. The centrality of historicizing citizenship, difference, and majority and minority distinctions remains therefore even more germane to making sense of contemporary violence. We are reminded that promises of liberal freedom and the "powers of the secular modern" remain not only hegemonic but also intensely chimerical and inadequate both to think with and to construct political community out of.

Our current predicaments petition us to revisit—as we do here—questions that *Citizen and Subject* posed to us: inquiries about the inheritances of citizenship defined by imperial and colonial rule and the challenges these continue to pose for the promises of emancipation and equality for political subjects who might be said to always be defined by attachments.

This book critically appreciates this seminal text by inviting an intergenerational group of scholars across the world, some of whom are among the most prominent writing on these questions today, to reflect on contemporary political violence and citizenship, as interlocutors.

More specifically, it is a volume of chapters that takes Africa as the entry point to the question of how to theorize predicaments of postcolonial freedom in most of the world—a world inaugurated to political modernity through the colonial encounter. It takes a seminal text written about Africa by an African intellectual to excavate a method of theorizing. But it does not confine that theorizing to the boundaries of area studies or of disciplinary reason; neither is it limited to African studies nor to political science. Rather, we take the text and an engagement with its author as an invitation for historicizing the legacy of the past on the present and for thinking political futures on a worldly scale.

We find affinities here with a range of current scholarly efforts that have been animated by the injunction to decolonize knowledge and to produce "theory from the South." These range from works that have explicitly named their intentions as such, such as a volume of essays by the anthropologists Jean and John Comaroff (2012), to collective intellectual projects, such as the South Asian initiative, Subaltern studies,

---

[1]   I am drawing on conjuncture as theorized in Scott (2001).

to the Latin American group affiliated to "Decolonial Thinking" (see Mignolo and Vasquez, 2013). What loosely resonates across these heterogeneous intellectual efforts is a shared weariness of the claims of historicism and its teleological assumptions that present Europe's past as the future of those waiting or struggling to catch up, with the rest considered deviations from the norm. But unlike some of these texts and scholars, for example, Jean and John Comaroff's theorizing of the question, and Achille Mbembe's insights on the post-colony (2001), taken explicitly as works of "theory," this volume places its accent elsewhere—less on diagnosing the present as a pathological and dystopian condition. Nor is its gesture in reversing the gaze by finding in the present of the South the future of the North. Where Mbembe's oeuvre conceptually seeks to release us from "history" in favor of a critique of postcolonial agency, it might be said that the emphasis on the *colonial legacy* in *Citizen and Subject* suggests that the institutional forms of colonial rule have not only structured postcolonial responses but also enabled forms of resistance to it that we think cannot be disavowed theoretically. The volume therefore places its accent on *historicizing* the present. It takes the question of historical legacy as a political-methodological frame—though it must be said, not an overdetermining limit—within which to think about how postcolonial politics has unfolded, and politically as the terrain that a decolonized political community will have to create, by itself.

This book is organized around two themes. The first theme deals with *methods, stakes, and styles.* The first chapter offers what might be considered a broad introduction and biographical sketch. Chen provides an important interpretation of Mamdani's critical works from 1972 to the present, which, as a whole, constitutes what Chen argues is a "third-world" mode of thought. Inspired by his recent work on imperial human rights, decolonizing the university, and settler colonialism, among others, Chen proposes a programmatic agenda on "Decolonizing the earth: For a grounded global intellectual movement" to transform the world via a "return" to the *minjung* (people or popular) world as a basis to move toward a more livable earth beyond colonialism, imperialism, and the Cold War.

In the second chapter, Grovogui offers an allegorical interpretation of *Citizen and Subject* that highlights analytical, disciplinary, and institutional dimensions of the book that are eclipsed by the criticism that it has received. The chapter outlines some of these critiques and offers three arguments. The first is that the text may be read as a commentary on the inadequacies of the disciplines concerning our time, Africa, and the political experimentations required to confront its current crises of state, society, and institutions. There is a need to desacralize the disciplines as they exist in order to develop appropriate understanding of contemporary Africa. The second, flowing from the first, is that the text also debunks the algorithm of indexes and catalogs of metaphors, truisms, facts, methods, logics, and the like that constitute the operational archives of African studies. Finally, Grovogui argues that it brings into focus the relationships between the vocation of the intellectual and its attendant commitment, particularly in regard to the pertinence of scholarship and social projects.

Other chapters deal with the theme of *critical extensions.* Asad argues that *Citizen and Subject* deals with institutional segregation between European and non-European races in Africa as well as between urbanized citizens and rural subjects that represented rights-based civil society and custom-based tribal society, respectively, dichotomies that defined at once the system of colonial rule and the character of the resistance it generated. Asad asserts that the book's overall argument is that in the colonial period "ethnicity [was] a dimension of both power and resistance, of both the problem and the solution." Once racial segregation was done away with after independence, the real structure of power emerged more clearly, based as it was, not on exclusion but on the incorporation of ethnic groupings into the modernizing state. Consequently, the challenge raised in the present predicament of African states is this: "[I]f power reproduced itself by exaggerating difference and denying the existence of an oppressed majority, is not the burden of protest to transcend these differences without denying them?" This chapter further explores Mamdani's insight by agreeing with it and also by turning it around and extending it to the liberal democratic states of Euro-America: Yes, he argues, the power of the majority and its ability to resist those who control the state (as well as its relationship to how the state identifies itself) need to be problematized. But it is the sovereign nation-state that, for all the good things it now offers its citizens, also needs to be problematized. The chapter pursues this point by reference to the way the modern state has been formed: first in Egypt (an African country that was also subject to European colonial rule) and then, through a discussion of Michel Foucault's idea of "governmentality," in Euro-America.

In the following chapter, Menon notes that bringing women into the ambit of individual property rights has long been one of the key issues in feminist practice and scholarship. Her chapter focuses on land ownership and the growing recognition that in the face of large-scale land acquisitions for corporate globalization, the only real challenge to capitalist ambitions is posed by collective ownership of land and strong assertions of the commons. At the same time, what is produced as "customary laws" of land ownership in postcolonial societies is dense with colonial interventions, as Mamdani's work has shown. This chapter considers feminist understandings of land rights for women in the twenty-first century, drawing largely on the Indian experience but also learning from how these issues play out in Africa as well as with movements of indigenous people globally.

El-Affendi's chapter illustrates that the power configurations that enabled the colonial order to sustain itself had also shaped the modern African state and continues to influence its character and trajectories. For example, the "sacredness" of the colonial borders was not just a principle adopted by the Organisation of African Unity (OAU) but also a real marker of lines of identity that continued to operate even against the OAU's own stated principle. The only African states to fragment (Somalia, Ethiopia, and Sudan) had done so along colonially constructed lines. However, enduring the impact of the colonial power configurations, the mechanisms that sustained the "decentralized despotism" of indirect rule remain only a small part of the picture, he suggests. The macro-explanations regarding "imperialism" and "new colonialism" (including dependency theory, world systems theory, etc.) also fall short of providing a fuller explanation. They often fail to account to the differential impact of the "world system" on specific cases. In this chapter, El-Affendi asks: What alternatives are there to the "decentralized despotism" of indirect-rule colonialism when dealing with external hegemonies in the postcolonial era? More to the point: do such alternatives exist? Is the much-vaunted South African "miracle" not just another enactment of this self-perpetuating colonialism? Is the postcolonial experience as a whole anything other than colonialism without (the physical presence and direct involvement of) the colonialists? Can scholarship, he provocatively asks, offer anything more substantial than lamenting this trap of "perpetual colonialism"?

In the following chapter investigating the processes of identity formation in the Harar and Jijiga localities of eastern Ethiopia during the period of the British Military Administration (BMA) from 1944 to 1954, Matshanda examines the impact of the antagonistic relationship between the Ethiopian state and the BMA. She illustrates how this period was characterized by the threat posed to Ethiopian sovereignty by the ambiguous presence of the BMA. The chapter demonstrates the significance of the presence of the BMA for people's perceptions of their national and ethnic identities in eastern Ethiopia. Matshanda argues that when Britain administered parts of eastern Ethiopia, there emerged a complex form of "decentralized despotism" where Ethiopian and British forms of domination collided in a bid to assert their authority. The focus of the contestation was to establish hegemony over sections of the population by categorizing them as either subjects or citizens. This collision was motivated by the contestation over Ethiopia's territorial claims in the region and Britain's attempts to "rectify" the "territorial problem." This chapter draws our attention to the more recent source of the complex and ongoing processes of identity formation in Ethiopia's eastern periphery. The current federal system in Ethiopia underscores ethnic identity where decentralization has introduced different and new forms of relating to both space and identity. However, this model has been shrouded in contradictions that challenge its ethnic basis. This chapter demonstrates that current discourses on identification in this area are not a post-1991 phenomenon but are part of an ongoing historical process of negotiating identification on the margins of the state.

The next chapter contends that political identities are neither natural nor cultural but the specific and direct consequence of state formation, in this case, colonial state formation. Mantena extends this insight by attending to the dynamics of democracy that have contributed to the politicization of identity and exacerbated political conflict and violence. She offers an account of "majoritarianism" and the concomitant increase in minority exclusion and vulnerability that seem coincident with deepening democratization. If law was the primary mode by which the colonial and postcolonial state inscribes, institutionalizes, and enforces political identity, in the case of democracy, we might, she argues, look to formal processes like elections where communal identities have proven especially resilient bases upon which to build political parties, coalitions, and patronage networks. Perhaps even more important and more elusive, Mantena concludes, are the deeper informal transformations of political imaginaries that accompany the logic and history of democracy.

In this chapter, Ossome asserts that the possibility of pursuing feminist emancipatory politics within liberal democracy remains a much-touted possibility in feminist scholarship. Yet the valorization of multiparty politics as a means of containing violence and stabilizing political contestation has not been borne out by experience in a number of African countries (Zimbabwe, Kenya, Côte d'Ivoire, Uganda). In those contexts, the increase in violence/gendered violence attached to politics lends multipartyism a particular paradox: an apparent consensus between normative freedom and violence. Furthermore, a significant body of scholarship shows the dialectical ways in which the liberal democratic pact is undermined by ethnic politics and the ways in which the politicization of ethnicity tends to deploy generalized and gendered violence in contexts of political competition. This latter problem, feminists have argued, can be traced to the complex ways in which ethnicity tends to map on to the bodies of women. For feminists struggling to make sense of violence amid democratization, argues Ossome, the contemporary predicaments foreshadowed by Mamdani's critique are twofold: first, that popular democracy inaugurated through multiparty politics cannot, in seeking to include everyone through its universalism, mediate an emancipatory path without apprehending the limits of its own identitarianism; and second, that particular injuries suffered by individuals and groups based on their class, racial, gender, or ethnic subjections are no longer apparent when examined within the very structures (of the liberal human rights discourses) that reproduce them as injuries. The violence that today accompanies the politicization of ethnicity may in this sense be regarded as the necessary means through which marginalized subjects of democracy seek to exceed identitarian boundaries to gain legibility within the democratizing state. Yet we must ask what it means for feminist emancipatory politics to similarly locate gendered violence associated with democratic contestations within the realm of the excess: what does it mean to lay claim on an ethnicized state that has historically tended to trivialize discourses (such as feminism) that fall outside of its parameters? Tracing the possibilities of feminist emancipatory politics through the dialectics of politicized ethnicity, Ossome explores the limitations inherent in the liberal construction of rights and how these limitations structure violent power—or power *as* violence—within the democratizing neoliberal state.

Friedman's chapter underscores that Mamdani's distinction between citizen and subject lies at the core of a contemporary South African reality—the society remains divided between those who enjoy substantive citizenship and those who are subject to coercive power. He asserts that the themes discussed in *Citizen and Subject* are particularly salient at a time when the divisions between citizen and subject, rural and urban, and civil society and the lived reality of the majority increasingly define politics—one symptom of which is an attempt by a section of the governing party to empower traditional authority structures. But, while Mamdani locates this division in the bifurcation of the state, Friedman argues that it is the bifurcation of society that creates and sustains this dichotomy between citizenship and subjection: the core reality in post-1994 South Africa is not the retention of the colonial state but that a change in state power has not altered the persistence of colonial power relations in society. The current attempt to impose traditional authority shows not the persistence of chiefly power but its erosion, argues Friedman—further evidence that bifurcation is a product of a social reality that the state did not create and which it is rarely able to influence.

In this chapter, Pillay scrutinizes instances of political tension in contemporary South Africa to explore the relationship between the legacies of the colonial administrative population categories and the political present. In particular, the chapter focuses on those population categories theorized by Mamdani as "subject races;" in the case of South Africa, these being Indian and "Coloured" minorities. The chapter, first, examines the inheritances of injustice and how they are playing out in post-apartheid South Africa, through a politics of space and a politics of naming from the vantage point of the "subject races." Second, it explores how these predicaments bring to the fore the relationship between a universal political subject of equality and particularist demands for justice, both of which can mobilize legitimate claims for recognition, situated along different chronologies of suffering. And more broadly, it is interested here in how contemporary political discourses wrestle with colonial categories of administrative-political difference in the making of a post-apartheid future.

In the following chapter, Chatterjee presents a stark reminder that the idea of territorial sovereignty as developed in Europe was imposed on the Eastern world largely to mutually demarcate European colonial possessions. He argues that this also produced the idea of graded sovereignty and protectorates. The anti-colonial movements rejected imperial sovereignty and insisted on the equal right to sovereignty of all nations. This was the call at the Bandung Conference of 1955. Consequently, it defined colonialism and racial discrimination as the greatest impediments to human rights. The chapter concludes by showing how the significance of human rights has changed, while the demand for equal sovereignty of nations remains unfulfilled.

In the concluding chapter, Mahmood Mamdani reflects on the key thematics and critiques of *Citizen and Subject*, not only restating but also reworking some of the central arguments from the vantage point of the present.

1

Decolonizing the World

On Mamdani's Thought

Kuan-Hsing Chen[1]

Introduction

For the Chinese readers living in mainland China, Taiwan, Hong Kong, Macau, and the Mandarin-speaking communities in Singapore, Malaysia, and elsewhere, we have considered the historical trajectories and structural position of the Third World. In addition, we have also shared broad common experiences with various regions in Asia, Africa, and Latin America, including colonialism and its legacy, civil war, Cold War, mass migration, refugee resettlement, late-coming capitalism, compressed modernity, strongman politics, ethnic conflicts, democratic transitions, and so forth. However, shackled precisely by the burden of these bleak experiences, we have been fixated by our attention solely on the West in the vain hope of imitating and eventually surpassing their successes, while jeopardizing the possibility of developing more affirmative, concrete, and meaningful understandings on and interactions with other Third World countries with comparable experiences. Consequently, because we failed to intellectually connect with these diverse experiences in the postcolonial world, we have often misjudged our own situations and our own positions in the world. Especially in the so-called era of globalization, such lack of knowledge about the Third World has inevitably distorted our worldview.

Due to my own involvement in organizing the conference series, *Bandung/Third World 60 Years* (2014–16), I had the fortune of making friends with the African intellectual Mahmood Mamdani. Having studied his major works and worked directly with him, I was deeply inspired by his ideas and visions. And I hope concerned readers would be able to encounter his ways of thinking, displayed through his concise writings that could contribute to alternative lines of knowledge production. Unlike the dominant systems of knowledge that always purport to be objective and universal, Mamdani's

[1] The text was written as the introduction to *Decolonizing the World: A Mahmood Mamdani Reader*, a collection of essays published in Chinese, translated by Flaneur (Taipei) in September 2016. I wish to thank Kit Wong for the translation of an earlier version of the text and Mahmood Mamdani for his support and friendship. This version was also translated by Kit Wong.

theorization is not only extremely sensitive to the local conditions of a society but also grounded on solid historical analyses. His engagement is always insightful and capable of explaining specific situations. Furthermore, the impulse of Mamdani's theorization has often been accentuated by his characteristically tenacious attempt to provide an imagination for political alternative. Mamdani's mode of thought is, I think, a sensibility shared by many Third World intellectuals, but it has been his ability to frequently intervene in important public issues with scholarly research, accompanied by his full grasp of the situations and the sagacity in his theoretical reasoning, that has made him stand out.

In spite of the enormous differences in terms of our regional configurations, the historical experiences of Africa and Asia overlap in one way or another. By comparing and contrasting the manifold unfolding of these experiences, it is possible to mutually reveal new problematics that are central to our historical processes but somehow covered up by all kinds of blind spots. Interactions and exchanges among Third World countries have always been constructive. Through Mamdani and Sam Moyo (a great friend who unfortunately passed away in 2015), we were introduced to the pan-African intellectual network Council for the Development of Social Science Research in Africa (CODESRIA), a transnational and transregional forum that for the past five decades has been able to produce a modern intellectual tradition for Africa and strategically channel analyses and visions for Africa's future. Due to the pioneering works generated, CODESRIA has become a world-renowned institution. The (inter-)Asian intellectual community could only stand in awe of these phenomenal achievements. Therefore, by critically introducing Mamdani's thought to the Asian context, I hope that it would engender a productive dialogue among Third World intellectuals. Built on the works of our predecessors, we hope that the intellectual communities in Asia, Africa, and Latin America would find ways of directly connecting with each other in order to produce constructive solidarity.

Mamdani's Thought and His Time

Mahmood Mamdani was born in Mumbai in 1946 as a third-generation Ugandan citizen of Indian descent.[2] He grew up in Kampala, Uganda, and experienced firsthand the impacts of colonialism and the racial segregation system imposed by the British colonial rulers. As a result, he was drawn to the anti-imperialist nationalism movement, which subsequently informed his political consciousness and intellectual worldview. After Uganda's independence in 1962, as part of its global project during the Cold War, the United States offered scholarships to Ugandans as an "independence gift." Due to his outstanding academic achievements, Mamdani received this scholarship in 1963 to study engineering at the University of Pittsburgh. However, he quickly turned his attention to politics as he became more politically involved in the student movements and civil rights movements of the 1960s. After he left Pittsburgh in 1967 with a

---

[2] This section is largely based on an interview with Mahmood Mamdani. See Chen et al. (2016).

bachelor's degree in political science, he continued to the Fletcher School of Law and Diplomacy at Tufts University in Massachusetts to study political and economic development (1967–8) and then law and diplomacy (1968–9). As a PhD student in government at Harvard University (1969–74), he completed a far-reaching semester paper on the subject of population control, which was subsequently published as his first book, *The Myth of Population Control: Family, Caste and Class in an Indian Village* (Mamdani, 1972). Based upon the study of experiences in an Indian village, this book argues that the failure of population control policy in the Third World cannot be explained by the irrational attitudes of the peasantry but has to be placed in the overall harsh conditions of the society; and to create conditions to change the attitude of the peasant population, wider structural problems embedded in poverty, caste, and class need to be changed first.

In 1972 Mamdani returned to Kampala and started working as a teaching assistant at Makerere University while conducting fieldwork for his PhD dissertation. Unfortunately, within one year he was expelled from Uganda by President Idi Amin's "economic war" against the Asian minority (formally known as the "Africanization in Commerce and Industry") in which Indians were stereotyped as being "only traders" and so "inbred" to their profession. Mamdani was then in exile in a refugee camp in London, where he completed his second book. *From Citizen to Refugee: Uganda Asians Come to Britain* is a touching story of how Indians were scapegoated by the Amin regime, providing the political economic background for Uganda's postcolonial politics (Mamdani, 1973). Shortly after the publication of that book, Mamdani secured a teaching position at the University of Dar es Salaam in Tanzania in 1973, and that was the beginning of his over forty-year-long academic career.

In 1974, he completed his PhD dissertation, which was later published as the book, *Politics and Class Formation in Uganda* (Mamdani, 1976). The monograph has become an indispensable work on contemporary Ugandan history, especially about the political shifts that took place during the 1950s and the 1970s. In it, Mamdani not only demonstrates his competence in Marxist political economic analysis but also starts to reveal his impressive sensibility in historicizing and theorizing the object of analysis, which has become the basic characteristic of his mode of thought. Mamdani's tenure at the University of Dar es Salaam continued until the overthrow of Amin in 1979, and that was the crucial period of the young teacher's intellectual formation. The 1960s and 1970s were times of intellectual upheaval. After Tanzania declared independence in 1963, its leader Mwalimu Julius Nyerere was heavily influenced by socialism and Mao Tse Tung's collectivization policy of agriculture in China. As Tanzania was undergoing radical social transformation, intellectuals also began to organize various socialist or communist reading groups in universities, where they discussed Karl Marx's *Capital*, the *Communist International*, the revolutions of the Soviet Union and China, peasant economy, and the political society of Uganda, among others. Thus, Marxism (political economic analyses) and the ideas from the Third World became the main theoretical resources for understanding problems in Africa, in part because they allowed students to historicize their postcolonial realities. It was around the late 1970s when Mamdani began his connection with the newly formed transnational civil society forum, CODESRIA, where his own "Pan-

Africanism" found an intellectual belonging, until today. And most importantly, through long-term interaction, mutual learning, and debates among members of the group coming from different locations, his sharp analytical ability to analyze Africa as a whole began to be molded and cultivated. For many African scholars, CODESRIA was thus the nurturing place where they could debate and develop a postcolonial vision for Africa.

Mamdani returned to Uganda after the fall of the Amin regime in 1980 to become a senior lecturer in political science at Makerere University. However, shortly after the new Milton Obote government took office, the Ugandan civil war (1981–6) broke out, and the space for public intellectual discussions generally deteriorated. Due to the close ties between the Obote regime and North Korea, Mamdani joined his friends to establish the Ugandan and North Korea Friendship Society, setting up some fifty branch offices in schools, factories, and villages throughout the country, organizing study groups and supporting the underclasses. That earned him a chance to visit Pyongyang via Beijing at the beginning of the 1980s. His 1984 book, *Imperialism and Fascism in Uganda*, was based on his political involvement during this period and was originally written for the railway workers as their study materials during their reading sessions (Mamdani, 1984). In this book, Mamdani carefully analyzes the role of transnational cooperation in exploiting Africa's agricultural economy and the complacency of the Amin regime regarding this project. He draws on the idea of "neocolonialism" to articulate the characteristic relation between domestic fascism and external imperialism. This insightful analytical framework is not only useful in understanding Uganda's political history but also sheds light on the nature of many postwar authoritarian regimes in Third World countries (exemplified by strongmen like Chiang Kai-shek, Park Chung-hee, Lee Kuan Yew, Suharto, etc.). Put simply, under the bipolarity of the Cold War, newly independent states very often found themselves in chaotic economic situations, lacking resources, and the emergence of various political forces, which provided the seedbed for imperialist interventions. "Neocolonialism" around this time often took the form of proxy politics in alliance with the local strong military leaders; through foreign aid and military supplies, the "old" colonists were able to establish authoritarian regimes in the Third World working in their favor. This proxy politics allowed the imperialists to maintain strong control over their former colonies or neocolonies. In many cases in Asia, Africa, and Latin America, this basic structure of Cold War proxy politics has lasted until today. Shortly after the publication of this book, Mamdani's citizenship was suspended in 1984 by the Obote regime due to his criticism of the government. He once again returned to Uganda in 1986 after the fall of the Obote regime and, realizing the importance of an independent research institution amid Uganda's political turmoil, in 1987 he established the Centre for Basic Research (CBR) in Kampala, with the support of CODESRIA. The aims were to create an independent intellectual network outside of the influence and boundary of the state and to connect the basic research of local politics, economy, and society with the wider Pan-African vision.

In 1991, Mamdani married Mira Nair, the leading Indian feminist filmmaker. Although he is of Indian descent, his African identity has always been paramount. This relation has deepened his lifelong connection with South Asia. Together with his later career in New York, Mamdani has become one of the very few tri-continental global intellectuals.

During his time serving as the executive director (1991–6) of the CBR, Mamdani extended the scope of his analysis to the southern part of Africa. In 1996, he published the classic *Citizen and Subject: Contemporary Africa and the Legacy of Late Colonialism*, in which he addresses two related questions. First, how has the structure of power in contemporary Africa been organized in the dynamic historical processes? Second, how has this mode of power structure conditioned and fragmented the possibility of popular resistance? In other words, Mamdani develops a historically grounded theory to explain the political impasse of contemporary Africa. The key lies in the lasting formation established in the process of colonial history: bifurcation between "race" (those who were identified as "citizens") and "ethnicity" (those who were identified as "subjects") in turn fragmented popular resistance and sustained (decentralized) state despotism. It is easy for an outsider to mistake the source of this postcolonial violence and neglect the colonial legal and social institutions without which systemic racism could not take place. However, Mamdani is able to identify the colonial system of "indirect rule," the institutionally enforced divisions of populations into separated "native authorities" governed by different sets of "customary laws," as the ultimate source of social and political division. In the context of Africa, colonialism sought to maintain a system of "decentralized despotism" by the "management of identities," which engineered the political partitions of a population into various "tribes," in effect, to prevent any united uprising against the colonial despotic regime. Furthermore, these colonially crafted identities could function well after the end of colonialism: as the postcolonial "democratization" of African nations was not able to overcome or decolonize those legal or political institutions that were directly responsible for these social divisions, they continue to be the source of racial conflicts and reproduce the dual legacy of colonialism. To sum up, the colonial systems of governance, in which (white) settlers were identified as "citizens" (governed by civil laws) and natives were identified as "subjects" (governed by customary laws), were reproduced in Africa's postcolonial period because the institutional decolonization of these societies had not taken place on these levels. In the postcolonial period, those who live in the urban areas have become "citizens" and those who live in the rural area remain as "subjects." Even though the central political power was handed over to the Black people as a result of national independence, the local or rural politics and the economy still functioned as they did in the colonial "despotic" period. This sophisticated theoretical framework, based on a comparative analytic perspective of Africa's political systems, as outlined in *Citizen and Subject*, provides the foundation for Mamdani's later work. This kind of grounded and transnational mode of analysis would be an extremely valuable source of reference for the (inter-)Asian intellectual community.

In 1996, Mamdani was appointed to the A. C. Jordan Chair in African Studies at the Centre for African Studies (CAS) at the University of Cape Town (UCT), Africa's first Chair in African Studies. For this post, the university required him to draft a syllabus for a class on "African Studies," mandatory for all students. As his class "Problematizing Africa" touched on many controversial issues that were politically sensitive especially in the post-apartheid period, such as the role of South Africa in the transatlantic slave trade, it was challenged by other existing opinions within the humanities faculty and triggered a public debate, attracting a very large audience. Following that debate, Mamdani delivered his inaugural lecture with the deliberately controversial title, "When does a settler become a native?" to a captive audience. In that lecture, Mamdani argued that the notion of "native" is a colonial construct, a prescribed political identity undergirded by colonial legal and political institutions, invented by the settler-colonists in the time of crisis. Therefore, the notion of "native" and its counterpart "settlers" (which is a political identity not always synonymous with "non-native") are both colonial concoctions sustained by the same legal distinction. The difference between them is not a cultural one alone but a political difference. Hence, Mamdani contended, there is really no way for the "settler" to become "native," since, if the difference between them were to be collapsed, both political categories "settler" and "native" would no longer exist as they were. Alternatively, the (legal as well as political) relationship between these two terms has to be transformed into something else entirely in order to end the reproduction of colonial indirect rule.

In the middle of the 1990s, when South Africa was in transition to become a post-apartheid society, reconciling the tension between white people and Black people, Mamdani's theoretical insight provided the basic framework under which true reconciliation could take place. Underlying Mamdani's theoretical intervention in these fundamental notions concerning political-colonial identities, it was also a larger project of decolonizing the universities, centering on the structure and content of the curriculum. Later labeled as the "Mamdani Affair," this event demonstrated his exceptional strength in countering popular opinions by elevating political dialogue to the level of public intellectual discussion, and he did it without sacrificing the theoretical originality of his thought. This resilience against populism and insistence on intellectual honesty has become Mamdani's style of thinking: in the following decades, in the face of enormous pressure, he continued to make interventions in many difficult public controversies, such as the Rwandan "genocide," the post-9/11 War on Terror, the war in Darfur and the "Save Darfur" movement in the United States, the imperialist agenda behind contemporary human rights movements, the decolonization of American settler colonialism, and so on.

In 1999, Mamdani left the African continent temporarily to take up a post at Columbia University, where he was appointed as the Herbert Lehman Professor of Government at the School of International and Public Affairs. Shortly after his arrival at Columbia, Mamdani published one of his most important books, *When Victims Become Killers: Colonialism, Nativism, and the Genocide in Rwanda*. The book is based on Mamdani's account of the root of the "unthinkable" 1994 Rwandan genocide. Living in Uganda, the neighboring country to Rwanda, Mamdani once again was able to historicize the colonial process that inevitably became the source of racial conflicts in postcolonial Africa and sought reconciliations in the decolonization of colonial institutions that were still functioning in the social fabric. Following his theoretical framework developed in *Citizen and Subject* that historicizes the crisis of civil rights in postcolonial time, *When Victims Become Killers* is an in-depth theoretical investigation of the regional histories of Rwanda. Mamdani traces the colonial-historical origin of the political identities of the "Hutu" and "Tutsi" and the shifting political functions in supporting colonial rules. Historically, inhabitants of the African Great Lakes region shared a common language, Kinyarwanda, but were politically and economically divided by European colonizers in the eighteenth and nineteenth centuries. By the 1920s and the 1930s, the Belgian colonial power imposed the identities of (or division between) "Tutsi" and "Hutu" onto the population based on cattle ownership and church records. Thus, Hutus were constructed as "natives," and Tutsis were framed as "foreigners." This "racially" defined difference had become the political origins for later conflicts. After the independence of Rwanda in 1962, similar to many other Third World countries, these colonially generated "racial" or "ethnic" differences continued to incite political conflicts, causing different "groups" to fight against each other in order to take control of the state. After thirty years of political deadlocks, the Rwandan Civil War and the "genocide" finally broke out. By historicizing the tragic trajectories in Rwandan history, Mamdani succeeds in explaining with clarity the "unthinkable" violence and proposing valid solutions. For the two opposing groups to peacefully live together, he argues, "justice" can no longer be understood as a monopoly by the victor and needs to be redefined as something shared by all the survivors. Justice, Mamdani maintains, ought to take the form of survivor's justice. Put simply, justice should not belong only to those in power, and it has to be based on a democratic process of reconciliation and negotiation in order to transcend the colonially established xenophobia or ethnocentrism. It is only by giving equal rights to all inhabitants of a country that racial and political conflicts can truly be settled. This powerful and passionately argued conclusion of *When Victims Become Killers* has become the basis for Mamdani's later writing on racial conflict and reconciliation.

When 9/11 happened in the United States in 2001, Mamdani was teaching at Columbia University and witnessed the public discussions that were unfolding. With the capacity cultivated in Africa to intervene in political society, he soon became involved. One week after 9/11, he participated in a New York City public forum to start discussing how to interpret this globally shocking event. Mamdani then spent the next one and a half years completing his most influential book to date, *Good Muslim, Bad Muslim: America, the Cold War and the Roots of Terror* (2004), which was immediately translated into seven languages after its publication. The title of the book is in part a reference to the idea that the American administration tries to incite divisions among Muslims and encourage those who are pro-America (the "Good Muslims") to conquer those with anti-American sentiment (the "Bad Muslims"). Against this imperialist approach to American foreign policy, Mamdani situates 9/11 in the context of the global history of the Cold War and argues that the perceived ideological connection between Islam and terrorism was an example of the politicization of culture. Specifically, it was the United States's failure in the Vietnam War that led Ronald Reagan to embrace the highly ideological politics of "good" against "evil" by conducting a proxy war with the militant nationalist governments in the Middle East. Reagan's central plan was to incite a religious schism inside Islam. However, after the end of the Cold War, America's proxy war against the Soviet Union backfired and paved the way for the growth of anti-American sentiments in the Middle East and "Islamic terrorism." In the face of the great public commotion after the events of 9/11, Mamdani once again succeeded in intervening in public discourses with his characteristic solid research and sound arguments. In 2008, Mamdani was listed as one of the "Top 20 Public Intellectuals" by *Foreign Policy* (US) and *Prospect* (UK) magazines.

Shortly after the publication of *Good Muslim, Bad Muslim*, Mamdani traveled back and forth between Darfur (Sudan) and New York for the research of his next book, *Saviors and Survivors: Darfur, Politics and the War on Terror* (2009). It would not be an overstatement to say that this book is an example of intellectual intervention in public political discourse *par excellence*. *Saviors and Survivors* challenges the basis of the US-based humanitarian advocacy group, the "Save Darfur Movement," comprised of nearly one million participants. Mamdani's analysis exposes how, in framing the crisis as a "genocide," the popular movement is completely out of touch with the reality in Darfur. The movement attempts to fit the crisis into a "rescue narrative" so that the United States could act as the "saviors" to "humanitarianly intervene" in the civil war in Darfur, while overlooking the fact that colonially tribalized Darfur is the victim of America's twenty-year-long interventionist policy in Chad and Sudan. Mamdani thus warns against any imprudent "humanitarian intervention" from the West that would very likely worsen the political situation in Darfur by furthering its internal political divisions. Mamdani vigorously demonstrates how these calls for humanitarian intervention lack the understanding of the historical source of postcolonial violence in Africa and of the recent changes in Darfur. Mamdani explains that the conflicts between the nomadic tribes from the north and the peasant tribes from the south originated from the colonial divisions of the population into "native" and "settler" and from the land policy that favored only the peasant tribes. Another factor was the failure of the Sudanese government to resettle the nomadic population when the country won its independence in the 1950s.

Based on the theoretical framework developed in *Citizen and Subject*, *Saviors and Survivors* shows Mamdani's capability to go against the popular movement supported by the state and nearly one million people and his insistence on intellectual analysis by historicizing the source of postcolonial violence that takes into account the local, national, and global conditions. He ultimately illustrates the power of historical analysis by arguing that historically, the nomadic groups in northern Darfur and those cultivating the land to survive in the south could peacefully coexist. English colonialism changed the conditions to tribalize the population in the first half of the twentieth century. Land policy gradually distinguished the nomads from the cultivators; the former became "settlers," and the latter became the "natives" who owned the land, which paved the way for conflict and crisis. In the 1950s, Sudan became independent, and the problems of the nation-state began to surface. To survive, especially when the weather was dry, nomads had to move to the areas owned by the peasantry. During the 1980s, these waves of contradiction escalated. The "land ownership right" (peasantry) versus the "civil right to survive," expressed in the form of "ethnic" conflict, eventually became a quasi-civil war, but never in the form of "genocide or ethnic cleansing," as alleged by the outsiders, such as the "Save Darfur Movement."

In the end, Mamdani proposes an alternative solution to US and UN military "humanitarian intervention." He advocates a negotiation mechanism for the political forces within Sudan in cooperation with the African Union, and the regional governments, in order to achieve a peaceful resolution for all parties through dialogues.

From *Good Muslim, Bad Muslim* to *Saviors and Survivors*, Mamdani has extended the scope of his internal comparative analysis of postcolonial African countries to address issues of global powers. To borrow a phrase from the prominent Japanese thinker Mizoguchi Yuzo, we could say that Mamdani's analytical scope has become "Africa as method, world as end." This line of thought continued in his later writings.

During the ten years of his full-time teaching stint at Columbia University (1999–2010), Mamdani maintained close ties with Africa. From 1999 to 2002, he served as the president of CODESRIA and succeeded in guiding the organization through its transitional period. During his academic leave in 2003, he returned to Makerere University and organized a research team to conduct a four-year investigation. The result was the publication of *Scholars in the Marketplace: The Dilemma of Neo-Liberal Reform at Makerere University, 1989–2005* (Mamdani, 2007). Focusing on the recent shift at Makerere University, the book brings to light the reality of the so-called "structural readjustment," rhetorically and strategically formulated by the World Bank. He regards this as a blatant neoliberalist attempt to change the direction of modernization projects developed in the Third World through market-oriented privatization and commercialization. In the sector of higher education, private interests should in the end overshadow public interests—a fundamental shift away from the university as a public institution. Through this analysis, Mamdani captures the central problems faced by African universities.

Mamdani's concerns with how to continue critical scholarship for knowledge production in Africa had facilitated his decision to return to Makerere University in 2010, where he became executive director of the Makerere Institute of Social Research (MISR), a position he retired from in 2022. Based on Mamdani's vision, MISR launched an interdisciplinary doctoral program in 2012 that provides basic training in social theory, history, political economy, and the study of culture. This program facilitates a network of Africa-based intelligentsia who are instrumental in driving continent-wide initiatives. In the design of the interdisciplinary doctoral program's syllabus, it was essential to read the history of intellectual debates in contemporary Africa, and also to establish connections with other intellectual traditions in the world, in order to develop a more comprehensive worldview and more global perspective. To a certain extent, this program is a continuation of the long-term intellectual endeavor of CODESRIA, with a specific emphasis on graduate-level training that was unfortunately lacking in the past. This doctoral program follows in the footsteps of Pan-Africanism and at the same time initiates the dialogues with different parts of the world.

Besides the impressive list of monographs written, Mamdani also edited six other important books and wrote numerous journal articles, columns, and media interviews for public affairs that deserve attention. One of his latest works, *Define and Rule: Native as Political Identity* (Mamdani, 2012), is based on three lectures (the W. E. B. Du Bois lectures) that he delivered at Harvard University. It contains his seminal thesis, developed over four decades, about the political structure of contemporary Africa. Tracing the intellectual formation of "indirect rule" back to the process of nineteenth-century colonial history, the book explores how the crisis of governmentality forced the empires to readjust their operating logics in India, British Malaya, and the Dutch East Indies, and then expanded and transplanted to Africa in the early twentieth century. Central to this new form of politics, he argues, is the idea of "define and rule" instead of the classical "divide and rule." The new policy of "native administration" classifies natives into different groups and then actively defines, restores, and preserves their culture and tradition, through legal systems and political institutions, to shape the subjectivity of the "native." In other words, notions such as "native," "tribe," and "settler" were all colonial inventions. Prior to that, in the cultural and economic lives, there was no clear system of classification and no clear boundary. With the colonial regime of the modern state, the governing machine actively incorporated classification and introduced boundaries into the political processes. In the process of "state formation" in colonies, identity was politicized and rigidified through legal and administrative practices; and the establishment of the tribal boundary in turn rediscovered the tradition to normalize and discipline the behavior and forms of life. In short, the political identity of "native" is never a natural given to begin with but a result of political practices. It was in the history of colonialism that theory and practice was articulated into knowledge production, becoming the basis for this new form of governmentality. The effect of this colonial knowledge has had a tremendous long-lasting impact and continued to function long after the independence of these nations. Even today, these colonially inscribed identities still govern the way in which we understand and identify ourselves. Therefore, how to liberate from the national history produced by the nation-state as a political system is an urgent task. How to decolonize and deconstruct a colonial worldview, how to dismantle the legacy of indirect rule, and how to rebuild political and legal systems are questions not simply for the African continent but for the entire postcolonial world, if not the globe.

The Problematics of Decolonization

In the previous discussion, we followed the course of Mamdani's thoughts and intellectual concerns formulated in his major works. In the remaining pages, we focus on three recently published essays written by Mamdani in order to highlight the problematics of decolonization. These essays have become the backbone for his most recent book, *Neither Settler nor Native: The Making and Unmaking of Permanent Minorities* (Mamdani, 2020).

Challenging the Imperialist Human Rights

"Beyond Nuremberg: The historical significance of the post-apartheid transition in South Africa" is an intervention to challenge the dominant tendency in the contemporary human rights discourse and movement that uphold the Nuremberg trials as the basis for achieving justice. Drawing on the experiences of political negotiations from South Africa in the 1990s, this chapter points out that the Nuremberg model was a way for the victorious nations of the Second World War to establish the principle of "individual" responsibility for the violation of human rights. Mamdani argues that this tendency only narrows the meaning of justice to criminal justice and individualizes the notion of justice in neoliberal fashion. Hence, the Nuremberg model should not be viewed as only a legal procedure in history but a specific (international) political arrangement that seeks to punish certain individuals for mass violence. Further, the model is extremely limited when it comes to the conflicts in civil war. To simply punish the violence committed in the past cannot help to create conditions so that different groups in conflict can live together in the future. In contrast to the Nuremberg model, Mamdani maintains that the South African experience of post-apartheid transition, particularly the Convention for a Democratic South Africa (CODESA) focusing on negotiations, instead of simply punishments, would in fact be a more appropriate model especially for resolving internal conflicts or civil wars. Similar to apartheid in South Africa, wars in Uganda, Rwanda, and Mozambique, the February 28, 1947 Incident and the white terror of the 1950s in Taiwan, the Indonesian mass killing of 1965–6, and the Communist Insurgency War in Malaysia were all examples of internal confrontations that were deeply divisive to a nation and could not be resolved through Nuremberg's victor's approach. The more difficult problem that has to be addressed in these cases is the recognition that both sides are merely "survivors" who have to share a common future together. Therefore, political reconciliations have to be prioritized, and this was precisely the path that South Africa had taken during its post-apartheid transition.

The South African CODESA model, moreover, can also be applied to cases other than internal conflicts within a nation. In the context of human rights issues that involved interstate conflicts, according to Mamdani's analysis of the logic of CODESA, on the one hand, it is necessary to contextualize (instead of demonize) the criminal violence that took place by historicizing its social and political conditions. On the other hand, in order to truly resolve the source of violence, it is also unavoidable to conduct internal political and structural reform (instead of relying on external forces of interventions to settle the problem). Theoretically and methodologically, the CODESA model aims to be inclusive, whether perpetrators, victims, beneficiaries, or bystanders, all are defined in the category of "survivor." If this survivor's justice were applied in the Nuremberg trials, it would have had a long-term future orientation; and the bombing of Hiroshima and Nagasaki or the Holocaust might not have resulted in the nuclear arms race or the lasting Palestinian-Israeli conflicts because, instead of focusing on punishing the perpetrators, the Nuremberg trials could have been a peace-building process for the international community. In Mamdani's words: "by turning its back on revenge, it offers the possibility of creating new communities of survivors" (Mamdani, 2015a: 82).

To sum up, "Beyond Nuremberg" challenges the hidden assumption behind contemporary human rights movements and forcefully argues that ethical judgments alone are fundamentally incapable of resolving political violence: any meaningful reconciliation has to be based on political and historical analyses that contribute to long-term political and structural reform in order to eliminate the conditions that give rise to such violence. Without a deeper understanding of the historical and political conditions of violence, any well-intended attempt to resolve political violence by external (often military) interventions would not only be futile but could also be complicit in the imperialist agenda.

American Settler Colonialism

"Settler colonialism: Then and now" relocates the United States at the earliest global history of settler colonialism and argues that without undergoing the intellectual and political process of decolonization, America not only misrecognizes itself as "exceptional" (the absence of feudal tradition and democratic revolution) but also misses out the momentum to reflect on itself as its archetypical colonialism, thereby overlooking the colonialist elements within American society. Simply put, America still lives in the conditions of settler colonialism.

Mamdani carries with him the problematics of settler versus native, developed in the African context to study the history of America. He discovers that, surprisingly, in Africa, in both colonial and independent periods, the native has always occupied a place in the center stage, theoretically and politically, but in the dominant narrative of the making of America, the notion of native is either absent or the native question is suspended, and, in effect, history is constructed from the point of view of the settler. The consequence is that, without critical reflection on the First World settler colonialism, whites (erasing the identity of settler) have naturally become the masters of the American continent. But if European settlers were located in the center of colonial history, all the romanticized past would have to be fundamentally questioned. From the point of view of the native, the "American revolution" was not really a revolution but a resurgence premised on the domination of Native Americans. In Mamdani's words:

> America [was] not just the first new nation; it [was] also the first modern settler state. What [was] exceptional about America [was] that it has yet to pose the question of decolonization in the public sphere. (Mamdani, 2015b: 608)

Another popular claim is that America "inherited" equality without the need for the strong arm of a central power due to the absence of feudalism. However, this claim would appear to be utterly false from the point of view of Native Americans or of African slaves working in plantations in the South: such claim could only make sense if one was ignorant about the genocide of Native Americans and the link between feudalism and slavery.

Historically, the political relation between white settler and native has been changing. In the beginning, the compromised agreement was that, as soon as the natives would "behave," they could have seats in the Congress of the shared state structure to represent themselves. However, in the most hypocritical fashion possible, this "acculturation" policy, proposed by George Washington and supported by Thomas Jefferson, was quickly replaced in 1830 by Andrew Jackson's Indian Removal Act (the dual policy of genocide and confinement). The Jackson administration betrayed all the promises to Native Americans and began the ethnic cleansing of Indians from east of Mississippi, arguing that genocide was "an inevitable consequence of progress" (Mamdani, 2015b: 611). By the end of Jackson's presidency, every tribe east of Mississippi and south of Lake Michigan, except for two tiny bands in Ohio and Indiana, was brutally removed. In total, the Jackson administration was responsible for the removal of seventy thousand southern Indians from their homes; eventually by

1944, only a few thousand survived in swamps and mountains. The next great wave of genocidal violence began in 1950, after California joined the Union; Governor Peter H. Burnett stated that "[the] war of extermination [would] continue to be waged between the two races until the Indian race became extinct" (quoted in Mamdani, 2015b: 612). Since then, a "two-state solution" was proposed for a white state east of the Mississippi and an Indian state west of the Mississippi. As expected, this solution did not last long. With the end of the American civil war in the 1860s, the promise of a two-state solution was betrayed and concluded with the idea of Indian reservation. From the point of view of the native, their fate has been nothing but a series of dissolutionment and waves of genocide.

Indeed, the "reservation regime" is the first of its kind and it resembles the tribalism of British colonial "indirect rule." The concentration of power in the head of a reservation/tribe was established through the legal system of native authority ruled by "customary laws." At the same time, a "pass system" was instituted to regulate the movement of the natives, a technology of governmentality learned from the plantation of the American South to control the flow of Black slaves. After the independence of South Africa in 1910, the white settler regime sent a delegation to North America, specifically to the United States, to study the history of the management of tribal homelands. The result of which became the 1913 Natives Land Act that declared 87 percent of the land for whites and divided the remaining 13 percent into tribal homelands for the native population. South Africa's apartheid was precisely modeled on American reservation. Today, we need to acknowledge the US government as the inventor of racial segregation. The Nazis' concentration camps in the 1940s were also inspired by President Lincoln's arrangement of Indian reservation started some eighty years ago, to confine the Jewish population. All in all, by situating the early history of America in the context of the historic development of colonialism, one could see that what is really exceptional is that America was the pioneer of the political technologies of settler colonialism.

In other words, in contrast to Africa's postwar (anti-colonial) independence movements that defeated European settler colonialism, forcing the change of political regime (even also leaving the difficult problems of decolonization on all levels), American settler colonialism has triumphed, becoming an enduring legacy that continues to the present. Unlike other settler regimes (Canada, New Zealand, Australia, and South Africa) that were forced by historical circumstances to reflect on their violence toward the native, America had never begun this intellectual process of decolonization. To start this process would entail a reevaluation of the role of America in world history. If colonialism were still ongoing in the United States, it would no longer be merely an "American" issue but a global political task to put an end to American colonialism. Among the tasks ahead, rewriting its history (especially the notion of "American Exceptionalism") and reevaluating its own contribution to the history of the world's colonialism will be central. Mamdani cites the renowned Indian law specialist Felix Cohen to suggest that "the Indian plays much the same role in our American society that the Jews played in Germany" (2015b: 614). And Mamdani goes one step further to indicate that Palestinians will play the same role in the context of Israeli settler colonialism.

To re-start the discussion on settler colonialism challenges the over-romanticized understanding of America, and brings back the premises suppressed by a one-sided understanding of American democracy. Only when this country recognizes the genocide of natives as the foundation to the history of establishing the nation-state can it do justice to the Indians and to create conditions for imagining liberation in other places, such as Palestine.

In the context of the Third World, especially in East Asia, Cold War proxy politics gave birth to numerous pro-American and anti-communist political powers, which thus formed the regional hegemonic powers supported by US neocolonialism in the image of a super-emperor above everything. For more than seventy years, the political model of the United States has been upheld by the ideological campaign in these countries as the perfect incarnation of freedom and democracy. In turn, these proxy political powers underwent various degrees of "Americanization," to the degree that even the US military operations in the Pacific region have been described as "peacekeeping action." Even in "socialist" China, many people in the newly formed, new rich country have become increasingly obsessed with the "American Dream," and sectors of political forces secretly admire American lifestyles and the US system of democracy. Therefore, for the intellectual community, it becomes all the more urgent to expose the settler-colonialist nature of America, in order to initiate the global dialogue of decolonization.

The Project of Decolonizing the Universities

In the essay "Between the public intellectual and the scholar: Decolonization and some initiatives in post-independent African higher education," first presented in the 2015 Hangzhou (China) forum of the conference series *Bandung/Third World 60 Years*, Mamdani centers his attention on the challenging but substantive issue of epistemological decolonization, particularly the institutional locus of knowledge production. Although the focus is on the post-independent African context, his investigation had far-reaching global implications in different parts of the world, where scholars are beginning to develop similar lines of thought. In the past two centuries, the university system and its related knowledge production, based on European experiences, has been disseminated through imperialist and capitalist expansion as well as nationalist movements to every corner of the world. Consequently, the European model of the university has radically transformed (or simply replaced) existing intellectual traditions, worldviews, and self-understandings of the semi-colonized world, resulting in a tendency of homogenization or singularization of knowledge. There is increasing consensus on the real limits of the knowledge produced by the university to be able to explain the world and the necessity to find alternatives. Whether it is colonially imposed or voluntarily adopted (as a process of self-colonization) by the colonized society, it has become urgent to critically reflect on the European model of the university in a global context, not to mention the need to mobilize resources of thought to properly understand locally situated problems. Though the conditions to set the agenda for discussion on decolonizing the university are more ready in some places than others, African experiences can provide useful reference points.

Mamdani's analysis lucidly points out that the modern university, the gated social space whose major constituents are students, academics, and university administrators, is built on the notion of "disciplinarity," the institutional division, and management of knowledge and its production of "experts." This model originated from the establishment of the Humboldt University of Berlin in 1810, which was the embodiment of the European Enlightenment tradition. Under the European intellectual tradition, the category of "human" (the object of study in the human sciences) was essentially a reaction and a resistance to the Christian tradition. Being "human" entailed the notion of being civilized and being free from the dogma of tradition. Consequently, from this point of view, those who were "uncivilized," or, more precisely, those who were colonized, became "subhuman." Put simply, this was and still is the paradoxical position of (the European tradition of) the humanities: on the one hand it upholds a singular unity for all of humanity, a universal character of human, which is "reason," but on the other hand this reason is based on the European experiences alone. With its unilateral conception of history, this European reason has thus refused other cultures and sought to impose itself on the rest of the world; therefore, it becomes a form of Eurocentrism. In essence, the discipline of "humanities" in the modern university, including its historical assumption and disciplinarity, is based on this European conception of "human." Due to the differences in our historical trajectories, its applicability in the Third World would be extremely doubtful. This is thus the critical topic for epistemological decolonization. (For example, under the European Enlightenment tradition, "humanities" was born of, and conditioned by, a rejection of religious dogmas, but this historical or religious background did not exist in the East Asian region, among other places.)

The premodern system of knowledge production in Africa was transformed into the modern system of the European university during the colonial period in the eighteenth to the nineteenth centuries, as part of the colonial civilizing mission. The University of Al Azhar in Cairo was "modernized" according to the European model, whereas the University of Cape Town and the University of Witwatersrand were established by the colonizers. After the Indian Uprising in 1857, the British colonizers realized that higher education could bring troubles for governmentality and became cautious about the idea of establishing universities in the colony. Hence, universities were set up in central and eastern Africa since the early twentieth century to serve the purpose of colonial ruling. Thus, in these regions, most universities are not really a product of colonization but of national independent movements. For example, Nigeria had only one university in 1961 but has established as many as thirty universities after independence. Generally speaking, as part of the "modernization project," nationalism was responsible for the birth of universities in these places. Their primary goal was to produce a new class of trained technicians, in order to quickly replace the tasks left by those colonial personnel.

Against this background, the first wave of decolonization was "Africanization," the replacement of staff and students in universities by the Black population. It was seen as a way of countering or undoing the colonial racial discrimination and a fight for educational resources. In reality, the debate centered on the opposition between "rights" and "justice." Those who were privileged through racial discrimination would advocate for their "rights" to university access to protect their own interests, whereas those who were the victims of discrimination argued for a more equal Black population in the university. This form of debate and struggle began to surface during the 1960s at Makerere University in Uganda and during the 1990s at the University of Cape Town in post-apartheid South Africa, but it had not yet intensified in this first wave of decolonization.

The most intense debate was on the institutional reform, centering on disciplinarity and design of the curriculum. In a white settler-dominant university, the content of the curriculum was the European tradition of humanities and social sciences; the object of knowledge was based on European experiences. This whole set of educational materials had not much to do with Africa's own history and society. Discipline was in effect about the study of Europe, and even the supposed interdisciplinary research about Africa had been formulated from a European perspective. Therefore, the "Africanization" of the universities was no longer confined to demanding a change in the faculty and student body but also a change in curriculum and university organization and departments. In the 1960s, the University of Dar es Salaam (Tanzania) was the main base to start a debate on the directions of change. The radical position argued for a genuine reform to abolish all disciplines and to restructure the entire curriculum, whereas the moderates only wanted a degree of curriculum reform, and the conservatives resisted any structural change. Under the political climate at that time, the university eventually introduced an interdisciplinary program of development studies. However, it was highly controversial and met with hostile reactions from the student body, and faculty resigned in protest. In terms of organizational reform, the university founded the Institute for Development Studies, which would design a syllabus for the university's core curriculum, and the humanities and social sciences faculty would also teach their own courses focusing on East African society, history, and politics for the first year and technology, development, and planning for second and third years. With this change, many younger teachers also actively organized various forms of small reading groups, which generated a movement for alternative knowledge in the 1970s. In contrast to the University of Dar es Salaam's approach, the debate and reform at UCT in the 1990s took place in the context of the post-apartheid transition. The debate took the form of discipline versus area studies, with the former maintaining that the European experience was universal and the African experience was particularistic, whereas the latter questioned how it was possible to reform a postcolonial/post-apartheid university, under such historical and social conjuncture, and if it was sufficient to simply implement a core curriculum that focused on African Studies.

In both waves of decolonization, the underlying tension was over the positioning of the university: was it merely a place for (training and cultivating) "scholars" to strive for universal knowledge or was it a place for "public intellectuals" to serve the larger society? To use a contemporary frame, this has become precisely the debate between the coded words of "excellence" and its counterpart, "relevance." Those who argued for "excellence" were usually supportive of maintaining the status quo or beneficiaries under the apartheid system, and those who upheld "relevance" were challenging the practice of racial discrimination. However, today to reflect on the level of epistemological decolonization, it is no longer sufficient to be simply a "scholar" or a "public intellectual." In this era of neoliberalism, it is necessary to be both, in order to historicize and theorize today's political predicament. For instance, under the "structural adjustment" program of the World Bank in Africa, universities and think tanks have been incorporated into the political agendas of the state, leaving no room for anyone to simply be either a "scholar" or a "public intellectual." Therefore, those working in the universities must, on the one hand, continue to produce critical knowledge in relation to the state and, on the other hand, propose substantive alternatives to the public debates, in order to democratize the process of the making of public policy. The task has become increasingly difficult.

Mamdani's intervention in the role of universities and their knowledge production allows us to see the urgency of epistemological decolonization, which is not only about the assumptions of knowledge, legitimacy, and adequacy of the imported academic disciplinary divisions and classifications but also about the practical reorganization of universities. In particular, it is about finding new alternatives to a system of knowledge production that has been surviving for more than a century. To this end, we will first need to break any myth of "singularity" and hence refuse to be hijacked by the system of global ranking that bureaucratically orchestrates a universal set of measurement. We will need to create conditions favorable to the alternative knowledge already produced by the established intellectual traditions grounded in the local/regional history and problematics. But universities have never been isolated from the social, economic, and political conditions of existence. Therefore, different places have different specificities of the institutional forms and practices. To reflect on these issues together, across the regions and continents, would undoubtedly be a laborious and difficult task.

Given this line of thought, the decolonization of the universities, especially in the Third World, would be an extremely challenging, if not impossible task. Because what is at stake is not just a difference in thought, it is also about changing the organization of an established institution on which many people's livelihoods and sense of security depend. One of the most difficult tasks is to shake the belief in and loyalty to disciplinarity, including the distribution of resources. However, if we were to understand the crucial role knowledge plays in social transformation and the necessity of such radical transformation in our world, we would have no choice but to face the difficulty of these issues, to criticize today's dominant intellectual climate, and to find an alternative against all odds. Otherwise, there would be a dim path to the future. This calls for all those who are inspired by the African experience to work together in this changing environment to find a solution for the future.

On the whole, if there is an intellectual project in appreciation of Mahmood Mamdani's work, this author argues that "decolonizing the world" would be a pertinent frame to mark the driving force of his ideas and insights. If the contemporary world is to be understood as a result of the history of colonialism, imperialism, and capitalism, it will require the decolonization and de-imperialization of the harms and legacies produced on several levels—psychological, material, and intellectual—as well as on the legal systems, institutional forms, and political economic structures. The onus is on fellow intellectuals to discover and rediscover more sources of thought, such as Mamdani's, to move toward a more open, more livable, more equal, and more democratic world.

References

Chen, K. H., Gao, S. M. and Tang, X. L. (2016). "The formation of an African intellectual: An interview with Mahmood Mamdani." *Inter-Asia Cultural Studies*, 17(3): 456–80.

Mamdani, M. (1972). *The Myth of Population Control: Family, Class and Caste in an Indian Village*. New York: Monthly Review Press.

Mamdani, M. (1973). *From Citizen to Refugee: Uganda Asians Come to Britain*. London: Frances Pinter Ltd.

Mamdani, M. (1976). *Politics and Class Formation in Uganda*. London: Heinemann Educational Books.

Mamdani, M. (1984). *Imperialism and Fascism in Uganda*. London: Heinemann Educational Books.

Mamdani, M. (1996). *Citizen and Subject: Contemporary Africa and the Legacy of Late Colonialism*. Princeton: Princeton University Press; Cape Town: David Phillip; London: James Currey.

Mamdani, M. (2001). *When Victims Become Killers: Colonialism, Nativism and Genocide in Rwanda*. Princeton: Princeton University Press; Cape Town: David Phillip; Kampala: Fountain Press; London: James Currey.

Mamdani, M. (2004). *Good Muslim, Bad Muslim: America, the Cold War and the Roots of Terror*. New York: Pantheon.

Mamdani, M. (2007). *Scholars in the Marketplace: The Dilemmas of Neo-Liberal Reforms at Makerere University, 1989–2005*. Kampala: Fountain Press.

Mamdani, M. (2009). *Saviors and Survivors: Darfur, Politics, and the War on Terror*. New York: Pantheon.

Mamdani, M. (2012). *Define and Rule: Native as Political Identity*. Cambridge: Harvard University Press.

Mamdani, M. (2015a). "Beyond Nuremberg: The historical significance of the post-apartheid transition in South Africa." *Politics and Society*, 43(1): 61–88.

Mamdani, M. (2015b). "Settler colonialism: Then and now." *Critical Inquiry*, 41(3): 596–614.

Mamdani, M. (2016). "Between the public intellectual and the scholar: Decolonization and some initiatives in post-independent African higher education." *Inter-Asia Cultural Studies*, 17(1): 68–83.

Mamdani, M. (2020). *Neither Settler Nor Native: The Making and Unmaking of Permanent Minorities*. Cambridge: Harvard University Press.

2

Of Citizen(s) and Subject(s)

Mamdani on Research, Methods, and Commitments in Postcolonial Africa

Siba N'Zatioula Grovogui

Introduction

It has taken me an inordinate amount of time to know how to write about Mahmood Mamdani's *Citizen and Subject* because the twentieth anniversary of the book corresponds to tumults in African politics to which its theses might apply. I say might apply because policy makers, scholars, and other analysts may also be in denial about the profundity of the origins of the crises. For these and other reasons, I have agonized over my own starting points, the choice of a mode of argumentation, and, more importantly, a focus. I have also had to think carefully about the manner in which I should broach the question of citizenship as it relates to an avowed citizen-scholar whose commitments extend beyond the classroom to society and to the academy itself. I have settled on a format, and I can only hope that it meets the purpose of this "anthology." The format is to talk about the substance of critiques of the book without engaging the particulars of individual authors' arguments. This may be maddening to some, but my focus is the contribution of *Citizen and Subject* to the field of African studies more broadly. I conclude by making connections between scholarships, global academic citizenship, and policy writ large.

I begin with the common knowledge that the central themes and arguments in *Citizen and Subject* came into focus while Professor Mamdani lived in South Africa. This fact would be insignificant if Mamdani's time in South Africa had not coincided with hope, anxiety, and tumult resulting from the political undoing of the apartheid state. It was during this time that consciousness set in that the state had vanished but perhaps not its regimes of culture, politics, law, and economy, among others. The seeming intractability of apartheid in the supposed post-apartheid quotidian led many to posit an episteme of apartheid exceptionalism. The related argument focused on the specificities of the apartheid system, particularly its racial regimes of truth and their underlying institutions. This argument also laid bare the scorn for the system's racial hierarchies, federated system of racial provinces and "homelands," differentiated educational systems, and their modes of subjectivity: the structures and legal and social qualities of existence resulting from psychic and moral imaginaries of persons based on race and ethnicity as well as modes of existence.

Mamdani does not hold the view that apartheid was unique in racial and racialized ontology and not even in its politics. He resists what he perceives to be a facile empiricism, or rather a perverse positivism, which loses sight of the universal features of the moral (or ideological) predicates of colonialism. This applies particularly to the near-uniform structuring effects of the instruments of colonial governance. The book is therefore in its essence unapologetically anti-positivist and anti-normative. It stipulates emphatically that, as an historical event, colonialism inheres from a widely shared ideology among its adepts. This ideology structured the making of institutions that, in the end, retained common genetic inheritances so that one may attribute to them familial relations.

This insistence on a genetic mapping of colonialism as a form of authority that is not reducible to its outward or pragmatic bureaucratic structures has invited suspicions about method, data, and analysis (see, e.g., Chege, 1997; Greenstein, 1997; Himmelstrand, 1997; Wiseman, 1997; Copans, 1998; Freund, 2000; Murray, 2000). There is also disquiet that Mamdani departs from disciplinary conventions on decolonization and the nature of the postcolonial state in Africa. For instance, Michael Chege (1997) objects that *Citizen and Subject* elides historical differences between, on the one hand, British and South African indirect rule and, on the other, French direct rule and policy of "association." Copans (1998) endorses this view by pointing to a lack of empirical specificity about the nature of different colonial empires, particularly as this relates to configurations of urban-rural administrations. There are in these and other critiques a willful resistance to admitting the validity in social scientific and historical methods of both the generic, which consists of characteristics relating to a class or group of things, and the genetic, which relates to the origin or a point of origination common to a class of things.

This is not without its ironies. For instance, while insisting on empirical and historical accuracy, Chege (1997) draws parallels between dimensions of Mamdani's approach and those of canonical European figures (for instance, Machiavelli and Weber). This move caught my attention for what it says about disciplinary practices in which reference to canonical exegeses often substitutes for analysis. The logical outcome is the casting of disrepute to work that diverges from the canons. The invocation of empirical inconsistency thus serves to dispense with otherwise valid epistemic stands, logical derivations, or philosophical speculations. As foreground to critique, the move is troubling on two grounds. This underlying epistemic deference accords eternal universal status to "canonical" truisms, maxims, axioms, and the methods through which they are attained. Hence, canons are applicable to the "African" context, although their own contexts of origination may be separated from the African events to which they are applied by time lags and geographical distance. This would be tolerable if then "Africanists" did not adhere (epistemologically) to African particularisms (as ontology) according to which African events, thoughts, institutions, and their mechanisms and modes of operation held no universal or comparative dimensions. Such particularisms apply to events authored by Africans as well as those to which they are subjugated.

There are criticisms of *Citizen and Subject* that impugn the credibility of its theses by pointing to a pathos, or the social context and life experience of the author, including growing up in Uganda and experience of the academic world of post-apartheid South Africa. The associated subjective inferences are thought to affect both the modes of argumentation and the nature of the "scientific" observations at the heart of analytical claims of the book. The review by Bill Freund (2000) does not quite fit this description but I will use some of his comments to return to related points, including what in African studies appears to be the obverse of Louis Althusser's theses on symptomatic reading (Bewes, 2010). In this sense, critics have elided the theses on the production and reproduction of racial ideologies in the institutional contexts of colonialism in favor of a focus on the intractability and incommensurability of differences in both the enacting colonial policies and Africans' reactions to them. In the context of *Citizen and Subject*, the most common form of symptomatic reading also appeals to a moralism that wishes to hold apartheid to account by pointing to the insidiousness of that system, in contrast to other forms of racism of European colonialisms. Robert L. Tignor (1997) comes close to this point, although I elect not to choose the worst-case scenarios.

The three examples cited earlier represent three forms of criticism that point more to deficiencies in African studies than they do Mamdani's work. As I show, even sympathetic readers have looked for factual or empirical details to support or invalidate various points. In so doing, many have deceived themselves into the logical fallacy that mistakes variations for divergences and as a result rejected the syllogism in much of the argumentation that points to the shared genetic of otherwise distinct propositions in colonial administration. In effect, *Citizen and Subject* is constructed in contrast to academic practices whose episteme often mirrors, reinforces, or validates colonial structures of governance and associated modes of knowing—which I do not conflate with knowledge per se. This is to say that *Citizen and Subject* is not merely a contribution to an existing anthology on the postcolonial state—or, for that matter, late colonialism. It emphatically rejects the two central tenets of African studies to which I alluded earlier: a racial epistemology of difference and related modes of differentiation, on the one hand, and, on the other, their underlying algorithms of facts, events, and other ontologies permitted by extant disciplinary modes of constitution.

It is not my intention to reprise, refute, or rebut the arguments of either *Citizen and Subject* or its critics. Instead, I offer an allegorical interpretation of *Citizen and Subject* that highlights analytical, disciplinary, and institutional dimensions of the book that are eclipsed by the sorts of criticism that it has received. I offer three arguments. The first is that *Citizen and Subject* may be read as a commentary on the inadequacies of the disciplines on our time and Africa on two scores: (1) colonial governance and institutional experimentations; and relatedly (2) postcolonial tribulations in confronting the crises of state, society, and institutions. The second point, flowing from the first, is the need, as *Citizen and Subject* does, to debunk the algorithm of indexes and catalogs of metaphors, truisms, facts, methods, and logics that constitute the operational archives of African studies. Finally—and this is my point and not Mamdani's—*Citizen and Subject* brings into focus the relationships between the vocation of the intellectual and its attendant commitment, particularly in regard to the pertinence of scholarship and social projects.

Knowledge, Discipline, and Empire

A common assertion that passes off as criticism of *Citizen and Subject* is that it defies conventional methods and disciplinary paradigms in African studies. It is an assertion that ought not to be taken necessarily as a criticism. The fact of defying convention appears as an affirmative statement if one agrees with the premise that African studies require epistemological and methodological interventions of its own. Defying convention becomes hazardous if one takes disciplinary conventions to be sufficient to the tasks assumed by analysts. The quandary for most of Mamdani's critiques is thus that they reproach the author of *Citizen and Subject* of eschewing specificity, one that highlights inherent differences in regions and modes of colonial administration, while denying the historical specificity of Africa, and the conditions under which it undergoes colonialism are not specific enough to require epistemological and methodological innovations. The latter position is at once ahistorical and anti-scientific.

The social scientific disciplines and humanities as we know them today got their last makeover during the nineteenth century when the actuality and requirements of social and cultural life mandate new scientific perspectives. Indeed, the authors often cited to deflate points made by Mamdani—Hegel, Weber, Durkheim, and Marx—made significant methodological interventions based on lived life or social existence: the phenomenology of the mind (Hegel); the definition of the state as an autonomous entity (Weber); the ability of society to maintain its coherence (Durkheim); and material existence under capitalism (Marx). These individuals have been commonly cited as the principal architects of modern social scientific disciplines—and historiography (for Hegel). The figure frequently omitted from the aforementioned list is W. E. B. Du Bois. This omission is not racial or racist, or at least not directly so. Du Bois posited different theses on the mind, particularly consciousness, that pointed to a distinct phenomenology of the mind: double consciousness as opposed to Hegel's consciousness and Marx's false consciousness. (There is a thesis to be made that the dual life of the mind and its ramifications into structures of existence are not merely a condition of the oppressed but also that of the oppressor. There is so much to say on this matter).

It is a paradox therefore that critics would wish to reinsert Mamdani's appreciations of African politics (as analytical object) and approach (or the applicable methods) into categorical indexes that belong to scientific practices, structures of thought, methodologies, logics, and rationalities that Mamdani holds suspect. Unless, of course, the permission to do so is not "authoritatively" granted and the credibility and competence of the author is in doubt. Few have the courage to stipulate such things. Nor are they aware of the irony of the demand that African practices, archives, and indexes of social existence conform to cognitive entities that flow from nineteenth-century practices associated with ethnography, sociology, political theory, legal anthropology, and public policy, among others.

Following developments during the Renaissance and the Enlightenment, nineteenth-century disciplines invariably reflected structures of thought, methods, logic, and rationalities as well as modes of evidence and classification that transformed both science and the archives to two ends. The first is Eurocentrism, which itself consists of at least three nonentirely convergent dispositions. At its root, Eurocentrism advocated the study of Europe and its cultures and traditions as self-contained integers. This initial supposition led to belief and methods thereof that studies of Europe may serve a comparative paradigm or template to reflect on historical developments from without Europe. In its most pernicious sense, Eurocentrism assumed that European sociopolitical, cultural, and institutional experiments were at once unique and superior to others and therefore should serve as templates for the salvation and redemption of regions deemed backward.

The proclamation of the supposed Western genus was one of the primary achievements of the Renaissance. The Renaissance had inherited from the Greeks and Romans a number of sciences. Philosophy (which pertained to ideas, morals, and wisdoms) and Mathematics (which applied to numbers, their functions, and distributions) were the primary or fundamental sciences because they were associated with thought itself. They were seconded by sciences of language (philology) and of nature: physics (related to motion, matter, and things); physiology (medicine, human body); geography (for landscapes and the properties of lands); and ethics (which stood for the sciences of what now passes for politics). These fields privileged the functions of integration over differentiation. They appeared as unitary fields that admitted parts from everywhere so long as they could be integrated into the whole. In other words, up to this point, particular ideas or thought forms could be assigned points of origination but their universality flowed from the fact that the implied human activities appeared elsewhere in recognizable and identifiable forms.

Post-Renaissance human and social sciences—themselves already integral distinctions—introduced radical overhauls of the existing disciplines in manners that fundamentally set the tone for the new disciplines, their methods, epistemologies, and the like: namely, history, anthropology, cultural studies, moral and political thought, and political economy, to name but a few. These fields were intended to give new life or instrumentality to knowledge, which functioned as the central ideological pulse of the political project leading to the hegemony of Europe—and later the West. The new (disciplinary) fields gave new significations to the idea of the human by generating new concepts of humanity and the purpose of human life. Again, these converged toward justifications of the emergent commons: state and international orders, kingdoms, and empires.

This process was predicated upon a logic founded on predictive distributional patterns, or algorithms. The logic, to which I have already alluded, was the appearance of the human and science as self-contained classes of things marked by common but exclusive characteristics. From then onward, Western conceptions of humanism and universalism—and therefore the humanities and social sciences—gave primacy to a certain unity of the human species and a unique place within the chain of beings. Long before the nineteenth-century introduction of the biological concept of ontogeny to support developmental and differentiated histories of societies, sixteenth-century European thought had established "Western science" not merely as the principal genus of all modes of thought but as genus unto itself and an exclusive one at that. Since the seventeenth century, this belief in the originality, specificity, and unique status of European populations, science, methods, and values has dominated European/

Western thought. As a mode of classification, a genus necessarily comprises and is related structurally or phylogenetically to other species based on identifiable modes of differentiation.

This notion of the Western genus provided logic as well as organizing structure to modern archives, which are at once distinguishable and indistinguishable from imperial and colonial archives. The "West" now appears to have a unique and unparalleled access to all essential moral and physical or natural cosmologies. The emergent cosmoses are thus reducible to a parochial principle (discernable through reason alone) and the instrumentalities of knowledge: the construction as discovery of self-serving social, moral, affective, and institutional cosmologies. The condition of science in this context is to render concrete and therefore particularly images of social life as universal teleology (by reason). The purpose of science would be to provide "scientific" justifications to specific fields of knowledge (including academic disciplines) and professionalization (through mentoring or the sanction of guilds). The underlying processes only the principles of power, hegemony, and exploitation that have defined the organizations of national and international societies upon Western ascension to hegemony.

It would take credulity to imagine that there are no temporal relations in the colonial project between thought (whether in the form of academe knowledge or ideological commonsense as attained under natural law), political rationality, and political action, including in the form of institution building. To affirm this view is not to claim a perfect alignment between the design of colonial institutions in the European context and their implementation in Africa. Mamdani's critics therefore allow the simple truism that institutional design depends on a host of factors, including their local contexts, but historically speaking, institutions that differ may still hail from the same rationality. This is why it is not incongruent to propose, as Mamdani does, that, as an historical event, colonialism inheres from a widely shared ideology among its adepts and this ideology structured the making of institutions that, in the end, retain genetic resemblance such that one may attribute to them familial relations.

From this perspective, one can hold two convergent truths. The first is that the design of apartheid necessarily reflected historical dynamics that are proper to its Southern African contexts at the time of its enactment. It also reflected choices structured on imperial and racial ideologies. The outlook of the enacted system therefore is a matter of design, which itself depends upon not only intellectual faculties and mental resources but also, politically speaking, pragmatism. In this sense, British, French, and Portuguese colonial powers made different choices, as a matter of judgment and rationality, but their inspiration and related structures of thought as well as political and ideological rationalities converged with those of the apartheid regime in South Africa. This is the second truth. One does not negate the other.

It is also true, from the perspective of the disciplines of History and Anthropology, that institutional design is actualized against the backdrop of local realties. This backdrop is the canvas of the institutional engineer, where desire as manifested in institutional design meets the ego (or the conscience and dispositions) of the other: those subjected to the operations of institutions. In this sense, it is almost self-evident that one should allow differences across space and circumstances in the implementation of institutional designs meant to draw lines of subjectivities (including citizenship or membership in the political community). It therefore stands to reason that the political realities and circumstances of the Zulus are not similar to those of the Igbos at the time of the implementation of customary laws. Nor would their reactions to colonial racism and its institutionalization be similar. Nor is apartheid as an instrument the same as the federated colonial system implemented in Nigeria. Yet, it is undeniable, for instance, although stipulated explicitly by Lord Lugard (1922), the dual mandate and the ideology that inspired "Whites" to assume trusteeship over Africans and colonized populations inhered in colonial contexts under different guises and denominations.

I am hinting here analogically to the relationships between designs, canvas, and tools—as between historical motivations and rationalities; historical institutions; racial policies. In this analogy, design reflects an ideological function leading the intention to create a plan and process toward the construction of a system. Yet, the intended system has to be translated on the ground (the canvas) into actionable policies that are administered necessarily within the contexts of negotiation, contention, and resistance—all of which determine the staying power or "legitimacy" of the related institutions (or mechanisms) and policies (instruments).

A Janus-Faced Metaphysics of Difference

At its core, *Citizen and Subject* is a commentary born of an observation on the epistemic manifestations of a colonial metaphysics of difference, as they are many, that stipulates analytical principles and concepts, according to which the substance and identity as well as the manifestations of time in Africa are different from those of other regions, particularly Europe. This metaphysics functions differently in research and publications in African studies. Some use the underlying principles affirmatively in highlighting African specificity as a constant, while others point to its deleterious effects of the related institutions, instruments, and policies and processes in time and localities. Mamdani is in the second category, while some of his critics fall in the first. Since Mamdani is in the second category, his theses do not lend themselves to some of the predicates of the metaphysics of difference of the colonial project. Like, and much to the chagrin of some of his critics, Mamdani does not abide by congruent disciplinary modes of knowing, including methods and ontological systems.

The difference in the perception of the veracity and utility of the colonial and now disciplinary metaphysics of difference has analytical implications begging for commensurate hermeneutics: a proper appreciation of its analytics based on the embedded semiotics or algorithms of facts, truisms, modes of knowing, predicates, suppositions, presuppositions, subtexts, pretexts, and the like. From this perspective, Mamdani's critics are mistaken in one singular respect: to measure the veracity of his theses against ontologies or truisms and their modes of inquiries or methods. The related undertakings have been more than tedious and less enlightening.

Mamdani has a specific observation to which he applies a scientific approach, not unlike one faced by geneticists outside of the humanities and social sciences. This is the problem of identifying and developing modes of inquiries for solving problems or outcomes. The problems under review here are the constitutionally assigned utilities of citizenship and membership in ethnic groups that appear in different colonial policies as disparate and incoherent. The reality, as Mamdani sees it, is that the related phenomena appear outwardly to be disparate but they are, in fact, born of genetically connected systems of mental categories, cognitive tenets, logical principles, and institutional functions. Appearing analogically in the likeness of a genetic algorithm, one would expect that the underlying categories, tenets, principles, and functions would have to evolve over time in the implementation of policy for their optimization. It would be ludicrous therefore to assume that colonial governance would look the same everywhere and over time. In this sense, Mamdani is mining data and sets of them that are not congruent with those drawn on colonial historiography or anthropology. He is looking for something else.

To me, the question that *Citizen and Subject* poses is twofold. The first is whether the effort and direction of *Citizen and Subject* is desirable. (The other, to which I return later, is whether Mamdani makes his arguments persuasively.) This question supposes rightly that Mamdani has both the authority as a scholar and the credibility as an engaged intellectual to take the steps required to this end. There is no doubt that over the course of the last twenty or so years, Mamdani has redefined what it means to be an intellectual in the postcolonial context. To say that Mamdani is an intellectual is not to say that his critics are not. To the extent that all humans apply their intellect or mental and cognitive faculties to thought, action, and judgment, we are all intellectuals. In the mere specialized deployment of the term, any person who is trained or instructed into an art, method, or analytical form that applies to dimensions of life, nature, and relationships is also an intellectual. It goes without saying therefore that all academics are intellectuals, trained, as we are to carry out inquiries and analyses within the strictures of our respective disciplines and fields.

To say that Mamdani is an intellectual is not to state the obvious: that he has extensive knowledge or that he is an erudite scholar. It would be condescending. I refer more specifically to an aptitude that can be traced or connected to appropriate exercises, that leads one to develop a practice, form, or culture of their own as these relate to inquiries, research methods, epistemic orientations, and, yes, affective dispositions. These necessarily relate to time, a consciousness or appreciation of the relative position of political entities within time, time-related political projects and experimentation, and the discreet analytical, moral, and ethical spectrums within which the human trajectory is inscribed. I stress yet again that it is not my intention to imply that Mamdani is more or less intelligent than his contemporaries, and more specifically his critics. I am saying that he has developed an orientation toward the idea of Africa, the actuality of Africa, and the relative position of Africa in time. The underlying intellectual project requires mental dispositions, methodic applications, and epistemic inferences that deserve their own modes and criteria of indexation.

At this point, I am going to shock my readers who are still beholden to the other side of the metaphysics of difference, which is that African scholars and scholarships may not be indexed alongside supposed classics inhering from disciplinary canons. Yet, this is exactly what I am going to do. I begin with the vocation of the intellectual without again postulating now that Mamdani has been persuasive in his arguments in *Citizen and Subject*. Max Weber, whose theory of state, subject, and society has been recalled incessantly in opposition to Mamdani's view of the African state, would most certainly endorse the idea that the historical state has temporal cultural predicates that are not easily transferable from one era to another or one region to another (Weber, 1919). Hence, Weber states emphatically, "There is no analogy"—regarding the processes related to the emergence of the administrative state in the Occident (his words)—"to be found in any area of the world" (Weber, 1919: 27). To borrow from Weber, the postcolonial African state did not proceed in the same fashion as in Italy or in Germany, where the state came about as a result of power struggles among local princes. Nor does the postcolonial African state correspond to culturally uniform norms and politically understood institutions besides attempts to put inherited structures of subjugation in the service of emancipation.

Hailing from a different part of the world and from an historical and cultural context that differed drastically from Weber, Mamdani remains unimpressed and is not convinced by the genealogy of the state, as stipulated by Weber and other modern Europeans in the European context. For this and other reasons, although Mamdani may share Weber's vocation, he looked inward (like Weber) as a matter of vocation for his own epistemic lenses and methodological instruments based on observation of phenomena before him. This posture is indeed the proper vocation of the intellectual.

Like Emile Durkheim (1982: 50–9), Mamdani understands that sociological or anthropological analysis and political theory do not proceed from induction alone. They also flow from social facts: phenomena that occur in society that "are separable, because of their distinct characteristics, from those that form the subject matter of other sciences of nature" (Durkheim, 1982: 51). Customary law and the attendant forms of regulations, or governance, in the colonial context were social facts that could be isolated not only as ontologically distinct from their prior categorizations and instrumentalities but because of their status as something other than modern and therefore inapplicable to the exigencies of urban life. The characteristics of customary law thus construed may be "local" and "legitimate" from some perspectives, but their incorporation in political life as instruments of government flew from rationalities that cannot easily disappear—certainly not upon the sort of nominal decolonization that occurs in Africa. I agree with Fernand Braudel about historical time—that the temporalities of everyday politics and those of the cultural and ideological structures upon which they are predicated are not the same (Tomich, 2011).

As Weber pointed out, and Durkheim confirmed, social entities embody cultural capital to which they ought deeply ingrained habits, skills, and dispositions that, at times, last lifetimes. This latter wording belongs to Pierre Bourdieu's concept of "habitus" (Bourdieu, 1980). The concept of habitus may be ambiguous but it runs counter to some theses on self-realization, self-consciousness, and reason often found in the writing of idealistic Enlightenment figures like G. W. F. Hegel (2001). Although critics have alleged that *Citizen and Subject* eschews Mamdani's early Marxism, the materialism, or rather the materiality of race and ethnicity, foregrounds many of the latter's theses. Hence, the parts of *Citizen and Subject* that read like a phenomenology of the colonial mind read so only in the context of the instrumentalities and logics of institutions. Institutions inject a sort of dialectics in human relations. For instance, the law affords rights in the form of entitlements but also privileges, immunities, and other sorts of claims that trigger not only judicial contests but also social conflicts or harmonies, depending on the political circumstances and social positions or conditions of political subjects and the object of contestations. This is a matter of positioning. It means that *Citizen and Subject* arrives at a public utility from opposing positions in all contexts, which does not preclude similarities in outcomes. Individual actors and agents retain moral and other dispositions that are particular to them, that also lead them to perceive the ends of contestation differently. Again, to paraphrase Bourdieu (1980), not everyone feels for the political games and/or social institutions the same way; again, per Bourdieu, individuals and subjects enter and confront the hustle of life with the hand dealt to them by social structures, myriads of networks, and resulting social capitals. The multiple pragmatisms on the part of both the colonizer and the colonized that account for temporal and spatial variations are as varied as the outcomes that they generate. This picture does not negate the structuring effects of social facts: in this case, the taste for the metaphysics of difference and its structuring effect as logic of practice or institution.

Indexation and Criticism

In *Politics as a Vocation*, Weber (1919) posited that students of politics either lived "for" politics or lived "off" it. This was a way of reflecting on the relationships between scholars and the objects of their investigation or scholars' interests in, or at times, motivations for, embracing research that they do. Mamdani is obviously not tempted to reproduce the strictures of disciplinary boundaries. This is not because they are functional. They are. Yet, his approach to the categories of the "native," "customary law," and the "colonial subject" is not meant to examine the nature of either race, ethnicity, or native self-rule. I imagine Mamdani's interest to be a desire to offer a science of the phenomenon of "native rule" and why the latter is bound up in "despotism." The efficacy of the arguments does not depend therefore on the already available disciplinary registers, indexes, and/or their archives.

The efficacy of the book depends on an epistemic disposition toward the sort of hermeneutics required to argue the point. Specifically, Mamdani's is not sentimentally normative. Nor is it intellectual moralism. There is no doubt from the passion behind the arguments of the book that the excesses of apartheid shocked Mamdani as they would the senses of anyone sensitive to racial discrimination. The core of his arguments is the following: in the ontological instance, there is an ethical kinship between the politics of apartheid and colonial rule that exceeds political and institutional pragmatics. In this reading, the institutional particularities of apartheid and policy differences between that regime and other colonial states are but manifestations of localized dynamics in opposition to policies and politics genetically connected to apartheid: white settlement, colonialism, separate administration, the subordination of the native, and white control of the central administration and the logic and processes of government. The predicates of the implicated institutional arrangements are to be found everywhere in whatever name. For instance, although Mamdani has been chided for not exploring the particularity of the French *mission civilisatrice*, nothing about it belies his own theses. The appellation may be pretentious but the "civilizing mission" was as banal in its racism and in espousing the ideology of white trusteeship over Blacks as was the dual mandate of Frederick Lugard (1922). Similarly, Mamdani does not admit the pragmatics of apartheid as signs of unenlightened colonial boorishness. Rather, the culture and policies of apartheid are troublesome indiscretions that threaten to undermine a contrived difference between "cultured" or even decent colonialism, on the one hand, and on the other, nonculture, inept, misguided, and even cruel colonial settlers. The intellectual moralism that underlies such positions passes off an undisclosed defense, near-absolution, and/or justification of the colonial enterprise as a mere manifestation of an otherwise universal hermeneutic of power, relations, and their political economies.

On the other hand, Mamdani's vocation as a moral intellectual becomes obvious when *Citizen and Subject* is read against a long list of his publications. In this sense, Mamdani's vocation is not different from those of Niccolo Machiavelli, G. W. F. Hegel, Max Weber, Emile Durkheim, and the like. For instance, in its concern, *Citizen and Subject* has the flair of Hegel's phenomenology; *When Victims Become Killers* (Mamdani, 2001) has the advice-giving intent of Machiavelli's *Prince*; *Saviors and Survivors* (Mamdani, 2009) has the social temper of Durkheim's *Suicide*; and *Good Muslim, Bad Muslim* (Mamdani, 2004) has the historical materialism of Marx. There are significant differences between these analogized texts: of course, time, space, and object oblige.

I wish to extend the analogy, however, to the dimension of indexation, or the manner in which practitioners assign meanings to scholarships, label them through both subjective and objective systems of categorization, and catalog them into substrata of archives for the purpose of their curation as data or information by researchers and others. It is in these regards that I think Mamdani and *Citizen and Subject* have suffered the most from the insidious side of Eurocentrism. I do not mean to dismiss the notion that Europe has cultures and institutions that deserve awe. Nor do I wish to dispense with the notion that some of those have universal valences. I am concerned with that part of Eurocentrism that imagines the European experiments and related observations to be unique and inimitable. And so it goes. It is obvious from this anthology that *Citizen and Subject* has been widely read across the globe. Notwithstanding this fact, few have read the oeuvre of which it is part, as the basis for reflecting back on the canons and the human experiment writ large that they aspire to portray. This means that *Citizen and Subject* seldom appears among so-called classics on the continuum of indexation extending from the particular, specific, singular, and unique to the generalizable, universal, and/or a model study with comparative value. Again, I understand the sleight, but it is not my concern in this space. I am concerned that a Eurocentric-inspired parochialism, which disguises itself as universalism and rationalism, has so affected Africanists themselves that many of them fault Mamdani for veering away from the truisms of the positive sciences of yore.

To make my point, I return to Durkheim's study of suicide, which is inseparable from his status as one of the greats of sociology. The study explores the differences in suicide rates among Catholics and Protestants in which he selected "strong social control" and "social integration" as variables. Durkheim found differences between Catholics (strong social control) and Protestants (less social control). He also noted an emergent pattern among young unmarried people, especially unmarried men, who were less bound to the stable social norms and goals provided by society. The method that Durkheim used for this study was not commonsense for his time, which is what makes him great. Few have ever dismissed the singularity of Durkheim's analysis because of either its particularity and specificity or possible flaws in the selection of samples, which could easily be done, given today's advances in that domain.

Durkheim's study corresponds to a period of great instability due to a number of factors, including the onset of the industrial revolution, the explosion of bourgeois lifestyle, and the ensuing social dislocation. Durkheim derives the term "anomy" from these circumstances to signify a condition of instability due to the breakdown of standards and values or from a lack of purpose or ideals. European scholars at the time did not think that sociology applies to Africans. After all, sociology applied to society, whose modern instantiation Africa presumably lacked. The work of sociology in Africa was better left to anthropologists, particularly ethnographers. Further, unlike sociology, anthropology was constructed on numerous predicates, but these predicates were not only unchanging, the models from which they were derived were comparatively European. The central epistemological fact is that nothing about Africa is generalizable to the human experiment as a whole or universal for the purpose of abstraction. Since the nineteenth century therefore, Eurocentrists never imagined African knowledge (which contrasts with knowledge of Africa) to form a nucleus, or central or most important component of any universal phenomena, for the purpose of reflection. African activities, including cognitive ones, are not so dignified.

To return to my central point, the end of empire was in itself an indictment of the intellectual, moral, and psychic predicates of colonialism. So too was decolonization meant to undo or transform the institutions, mechanisms, and structures of colonial governance into nonoppressive forms. The fact that decolonization in the above sense was a universal failure leaves the scholar with multiple explanatory models that are reducible to two poles. One reverts to the metaphysics of difference to highlight the prevalence of non-normative behaviors among African rulers: corruption, incompetence, and lack of institutions. The other possibility is to reach beyond the description and appearances of non-normative behavior for a theory that places the general relativity of postcolonial dysfunctions into the large structures of the modern state system, the international order, and their political economies. Modern social sciences seem to concur at this level that every society is subject to fundamental forces that operate concurrently on three scales: atomic—in this case, the state; subatomic—social entities or units of the state; and supra-atomic—the international order and its economies of power, cultures, and markets. *Citizen and Subject* aligns with the second approach.

The Legacy of Late Colonialism

While it may soothe moral indignation to point to postcolonial dysfunctions, there is no point in denying that the legacy of late colonialism plays a significant part in the contemporary crises of the African state, society, and institutions. The relevant question is thus whether Mamdani's arguments are persuasive in this regard. This is where methodological and ideological preferences about the future of Africa necessarily interfere with one's reading of *Citizen and Subject*. On this score, I revert to an old French diction: *Les gouts et les couleurs ne se discutent pas, pas surtout en démocratie!* Indeed, there are numerous opinions about the most favorable denouement of the crises. I focus therefore on the practices of knowledge required for the moment.

One need not impugn the motives of non-Africans to imagine the weight and responsibility of an African who opts for a vocation in African studies. There are parallels here again in the options faced by nineteenth-century European scholars and twenty-first-century Africans. In the nineteenth century, after centuries of tumult, Europe finally awoke from the yoke of reactionary dynastic systems to rise up to the demands of revolutionaries in politics, arts, the academy, and other aspects of civil and public lives. It was unusual then, throughout the continent, to self-consciously commit to the betterment of the "nation," its "ideals," and "destiny." To stick to my example, this is what explains Weber's proclamation of vocation as well as his examination of its implication. It is also why the disciplines of the human and social sciences today are at once parochial in their inception and universal in their outlook. The latent universalism of thought, even nationalist ones, was the result of the inherent motion in the minds or spirits of scholars that happen to match the rate of social changes and the temporal aspirations of their leaders and ministers. It remains, however, that the disciplines are indebted to those circumstances for their facts, methods, and imaginaries.

Africa is at a similar junction in its history, burdened by the legacy of late colonialism, weighed down by the politics of its present, and yet desiring to move forward to better horizons. The author of *Citizen and Subject* is conscious of these historical crossroads or temporal convergences. The convergence of three temporalities into a singular methodology is not an easy feat, and I am not saying that Mamdani has had the last word in this regard. But he cannot be faulted for fudging history, political science, anthropology, and philosophy. There is a philosophical thrust to history, as Hegel's famed *Philosophy of History* (1837) suggests. Mamdani seems keenly aware of it. The first sign of this awareness is that the past does not surrender to the senses in *Citizen and Subject* simply as an agglomeration of facts. Nor does Mamdani succumb to the sort of historicism aptly described by Dipesh Chakrabarty in *Provincializing Europe* (2000). The past had a Geist, or spirit, that felt to the colonized more like a virus that caused a debilitating infection to the body politic. In this logic, the body does not recover merely by ridding itself of the debilitating agent of its disease. In other words, the passage from the colonial administration to the postcolonial state does not eliminate the sequela of colonialism. Diseases inherently leave sequela, or a condition that is the consequence of the prior condition.

How fast the body recovers from the disease depends on many factors, which most certainly include the prior constitution of the body, the depth of the sequela, and the nature of remedies brought to it. But, just as is required to bring the sick body to health is a matter of politics, the constitutional recovery from late colonialism does require multiple and complex formulas. Put differently, politics requires artful engagement, institutional wisdom, and ethical determination, all of which depend on understanding the moment (as would an epidemiology). This is why politics is not reducible to policy or a normative or prescriptive science. Political science thus requires not only engagement with the organs of the state (as Hegel does for civil society in the *Philosophy of Right*), the function of the state (something Weber does with the monopoly of the means of violence), and the anomies of the state (to which Durkheim so famously hinted). In this sense, good political science requires not only good historiography (not merely history) but also ethnography and hermeneutics. This is why the current focus in Africanist political science on patrimonialism, corruption, rule of law, and so on, seems so superfluous to the conjuncture, or state of affairs in Africa today. An Africa with vocation to political science must by necessity cast a critical eye on the past, a skeptical mind on the present, and a hopeful gaze toward the future. Political science is thus, and rightly so, an artful science. It is, after all, the science of an art. It must also be a healing science. I do not mean a science for the ego. No. I mean a science that injects needed dynamism and ambition in the intellectual enterprise.

It is therefore missing the point to bemoan the fact that *Citizen and Subject* wanders off analytic orthodoxy or that its taxonomy does not paradigmatically appear scientific. Such a complaint portends to "bad" (as in disingenuous) reading. Mamdani is not given to rhetoric, but his style does not lack rhetoricity, or a deliberate style or patterned mode of writing that appeals to more than the supposed (but nonexistent) scientific reason. *Citizen and Subject* and all of Mamdani's other books, book chapters, essays, and interventions are in the style of the academic citizen—yes, a citizen of his epistemic community, the nation, and the world that he wishes to be fully decolonized.

Citizenship has its exigencies and requirements. For the citizen, the demands of the practice of the academy are not reducible to proficiency in the reproduction of knowledge within existing paradigms. As Weber noted, the citizen social scientist does not live solely off his observations of social processes or ills, however eruditely done. The citizen is required to respond to society and to reflect on its need of society—not as a subordinate of it, nor a functionary of its rulers or the state. To the citizen, society is an objective entity, with objective and subjective dimensions, including a general or sovereign will. To the people, the general will of society is the sovereign will. It is subjective in character, but its manifestations are not. The latter are subject to history, particularly to cultural productions and institutional experimentations. Yet, they appear to the senses as expressions of the present. For instance, after the Second World War, the expression of the general and/or the sovereign will appeared under the designation of self-determination. As a right, self-determination appeared in the larger context of global politics as an empty signifier, but each locale, territorial entity, or region gave it concrete historical meanings. The anti-colonial citizen thus knows that citizenship is tied to self-realization or self-actualization. There is no prospect for this self-realization as social, cultural, and political ends until a promise to self (the public, citizens, or the people): that postcolonial sovereignty is predicated upon a constitutional order and government that is an organization of the nation in which all citizens are equal in duty, obligation, responsibility, immunity, privileges, and other dispensations.

As it happened, the attainment of this end and the possibility of enacting an historical project to this end run up against objective impediments. One is what society knows of itself, both as a matter of self-examination and as a means to the required experimentations toward self-actualization. Knowing in this sense is not an esoteric exercise. Self-examination must be concrete. In Africa, it must incorporate reflection of the legacies of the politicization of racial identity under colonialism as well as its reproduction of the related pathos after "independence." It is an open question whether the deracialization of politics was more efficacious in one country, or region, linguistically connected or not. The idea that the white citizens of former settler-colonial entities were at a disadvantage is more than wishful thinking. Mamdani is correct in this regard that the mental and psychic ills injected through the polity through the categories of the native, indigene, évolué, chief, and so on, left deep sequelae that manifest themselves even today in the concepts of tradition, custom, tribe, and the like.

This is why the citizen must confront the politics of ethnicization as a constitutional principle—and not merely as a matter of an ever so ephemeral political goodwill (think analogically here of Hegel's *Philosophy of Right*.) This principle—and not just pragmatism—is also the reason to deracialize the postcolonial political economy (this is a question faced in a different context by Adam Smith, Karl Marx, and, in earlier time, the Levelers and Diggers.) The two go hand in hand for moral and ethical reasons.

The academic citizen, thus situated, reflects on the telos of intellectual production beyond the academy. Here, I am grateful to my peers who have already expounded on the invaluable role played by Mamdani in the revival of the Makerere Institute of Social Research (MISR). I would add simply that Mamdani's academic life is inseparable from institution building, and I do not mean merely student training. It seems that his tenures and efforts in the North American academic scene and his roles in the operations of foundations stand alongside his mentorship of African scholars at institutions such as CODESRIA. Observers and followers would note that he always pushed a number of questions. I have already alluded to one, but a rephrasing might be in order: whether the purpose of research and analytical methods must respond to the exigencies of life and its material and psychic conditions. The related question, which comes as a response in his writings, is whether the requirements of time and space require specific research questions, ones that correspond temporally to the imperatives of life, politics, cultures, and their economies in the postcolonial state.

Conclusion

In the academy, as in life outside of it, systems of thoughts connect necessarily to other orders of morality, culture, political economy, and their institutions and norms. These entities represent the foundations of the commons when reflecting spatial denominations. There is no doubt that the commons are in crisis. The challenge is for all of us to identify and characterize the nature of the crisis. Whether one sees the crisis as a prelude of the abyss or representing a moment of transition remains open. It is not an open question, however, whether Africa is undergoing a moment not unlike the time before the European Renaissance, when the old analytics axioms, ideological configurations, political horizons, ethical scopes, and moral orientations no longer sufficed. A critique of *Citizen and Subject* in this light or direction is yet to materialize. This is a shame.

The thesis and methodology of *Citizen and Subject* could be expanded today to deal with the crises of legitimacy in Africa that reflect sets of dual crises of institution, legitimacy, culture, and political economy. The dual dimensions of these crises are in evidence everywhere. A new dialect between the local and the global seems to be in operation everywhere, particularly in Africa, that is no longer epistemologically avoidable, despite the normative (or normalizing pull) to do so. It stands to reason, for instance, that the crisis of the constitutional order, state, culture, or imagination, and their political economies in the context of Africa can no longer credibly be disentangled from the crises of the global order, neoliberalism, global alienations of population, and the operations of the global political economy. In this latter instance, there seems to be a pushback against the reproduction in other guises and forms of colonial and imperial privileges and their institutions, instruments, and norms of adjudication of the desserts, rewards, and sanctions in international or global life. In this sense, the rise of xenophobia, the increasing wealth gap, racialized poverty, and the social dislocations of the poor (white) in the "West" are merely symptoms. As a result, they cannot be resolved through discreet and overt forms of discrimination, surveillance, and control of "undesirable" populations, and identity-based violence against Blacks and Brown people, Muslims, and the sexually queer. These are the challenges of citizens everywhere. They are what *Citizen and Subject* beckons us to turn our attention toward, once we properly diagnose and disavow the legacies of late colonialism.

Salaam.

References

Bewes, T. (2010). "Reading with the grain: A new world in literary criticism." *Differences: A Journal of Feminist Cultural Studies*, 21(3): 1–33. https://doi.org/10.1215/10407391-2010-007.

Bourdieu, P. (1980). *The Logic of Practice*, translated by R. Nice. Stanford: Stanford University Press.

Chakrabarty, D. (2000). *Provincializing Europe: Postcolonial Thought and Historical Difference*. Princeton: Princeton University Press.

Chege, M. (1997). "Review of: *Citizen and Subject: Contemporary Africa and the Legacy of Late Colonialism*, by Mahmood Mamdani, 1996. Princeton: Princeton University Press." *African Studies Quarterly*, 1(1): 47–51. https://sites.clas.ufl.edu/africanquarterly/files/Book-Reviews-Vol-1-Issue-1.pdf.

Copans, J. (1998). "Review of: *Citizen and Subject: Contemporary Africa and the Legacy of Late Colonialism*, by Mahmood Mamdani, 1996. Princeton: Princeton University

Press." *Transformation*, 36. http://pdfproc.lib.msu.edu/?file=/DMC/African %20Journals/pdfs/transformation/tran036/tran036007.pdf.

Durkheim, E. (1982). "What is a social fact?" in S. Lukes (ed.), translated by W.D. Halls, *The Rules of the Sociological Method*. New York: Free Press, pp. 50–9.

Freund, B. (2000). "Democracy and the colonial heritage in Africa: Revisiting Mamdani's *Citizen and Subject*." *Left History*, 7(1). https://doi.org/10.25071/1913-9632.5414.

Greenstein, R. (1997). "'Colonial legacies and the post-colonial African state,' in 'Review Symposium: Mahmood Mamdani and the Analysis of African Society.'" *African Sociological Review*, 1(2): 1–11.

Hegel, G. W. F. (2001). *The Phenomenology of Mind*, translated by J. B. Baillie. Blackmask Online. http://www.naturalthinker.net/trl/texts/Hegel,G.W.F/Hegel,_G.W.F._-_The _Phenomenology_Of_Mind.pdf.

Himmelstrand, U. (1997). "Mahmood Mamdani and the analysis of African society: Review Symposium." *African Sociological Review*, 1(2): 96–144.

Lugard, F. J. (1922). *The Dual Mandate in British Tropical Africa*. London: W. Blackwood and Sons.

Mamdani, M. (2001). *When Victims Become Killers: Colonialism, Nativism, and the Genocide in Rwanda*. Princeton: Princeton University Press.

Mamdani, M. (2004). *Good Muslim, Bad Muslim: America, the Cold War and the Roots of Terror*. New York: Pantheon.

Mamdani, M. (2009). *Saviors and Survivors: Darfur, Politics, and the War on Terror*. New York: DoubleDay.

Murray, M. (2000). "Review: Configuring the trajectory of African political history." *Canadian Journal of African Studies/Revue Canadienne des Études Africaines*, 34(2): 376–86.

Tignor, R. L. (1997). "Review of: *Citizen and Subject: Contemporary Africa and the Legacy of Late Colonialism*, by Mahmood Mamdani, 1996. Princeton: Princeton University Press." *The American Historical Review*, 102(5): 1541.

Tomich, D. (2011). "The order of historical time: The *longue durée* and micro-history." *Almanack. Guarulhos*, 2: 52–65. http://dx.doi.org/10.1590/2236-463320110204.

Weber, M. (1919). "Politics as a vocation." https://www.balliol.ox.ac.uk/sites/default/files/ politics_as_a_vocation_extract.pdf.

Wiseman, J. A. (1997). "Review of: *Citizen and Subject: Contemporary Africa and the Legacy of Late Colonialism*, by Mahmood Mamdani, 1996. Princeton: Princeton University Press." *The Journal of Developing Areas*, 31(2): 273–5. https://www.jstor.org/ stable/pdf/4192672.pdf.

3

Thinking with Citizen and Subject

Talal Asad

Introduction

Mahmood Mamdani's academic work has helped many of us to think more deeply about colonial and postcolonial politics. But more important: his publications constitute an intervention by an outstanding public intellectual in some of the most vital debates of our time. His most famous book, *Citizen and Subject* (1996), is rightly regarded as a path-breaking work that helps us understand important aspects of European colonialism. I want to suggest that it also raises crucial questions about the nature of modern (i.e., Euro-American) rule toward which postcolonial states aspire.

Citizen and Subject deals with institutional segregation, between European and non-European races in Africa as well as between urbanized citizens and rural subjects, that represented rights-based civil society and custom-based tribal society, respectively, dichotomies that defined at once the system of colonial rule and the character of the resistance it generated. The book's overall argument is that in the colonial period "ethnicity [was] a dimension of both power and resistance, of both the problem and the solution" (1996: 8). Once racial segregation was done away with after independence, the real structure of power emerged more clearly, based as it was not on exclusion but on the incorporation of ethnic groupings into the modernizing state. Consequently, the challenge raised in the predicament of modernizing African states is this: "[I]f power reproduced itself by exaggerating difference and denying the existence of an oppressed majority, is not the burden of protest to transcend these differences without denying them?" (1996: 8).

In what follows, I want to think about Mamdani's insight by agreeing with it and also by turning it around and extending it to the liberal democratic states of Euro-America: yes, the power to represent the majority and the ability of citizens to resist those who control the state (as well as their relationship to how the state is identified) need to be problematized. But I think he would agree that it is the sovereign nation-state that, for all the good things it now offers its citizens, or promises to offer them, also needs to be problematized. I pursue this point first by reference to the way the modern state has been formed: first in Egypt (an African country that was also subject to European colonial rule) and then, through a discussion of Foucault's idea of "governmentality," in Euro-America. I argue that it is not easy for the modern state to transcend the cultural differences it has inherited (without denying them) because the interests that articulate the social groups based on those differences can be secured only by agonistic political means.

The Birth of the Secular Citizen

The Enlightenment ideology of progress, equality, and self-regulation involves the moral criticism of old beliefs and practices ("superstitions") from a transcendental viewpoint (see Tylor, 1871; Benveniste, 1973; Belmont, 1982)[1] and the moral reconstruction of political subjects. This is what connects the Enlightenment project essentially to the construction of the modern state, because it is the modern concept and practice of government that universalizes the individual not only as the subject of rights but also of cumulative knowledge and continuous moral self-reconstruction.

It is widely recognized that the ideology of progress generated, first, the discourse of "civilization" (in the eighteenth and nineteenth centuries) and, then (in the second half of the twentieth century), the discourse of "development." But as Arendt (1970: 25–6) reminds us, the idea of progress has undergone a remarkable transmutation since the seventeenth century. For at first it simply meant the accumulation of knowledge, and only in the eighteenth century was it thought of as a collective human growth—"an education of mankind"—although even then it was conceptualized as having an historical terminus. It was in the nineteenth century that progress acquired its present sense of an endless improvement in material and moral conditions. Bowler (1989) has recently described the way in which embryological concepts of growth cycles came to be synthesized with progressivist ideas to create Victorian models of evolution:

> Once we begin to think of the history of civilization, or of life on earth, as following the same pattern as the growing embryo, we are locked into a model in which evolution is seen as the ascent of a ladder towards ever-higher states of development. . . . (T)he more self-confident Victorians certainly saw the spread of European power around the globe as an indication of their own cultural maturity. (1989: 10–11)

Intimately connected with this conceptual transmutation is another, that of the increasing salience of "the individual." The concept of the individual as a self-creating

---

[1]   According to the etymology supplied by Benveniste, "superstition" comes from the root that means "surviving." Initially, therefore, there was nothing pejorative about the word, but when theologians used it to refer to pagan beliefs and practices persisting in a Christianized population, it acquired a sense at once historical and value-laden. In her interesting article on superstition and popular religion in societies, Belmont states that Victorian anthropologists cleared the notion of its theological overtones by translating it as "survival." But the concept of beliefs and practices that have outlived their proper time is itself a product of transcendental judgment, which is essential to the idea of progress. And when Tylor writes that "the term superstition now implies a reproach, and . . . this reproach may be often cast deservedly on fragments of a dead lower culture embedded in a living higher one" (1871: 72), he affirms the theological basis of such judgments; he does not deny it.

subject goes back in Europe only to the fifteenth and sixteenth centuries, as an integral part of bourgeois political economy and the Protestant culture that accompanied it.

The emergence of authoritarian regimes in the Middle East has sometimes led commentators to overlook how much they have in common with liberal ideology that combines the idea of an indefinitely progressive future with that of an emancipated and self-creating individual. Cultivating new, free, human beings is at once the precondition and the objective of such a future, as President Gamal Abdel Nasser of Egypt fully understood. Thus, in his opening speech at the first session of the National Assembly on July 22, 1957, Nasser declared:

> We must ever keep in mind that the most important, the most difficult and the most crucial of our problems is to rear in this part of the world a lively, vigilant and conscious nation and that human beings are the raw material of which such a nation is made. The real effort, therefore, in building the new Egypt lies in the adequate development of the latent potentialities with which the Creator has endowed this raw material . . . (B)uilding factories is easy, building hospitals and schools is possible but building a nation of men is a hard and difficult task. (Garzouzi, n.d.: 5)

Nasser's metaphor of "raw material" belongs to a particular vocabulary of the transformative moral project.[2] It captures nicely the twin features that characterize the individual *citizen* as the basic unit in liberal political theory: at once subject and object and capable of being grouped numerically into different categories. It is the sovereign state's duty to help mold that raw material the right way—and by a curious paradox, a "progressive" government that is also representative of every single citizen becomes the means by which citizens reproduce themselves as a collective subject— "a lively, vigilant and conscious nation."

But of course, Nasser did not invent the project in Egypt. Lord Cromer (born Evelyn Baring), virtual British ruler of Egypt from 1883 to 1907, was equally committed to it, although he employed quite another metaphor. In reviewing the extensive reforms (fiscal, legal, agricultural, military, educational) carried out under his authority, he observed, "A new spirit has been instilled into the population of Egypt" (Cromer, 1908: 556). He then concluded with characteristic imperial confidence:

> Where once the seeds of true Western civilization have taken root so deeply as is now the case in Egypt, no retrograde forces, however malignant they may be, will in the end be able to check germination and ultimate growth. The seeds which [Egyptian governors prior to British occupation] planted produced little but rank weeds. The seeds which have now been planted are those of true civilization. They

---

[2]   Its lineage can be traced to the aftermath of the French Revolution, when "history" came to be makeable in the modern sense—cut off decisively from the past ("tradition") and oriented entirely to a beckoning future. As Malchus, state councilor appointed by Napoleon to Westphalia, declared in 1808 that "in a state like ours, founded on victory, there is no past. It is a creation, in which—as in the creation of the universe—everything that is present is but raw material in the hand of the creator by whom it is transformed into existence" (cited in Koselleck, 1985: 35).

will assuredly bring forth fruit in due season. Interested antagonism, ignorance, religious prejudice, and all the forces which cluster round an archaic and corrupt social system, may do their worst. They will not succeed. We have dealt a blow to the forces of reaction in Egypt from which they can never recover, and from which, if England does her duty towards herself, towards the Egyptian people, and towards the civilized world, they will never have a chance of recovering. (Cromer, 1908: 558–9)

In his conception of governmental practice, the imperialist gardener is clearly as radical as the nationalist artisan. For what brings the two together, despite their opposed views about the role of the state in the economy and in society, is their concern for the total transformation of a population's everyday life. Both of them in their different ways recognize that this transformation requires not only the making of a newer and more truthful existence but also the elimination of one that is less worthy. It is the *scope* of governmental concern, including the continuous critical evaluation of the lives of political subjects by governors and governed, that makes the modernizing project revolutionary.

Of course, I am not speaking here about practical achievements but about the ideas of the ruling elite that those practical achievements are meant to be guided by. Many historians have repeated the Egyptian nationalist accusation that the British colonial government did not undertake sufficient reforms (especially in the sphere of industrialization, education, and social equality), while others have defended the British record by insisting that only what could realistically be done was attempted (see, e.g., Tignor, 1966; Al-Sayyid, 1968). My intention here, however, is not to enter into this debate but to emphasize that something radical has occurred in the historical landscape of Egyptian state and society when such a debate can take place[3]—even though some Europeans expressed doubts about the possibility of introducing Western political institutions into Egypt.[4]

Lord Milner, Cromer's undersecretary for finance and later head of the 1920 Commission of Inquiry, described the inexorable logic of Britain's involvement in Egypt following its military intervention to what they claimed was the restoration of civil order in 1882:

[3]   Thus, when the liberal nationalist reformer Hafiz 'Afifi Pasha (1938: 3) thanks God for bestowing on Egypt all the means for effective reform and proudly maintains, "Our country is rich in raw materials and various other benefits; we are a harmonious nation, from a single stock, speaking a single language, and our hearts are stirred by a single emotion—love of Egypt. All of us live for one hope: to work for her elevation, and her advancement. We are not afflicted, as other countries are, by the plurality of races and the multiplicity of languages and disagreements over aims," he employs a language that was inconceivable in Egypt a century earlier. The valorization of racial homogeneity and national advancement, and the absence of any allusion to religious identities or commitments, now echoes the secular discourse of European social evolutionism.

[4]   "It cannot be too clearly understood that whether we deal with the roots, or the trunk, or the branches, or the leaves, free institutions in the full sense of the terms must for generations to come be wholly unsuitable to countries such as India and Egypt. If the use of a metaphor, though of a less polished type, be allowed, it may be said that it will probably never be possible to make a Western silk purse out of an Eastern sow's ear; at all events, if the impossibility of the task be called into question, it should be recognized that the process of manufacture will be extremely lengthy and tedious" (Cromer, 1913).

This then, and no less than this, was meant by "restoring order." It meant reforming the Egyptian administration root and branch. Nay, it meant more. For what was the good of recasting the system, if it were left to be worked by officials of the old type, animated by the old spirit? "Men, not measures," is a good watch-word anywhere, but to no country is it more profoundly applicable than to Egypt. Our task, therefore, included something more than new principles and new methods. *It ultimately involved new men.* It involved "the education of the people to know, and therefore to expect, orderly and honest government—the education of a body of rulers capable of supplying it." (Milner, 1899: 23)

The "order" that Milner writes about is evidently a very *specific* arrangement. Milner enunciates quite clearly the government's need to create the necessary conditions for its own revolutionary existence: subjects (in both senses) formed by new moral awareness, which would enable them to criticize their state (in both senses of "state"), and a new body of rulers able to respond positively and practically to the moral critique of government. The British knew that they were aiming at more than the restoration of just governmental practices, that they wanted to institute an entirely new conception of political justice and ethical behavior.

European imperialists were aware that their civilizing mission had strong roots in Christian morality,[5] but this did not inhibit them from carrying out their educational task in non-Christian societies—after all, the state they were shaping there was "secular" in the sense of being committed to religious neutrality in quite unprecedented ways. It was precisely because the state was secular that the claim could be made that "real Islam" would not be adversely affected. So, although the modern secular state emerged in Europe out of an imposed solution to the widespread destruction wrought by religious wars in the seventeenth century between Protestants and Catholics, its development and ideological plausibility owe much to later European imperial experience and sense of destiny.

Absolute princely power in seventeenth-century Europe disarmed antagonistic sectarian forces by forcibly redefining their claims. But the subversion of theological authority, together with the privatization of moral conscience and its separation from the sovereign's public realm (even from the sovereign's own moral conscience), contributed initially to the formation of a morally empowered and politically powerless Christian subject (Koselleck, 1988).[6] Viewed in this light, religious toleration consisted

---

[5] In England this included the influential trend known as liberal Anglicanism, represented by men such as Frederick Temple (whose famous essay *The Education of the World* caused great controversy) and Thomas Arnold, who argued for a controlled form of social change and social progress. A recent history of Victorian ideas of evolution notes that Arnold, as headmaster of Rugby school, "was in a position to direct the education of the natural leaders who would govern the country's future evolution. One of his chief goals was to instill a new respect for the natural foundations of western culture. This included not only the creation of a new and more vigorous approach to Christianity, but also a revolution in the teaching of classics" (Bowler, 1989: 53). According to Arnold, the direction of mankind's spiritual growth depended finally on Europe: "If our existing nations are the last resources of the world, its fate may be said to be in their hands—God's work on earth will be left undone if they do not do it" (cited in Bowler, 1989: 55).

[6] I have drawn on this provocative study in the following paragraphs, but this should not be taken to signify that I accept Koselleck's analysis in its entirety.

not in a new attitude of forbearance toward *different* beliefs and practices but in the fact that religion was rendered tolerable to an absolutist political order.

Restoration England was not, of course, absolutist in the Continental European sense, but its forcible suppression of sectarian conflict and its attempt to draw a firm boundary between civil government and religious belief anticipated the absolutist pattern described by historians. Needless to say, there were different kinds of adjustment between state and church (including Catholic, national, and nonestablished Protestant) in different European countries. But everywhere the attempt was made to define and contain the church's powers, and that meant a politics in which the objective of a sovereign state in control of the church helped to bring deists, absolutists, and Enlightenment critics together for a time as allies. When this objective was achieved, oppressed dissenting sects continued to be among the most vigorous critics of the established state. This is borne out by Jacob (1991: 487):

> Under certain circumstances, traditionally religious communities could also possess political postures and articulate opposition to authoritarian or established governments or elites. Methodists and Unitarians in Britain, Mennonites in the Dutch Republic, and especially Jansenists in France could and did speak politically.

Initially, Enlightenment criticism was deployed within the nonpolitical realm to which religion had now been confined by secularizing princely power—and thus against the knowledge that religion authorized and depended on. From the latter part of the eighteenth century the critical offensive was increasingly directed also at the nonmoral foundations of absolutist politics, as Koselleck (1988: 5–6) explains:

> The eighteenth century witnessed the unfolding of bourgeois society, which saw itself as the new world, laying intellectual claim to the whole world and simultaneously denying the old. It grew out of the territories of the European states and, in dissolving this link, developed a progressive philosophy in line with this process. The subject of that philosophy was all mankind, to be unified from its European centre and led peacefully towards a better future.

It was in this context that probability theory developed as a central part of the language of statistics (information collected by the state for purposes of government). The construction of a *public* realm of power and knowledge beside a *private* realm of religious belief and moral conscience was a momentous outcome of the new secular order. It involved, first, a criticism of the political and moral claims of theology and, then, an attack on the static and amoral orientation of absolutist government. In Europe the new secular order gave the bourgeoisie the (private) space to create a society that would eventually invade and attempt to moralize the state. In colonial Egypt, by contrast, the autocratic state was the precondition for a massive project of moral transformation from above; that project was the mode in which the state invaded—or rather, constructed—"society." The critical, progressive subject had to be forcibly created before a private space could be secured for it to inhabit.

Parts of this project were assembled long before the commencement of British rule in Egypt, immediately after the French invasion and withdrawal (1798–1801). Muhammad Ali, the Ottoman viceroy, centralized and strengthened his financial and administrative grip over the entire country and reformed the army and education along European lines.[7] This was done, of course, for reasons of personal and dynastic ambition. Unlike his grandson Ismail, Muhammad Ali never spoke of "civilizing" his subjects.[8] But what concerns me here are effects, and not motives. For the project, whose elements are beginning to be brought together under Muhammad Ali, is not essentially a matter of centralized political control—although centrally coordinated administrative routines were essential to it. The project that would eventually be formed has to do with the ambition to improve continuously the moral and material conditions of an entire population.

The decisive subjection of the *'ulama* (men learned in the religious law) was a crucial part of Muhammad Ali's political restructuring.[9] Depriving them of their independent economic base, and the twentieth-century imposition of bureaucratic and curriculum changes on what became the Islamic University of Azhar, resulted in an official religion being constituted as a subordinate part of a modernizing state—an important sign of future trends.

But the population of Egypt was not entirely Muslim. Even in the nineteenth century there was a significant proportion of Copts—who have been referred to retrospectively as "a minority." Their identity has been seen as a problem for the postcolonial Egyptian state, and not simply because of the policies of the British during the colonial era but because of the very structure of the modern sovereign state.

In her excellent book on political secularism and minority rights in contemporary Egypt, Saba Mahmood (2016) shows that far from being a solution to the problem of religious conflicts in that country, secular government policies hardened the

---

[7] For standard accounts of economic reorganization under Muhammad Ali, see Crouchley (1938), Rivlin (1961), and Owen (1969). On educational reforms, see Heyworth-Dunne (1939). A synoptic account of economic, political, and cultural evolution from a strongly nationalist viewpoint is contained in Abdel-Malek (1969). A more recent nationalist account by an Egyptian scholar is Al-Sayyid Marsot (1984).

[8] In order to impress the European powers, who were also his creditors, Ismail convened an advisory Chamber of Delegates (the *Majlis Shūra al-Nuwwāb*) in 1866. While this "was meant to ensure Egypt a place among the 'civilized' countries, within Egypt it was intended as a 'civilizing' instrument. Nubar [Ismail's representative in Paris] declared to the French Foreign Minister in December 1866 that 'notre parlement est une ecole au moyen de laquelle le gouvernement, plus avancé que la population, instruit et civilise cette population'" ["our parliament is a school by means of which the government, more advanced than the population, educates and civilizes this population"] (Schoelch, 1981: 15).

[9] As Clot Bey, Muhammad Ali's French advisor, wrote: "Autrefois ils [the *'ulamā*] avaient une grande influence sur l'esprit du peuple, ils dirigeaient l'opinion, ils excitaient ou arretaient souvent les mouvements politiques. Ce haut ascendant a ete detruit par le vice-roi, qui leur a enleve les grandes richesses territoriales qu'ils devaient a la superstition et a l'ignorance de leurs compatriotes. Ils ont maintenant peu d'influence et n'exercent aucune action sur le gouvernement qui se trouve entierement concentre entre les mains des Turcs" ["Formerly they [the *'ulamā*] had a great influence on the minds of the people, they ruled opinion, they often stirred up or stopped political movements. This high ascendancy was destroyed by the viceroy, who deprived them of the great territorial wealth which they owed to the superstition and ignorance of their compatriots. They now have little influence and do not exercise any influence over the government which is entirely concentrated in Turkish hands"] (Al-Sayyid Marsot, 1968: 271).

boundaries between Copts and Muslims and thus helped to intensify tensions between them. She writes that the very act of the government having to separate "religion" from "politics" serves to transform what is retrospectively now seen as historical inequality into something new in a state aspiring to the liberal value of equality:

> While Islamic concepts and practices are crucial to the production of this inequality, I argue that the modern state and its political rationality have played a far more decisive role in transforming preexisting religious differences, producing new forms of communal polarization, and making religion more rather than less salient to minority and majority identities alike. (Mahmood, 2016: 2)

Strictly speaking, the political categories "minority" and "majority" are entirely modern. Mahmood points out that under the Ottoman system of *millets*, which was a crucial part of premodern Islamic governance and that now constitutes part of Egypt's judicial legacy, Christians and Jews were regarded not as "minorities" but as "People of the Book" and therefore entitled to autonomy—especially in regard to what is now categorized as "family law."

However, what needs to be stressed is that it is the discourse of "national culture" that proves to be highly significant in the modern secular state and that has now become entwined with the central doctrine of representative democracy. It is with reference to a transcending "national culture" that "majority" and "minority," originally contingent devices for resolving particular disagreements, have become foundational in the definition of "the nation-state." And although many secular nationalists, Copts as well as Muslims, challenge the label "national minority" being applied to the former— on the grounds that the British used that term to promote division and antagonism between Muslims and Christians—there are various forces that combine to reinforce that liberal designation. For most Muslim citizens who are induced to think of Egypt's "national character," the Islamic heritage is its single most important element. The Coptic Orthodox Church claims to represent the interests of all Copts, as individuals and as a community, a claim that is ratified and formally institutionalized by the Egyptian state for administrative convenience—and also, incidentally, as a signal to progressive Europeans that Egypt recognizes the principle of "religious freedom."

But there is another point to be made here: rights, whether held by groups or individuals, are closely connected with sovereignty and the law mandated by it. The concept of sovereignty has been much debated, and Foucault has famously contrasted it with governmentality in the evolution of the modern—and modernizing—state.

Individuating the Population

In his essay entitled "Governmentality," Foucault (1991) describes a kind of state power that is distinctive of our epoch, by tracing its genealogy from early modern beginnings in Western Europe. The most striking thing about the essay is a silence: there is no serious interest in "religion." Why, in our secular age, should this silence be important? Because the liberal democratic state is supposed to be secular. But there is more to be said on the subject. Consider, first, this well-known passage from Foucault (1991: 87–8):

> How to govern oneself, how to be governed, how to govern others, by whom the people will accept to be governed, how to become the best possible governor—all these problems, in their multiplicity and intensity, seem to me to be characteristic of the sixteenth century, which lies, to put it schematically, at the crossroads of two processes: the one which, shattering the structures of feudalism, leads to the establishment of the great territorial, administrative and colonial states; and that totally different movement which, with the Reformation and the Counter-Reformation, raises the issue of how one must be spiritually ruled and led on this earth in order to achieve eternal salvation.

The double process of political centralization and religious fragmentation to which Foucault draws attention here is familiar to all historians of early modern Europe. However, Foucault does not examine the implications of the breakup of the unity of the Catholic Church—still less of the European encounters with non-Abrahamic "religions" across the globe—and the implications of individualist forms of Protestant Christianity for "governmentality." He discusses the categories of politics, law, and the economy but not how modern "religion" emerges together with modern "politics." Consequently, he does not consider secularism (i.e., political neutrality) as a central feature in the formation of the modern sovereign state.

In the seventeenth century, the construction of religion as a universal category was an integral part of the general reorganization of knowledge and power. "Maybe," observes Foucault, "what is really important for our modernity—that is for our present—is not so much the *étatisation* of society, as the 'governmentalization' of the state" (1991: 103). The modern concept of religion as properly belonging to "the private sphere," of the individual as the subject in whom the right to be free is vested, of civil society as the domain of free exchange, of the state as the guardian of religious freedom and legal equality, of science and technology as *the* model for the disinterested pursuit of truth—all have closely connected genealogies at the institutional and ideological levels.

Political power is, of course, the primary focus of Foucault's writings on governmentality. In this context, he suggests that although early discourses on "the art of government" distinguished between different types (governing the self, governing the economy, governing the state) they often assume an underlying continuity across them. Hence, Foucault (1991: 91) writes,

> [W]hereas the doctrine of the prince and the juridical theory of sovereignty are constantly attempting to draw the line between the power of the prince and any other form of power, because its task is to explain and justify this essential discontinuity between them, in the art of government [governmentality] the task is to establish a continuity, in both an upwards and a downwards direction.

In other words, electoral democracy is the means by which the sovereign people (not the sovereign prince) simultaneously claim, bestow, and receive the right to act freely.

Quentin Skinner (1978, 1989), in his account of the history of the state, alerts us to the fact that the medieval theory of *status regni*, which was revived by seventeenth-century absolutists, and the tradition of popular sovereignty—evident in, say, Locke—drew very different lines of continuity and discontinuity between the power of the prince and any other form of power. Hobbes (1651), in contrast to both these traditions, argued that sovereign power belonged neither to the actual ruler nor to the people but was vested in "an artificial man" he called *Leviathan*.

Whether Foucault is correct in asserting as a matter of course that the juridical theory of sovereignty is constantly attempting to draw a line separating the power of the monarch from all other forms of power depends on whether the theory in question postulates a concept of indivisible sovereignty, or one that is divisible. Thus, in the context of debates in earlier years about the European Union, a British historian, Clark (1991), has maintained,

> [B]ecause of its dynastic and religious track record, England is heir to a conception of sovereignty which still contrasts with that of her continental neighbors, so that the integration, merging or sharing of sovereignty is an easier intellectual exercise within the traditions of thought to which Germany, France, Holland, Italy or Spain are heirs. Until the eighteenth century continental composite states, most notably France and Spain, similarly stressed their monarchies as unifying principles: but their Roman law traditions, the entrenched local privileges which Roman law countenanced, and the ultramontane claims of the Roman Catholic Church for long inhibited any idea of a unified sovereignty that could not be shared, and when dynastic regimes were swept away after 1789, jurists henceforth attributed sovereignty not to an indivisible person or institution but to an abstraction, "the republic." (1991: 59)

But this still does not tell us precisely what the power of sovereignty consists in or how the modern state asserts its power over its subjects.

Although Foucault appears to be saying that a state constructed in terms of theories of *sovereignty* is quite unlike one built on the *art of government*, his argument is not as clear as one might wish. We may think he is talking about different kinds of historical states. And certainly that is the impression one gets when he points to two historical developments that help to explain the emergence of governmentality: (1) on the one hand, a shift in meaning of the word "economy" from the sixteenth century (when it signified a form of regulation) to the eighteenth century (when it designated a specific field of intervention); and (2) on the other hand, the gradual formation of a set of practices concerned with "the right disposition of things, arranged so as to lead to a convenient end" (1991: 93).

Thus Foucault thinks of governmentality as a type of state that emerged in the seventeenth century and began to flourish in the eighteenth in which governing consists of manipulating things in a way that achieves the desired end, in contrast to governing through the principle of sovereignty: "The art of government could only spread and develop in subtlety in an age of expansion, free from the great military, political and economic tensions which afflicted the seventeenth century from beginning to end" (1991: 97). As Foucault points out, this does not mean that sovereignty and governmentality are mutually exclusive principles of state but only that they are different. We are to understand that unlike theories of sovereignty, which are concerned with founding the prince's (or modern state's) legal power to command, governmentality refers to the processes by which a rational order is secured by individuals who act without being commanded—and who therefore act apparently freely.

Foucault concedes that theorists of sovereignty are also concerned with the ruler's duty to maintain "the common good," and that therefore they too might be thought of as being concerned to secure a particular state of affairs. But he insists that *this* notion of "the common good" is essentially a matter of everyone obeying the law—whether human or divine—and *that* means that the purpose of sovereignty is ultimately no more than the exercise of sovereignty itself. The concept of "government," he maintains, is quite different:

> With government it is a question not of imposing law on men, but of disposing of things: that is to say, of employing tactics rather than laws, and even of using laws themselves as tactics—to arrange things in such a way that, through a certain number of means, such and such ends may be achieved. (Foucault, 1991: 95)

Foucault does not deny that the state essentially characterized by governmentality makes use of the law as command; he simply emphasizes the use of law as one manipulative instrument among others.

In an important respect, this is reminiscent of Max Weber's famous essay "Politics as a Vocation," in which the state itself is defined instrumentally. The difference is that Weber (1948: 78) defines the distinctive means of the state as the "monopoly of the legitimate use of physical force," while Foucault separates the concept of governmentality both from the sovereignty of the state (because it embraces agents in civil society as well as the state) and from the force used by it.[10]

Foucault (1991: 101–2) refers to force implicitly when he talks about discipline in the sense of order established on the basis of command. Hence the concept of discipline is not regarded as part of the concept of governmentality, but as being "in tension" with it, because both are actually parts of the state:

> As for discipline, this is not eliminated when the art of government begins to become political science; clearly its modes of organization, all the institutions within which it had developed in the seventeenth and eighteenth centuries— schools, manufactories, armies, etc.—all this can only be understood on the basis

---

10 For Carl Schmitt (1985: 9), the essence of sovereignty is neither (tautologically) the exercise of sovereignty itself nor simply the imposition of law on men. Although force (both internal and external) is crucial to the exercise of sovereignty it does not in itself define it. Nor is it the application of the law as norm that defines the sovereign, because that is something that all bureaucrats do. He denies that sovereignty can be defined in terms of routine and insists, famously, that "even the seventeenth-century authors of natural law understood the question of sovereignty to mean the question of the decision on the exception."

of the development of the great administrative monarchies, but nevertheless, discipline was never more important or more valorized than at the moment when it became important to manage a population; the managing of a population not only concerns the collective mass of phenomena, the level of its aggregate effects, it also implies the management of population in its depths and its details.

Thus, although discipline involves force, and is crucial to the administration of the state, Foucault thinks of it as being external to the concept of governmentality—in the way that Weber thinks of the monopoly of the legitimate use of force as intrinsic to the concept of the state (or Schmitt thinks of the ability to declare the exception as intrinsic to the concept of sovereignty). That is why Foucault (1991: 102) speaks of "a triangle, sovereignty-discipline-government, which has as its primary target the population and as its essential mechanism the apparatus of security." Governmentality does not—cannot—do without the use of force and without the ability to make distinctions.

So, governmentality refers to a particular aspect of liberalism that is sometimes referred to as civil society (the domain of the free exchange of goods, labor, and ideas) and to the idea of equality that is essential to the aspiration of liberal democracy. Foucault does not reject the familiar components of the liberal democratic state (civil and political rights, the neutrality of the law, etc.) but incorporates them into a neo-Machiavellian model in which emphasis is put on the state's *indirect regulation* of its population: "With government it is a question not of imposing law on men, but of disposing of things" (Hirschman, 1977: 78). It is not that direct command is absent in liberal democracy but that it is minimized. Like many other modern thinkers, he seems to be implicitly suggesting that *authority* is quintessentially a religious (and therefore externally imposed) power and contrasting it with the moral self-regulation of individuals (the political freedom of citizens) in secular life and the neutrality of the state toward religious and ethnic group identities—a function that leads the secular modern state to reinforce those identities. As in nineteenth-century liberalism and Protestantism, the sovereign state (the source of secular commands), like God (as the source of religious authority), is kept at a distance but not done away with. That distance is how the modern idea of freedom is defined. Under governmentality (whether in the narrower sense of the state's domain or the broader sense of civil society), each individual chooses their beliefs, fashions and regulates themself, and is subject only to their own reason; and yet a spontaneous form of social order results. Like nature that no longer requires the intervention of God, civil society maintains its own coherence by promoting the free exchange of goods, labor, and ideas. It guards individual liberty by invoking the neutrality of the state and the inviolability of privacy and property.

Foucault's governmentality presupposes the existence of liberal political virtues. Acceptable *public* conduct has to be cultivated and regulated and is sanctioned by a discourse of rights and the authority of moral conscience. In the system Foucault calls governmentality, the liberty of the individual to speak and act freely in public is a right and toleration of other people's publicly expressed beliefs and practices, however scandalous, a duty. But just as the Puritan had to confront a dilemma between his duty to obey the magistrate and his duty to disobey ungodliness, so the liberal must juggle between, on the one hand, the right of each individual to act and speak freely and the duty of all individuals to abstain from harming the person or property of others.

So, a central aspect of governmentality, as Foucault points out, is the *individualization* of subjects as separate but equal citizens and their *totalization* in which the unity of the nation-state is expressed. It is in this connection that he draws attention to the principal technique used in the modern state for handling harms and benefits accruing to its population: statistics. *How much* harm becomes more important than *by what means* the harm is done—and therefore the necessity of calculating welfare becomes equally important. Foucault reminds the reader that originally the word "statistics" referred to information collected for the prince—as the head of a vast family—in order to rule his people as the patriarch rules his household. With increasing quantification and standardization, statistical information revealed its own regularities that were irreducible to the family conceived of as a dominant political metaphor. The family—Foucault notes—has now clearly emerged as the elementary unit of the entire national population, and as the locus of its reproduction. But the target of statistics is not only the collectivity; it is also and in a more profound way the individualization of populations.

Conclusion

The knowledge now available to the sovereign state, makes for a significant increase of its authoritarian power. The centrality of statistical data collection to governmental power makes it clear that it is not the *absence of equality* that is significant in the modern—and modernizing—nation-state but the *necessity of inequality*.

From being a body, whose members are subject to the authority of the patriarch in accordance with divinely instituted laws, the family becomes an object to be manipulated for the ends of secular society, an instrument of government policy. The locus of power (from the family to the state) and the form of that power (from command to manipulation) have changed. The changes give us a glimpse of a more fundamental transformation: the building up of the modern understanding of religion as belief (divisive) in opposition to secular reason (unifying). The individual freedom promised by governmentality and the secular reason (modern techniques of power, both material and mathematical), central to both state and corporation, together create an increasingly powerful political-ideological center.

It has become a cliché to say that the collection and manipulation of statistical data is an important means for the nation-state to profile individuals who might break the law—whether as petty criminals or as terrorists or as protesters disruptive of the national order—and thus to disable all those who constitute a challenge to its authority. But profiling is simply one way of identifying suspicious individuals by targeting suspicious groups to which they belong. However, the state shares statistical techniques with commercial corporations. Perhaps the most important of these are the techniques that begin not with a priori categories (such as ethnic or religious affiliation) but with the personal characteristics (behavior, beliefs, interaction patterns, tastes, etc.) of vast numbers of individuals in order to identify clusters by which groups of individuals might be identified and thus targeted not only as potential criminals but also as potential consumers or voters. The social groups that emerge in this process are the products of computational methods; they are not a priori starting points. Because the groups constructed mathematically by information-collecting agencies (private corporations and state departments or the two in collaboration) are unknown to the individuals who belong to them, the state and business enterprises have a firmer grip on them. In this sense the relative strength of self-constituting groups (whether inherited or not) in confronting the increasing power of the state is greatly diminished.

Whether there is a happy solution to this state of affairs is not easy to say. But my concern is that transcending sectarian and ethnic groupings *within* the modern state in order to achieve equality and unity—while at the same time allowing space for organized citizen groups to protest against injustice—may not be possible. This for at least two reasons: first, the sovereign state is typically committed to the notion of "a national culture," and that creates "marginal groups" whose precariousness renders them easy to represent other groups as possibly threatening and encourages all groups to see themselves as competing. The second reason is the strengthening of *individualization* (both as a social ideology and as a statistical technique of governmentality) that makes it difficult to organize collective groups for resisting state injustice. The sovereign state remains the engine of "progress" and "civilization," and "liberal democracy" comes to mean commitment to the computation of equal units (citizens), a commitment that serves to hide the dominance of a given cultural group—whether based on economic, tribal, racial, or religious categories—as majority rule within the modern state.

References

Abdel-Malek, A. (1969). *Ideologie et Renaissance Nationale: L'Egypte Moderne*. Paris: Anthropos.

'Afifi Pasha, H. (1938). *'Ala hamish as-siyasa: Ba'd masa'ilna al-qawmiyya*. Cairo: Daral-Kutub al-Misriyya.

Al-Sayyid Marsot, A. L. (1968). "The beginnings of modernization among the rectors of al-Azhar, 1798–1879," in W. R. Polk and R. L. Chambers (eds.), *Beginnings of Modernization in the Middle East*. Chicago: University of Chicago Press, pp. 277–9.

Al-Sayyid Marsot, A. L. (1984). *Egypt in the Reign of Muhammad Ali*. Cambridge: Cambridge University Press.

Arendt, H. (1970). *On Violence*. London: Allen Lane.

Belmont, N. (1982). "Superstition and popular religion in societies," in M. Izard and P. Smith (eds.), *Between Belief and Transgression: Structuralist Essays in Religion, History, and Myth*. Chicago: University of Chicago Press, pp. 9–23.

Benveniste, E. (1973). *Indo-European Language and Society*. London: Faber and Faber. http://nrs.harvard.edu/urn-3:hul.ebook:CHS_Benveniste.Indo-European_Language_and_Society.1973.

Bowler, P. (1989). *The Invention of Progress: The Victorians and the Past*. Oxford: Blackwell.

Clark, J. C. D. (1991). "Britain as a composite state." *Culture and History*, 9(10): 55–84.

Cromer, L. (1908). *Modern Egypt*, Vol. II. London: Macmillan.

Cromer, L. (1913). *Political and Literary Essays, 1908–1913*. London: Macmillan.

Crouchley, A. E. (1938). *The Economic Development of Modern Egypt*. London: Longmans, Green, and Co.

Foucault, M. (1991). "Governmentality," in G. Burchell, C. Gordon and P. Miller (eds.), *The Foucault Effect: Studies in Governmentality*. Chicago: University of Chicago Press, pp. 87–104.

Garzouzi, E. (n.d.). *Old Ills and New Remedies in Egypt*. Cairo: Dar al-Maarif.

Heyworth-Dunne, J. (1939). *An Introduction to the History of Education in Modern Egypt*. London: Luzac and Company.

Hirschman, A. (1977). *The Passions and the Interests*. Princeton: Princeton University Press. https://doi.org/10.1177/000271627843500165.

Hobbes, T. (1651). *Leviathan: The Matter, Forme and Power of a Commonwealth Ecclesiasticall and Civil*. London: Printed for Andrew Crooke. https://quod.lib.umich .edu/cgi/t/text/text-idx?c=eebo;idno=A43998.0001.001.

Jacob, M. C. (1991). "The enlightenment redefined: The formation of modern civil society." *Social Research*, 58(2): 475–95.

Koselleck, R. (1985). "Historia magistra vitae: The dissolution of the topos into the perspective of a modernized historical process," in R. Koselleck (ed.), *Futures Past*. Cambridge: MIT Press, pp. 21–38.

Koselleck, R. (1988). *Critique and Crisis: Enlightenment and the Pathogenesis of Modern Society*. Cambridge: MIT Press.

Mahmood, S. (2016). *Religious Difference in a Secular Age: A Minority Report*. Princeton: Princeton University Press. https://doi.org/10.2307/j.ctvc77k82.

Mamdani, M. (1996). *Citizen and Subject: Contemporary Africa and the Legacy of Late Colonialism*. Princeton: Princeton University Press.

Milner, L. (1899). *England in Egypt*. London: Edward Arnold.

Owen, E. R. J. (1969). *Cotton and the Egyptian Economy, 1820–1914*. Oxford: Clarendon Press.

Rivlin, H. A. B. (1961). *The Agricultural Policy of Muhammad Ali in Egypt*. Cambridge: Harvard University Press.

Schmitt, C. (1985) [1922]. *Political Theology*. Cambridge: MIT Press.

Schoelch, A. (1981). *Egypt for the Egyptians! The Socio-Political Crisis in Egypt, 1878–1882*. London: Ithaca Press.

Skinner, Q. (1978). *Foundations of Modern Political Thought*, 2 vols. Cambridge: Cambridge University Press.

Skinner, Q. (1989). "The state," in T. Ball, J. Farr and R. Hanson (eds.), *Political Innovation and Conceptual Change*. Cambridge: Cambridge University Press, pp. 90–131.

Tignor, R. L. (1966). *Modernization and British Colonial Rule in Egypt, 1882–1914*. Princeton: Princeton University Press.

Tylor, E. B. (1871). *Primitive Culture*, 2 vols. London: Oxford University Press.

Weber, M. (1948). "Politics as a vocation," in M. Weber, H. Gerth and C. Wright Mills (eds.), *From Max Weber: Essays in Sociology*. London: Routledge & Kegan Paul, pp. 77–128.

4

Beyond the Custom/Market Dichotomy

Women's Rights to Land and the Challenge of the Commons

Nivedita Menon

Introduction

This chapter is shaped by two insights that I draw from Mahmood Mamdani's work. First, the imperative not to do "history by analogy" as he puts it, that is, using conceptual apparatus developed from another experience, another spatiotemporal configuration, to understand experience and history elsewhere. Second, his problematization of the idea of the "customary," which across colonial practices in Africa and South Asia was both produced from existing cultural material in particular ways and reified.

Bringing women into the ambit of individual property rights has long been one of the key issues in feminist practice and scholarship. Focusing on land ownership rights, this chapter asks what happens to the feminist understanding of land rights for women in the face of large-scale land acquisitions for corporate globalization. The only real challenge to capitalist ambitions today is posed by collective ownership of land and strong assertions of the commons. What does this recognition mean for feminist campaigns of land rights for women? This chapter draws largely on the Indian experience, but I suggest that scholarship and activism across Africa and Latin America raise similar questions.

This means that I am setting aside for the moment as undisputed from a feminist perspective, the rights of women to nonlanded property in natal and matrimonial families and to the matrimonial home. I consider as undisputed too, the right of women to maintenance upon divorce, justified by a feminist understanding of the sexual division of labor that makes women in a heterosexual marriage or domestic partnership solely responsible for doing or organizing reproductive labor. I make this clarification because several recent court judgments in India have disallowed maintenance to divorced women if they are employed or childless. In other words, women's rights to property in general is not the focus of this chapter, and it focuses on land rights in particular.

I think that at this moment in time, several kinds of political movements and several strands of scholarship from the end of the twentieth century onward, for about three decades or so, are coming together to alert us to a need for a shift in feminist perspective on land rights for women.

Land Struggles in India

Let me begin with what we learn from struggles against the accelerated and large-scale land acquisitions by the state for use by private corporations. Activists in these movements and scholars engaged in understanding land relations are increasingly coming to the recognition that the Indian state is now very amenable to joint *pattas* (title deeds), which has been the main demand of women's movements for decades— that is, joint title deeds for husband and wife to family land. However, as Smita Gupta (2018) argues, while joint *pattas* are important, a sole preoccupation with them is a problem, thrust upon us by international agencies with a neoliberal agenda. The women's movement must, says Gupta, focus far more on dispossession, land use change, lack of access to commons, and depletion/degradation of the commons. Small individual plots in a context of rising and widespread agrarian distress will, in fact, increase women's drudgery. Gupta believes that collective farming with state support is the way forward (Gupta, 2018). Individual land rights, whether to men only or also to women, restrict farmers to family plots by giving them formal title deeds, even joint *pattas*—while the state takes control of common and public lands. Enclosures, evictions, and land use policies are all state strategies for taking over common and public lands, and of course, title deeds are no magic potion against land acquisition. Rather, individual title deeds facilitate land acquisitions by the state. Furthermore, it has long been understood in the context of land reforms that joint *pattas* in effect sideline the question of land redistribution and, in that sense, are not a radical agenda. As Mercia Andrews, land rights activist from South Africa, puts it, no effective land struggle is possible without breaking up the nuclear family (Andrews, 2014).

Roma, an activist with All India Union of Forest Working People, is opposed to the *patta* as such, which she sees as looking at land use and ownership exclusively through the prism of the family. In her experience, she says, only collective ownership can fracture patriarchy, and her organization works with movements that collectively cultivate land. Such a movement would be a movement of the landless, not of middle and upper peasantry. There is thus, in this understanding, a contradiction between the interests of peasants and the interests of the landless, largely Dalits, who use common lands. In her understanding then, an alliance of marginal farmers and the landless needs to be built, and this would have to address the caste divide as well (Roma, 2014).

Common lands that embody layers of customary usufruct rights are the biggest challenge to market relations, and prime among such lands are forests. It is in this context that land occupation movements by castes and tribes traditionally excluded from agriculture must be viewed and understood—for example, the occupation of Muthanga forest lands in Kerala by adivasis, violently evacuated by police in 2003. C. K. Janu, chairperson of the Adivasi Gothra Maha Sabha that spearheaded this struggle, said in an interview: "Adivasis are the real owners of land . . . [Our main slogan is] the right to live in the land where we are born till death" (Gatade, 2005).

This "occupation" of lands by the poor is in fact a *reoccupation* of common lands, which were turned into state-owned land overnight through colonial legislations such as the Indian Forest Acts of 1878 and 1927, equally fiercely enforced by the post-independence Indian state as well.

Globally the trend is toward the legitimization by states and World Bank institutions of property titles for the poor and for women, even as these states engage in large-scale land acquisition in the interest of extractive capital. We will see that this is not a contradiction and how the first works in the interests of the second.

Is there then a disjuncture between women's individual rights to land and struggles against land acquisition to protect or create a commons? It seems that something counterintuitive with regard to feminist common sense is being articulated in these contexts, a possibility this chapter explores.

Land Rights through Custom and Tradition in India

There are three kinds of access to land rights in India—through religious Personal Laws to agricultural land, through Forest Acts to forests, and through Customary Laws to agricultural and forest lands occupied by tribal people. It is important to keep in mind that neither Personal Laws nor Customary Laws are, in any pure sense, traditional or indigenous. A large body of scholarship has shown that even up to the eighteenth century across India, there was a considerable range of authorities offering different types of justice and a multiplicity of scriptural and customary sources of right. The colonial state's efforts to consolidate a body of Hindu and Islamic law to vindicate its claim to be ruling on the basis of the laws and customs of the people, in fact, resulted in a body of jurisprudence that modified both "scriptures" and "custom" in keeping with official objectives wherever necessary. The dynamic interaction between textual law and nontextual custom, which had gradually evolved in pre-British India, was henceforth rigidly fixed, through the authority of Brahmin scholars (for Hindu law) and *maulvis* (for Muslim law) whom the British treated as authoritative and representative, while retaining as overriding the imperatives of British rule in India. British colonialism, in effect, constructed both custom and scriptures in collaboration with Hindu and Muslim elites, while maintaining the latter's subordinate status in the process of crafting British dominance (for instance, see Derrett, 1968; Nair, 1996; Anderson and Guha, 1998; Singha, 1998).

Similarly, regarding the customary laws of tribal people of Northeast and Central India, while the British claimed to leave them to be governed by their customary practices, in fact traditional communities were reshaped as viable revenue-generating areas (Kurup, 2008) and colonial village heads such as *gaonburha* were established parallel to traditional chieftains. Colonial control of the Northeast was important for strategic reasons, and Central India was rich in minerals. The form of control that was effected in tribal regions by the colonial government was "a system of exclusion premised on direct paternalistic rule by the Governor of the province through the district officers" (Prakash, 1999: 117). The exclusion was supposedly to protect tribal culture but with British rule and introduction of the formal law, customary regulations acquired secondary status. During the colonial era, Indian courts attempted to integrate customary rights into the modern legal framework that was emerging. Forests and village commons began to be controlled by the colonial government. The Indian Forest Act of 1927 treated communities that had lived in the forests since time immemorial as criminal trespassers. Nevertheless, local communities continued to live in the forest and depended on nontimber forest produce for their survival and continued to be guided to a great extent by traditional and customary practices in the usage of natural resources (Krishnan, 2000). In short, aspects of tribal practices were left alone while there was also considerable intervention by the colonial state in keeping with its economic requirements as well as along the lines of British cultural and social norms of the time, which were decidedly Victorian and patriarchal. It is impossible today, therefore, to excavate any purely indigenous practice. It is also important to note the continuity of tribal policy between the colonial and post-independence Indian state.

Women's Rights to Land in Personal Laws

The question that we need to address is, as we noted earlier, why are land struggles finding the Indian state so amenable to joint *pattas* by the early twenty-first century, and why are women's rights to land *now* recognizably "centrally located in the national policy agenda"? (Rao, 2008: 6). After all, feminist scholars like Bina Agarwal have argued for over a decade and a half for women's "independent rights in land" on grounds of welfare, efficiency, equality, and empowerment (Agarwal, 1994: 27). Agarwal has pointed out that it has been easier to push the welfare and efficiency arguments with state planners than equality and empowerment of women. The former are more easily understood within a poverty alleviation framework, she suggests, while the latter run counter to "deep rooted notions of appropriate gender relations shared by many men who make and implement policy," for whom more equal gender relations appear as "threatening to existing family and kinship structures" (1994: 45).

Certainly nothing leads us to think that these attitudes have changed; on the contrary, policy makers continue to express the most appallingly sexist and misogynist opinions quite freely. And yet, in 2005, the amendment to the Hindu Succession Act (HSA) of 1956, which amended Clause 6 and omitted Clause 4 (2) of the HSA to give women rights to ancestral property, was declared "passed unanimously" in both houses of the Indian Parliament, first in the upper house Rajya Sabha and then in the lower house Lok Sabha the same year. Several states had already passed such legislation between 1986 and 1994—Andhra Pradesh, Tamil Nadu, Karnataka, and Maharashtra, while Kerala abolished the joint family system as a legal entity altogether in 1975.

What did the HSA Amendment Act of 2005 accomplish? Bina Agarwal (2005) calls it a landmark, because it established gender equality on agricultural land and in coparcenary joint family property. Interestingly, during the debate in the lower house of Parliament, Lok Sabha, several Members of Parliament (MPs) who supported the amendment demanded that it be extended to include agricultural land which,

Agarwal points out, was already part of the amendment. Thus, the debate on the HSA Amendment Bill in Lok Sabha is intriguing, partly because of the enthusiastic support from many MPs who had clearly not read the proposed amendments with any care, but even more so because in fact several MPs had very negative responses to the Bill.[1]

Shailendra Kumar of the Samajwadi Party tied together the Domestic Violence Act (passed in 2005), the pending Bill for women's reservations in Parliament, and the HSA Amendment Bill to accuse the Congress-led ruling coalition United Progressive Alliance (UPA) of "playing the politics of women's vote bank." He said that instead of giving women equal rights to property in their natal home, they should instead be educated and self-reliant and after marriage after all, they are "fully entitled to right of property in [the] in-laws' home." This Bill could create "wide gulfs" in a family, especially between brother and sister, he added.

Rajaram Pal, a Congress MP, said these measures would "further diminish the size of cultivable land," a very old argument against land rights for women, which Bina Agarwal has dealt with conclusively in her work through both empirical evidence and the argument that fragmentation of land would never be used as an excuse to deny land rights to many sons.

B. Mahtab of the Biju Janta Dal began by giving illustrations of why the legislation did not go far enough—agricultural land was excluded and only unmarried women given rights to coparcenary property (both mistaken assumptions). But then he turned around to criticize the Bill because it increases inequalities *among* women in the family—between those born and those married into the family. (This is an anomaly that Agarwal (2005) points out as well, except that she suggests redressing it by abolishing the Mitakshara system[2] altogether, as it does not recognize individual rights to land.) Mahtab also argued that the new law increases the possibility of litigation in the Hindu Joint Family. He further asserted that the new law will encourage "female feticide" because if women can inherit ancestral property, that is another reason to kill them before they are born.

Kishan Singh Sangwan of the Bharatiya Janta Party (BJP) feared that litigation could result in the "deterioration in social structure" in families and added that female feticide may increase. Nevertheless, characteristic of his Hindu nationalist party, he added that the law should also be applicable to Christian and Muslim women.

Ruin of "our social fabric" through litigation and increased female feticide was presented by Tufani Saroj of the Samajwadi Party too, as possible outcomes of the Bill. He said that only physically challenged women and "girls who cannot get married" should get this right (Republic of India, 2005).

Despite these kinds of views being expressed across party lines, the Bill was unanimously passed in the Lok Sabha. Earlier, when the Bill was discussed in the Rajya Sabha, the media reported, "Only one male member (the rest were women)

---

[1] The statements of MPs that follow are all taken from *Lok Sabha Debates* (2005).
[2] The Dayabhaga and the Mitakshara are the two schools of law that govern the law of succession of the Hindu Undivided Family under Indian Law. The Dayabhaga school of law is observed in Bengal and Assam. In all other parts of India, the Mitakshara school of law is observed. The Mitakshara enforces unity of the coparcenary, whereas the Dayabhaga permits alienation and partition to a greater degree.

participated in the discussion that came at the fag end of the day. Some of the members pointed to the low attendance in the House during the debate" (*The Hindu*, 2005).

But there too, the Bill was unanimously passed and the Minister for Law, H. R. Bhardwaj, "expressed happiness at the unequivocal support given to the Bill by the BJP-led opposition National Democratic Alliance" (*The Hindu*, 2005).

As regards Muslims and Christians, the Shariat Act of 1937 that governs Muslims permits agricultural land rights to be governed by custom; as a result, in many states Muslim women are excluded from ownership of land. There has been an ongoing campaign to end this discrimination along the lines of the 2005 Amendment of the HSA (Agarwal, 2017). Christians and Parsis are now governed by the Indian Succession Act, which permits ownership rights to ancestral property to women.

But our concern in this chapter goes beyond asking whether women have equal rights to land, to why women's individual rights to land are so centrally on the agenda of the Indian state. As we saw, the debate in the Lok Sabha reflects on the part of many MPs, the same "deep-rooted notions" of gender inequality that Bina Agarwal noted, and many seemed to be unaware of basic provisions in the Bill. In the Rajya Sabha it seems to have not even attracted sufficient interest to warrant a debate. And yet the Bill was unanimously passed in both houses.

We need to ask ourselves therefore, what the transformation is, that is being brought about in the name of equal rights for women. Let us go back to about a century ago to seek some answers before we return to the moment of 2005.

Producing Modern Regimes of Property under Colonialism

Some interesting historical work started emerging in the first decade of this century, on Hindu law reform and codification in late colonial India, a process that has hitherto been debated in feminist scholarship exclusively in terms of enhancement or curtailing of women's rights to property. This work, that of Ritu Birla (2009) and Eleanor Newbigin (2009) for instance, is enabling a reframing of this codification as "the making of capitalist subjects" (Birla, 2009: 199).

In her study of the Indian Chamber of Commerce, Birla shows how "vernacular capitalists staked a place in the colonial global" through "the gendered production of the local, especially in defence of the joint family system" (2009: 200). Birla traces the complicated history of the "Hindu Undivided Family [HUF] as an alibi for the family firm" (2009: 203). Colonial commercial law of partnership "sought aggressively to place [the HUF] under the purview of contract" (2009: 203), in response to complaints of British traders regarding the unenforceability of contracts with indigenous firms:

> The constitution of native firms shifted depending on the birth of sons within joint families and the marriage of daughters into other families. This fluidity allowed the management of debt and transfer of capital between retail, wholesale and money-lending concerns. British traders worried that native firms' familial structure

helped them evade contractual obligations, particularly in the case of debt. (Birla, 2009: 205)

Birla further explains that one kind of response from Gujarati traders was to validate kinship-based capitalism through a defense of the HUF, representing it as a perfectly legitimate form of commercial organization (2009: 207). Through this intervention, they challenged the modern common sense, sought to be normalized through colonial law, that commerce as a public endeavor and family (expressed as authority over women and children) were mutually exclusive. Rather, they sought to produce the joint family as a *codified* (therefore modern) and not *customary* (traditional) arrangement (2009: 208). The colonial response was to then treat the HUF as analogous to the joint stock company through the Super-Tax Act of 1917, but to tax the HUF at source, while joint stock companies could deduct amounts paid to individual members or shareholders (2009: 209).

According to Birla, this "strange creature of the bazaar: the family firm" (2009: 216) was at the center of competing intra-community discourses of reform (which held that the ethical management of the joint family would be consistent with material development) and orthodoxy (which held that the joint family was a realm of Hindu culture, separate from public material concerns) (2009: 222). This "codified legal creature," the HUF, shielded the jointness and fluidity of kinship-based commerce (2009: 223). The debates over proposed amendments to the Special Marriage Act of 1872 that Birla outlines are productive for feminist rethinking on this legislation, which, like other legislations on family and marriage, has tended to be read as reflecting debates on the "status of women."

The 1872 Act was inspired by Henry Maine's proposals to remove "caste disabilities" (Birla, 2009: 224) and provided for civil marriage for those who professed no religion. However, since the Privy Council had declared that Hindus could not renounce their religion, and that Buddhists, Jains, and Sikhs counted as Hindus for the purposes of succession and marriage, an amendment was proposed in 1921 to permit civil marriage for those professing these faiths. Orthodox opinion of course reacted strongly to recognizing contractual forms of marriage as Hindu, but reformist voices within commercial castes like the Marwaris tried to support marriage reform while keeping coparcenary property relations outside their purview (Birla, 2009: 224–5). Thus, while "conservatives sought the HUF's autonomy from public regulation, social reformists attempted to align its patriarchy with the aims of national progress" (Birla, 2009: 230).

Although the discourse that circulates is that of social reform, it is clear from this account that the reforms are about creating modern entities amenable to capitalist economic arrangements, while accommodating the tension between the order of state and family.

The focus on Hindu law in this chapter is largely because through law reforms of the 1860s, colonial officials both created and formalized "personal laws," the effect of which was different on Muslim and Hindu personal law, as Eleanor Newbigin demonstrates. Koranic shariat law, the "outcome of the hybrid Company legal system" (Newbigin, 2009: 87), was presented as "traditional" as well as clear-cut and easily applied, under which "Muslim families were considered to comprise of property-owning individuals, whereas the natural condition of a Hindu family was assumed to be 'joint'" (Newbigin, 2009: 87). Contrary to later discourses about Muslim law being backward then, at that point, it was Hindu laws that were considered as requiring reform to bring them into the modern world of individual rights to property.

The impetus toward reform came, argues Newbigin, from conflicts between Hindu professional and mercantile elites, on the one hand, and agrarian elites, on the other. This put pressure on the Mitakshara coparcenary and "its system of joint, intergenerational property ownership" through which agrarian elites maintained their authority while for Indian merchants competing with European capital, this focus on "joint rights and its effect of locking away capital in land" was problematic. Of course, both groups were found in the same families, and younger men gradually opposed joint family living and collective property ownership in the emerging Anglo-Hindu law (Newbigin, 2009: 88).

The movement toward the legal abolition of matriliny in Kerala must be seen as part of the same process. The last vestiges of Nair matriliny that had gradually been delegitimized were finally removed with the Hindu Succession Act of 1956 that gave men equal rights to matrilineal ancestral property. Historian Pravina Kodoth has pointed out that this dispossession of women was produced within a narrative of historical progress and the newly emerging discourse of individual rights. That is, the end of Nair women's exclusive rights to natal property under matriliny was conducted impeccably in the language of rights—pitting the rights of the wife against those of the sister of the Nair man; the subject of rights was never, of course, assumed to be the Nair woman herself (Kodoth, 2001).

Newbigin draws our attention to the bill introduced to the Madras Assembly by Diwan Bahadur Ramachandra Rao in 1915, to facilitate partitioning of coparcenary estates and to grant women absolute ownership over property inherited from their husbands, on the explicit argument that this would "improve market relations and produce a more streamlined legal system" (Newbigin, 2009: 90). This was opposed by the "powerful landed elites" and never passed.

However, fifteen years later, in 1930, the Hindu Gains of Learning Bill drafted by Mukundrao Ramrao Jayakar did pass. Although this legislation is not about women's rights to land but to earned income, it is illustrative of the manner in which the figure of "women" and their "rights" get mobilized into the larger process by which commercial elites gain ascendancy over traditional patriarchs. Hence, although not strictly within the focus of this chapter, let us take a minute to consider it.

This legislation made income earned by a son, as a result of English education, his sole individual property, overriding the principles of the Mitakshara coparcenary, in which income earned from a profession was to revert to the joint family. Jayakar presented this bill as vital for improving the position of Hindu women, as widows could through it inherit their husbands' self-earned income and avoid a life of destitution. Jayakar also argued, "implying that the Muslim community was not hindered in the same way," that "joint family ownership undermined entrepreneurial drive and easy access to credit" (Newbigin, 2009: 92).

There were two achievements of this bill in Newbigin's reading. First, it secured "the economic and domestic power of the male Hindu commercial classes" over the older patriarchs or *kartas* over the Hindu family (Newbigin, 2009: 93). Second, it enabled British finance officials during the economic depression to expand the tax base, overriding attempts by Hindu professionals to include their salaries as part of their joint family tax return. The Hindu Gains of Learning Act thus, proposed as intended to give widows a means of subsistence, came in handy to pursue Hindu professionals and businessmen for larger tax payments (Newbigin, 2013: 105).

Meanwhile, it had come to be generally accepted that under Shariat law, daughters could inherit from their fathers and had rights to divorce and maintenance; it was therefore more progressive and modern than Hindu laws. So, Hindu men interested in producing the idea of an all-India Hindu community with similar progressive laws came together. G. V. Deshmukh introduced the Hindu Married Women's Rights to Property Bill in 1937 (the same year as the Shariat Act), including the widow and the daughter in the list of heirs to succeed absolutely to a Hindu man's property, including his share in the coparcenary. There was opposition from those in Northern India, while from the West and South there was more willingness to contemplate radical reform, and ultimately the law was redrafted along more conservative lines, excluding daughters and giving rights only to widows (Newbigin, 2009: 97).

These developments cannot be seen independently of the longer process of turning land into a commodity, which began with the Permanent Settlement of 1793 and culminated in the Land Acquisition Act of 1894—that is, the process through which "the rule of property" (Guha, 1996) was sought to be established over heterogeneous practices of land use and land relations, thus creating "a precise and definitive location of saleable property right" (Sarkar, 2014: 89). We should also note, however, that this process was far from successfully completed by the end of colonial rule, for as Guha argues, the grafting of a capitalist vision of land rights on to the Indian agrarian system without an understanding of the traditions on which it was based resulted in continuing forms of feudal land relations at independence (Guha, 1996).

The Nation-State and Modernizing of Property

The independent Indian state thus still needed to address the land question. Let us turn to the debate on the First Amendment to the Constitution in 1951, in which the right to agrarian property was significantly limited by an amendment to Article 31 through which the individual's right to property was made subject to the state's right to acquire property to resolve what then prime minister Jawaharlal Nehru termed "the land problem" (Republic of India, 1951). Through the insertion of Articles 31a and 31b, government acquisition of land could no longer be challenged on grounds of inadequate compensation, and the Ninth Schedule was created, in which land reform legislation was to be placed, protecting it from judicial review. We must see this amendment as part of the process of the nation-state in the process of establishing a capitalist economy through a "passive revolution."[3]

---

[3]   I refer here to Sudipta Kaviraj's well-known development of the Gramscian notion to explain the pattern of development adopted by the Indian state. That is, for a thoroughgoing bourgeois

Revealingly, the fact that these reforms were not meant to weaken property rights as such, but only landed property in feudal estates, was spelled out by Finance Minister T. T. Krishnamachari in a later letter to Nehru during discussions on the Fourth Amendment in 1954: "We have to move to the left on agricultural land, but moving left in industry will prevent expansion" (cited in Austin, 1999: 104). In the debate on the First Amendment, Hussain Imam, a big landowner, or *zamindar* MP from Bihar, protesting the lack of fairness and uniformity in compensation, demanded that not only feudal forms of property should be targeted. He said, "Whatever the law you may pass, it must not be for *zamindari* alone but for all kinds of property. Property must not be sacrosanct when it is held by blackmarketeers and industrialists and taken without compensation when held by simple *zamindars* of villages" (Republic of India, 1951). In a sharp retort reflecting modern capitalist notions of property, Pandit Krishna Chandra Sharma said firmly, "The other property a man creates. Land you have not created."[4]

It is significant that no voice in Parliament explicitly opposed the abolition of *zamindari* (large landholdings). The debate was over whether compensation should be "just" and "adequate." Here was the fledgling bourgeois state putting in place notions of legitimate and illegitimate property.

Soon, through the Hindu Marriage Act of 1955 and the Hindu Succession Act of 1956, far-reaching changes were brought about. These changes are presented as reform of Hindu laws to give women equal rights to property, rights to divorce, and so on. However, it has been convincingly demonstrated by Flavia Agnes (1999) and Madhu Kishwar (1994) that what in fact these legislations achieved was the codification of the heterogeneous practices of the many communities that were not Muslim/Parsi/ Christian, bringing them into conformity with what was assumed to be the "Indian" and "Hindu" norm—that is, North Indian, upper-caste practices. This process took away many practices that were better for women in other communities, while giving North Indian upper-caste women a few limited rights they did not have before. For instance, Kishwar (1994) shows how the Hindu Women's Right to Property Act of 1937, referred to earlier, that gave Hindu widows rights to their husbands' property, because it applied uniformly to all communities classified as "Hindu," empowered Brahmin widows but took away from Jain widows the much better provisions that they had under customary law. The "reformed" law thus worked to the detriment of communities that had better inheritance practices for women than Brahmins.

This trend was repeated in the Hindu Succession Act, which, for example, nullified the better position of daughters under matrilineal laws, making sons equal inheritors. The earlier proposal had been to exempt matrilineal communities from the purview of the Hindu Code, but the Select Committee headed by B. R. Ambedkar,[5] against his judgment, removed the exemption.

revolution to be effected, for industrialization to take place, a domestic market must be built up by reducing poverty in the countryside. This can only be done by effective land reforms, which have been legislated but never effectively implemented because of the influence of landed interests in the coalition of ruling classes. The entire planning process until the 1980s has therefore been an exercise in trying to promote industrialization without the radical transformation of agriculture (Kaviraj, 1988).

4   *Lok Sabha Debates*, Part II Vol XII 1951, Col 8965-6 (Republic of India, 1951).

5   Chairman of the Constitution Drafting Committee and first law minister of independent India.

At the same time, the safeguards for women that existed in the traditional coparcenary system were done away with. The main feature of the traditional Hindu Joint Family property had been its inalienability. But the English concept of alienation through testamentary succession was incorporated, while the protection granted to family members under English law was not. As a result, the earlier rights of daughters to be maintained from the ancestral property were lost while their new rights to a share of fathers' self-earned income were nullified by the new testatory rights that fathers simultaneously acquired, to write wills disinheriting them. Interestingly, Agnes (1999) points out that during the parliamentary debate, these very features disempowering daughters were specifically cited as the positive aspects of the new law, in order to persuade members opposing women's property rights that the new provisions could be circumvented.

I would argue that the personal laws on succession and property, such as the Hindu Succession Act, represent a point of conflict between the imperatives of the state and those of the family. The modern state requires legibility in order to mobilize resources toward capitalist industrialization, that is, it must be able to "see" and recognize the forms of property in existence. This need for legibility arises from two crucial imperatives of the modern state—taxation and revenue generation. Toward this end, the institution of individual rights to property is crucial. All forms of property must become completely alienable and transparent to the state—this development is essential for capitalist transformation of the economy. The family, on the other hand, has its own imperatives of controlling name, descent, and passing on of property, a project disrupted by individual property rights. However, the desire to "modernize" and to set up such a regime of property rights is also present in sections of the community, leading to debates between "progressives" and "conservatives." It is in light of this understanding that we must view the gradual granting of land rights to women under Hindu law, all the way up to 2005, when both married and unmarried daughters were given rights to coparcenary property as well. These changes are more than a simple triumph of a feminist perspective—they also represent the establishment of a bourgeois regime of property for the Hindu community, at least in principle, which makes land completely alienable by every separate individual owner. In the current climate of widespread resistance to land acquisition, this is a considerable achievement for the state, and for capitalist interests within the community, as it is always easier to pressurize or tempt individual owners rather than communities to sell land.

From the development and expansion of individual rights to agricultural land in Personal Laws, we turn now to forest lands and to customary land rights in tribal areas. Each of these three has a different historical trajectory.

Forests and Tribal Communities

Sumit Sarkar (2014) shows that prior to what he terms "the environmental turn" in history writing, rural India was assumed to consist of a multitude of peasant villagers engaged in settled agriculture. Extending cultivation to "cultivable wastes" was seen as "synonymous with the advance of civilization" (2014: 78). Environmental histories brought about a paradigm shift in this understanding, demonstrating that hunters and gatherers, pastoralists, and those who practiced shifting cultivation had "an extremely significant and far from marginal presence" down to late colonial times, when regulatory mechanisms of the state started drawing in on them (2014: 78). Through the Forest Acts of 1865 and 1878, the Forest Department came to control one-fifth of British Indian land area, and overnight, communities that had lived for generations in forests became "encroachers" on newly enclosed forest lands, and their everyday subsistence activities became crimes—cattle grazing, cutting low-hanging branches, gathering leaves, and so on. Other key legislations were the National Forest Policy of 1894, which further regulated rights and restricted privileges of "users" in forest areas for the public good; the Land Acquisition Act of 1894, which permitted compulsory acquisition of land for a "public purpose"; and the 1927 Indian Forest Act, which remains the main legal basis for depriving forest dwellers of their user rights to forest resources.

Sarkar (2014) asserts that there were two main purposes behind these moves—developing forests for the modern timber industry, through "scientific forestry," and expanding arable farming "at the cost of nomadic communities of pastoralists and hunter-foragers" (2014: 88). This was done for reasons of extraction of land revenue and enhancement of export surplus in food grains and cash crops, as that was "the principal channel of remittances to Britain of official savings, pensions and business profits from India" (2014: 88). This process of encouraging sedentarization was in continuation of land revenue policies since the eighteenth century, referred to earlier. "Sedentary ways of life were . . . valorized for being much more orderly and manageable" (2014: 489). Those who refused to settle down were branded as vagrants and criminals in a manner similar to the one noted by James Scott for Southeast Asia (Scott, 2009).

This process has carried on apace in independent India, with the National Forest Policy of 1952, which focused on protecting forest resources while commercially exploiting minor forest produce, and the Forest Conservation Act of 1980, which placed all forests under the control of the central government. The post-independence state also continued utilizing other colonial land acquisition laws for the "public good" in the name of development.

The Supreme Court has now integrated into Indian environmental jurisprudence the idea of "the state as trustee of all natural resources" (Rajamani, 2007: 294). Essentially, this marks a shift in state policy from the colonial objective of encouraging sedentarization to dispossessing forest dwellers so that forests can be handed over to private interests for more efficient extraction of forest produce. Parts of forests are also declared as national parks in the interests of protection of the "environment," over which the state is to be the sole authority. Once an area is declared a national park or sanctuary, forest communities that have lived in and sustained forests for generations overnight become illegal encroachers. It is in this context that we must understand the particular principle of international environment law referred to earlier, that of "the state as trustee of all natural resources."

During the UPA regime, movements of forest peoples, supported by left parties in Parliament, were able to get the Scheduled Tribes (Recognition of Forest Rights) Act 2006 passed. Since the advent of colonial rule, as we have noted, the usufructuary rights to land of millions of tribal communities and forest dwellers have remained disputed or unacknowledged due to lack of records of land rights. A Supreme Court judgment in 2001 put the final seal on the extinguishing of such rights when it issued a stay on the regularization of tribal villages in forest areas. The FRA 2006 was militantly campaigned for in order to recognize and formally codify these rights, but interestingly, the rights that are sought to be recorded are not only "individual rights to cultivated land in forested landscapes" but also collective rights to control, manage, and use forests and their resources as common property (Samarthan, 2012: 2). It also "stipulates the conditions for relocation of forest dwellers from 'critical wildlife habitations' only with their 'free informed consent' and their rehabilitation in alternative land" (Samarthan, 2012: 2).

It is clear that through the involvement of forest peoples' movements, it is not "traditional" rights that are being asserted through the FRA 2006 but new forms of collective rights and claims that are being fashioned. These movements represent the powerful presence of thousands affected by the "brutal violence of the forest bureaucracy" (Ramdas, 2009: 65). In an impressive display of solidarity, "from shifting cultivators, to pastoralists whose livelihoods banked on their access to forests to graze their animals, to internally displaced adivasi women forced to leave their homes and live as refugees in new forest regions" (Ramdas, 2009: 65), all of these came together to ensure the passing of the FRA 2006. However, Ramdas argues that the essentially unchanged patriarchal view of the state and its reluctance to grant claimants community rights to the land they were tilling for over a hundred years reveal that the state is still trying to subvert the intent of the law and to use it to integrate forests into the global capital markets. When it does hand out individual title deeds, the decision on what crop to plant—cash crops trending in global markets or local necessities—is also left to the individuals. Thus, the spirit of the legislation, which emphasized customary traditions and indigenous livelihoods, is subverted. These strategies are disastrous with respect to food sovereignty and gender justice, says Ramdas (2009).

Collective rights are, of course, not desirable from the point of view of either the Forest Department, which has set up patronage networks through bribery and giving selective permissions to the tribal people to use forest produce, nor for supporters of corporate investment-based development (Choubey, 2014). The provision in the FRA 2006, making it mandatory to take "prior informed consent" of the Gram Sabha (village council) for any diversion of forest land, is also an obstacle to corporate exploitation of forests. But within one hundred days of the current BJP government of Narendra Modi, the Ministry of Environment and Forests passed 240 of 325 projects held up for lack of environmental clearance and it emerged in the media that the government was planning to bypass the FRA 2006 by using the provisions of the Environment Protection Act 1986, which only requires a public hearing for giving permission to any project, not the informed consent of Gram Sabhas. This would not only undermine the Gram Sabha but would also establish the dominance of bureaucrats, experts, and politicians on decisions on diversion of forest land (Choubey, 2014).

It is, of course, also the case that the FRA 2006 is not fully implemented yet. For example, the West Bengal government is yet to notify the FRA 2006 in districts, and this results in draconian action by the Forest Department. In this regard, in 2015 the Forest

Department confiscated and destroyed canoes belonging to subsistence fisherwomen in the mangroves of Sunderbans; these women are fighting to be recognized as traditional small-scale fishworkers, with a right to fish for their livelihood. Other livelihood rights of forest-dependent people that are denied include wild honey, shell, and dry wood collection and result in continuous conflicts with the Forest Department (Sarkar, 2015).

The FRA 2006 that emerged from movements, and has enormous potential for rejuvenating forests and the collective livelihoods of forest people, can be a threat to expanded regimes of individual property rights amenable to capital and, not surprisingly, is itself under threat under corporate-friendly regimes.

Customary Laws

"Customary laws" is a term used to refer to the bodies of unwritten usages that govern the lives of communities called tribes, in Northeast and Central India. Tribes consider these intrinsic to their identity, culture, and tradition, but of course they have not remained unchanged through time. As noted earlier, although the colonial government formally did not intervene in customary practices, in practice it intervened extensively. Two sets of legislation, namely the Assam Waste Land Grant Rules of 1838 and the Assam Land and Revenue Regulation of 1886, facilitated land acquisition by the colonial state and these formed the basis for post-1947 laws that enabled state takeover of tribal lands.

The land tenure system is not uniform over tribal lands. There are different systems in place within both Central and Northeast India. A survey of scholarship on the Northeast shows great diversity in landowning patterns. Some tribes have complete community-based ownership with no notion of individual ownership till recently, and others combine individual with clan ownership. Some tribes practice shifting cultivation and so their villages did not have a fixed boundary or name, and communal ownership was the norm among them. Others allot land to each family in return for free labor for about a third of the year. Practices of community ownership were basic to intra- and intergenerational equity as well as the relatively high status of women, because even individually owned land was treated as a community resource inherited from ancestors that they could use to meet their needs but had to preserve for posterity according to ecological imperatives (Fernandes and Bharali, 2008).

The argument is not that tribal societies were free of gender hierarchy but that if resources like land, forests, and water bodies were community-owned, women would have more of a say in their management. However, the relatively high status it confers on them is based on their role as economic assets in the family, not in society. Most tribal traditions kept a clear separation between the family and society. Women were in charge of the family production and economy while men controlled social power. Even the matrilineal tribes like the Khasi, Garo, and Jaintia of Meghalaya are patriarchal in the sense that social power is with men. Men control the village council and other decision-making bodies and also take decisions concerning land alienation (Fernandes and Bharali, 2008).

A study of five tribes that are at different stages of the interface between customary law and the modern legal system notes that land relations are being modified by several factors—immigration and encroachment, but most crucially, the changes introduced by the modern legal system. When modern land laws enter such societies through the process of codification, it is found that the result is class formation and a stronger patriarchal ethos. The intervention of individual ownership-based laws first turns land without an individual title into state property, but this prepares the ground for transferring power from the community to a few elite men who took control of all decision-making and interpreted the customary law to their own benefit, thus deepening and entrenching gender and class inequality (Fernandes et al., 2008).

State policies further strengthen these processes, for example, by giving loans and subsidies for commercial crops only to individual landowning family heads, interpreted as men. Community property-oriented tribes are thus forced to change over to individual title deeds or *patta*s. For example, among the matrilineal Garo of Meghalaya, the state encouraged rubber plantation and gave subsidies and loans to individual owners, thus forcing them to get *patta*s. The administration treated men as family heads and consulted them alone in decisions concerning land use and transfer. Today women continue to inherit land but men wield more political and social power than in the past (Marak, 1997: 60–9, cited in Fernandes et al., 2008).

Women's organizations in the Northeast, for example the Arunachal Pradesh Women's Welfare Society and the Naga Mothers' Association, while pushing for land rights for women and equality in representative institutions, simultaneously defend the protection afforded by customary laws from land acquisition by the state and private corporations. Perhaps this is why reservation for women in local bodies, in accordance with the Indian constitution, is being so strongly opposed by the tribal male elite. Activists from the women's organizations that oppose land acquisition for ecologically harmful and capitalist purposes argue that while the male elite are open to transgressing customary laws in order to sell community lands to private corporate interests, they invoke customary laws only to prevent women from having a say in these matters.[6]

Codification and individual rights to land for women are seen as progressive, and some tribes are bringing about inheritance rights for women. For instance, the Paite Tribal Council in 2004 introduced provisions in favor of daughters, widows, illegitimate or adopted, and other disinherited sons (Kamkhenthang, 2005, cited in Fernandes et al., 2008). However, two decades ago, legal scholar and activist Nandita Haksar wrote critically of an initiative by Madhu Kishwar to press for individual rights to property for Ho tribal women over community rights. She saw the initiative as uncomprehending of the complex community practices that make up tribal understanding of property and its ownership and urged, rather, the need for a struggle within tribal communities to evolve new customs that are more egalitarian, rather than forcefully introducing from above, individual rights to property (Haksar, 1999).

[6] Jarjum Ete of the Arunachal Pradesh Women's Welfare Society and Rosemary Dzuvichu of the Naga Mothers' Association have publicly stated this at workshops of women's organizations at which this author was present.

Haksar's argument is all the more relevant today in the context of accelerated land acquisition by the state in the last few years, now not only for a "public purpose" but also for private capital. The "progressive" changes in customary laws that tend toward individual rights and now property rights for women must also be seen against the same background that we discussed at length in the context of "reforms" in Hindu Personal Law.

We return now to the first decade of the twenty-first century.

Property Titling for Capitalist
Transformation Around the Globe

In June 2010, a news report noted that Peruvian economist Hernando de Soto, hailed as the "poor man's capitalist," had arrived in India to prepare "a road map for slum development in the country," helping the UPA government to "merge the informal economy in the slums of the country with the formal or mainstream one" (Chatterji, 2010).

De Soto indicated that he had been invited by the Federation of Indian Chambers of Commerce and Industry (FICCI)—the tagline on its website is *Industry's Voice for Policy Change*—"to give a few conferences and to meet a few people in government that had an interest in the sort of things I was talking about." Among the people in government he met was the Prime Minister Manmohan Singh, who was later to present to the Union Minister for Housing and Urban Poverty Alleviation, two books written by De Soto, "for a better understanding of issues relating to urban poverty and slum development" (Chatterji, 2010). A government official said to a journalist: "The group led by De Soto will be providing us a methodology for changing the face of the informal economy through routes like property titles and land ownerships." Another official further clarified: "De Soto's approach is essentially based on capitalist economic principles. Our government will try to meld them into our socialist objectives." The news report added, from its briefing, presumably, that De Soto's Institute for Liberty and Democracy, a Lima-based nonprofit organization, "has advised governments in many countries to vest slum-dwellers with property rights to maximise the economic use of assets in slums, create organisational forms to increase the productivity of enterprises and *provide identity devices to allow entrepreneurs to operate in expanded markets*" (Chatterji, 2010, emphasis added).

The De Soto agenda has long been recognized by some scholars as a project of attempting to bring about capitalism globally through sustained state intervention. Timothy Mitchell pointed out that De Soto's two books, *The Other Path* (1989) and *The Mystery of Capital* (2000), became "the most widely cited studies of non-Western economic development in a generation," and that the Institute for Liberty and Democracy (ILD) in Peru, which carried out the research presented in these books, has been called the second most influential think tank in the world (Mitchell, 2007).

In Mitchell's rendering, De Soto's argument, based on findings from research in five countries, is that a large amount of their wealth lies outside the formal economy, trapped in forms that cannot enter the market and therefore cannot be invested to create further wealth. Described as "dead capital," this wealth consists principally of land and housing, to which most people in non-Western countries have no formal title registered with the state. "Live capital," according to De Soto, is created by transforming the value of material assets "into abstract forms, which can live an 'invisible, parallel life' alongside their physical existence." This abstract form is credit and capital (Mitchell, 2007: 248–9).

Mitchell points out, using the example of Egypt, one of the countries studied by De Soto, that "informal property arrangements" have not arisen because of ignorance of notions of private property or because the West did not try to "export its property system abroad." On the contrary, in the nineteenth century, Ottoman and European rulers in Cairo launched a series of attempts to transform property arrangements into systems based on an absolute right of private ownership. But Egyptian farmers were able to prevent the complete destruction of livelihoods that absolute property rights entailed because "Egypt controlled no overseas colonies or Indian territories to which to ship a dispossessed rural population, so could not afford the rates of dispossession that private ownership produced." Mitchell argues that the position of ordinary Egyptians "outside" the mechanisms of private property ownership was "the outcome of a long, often violent, but ultimately relatively successful objection to undergoing the dispossession inflicted on the rural populations of Europe or the complete marginalization or elimination of native populations in parts of the world where settler colonialism was carried through" (Mitchell, 2007: 253).

However, once De Soto's program was adopted from the late 1970s as part of neoliberal reforms in Egypt, and ILD-drafted legislation pushed through in the early 2000s to bring about a mortgage law, a property titling program, and new rules for licensing small businesses, the situation changed drastically. The government and the courts began to alter the laws protecting commercial and residential tenants, freeing property developers from the constraint of rent controls. The investment funds stimulated by the reforms flowed primarily into real estate and into exclusive concessions to provide services such as cell phones or McDonald's restaurants or to supply imports of electronics, cars, and other luxury goods. In other words, capital was transformed wherever possible into sources of rent rather than into productive activity. The share of manufacturing in the economy declined, nonoil exports fell, and no significant efforts were made to increase large-scale employment (Mitchell, 2007: 263).

Addressing De Soto's program, scholarship on other parts of Africa comes to the conclusion that the institution of formal and privatized systems of property rights is not fully implementable, even if desirable. One reason is that people prefer to go through locally recognized institutions of exchange (Joireman, 2008: 1237). This preference may be explained by Sindiso Mnisi's argument that there is a disjuncture between what is termed customary law in South Africa for example, which is merely "official customary law" applied in civil courts, and the "law that is lived in rural communities of South Africa" (Mnisi, 2007: 241). Mnisi uses the term "living customary law" to refer to "an array of varying, localized systems of law observed by numerous communities" as opposed to official customary law (2007: 241–2).

Mnisi makes a general argument that is not directly related to property titling, but the accommodation of living customary law alongside the state system, as Mnisi suggests, would certainly challenge the idea that universal individual rights to land are inevitable and desirable.

More significantly, rather than promoting security of tenure, titling efforts lead to higher levels of conflict over land. When it comes to women, because they are not entitled to own customary land autonomously, formal titling deprives them of even use rights recognized by the community. It is therefore being suggested that joint ownership for women should be instituted before formal titling takes place (Joireman, 2008; Sjaastad and Cousins, 2008). As Sjaastad and Cousins put it, "massive, nation-wide formalization programmes can be seen as risky social experiments that gamble with the livelihoods of the poor" (2008: 8).

A study based on extensive scholarship from countries of Latin America and Africa found that land titling programs have not achieved the benefits claimed by their proponents. There has been no increase of investment in land and housing or in access to formal credit, and municipal revenues have not increased noticeably more than under other tenure regimes, including those that allow many unauthorized settlements. There is no significant evidence of poverty levels being reduced. Not only does titling not provide increased tenure security but many alternative forms of tenure, including those in many informal settlements, also provide high levels of security. In addition, in many countries, land titles do not necessarily protect people from eviction and expropriation of their land (Payne et al., 2009).

All this evidence from India, Africa, and Latin America goes to show that individual rights to land is a strategy that achieves nothing more than opening up land for capitalist transformation, often via the state. De Soto's program was promoted powerfully by bodies like the United Nations Development Programme (UNDP) High Level Commission on Legal Empowerment of the Poor, and in fact India's introduction to De Soto's program was not in 2010, with his first visit. This High Level Commission, co-chaired by former US Secretary of State Madeleine Albright and Hernando de Soto, with India as one of the founding members, was set up in September 2005 (around the same time as the amendments to the HSA were being passed with such a puzzling lack of enthusiasm, but nevertheless unanimously, in the Indian Parliament).

The De Soto agenda involves, says Mitchell (2007: 268), "the movement of assets from the outside to the inside" of capital. The process advocated by De Soto, of property titling and the use of property as collateral, brings into being speculation, concentration of wealth, and the accumulation of rents. Mitchell states unequivocally that

> the outcome of a process of property titling and the mortgaging of property is that land and housing become even less affordable to the poor. They are further excluded from opportunities for the accumulation of capital. Yet at the same time they are "inside" the process, for it is their houses and their lives that must be transformed in order to carry out the production of this wealth. (Mitchell, 2007: 268)

Individual Rights to Land and Land Acquisition

Aditya Nigam (2013) asserts that the widespread *continuation* of "pre-capitalist" forms of production both in agriculture and in non-agricultural sectors is what "confronts capital's onward march" (2013: 509). Nigam argues that these are actually "non-capitalist" rather than "pre-capitalist" forms and "represent the recalcitrant other of capital and capitalism—that which capitalism must attempt to seize, discipline, control and subsume within its own domain but which constantly escape its logic" (2013: 509). The transformation to bourgeois private property, therefore, involves and has always involved, he says, "a violent decimation of all forms of common property and even non-capitalist private property" (Nigam, 2013: 504).

This is evident from the story of land acquisition legislation in contemporary India. In 2013, the Right to Fair Compensation and Transparency in Land Acquisition, Rehabilitation and Resettlement Act (LARRA) was passed, replacing the 1894 Act. Key provisions of this new legislation re-enshrined the state's power to dispossess land for private profit but ensured farmers a share of the profits that would accrue to capital in the form of higher prices for land and rehabilitation and resettlement benefits. Michael Levien sees this as an attempt to substitute one-time payouts for development. LARRA thus represents the contradiction between the land requirements of neoliberal capitalism and the pressures on the state due to electoral democracy. More importantly, this policy concretizes the shift from the state dispossessing land for public sector infrastructure, mining, and public sector heavy industry to the state in effect becoming land brokers for private capital (Levien, 2018).

However, corporate interests were not satisfied with this legislation, and with what they called the general "policy paralysis" of the UPA (which was constrained in its neoliberal ambitions because of the backing of social movements). The UPA itself diluted many of its provisions through an ordinance later in 2013, and the ordinance has since then been promulgated by the president for the third time in 2015 (i.e., without being passed by both houses of Parliament, twice by the government that succeeded the UPA). By this ordinance the government can acquire land for any private entity without obtaining the consent of affected people and can do so without the precondition of Social Impact Assessments. In addition, complaints regarding the state's failure to follow due process now need prior consent of the state to be filed.

Alongside this increased state power to acquire land is the big push toward enshrining individual rights to land, replacing community rights where they existed. We have noted the enthusiasm with which women's rights to land are being promoted by the Indian state. Community rights are also being gradually replaced by individual rights. In March 2018, the Arunachal Pradesh Land Settlement and Records Amendment Act was passed, giving individual ownership rights to indigenous people of the state of Arunachal Pradesh, who earlier had held lands jointly as a community. The state government said in a statement that echoes De Soto that with this legislation, "huge investments are expected, which will augment the economy of the state," and that with ownership rights, tribal people will be able to lease out their land and use it as collateral to get loans from banks (Chandran, 2018). As discussed earlier, none of these benefits actually have accrued in places all over the world where individual land titling has taken place. We also know that individual titles to land make land acquisitions for any purpose easier for the state, and their only purpose is commodification of land.

Michael Levien has starkly defined dispossession as "state sponsored redistribution of land from the poor to the wealthy" (Levien, 2015). It seems that "land rights for women" and "property titles for the poor" are the banners that fly before this process of dispossession leading toward an economy driven by capitalist imperatives.

From Ownership Rights to Use Rights as a Radical Agenda

Pascal van Griethuysen, one of the proponents of the degrowth movement, draws our attention to the fact that there are two different potentials in the institution of property. The first is the "possession aspect" of property, referring to different levels of use rights. The second potential, the "property aspect" of property, refers to "the possibility of engaging the security associated with the legal property title in a capitalization process, the most elementary one being the credit relation" (Van Griethuysen, 2009: 1).

A property-based economy thus involves a "capitalization process," in which owners of property accumulate more and more wealth, "the self-enrichment of proprietors being a spontaneous, consequence of property expansion," and nonproprietors get caught in "an ever-increasing poverty trap by being excluded from wealth creation (when not dispossessed from their own goods through enclosure, foreclosure and other appropriation processes)." The institutional framework becomes more and more influenced by proprietors and inclined to favor their vested interests (Van Griethuysen, 2009: 5).

Van Griethuysen says that as the property economy expands through capitalization and competition, the role of property is reinforced as a central institution in the organization of society:

> Such an institutional path-dependency has been strengthened and further accelerated by the industrial mode of development, which provided unprecedented responses to the particular pressures of property, along with industrial society's fundamental dependence on mineral resources. In such a process, every option that shows incompatibility with property requirements is discriminated against, and every proposition for alternative development paths is eluded. (Van Griethuysen, 2009: 5–6)

It is becoming increasingly clear that women's rights to land are an integral part of the agenda of forcibly constructing capitalism through the agency of the state.

Resisting the Co-Option of Women's Rights into the Capitalist Agenda

The discourse of women's rights arose at the historical moment of the rise of capitalism, and hence the focus on individual rights, but today that language must be radically rethought. This is the moment of the search for a new commons, a new language, and grammar of transformative justice.

From the perspective that this chapter offers, all three—the state, the traditional religious community, and the customary community—are equally problematic from the point of view of equitable access to land for women as well as other excluded castes and groups. A truly radical agenda would thus have to challenge all three factors simultaneously—state-led capitalist enclosures of commons, which is part of what Veltmeyer and Petras (2014) call the "new extractivism"; private individual land ownership; and gendered, casted, and other forms of exclusion from land use. This struggle would have to be waged in a context of accelerated decline of agriculture in an era of rampant dispossession.

We have seen that such movements are already on the ground, whether of forest people or farming communities. It is evident that a feminist agenda will have to radically rethink our old slogan of land rights for women within an individual-centered capitalist regime of property. Learning from the experience of movements for digital commons and intellectual property commons as the paradigm for the future, as well as from movements across the globe that emphasize collective ownership and renewal of the commons, feminist movements must work toward producing new forms of commons and anti-ownership, collective, *use* rights in land.

References

Agarwal, B. (1994). *A Field of One's Own: Gender and Land Rights in South Asia.* Cambridge: Cambridge University Press.

Agarwal, B. (2005). "Landmark step to gender equality." *The Hindu*, September 25. http://www.thehindu.com/thehindu/mag/2005/09/25/stories/2005092500050100. htm.

Agarwal, B. (2017). "Can we unify inheritance law?" *Times of India*, September 19.

Agnes, F. (1999). *Law and Gender Equality: The Politics of Women's Rights in India.* New Delhi: Oxford University Press.

Anderson, M. and Guha, S. (eds.). (1998). *Changing Concepts of Rights and Justice in South Asia.* New Delhi: Oxford University Press.

Andrews, M. (2014). "Theory and experiences from the field: Fostering rural women's access and ownership to land and collectives," Presentation at workshop on women and land rights, 14–15 May, Jawaharlal Nehru University, New Delhi.

Austin, G. (1999). *Working a Democratic Constitution: The Indian Experience.* New Delhi: Oxford University Press.

Birla, R. (2009). *Stages of Capital: Law, Culture, and Market Governance in Late Colonial India.* Durham: Duke University Press.

Chandran, R. (2018). "Individual land rights to India's indigenous people could be 'disastrous,' expert says." *Reuters*, March 15. https://in.reuters.com/article/india -landrights-lawmaking/individual-land-rights-to-indias-indigenous-people-could-be -disastrous-expert-says-idINKCN1GR1U8.

Chatterji, S. (2010). "UPA to try 'de Soto model' for slum development." *Business Standard*, June 29. https://www.business-standard.com/article/economy-policy/upa-to-try-de -soto-model-for-slum-development-110062900053_1.html.

Choubey, K. N. (2014). "'Red carpet' in forests." https://kafila.online/2014/09/28/red -carpet-in-forests-kamal-nayan-choubey/.

Derrett, J. D. M. (1968). *Religion, Law and the State in India*. London: Faber and Faber.

Fernandes, W. and Bharali, G. (2008). "Customary law–formal law interface: Impact on tribal culture," in T. B. Subba, J. Puthenparakal and S. J. Puykunnel (eds.), *Christianity and Change in Northeast India*. New Delhi: Concept Publishing Company, pp. 93–108.

Fernandes, W., Pereira, M. and Khatso, V. (2008). *Tribal Customary Laws in Northeast India: Gender and Class Implications*. Guwahati: North Eastern Social Research Centre. http://www.nesrc.org/Monographs/Customary-Laws.pdf.

Gatade, S. (2005). "Interview with Ms C.K. Janu, leader of tribals in Kerala." March 18. http://www.sacw.net/Nation/gatade18032005.html.

Guha, R. (1996). *A Rule of Property for Bengal: An Essay on the Idea of Permanent Settlement*. Durham: Duke University Press.

Gupta, S. (2018). "Women and land rights in India: Towards a democratic and gendered formulation of the land question," in P. Jha, A. Kumar and Y. Mishra (eds.), *Labouring Women: Issues and Challenges in Contemporary India*. Hyderabad: Orient Blackswan, pp. 267–77.

Haksar, N. (1999). "Human rights lawyering: A feminist perspective," in A. Dhanda and A. Parasher (eds.), *Engendering Law: Essays in Honour of Lotika Sarkar*. Lucknow: Eastern Book Company, pp. 71–88.

The Hindu. (2005). "Equal rights for women in parental property." *Special Correspondent*, August 17. http://www.thehindu.com/2005/08/17/stories /2005081705461200.htm.

Joireman, S. F. (2008). "The mystery of capital formation in sub-Saharan Africa: Women, property rights and customary law." *World Development*, 36(7): 1233–46.

Kaviraj, S. (1988). "A critique of the passive revolution." *Economic and Political Weekly*, Annual Number, 23(45/47): 2429–44.

Kishwar, M. (1994). "Codified Hindu law: Myth and reality." *Economic and Political Weekly*, August 13, 29(33): 2145–61.

Kodoth, P. (2001). "Courting legitimacy or delegitimizing custom? Sexuality, Sambandham and marriage reform in late-nineteenth century Malabar." *Modern Asian Studies*, 35(2): 349–84. https://doi.org/10.1017/S0026749X01002037.

Krishnan, B. J. (2000). "Customary law." *Seminar* 492, August.

Kurup, A. (2008). "Tribal law in India: How decentralized administration is extinguishing tribal rights and why autonomous tribal governments are better." *Indigenous Law Journal*, 7(1): 87–126. http://hdl.handle.net/1807/17375.

Levien, M. (2015). "Dispossession, development and democracy." *The Hindu*, February 4. https://www.thehindu.com/opinion/lead/lead-article-dispossession-development-and -democracy/article6853389.ece.

Levien, M. (2018). *Dispossession Without Development: Land Grabs in Neoliberal India*. New York: Oxford University Press.

Marak, C. (1997). "Status of women in Garo culture," in S. Sen (ed.), *Women in Meghalaya*. New Delhi: Omsons Publications, pp. 56–72.

Mitchell, T. (2007). "Properties of markets," in D. MacKenzie, F. Muniesa and L. Siu (eds.), *Do Economists Make Markets? On the Performativity of Economics*. Princeton: Princeton University Press, pp. 244–75.

Mnisi, S. (2007). "Postcolonial culture and the South African legal system: Understanding the relationship between living customary law and state law." *Zeitschrift für Rechtssoziologie (The German Journal of Law and Society)*, 28(2): 241–51.

Nair, J. (1996). *Women and Law in Colonial India: A Social History*. New Delhi: Kali for Women.

Newbigin, E. (2009). "The codification of personal law and secular citizenship: Revisiting the history of law reform in late colonial India." *The Indian Economic and Social History Review*, 46(1): 83–104. https://doi.org/10.1177/001946460804600105.

Newbigin, E. (2013). *The Hindu Family and the Emergence of Modern India: Law, Citizenship and Community*. Cambridge: Cambridge University Press.

Nigam, A. (2013). "'Molecular economies': Is there an 'outside' to capital?" in N. Menon, A. Nigam and S. Palshikar (eds.), *Critical Studies in Politics: Exploring Sites, Selves, Power*. Hyderabad: Orient Blackswan, pp. 482–514.

Payne, G., Durand-Lasserve, A. and Rakodi, C. (2009). "The limits of land titling and home ownership." *Environment and Urbanization*, 21(2): 443–62. https://doi.org/10.1177/0956247809344364.

Prakash, A. (1999). "Decolonisation and tribal policy in Jharkhand: Continuities with colonial discourse." *Social Scientist*, 27(7/8): 113–39. https://doi.org/10.2307/3518015.

Rajamani, L. (2007). "Public interest environmental litigation in India: Exploring issues of access, participation, equity, effectiveness and sustainability." *Journal of Environmental Law*, 9(3): 293–321.

Ramdas, S. (2009). "Women, forestspaces and the law: Transgressing the boundaries." *Economic and Political Weekly*, 44(44): 65–73.

Rao, N. (2008). *Good Women Do Not Inherit Land: Politics of Land and Gender in India*. Hyderabad: Orient Blackswan.

Republic of India (RoI). (1951). *Lok Sabha Debates, Part II*, Vol. XII. New Delhi: Parliament of India.

Republic of India (RoI). (2005). "Motion for consideration of the Hindu Succession (Amendment) Bill," Lok Sabha Debates, 29 August. Parliament of India, New Delhi. https://indiankanoon.org/doc/842089/.

Roma. (2014). "Theory and experiences from the field: Fostering rural women's access and ownership to land and collectives," Presentation at workshop on women and land rights, 14–15 May, Jawaharlal Nehru University, New Delhi.

Samarthan—Centre for Development Support. (2012). "Recognition of community rights under Forest Rights Act in Madhya Pradesh and Chhattisgarh: Challenges and way forward." http://www.undp.org/content/dam/india/docs/DG/recognition-of-community-rights-under-forest-rights-act-in-madhya-pradesh-and-chhattisgarh-challenges-and-way-forward.pdf.

Sarkar, S. (2014). *Modern Times: India 1880s–1950s*. Ranikhet: Permanent Black.

Sarkar, U. (2015). "A right to fish, a fight to live." https://ruralindiaonline.org/articles/a-right-to-fish-a-fight-to-live.

Scott, J. (2009). *The Art of Not Being Governed*. New Haven: Yale University Press.

Singha, R. (1998). "Civil authority and due process: Colonial criminal justice in the Banaras Zamindari, 1781–1795," in M. Anderson and S. Guha (eds.), *Changing Concepts of Rights in South Asia*. New Delhi: Oxford University Press, pp. 30–81.

Sjaastad, E. and Cousins, B. (2008). "Formalisation of land rights in the South: An overview." *Land Use Policy*, 26(1): 1–9. https://doi.org/10.1016/j.landusepol.2008.05.004.

Van Griethuysen, P. (2009). "Why are we growth-addicted? The hard way towards degrowth in the involutionary western development path." *Journal of Cleaner Production*, 1–6. https://doi.org/10.1016/j.jclepro.2009.07.006.

Veltmeyer, H. and Petras, J. (eds.). (2014). *The New Extractivism: A Post-neoliberal Development Model or Imperialism for the Twenty-First Century?* London and New York: Zed Books.

5

Empire in the Era of DIY Colonialism

Barbarism or Slavery in the (Post)Colonial Context?

Abdelwahab El-Affendi

Introduction

Regardless of the (intense) controversy provoked by Mamdani's seminal work, *Citizen and Subject* (1996), few dispute the importance of the focus it has brought on the issue of the enduring legacy of the colonial state in Africa. The power configurations that enabled the colonial order to sustain itself have also continued to shape the modern African state and influence its form, identity, and trajectories. One might (and in my case, will) disagree with some aspects of Mamdani's narrative regarding the nature of colonial power and the forms of its perpetuation. However, the focus on the colonial roots of current power configurations is absolutely central.

The key questions revolve around the "secret" of the colonial endeavor: the ability of some countries to rule foreign populations (often several times the size of the imperial country's own population, and with much vaster territories) against their will, their culture, and their interests, using only a handful of administrators and rather small armies. As Cooper puts it, it entails "the institutionalization of a set of practices that both defined and reproduced over time the distinctiveness and subordination of particular people in a differentiated space" (Cooper, 2005: 26). For Ypi, it is "typically understood as a practice that involves both the subjugation of one people to another and the political and economic control of a dependent territory (or parts of it)" (Ypi, 2013: 162).

Subjugation involves violence, in this case, plenty of it. The conquest itself was brutal, but the colonial state "was violent above all in its everyday, routinized exercise of authority, that is, in the colonial administration. Its administrative actions were constitutively despotic" (Von Trotha, 2006: 438). As is now well known, this violence took in many instances terroristic and genocidal proportions, especially when faced with resistance. However, what is more interesting is not the violence but the longevity of this arrangement and the effectiveness of the techniques. Violence "pacified" the colonies, given room for more subtle forms of co-optation.

Mamdani sees "late colonialism" in Africa as the outcome of a failed project, a "Plan B," so to speak, after the failure of its presumed "civilizing mission." The latter was abandoned in the face of setbacks (chief among which was the violent 1857 "Sepoy Rebellion" in India, in which the "native" troops in the colonial army turned against their masters). As a result, a shift occurred where the goal became that of civilizing the colonized "not as individuals but as communities" (Mamdani, 1996: 51). The outcome was "indirect rule," a colonial partnership with local tribal aristocracies that instituted a form of "decentralized despotism." In this disposition, the colonial state became a "bifurcated state," where urban areas were "governed directly by a civil power enforcing a civil law claiming to guarantee rights." In the rural areas, however, "the free peasantry was ruled indirectly through Native Authorities whose aim was to enforce custom through a customary law" (Mamdani, 1996: 182).

DIY Colonialism

I take issue with these claims in detail in the following. But suffice it to say here that identifying "decentralized despotism" as one of the key mechanisms that sustained colonial rule leaves its enduring impact and power configurations still a mystery. The macro-explanations regarding "imperialism" and "new colonialism" (including dependency theory, world system theory, etc.) also fall short of providing a fuller explanation, for they fail to account for the differential impact of the "world-systems" on specific cases. The issue with colonialism is not just one of techniques, such as "indirect rule," as well as terror and genocide. It was also the success of these techniques, and the continued efficacy of the colonial project, in its direct and indirect forms, mostly the latter, especially in the "postcolonial" era.

In this chapter, we start with the hypothesis that the "decentralized despotism" of "indirect rule" (or what I would like to call "DIY colonialism") is the essence of the colonial project and experience. It is also the key to understanding both the precolonial and postcolonial relationships of subordination of the periphery to the metropolitan center. The rural peripheries of various colonies were not the only regions that had been subjected to indirect rule; many so-called "independent countries" continue to be subject to indirect rule as well. Just as India had been run "indirectly" by the East India Company before the rebellion, and only became incorporated into the empire fully after it, "independent" countries have also reverted to indirect rule through multinationals and other devices. Those who resisted suffered grievous consequences, and most have now reverted to submission in various degrees, many not only willingly but also eagerly. The recent Arab stampede toward embracing Israel, when that problem country is under one of its worst regimes, and at its most vicious and nasty, is a case in point. The way in which some oil-rich Arab autocracies lavished money on Donald Trump's America is the most blatant case of the pay-to-be-colonized syndrome, of which more later.

This raises the key question: is the present generation at all better equipped to understand the mechanisms of foreign hegemony, let alone devising ways of countering them, than previous generations of the anti-colonial vanguard? The latter had ruined their countries in futile attempts to escape the capitalist system, only to come back into more abject submission. Can scholarship offer anything more substantial than lamenting this trap of "perpetual colonialism"?

Here, we may need to dwell on Mamdani's important distinction between the apparent perpetuation of "decentralized despotism" by the more conservative regime types and attempts by radicals to discard or reform the system in favor of a uniform and unitary system. The conservatives reconciled themselves to the state form inherited from the colonial era, making their peace and pacts with the local despots, co-opting them into the system. The radicals, however, went to war against that system but ended up imposing centralized despotism instead (Mamdani, 1996: 25–7).

However, this may be a rather limited—and somewhat distorted—focus on the internal dynamics of the operation. The conservative ("moderate") regimes, exemplified by the likes of post-independence Kenya and Côte d'Ivoire (one should add South Africa now and Zimbabwe before "going rogue"), have not only reconciled themselves with indirect rule. They were even happy to perform DIY indirect rule by reconciling themselves with the economic and political interests of the former colonial powers. In this regard, they expended minimal political capital on internal and external wars. Their countries relatively prospered and enjoyed some peace in the interim. The "radicals," by contrast, appeared to engage in perpetual (and immensely destructive) wars that weakened the countries and made them even more "colonizable" (to use Malik Bennabi's term, cited in Benlahcene, 2011). It is a supreme irony that the trajectories of countries like Ghana, Egypt, Iraq, Guinea, and Algeria have taken them from presumed fearless confrontation with hegemony to conditions of complete "reconciliation" with the powers-that-be (to use a euphemism). The irony is epitomized, in its most grotesque manifestation, in "revolutionary" Algeria, where repenting collaborators with colonial France, who joined the revolution *after* the eleventh hour (dubbed "France's generals" or "the Party of France") came to dominate the country from the 1990s (Roberts and Roberts, 2003: 352).

In any case, modern colonialism has distinguished itself from earlier forms of imperialism by perfecting indirect hegemony. In India and other remnants of the Muslim empires, as well as in Africa, it always started with "treaties" (or "capitulations," as some were appropriately named) with local princes and rulers: to permit trade, protect minority rights, allow diplomatic and consular privileges, and so on. Creeping control and, finally, conquest followed. In fact, it can be argued that the Indian Mutiny signaled the start of direct colonial hegemony, rather than the establishment of indirect rule. For what followed was the end of the earlier "rule" through the East India Company and similar nonstate devices and the takeover by the British state of direct control of India. Similar shifts happened in Africa, where coastal trading posts and other trade agreements were replaced by direct conquest during the notorious "Scramble for Africa" (Pakenham, 2015).

In Egypt, one of the earliest colonies in Africa, colonial domination started by sending "advisors" to help organize the country's finances. It soon became a rather advanced instance of "indirect rule," whose fictional layers were as ingenious as they were transparent. Officially, Egypt was an Eyala (governorate) of the Ottoman Empire. Its ruler, the Khedive, was an appointee of the Ottoman Sultan. This nominal suzerainty continued to be acknowledged, even as Egypt gained virtual independence under

Mohammad Ali and his descendants from around 1805. It also continued after the British invaded and took control in 1882. While the fiction was maintained that Egypt was ruled by an Ottoman-appointed Khedive, it was Britain that effectively appointed the man and dictated to him. The British consul-general in Cairo effectively ruled through his officials within the government. The Sirdar (commander) of the Egyptian army (who from 1898 also became the Egyptian-appointed governor-general of Sudan) was also British. Thus, there was a ruler of Egypt who was fictionally an autonomous appointee of the Ottoman Sultan (but was in fact a British appointee and employee), fictionally appointing the ruler of Sudan, who was also the commander of "his" army (Daly, 1983; Tignor, 2015).

In Egypt's case, the mechanisms of British control were multiple: financial, diplomatic, and military. The latter was the most decisive element, since it was the vanquishing of the Egyptian army in 1882 and putting down of the Urabi uprising against the Khedive, that enabled Britain to call the shots. However, before that Britain and its European partners had taken control of Egyptian finances from 1879, deposing the profligate Khedive Ismail and purporting to restore Egypt's financial health.[1] Many among the Egyptian elite were willing to cooperate, having entertained the illusion that Britain would leave Egypt once that task was accomplished. No less important was the fact that the British invasion had "saved" the Khedive Tewfik Pasha (Ismail's son and successor) from his own mutinous army, restoring him to power. This playing on internal conflicts represented another source of colonial power, since some powerful interests were willing to see Britain as an ally. The "light touch" colonialism had the effect of turning Egypt into a thriving economic center, even a haven for "free expression," toward which many intellectuals from surrounding areas converged (Cole, 1999).

In Algeria, as in India, the occupiers tried to cultivate the allegiance of the local community by purporting to safeguard religious freedoms and permit people to manage their own affairs, including running their own "religious courts." In the face of rebellions and mass migration from lands controlled by "infidels," both France and Britain sought and obtained from ulama in Al Azhar Mosque in Cairo and the Holy Mosque in Mecca fatwas, making it legal for Muslims to live under colonial rule. The pretext was that this rule permitted Muslims to perform their religious rituals without interference and to manage their personal affairs according to Islamic rule through "native courts." Thus, indirect rule was built into colonialism from its inception (Mahmud, 1997).

On the "Civilizing Mission": Liberalism's Eternal Paradoxes

The "civilizing mission" myth (together with the concomitant argument regarding the maintenance of "civil society" in urban areas) is also in need of more critical scrutiny. Even an ardent advocate of colonialism like Tocqueville was happy to admit that the European colonialists were acting more savagely than the "barbarians" they were

---

[1]　Ironically, the British asked the Ottoman Sultan to depose the Khedive!

presumed to civilize (Tocqueville, 2001: 25, 70). An advocate of "liberty" like Napoleon arrived in Egypt promising liberation from tyranny and respect for Islam. However, he was soon hanging clerics and bombing Cairo's crowded quarters indiscriminately. He even turned Al Azhar Grand Mosque into a stable for his army's horses and a toilet for his drunken soldiers. Many compared George W. Bush's claims to democratize Iraq to that earlier "civilizing mission," as both proved as barbaric as that of Attila the Hun (El-Affendi, 2010).

There is also a need to reexamine the argument that areas under direct colonial rule (in contrast to ones subject to indirect rule) enjoyed thriving civil society and civil rights. There was no "bifurcation" at all in the African state: it was either direct despotism or a delegated one. In fact, people in rural areas were in many senses freer than those under direct tutelage of the colonial administration, enjoying more rights and freedoms.

In this case, Mamdani's definition of "despotism" is counterintuitive, to put it mildly. It takes a lot of convincing for one to regard the authoritarianism of rulers like Museveni as "democratization." Sending "commissars" from the single party to lord it over rural people could also hardly be termed "democratizing" and "de-tribalizing," while the voluntary solidarity along tribal lines was deemed "despotic." In this regard, the prescription of radical politicians for embarking on another "civilizing mission" to liberate those falling under the sway of tribalism against their own (deluded) will has had, not surprisingly, disastrous consequences. More of the same will hardly be an improvement.

By the same token, one would hesitate to accept the description of the arbitrary dispossession of Asians and other "settlers" as a "deracializing" African politics. In fact, if anything, it would appear to racialize politics and contaminate it with irrational prejudice. We have seen the disastrous consequences of those policies, from Egypt, Tanzania, Uganda, and Sudan to Zimbabwe, and the ignominious and costly (and futile) reversals that had to be made. Radical politicians, like Idi Amin or Robert Mugabe, dispossess certain groups and ruin the economy in the process, then the same groups receive compensation at the expense of the very people purportedly being championed.

This is a reminder that colonialism started at home, in Europe. As Von Trotha reminds us, "It is all too easily forgotten that the modern territorial state is closely related to colonial rule with respect to its use of violence and the methods and conditions of power and domination in its incipient stages" (Von Trotha, 2006: 433).

It is often said that Ireland was Britain's first colony. However, Britain itself was once a Norman "colony," and its Welsh and Scottish extensions were colonies in some sense. The French "Republic" was itself a colonial project, where many of its "provinces" were brutally incorporated into the republican project. Some have even argued that the "so-called Westphalian system" was in itself "actually an imperial system of hegemonic and subaltern states" and not the system of "sovereign states" modern mythology depicts (Pitts, 2010: 233). In turn, European colonialism has helped shape the modern state in its European incarnation that later became a model for all to emulate:

> The dynamics of European expansion were always part of the dynamics through which the European nation-states emerged, consolidated, and competed among

one another. In the Age of Imperialism this force assumed a new quality. . . . It was a view of European power politics as world politics, and imperialistic colonial policies were seen as global power policies by means of colonies. (Von Trotha, 2006: 437)

This shaped and influenced modern thinking on world politics. The same can be said about modern "liberal" political thought in general. Not only were the most prominent architects of modern liberal thought directly involved in the colonial endeavor (as employees of the major companies of the colonial era, like Grotius, Mill, and Locke), but they were also legislators and activist-theorists (like Montesquieu). Additionally,

> More fundamentally, the key concepts and languages of European political thought—ideas of freedom and despotism, self-government, and the autonomous individual—were imagined and articulated in light of, in response to, and sometimes in justification of, imperial and commercial expansion beyond Europe. (Pitts, 2010: 215)

The apparent contradiction between the liberal ideals of Enlightenment theoreticians and their ardent advocacy of colonial subjugation is thus not an anomaly. Liberalism was equally and ardently supportive of the exclusion of the bulk of citizenry from the political sphere: the poor, the uneducated, women, and so on. These exclusions were easy to explain in terms of a deficit of rationality in those excluded. Grotius went so far as to describe natives in colonized countries as practically insane. Colonial authorities were thus seen as guardians of these pre-rational groups. This guardianship could be temporary in some charitable versions, but in practice it was seen as indefinite. It was thus accurate to speak of a "mutually constitutive" relationship between liberalism and empire (Pitts, 2010: 216).

In this context, indirect rule was part of the justification of this indefinite nature of colonial guardianship. It opts to perpetuate the colonial bond by first enlisting the "natives" as partners in their own enslavement and, second, by portraying this bondage as a form of liberation. The "natives" are now "free" to be who they are and what they want to be, living according to their own values within an overarching liberal framework.

Critics of these arrangements often neglect how constitutive of identity and self-sustaining they can be. Just as the partitioning of Africa has created "national" identities that are now fiercely (and frequently violently) defended by "patriots," the "native administration" partitions have also created "tribal"/regional identities that are equally powerful. Radical "nationalists" saw the disruption and dismantling of these constructs as acts of "decolonization." In this, they commit the same colonial sin of devaluing the agency of the subjects involved. Nowhere has this been more graphically (and tragically) illustrated than in the cases of Eritrea and Southern Sudan, where "nationalists" thought it right and expedient to regard the colonially constituted identities as "artificial," thus justifying the use of the same colonial tactics of violence, indoctrination, and manipulation to reverse the process and restore what should have been a "natural order" of things.

Sources of Colonial Power: The Case of Sudan

Some years back, I was visiting a friend at his family home at the outskirts of the Sudanese capital Khartoum, where I met his father for the first time. "Don't mention to my father that you have just come from Britain," the friend joked after the introductions, "or you will never get him to stop his nostalgic reminiscences about the era of British rule."

Curious, I insisted on asking our elderly host about what he liked so much about British rule. His answer was as succinct as it was thought-provoking. "They provided security," he said, "and left us more or less alone."

The family hailed from one of the nomadic tribes inhabiting the deserts of Western Sudan. So, one can see, in perspective, why they appreciated this minimalist approach to governance. His statement was also a criticism of the "busy-body" approach of post-independence administrations, which bothered the people with multiple tax burdens and endless new rules but provided little by way of security or services. It is interesting that most former subjects of colonial rule do not seem to appreciate the virtues of minimalist governance, except nostalgically and in retrospect. Deng and Daly (1990: 4–11) had tried to emphasize this "bonds of silk" side to colonial subjugation in a wider context, presenting the reminiscences of thirty-seven British colonial officials and seventeen Sudanese tribal leaders and other figures. The majority viewed the colonial era in suspiciously rosy terms. Daly partly corrected this perceived bias in his rather scathing account of British rule in Sudan (Daly, 1991). However, the Sudanese case remains a unique enactment of the principle of indirect rule, since British rule there was based on multiple fictions, chief among which was the depiction of British colonial rule as a joint venture with Egypt ("Condominium") (Collins, 2008: 33–68).

This fiction (like the previously mentioned and related fiction about British rule of Egypt) had far-reaching consequences for all three parties (Daly, 2004). The Egyptians, while acquiescing in this narrative, became initially collaborators in the colonial venture, supplying the military manpower for the invasion, and the first tier in this scheme of "indirect rule," even before the term was invented. At the same time, the experience fed Egyptian nationalism, making the "restoration" Sudan to Egyptian rule the focus of nationalist mobilization and aspirations. Boutros Ghali, Egypt's prime minister from 1908, was blamed (among other things) for surrendering Sudan to Britain by signing the 1899 treaty as foreign minister. He was assassinated in 1910 by a young Egyptian nationalist, mainly on account of this, but also for his role as one of the judges in the notorious 1906 Denshway trial. In that trial, a number of Egyptian peasants were hanged after being wrongfully implicated in the death of a British officer (Goldschmidt, 1993). (This incident may also problematize Mamdani's rather favorable characterization of the colonial judicial system.)

It was another irony that, as it fought to regain independence from British colonial rule, Egyptian nationalism foregrounded regaining exclusive "colonial" control of Sudan at the same time! More ironic was the way in which Sudanese nationalism bought into this narrative, playing the presumed colonial partners against one other, and at times even believing in a joint Egyptian-Sudanese destiny and a common cause against British colonialism. However, the complex dynamics at play here reinforced the drive toward "indirect rule" and shaped its contours in the Sudanese case.

As everywhere else, brute force was the main instrument of colonial dominance in Sudan as well. However, unlike many other African "countries" where colonial rule was a creeping phenomenon, often creating "colonies" out of a patchwork of tribal fiefdoms, Sudan was a fully fledged independent state when the British invaded in 1896. As an integral state, Sudan came into being following an invasion by a resurgent Egypt under Muhammad Ali in 1821, when at least four independent kingdoms were merged into one country named Sudan. Modern-day South Sudan was annexed in the process. Egyptian rule was overthrown by the Mahdist uprising in 1885. Under Mahdism, Sudan even became a "radical" expansionist state, with its own world-conquering ambitions and a messianic ideology to match. It had a formidable army with determined fighters. However, what settled the matter was the unchallengeable military superiority of the invaders, who deployed railroad, armed steamers, and the formidable Maxim machine gun. This killing machine saw its first major field test on the outskirts of Omdurman in September 1898. The bravery of the fanatical Mahdist troops was to no avail, as the machine guns and cannon fire wiped out most of the army in under four hours. This decisive crushing of resistance established an unchallengeable military power, dictating who was the boss from then on. Any rebellion was brutally and efficiently put down (Daly, 2004; Collins, 2008).

However, divide-and-rule tactics were additionally applied here early. The Mahdist state was despotic and rather brutal under the Mahdi's *Khalifa* (successor), alienating many key Sudanese tribes and religious brotherhoods. The British relied on those components to isolate and alienate dissent. Economically, the British also deployed "strategic benevolence" to win hearts and minds. Sudan had suffered devastating famines during the Mahdist era, wiping out nearly half of the population, according to some estimates. During the first part of his two-year rule, Kitchener's policies made things worse in some respects. However, more prudent policies (including low taxation due to reliance on "Egyptian" subsidies, distribution of imported grain, etc.) helped ease the hardships in subsequent years. A threatened famine in 1913 was averted by importing sorghum from India and selling it cheaply, impressing the locals (Daly, 2004).

Later, "indirect rule" became the chief component of colonial divide-and-rule tactics, when it began to be applied seriously only after the 1924 popular uprising and officer mutiny. Since it was mainly the new modern-educated elite, inspired by Egyptian nationalism, that began to challenge the new regime, colonial administrators evolved "indirect rule" as a deliberate counterstrategy to replace the "unreliable" officers with tribal chiefs.

The rebellion had been partly provoked by moves championed by the Sudan Political Service (SPS, the corporate body of British colonial officials in Sudan) to end the fiction of joint Egyptian-British sovereignty over Sudan, making the status quo of unilateral British hegemony official. This in turn fed more dissent among the emerging Sudanese national elite. June 1924 witnessed the first wave of popular protests, followed in August by a mutiny among cadets in the military academy and a rebellion among Sudanese officers in the (Egyptian) army. Like the Indian Mutiny, this was a deep shock to the British establishment, which had until then trusted in the loyalty of the graduates of its own institutions. A decision was immediately taken to close the military academy. When, in November 1924, an Egyptian nationalist assassinated the governor-general of Sudan, Sir Lee Stack in Cairo, the SPS and Britain found it opportune to eliminate the Egyptian military presence in Sudan. The newly elected government of nationalist hero Saad Zaghloul (which came to power only in February 1924) was given a 48-hour ultimatum to withdraw Egyptian units from Sudan, forsake rights in the Nile waters, and accept other punitive measures. Zaghloul could not stomach the humiliation and had to resign, with Egypt instantly returning to "indirect rule." The monarchy and sections of the elite were happy to play along (Beshir, 1974).

In Sudan as well, the nationalist upsurge and its links with Egypt provoked fears among the traditional religious and tribal elites, incensed by the leadership claims of "upstarts," with no pedigree in the tribal or religious aristocracies. They thus worked to create a rival bloc, which backed the planned removal of Egyptian influence from Sudan and accepted Britain alone as a "guardian" to steer Sudan toward eventual independence. The slogan raised was "Sudan for the Sudanese," in opposition to the nationalist advocacy of unity with Egypt. Thus, ironically, the local elites in both Egypt and Sudan were actively advocating "indirect rule" by seeking colonial protection against the emerging nationalist threat to the precolonial order of privilege. For the militant nationalists, ironically, the slogan "Sudan for the Sudanese" was not seen as call for freedom and independence but a treacherous advocacy of continued colonialism. The British loved it: a nationalist slogan in favor of colonial rule!

There is a background to this, given that Egypt was the former "colonial" power in Sudan in the pre-Mahdist era. It was Muhammad Ali's brutal conquest in 1821, and the increasingly oppressive rule of his heirs, that had both forged modern "Sudanese" identity, and provoked the Mahdist revolt of 1881, and facilitated its success. The increasingly influential neo-Mahdist movement, which emerged in the second decade of the twentieth century, nurtured a deep animosity toward the former colonial rulers. With its allies, it depicted the call for unity with Egypt as an advocacy for a return to those "bad old days." This was another irony, since the "nationalists" appeared to be advocating an alternative form of "foreign" rule, helping exacerbate the divisions, to the benefit of the actual colonial rulers. Another irony was that Gamal Abdel Nasser's accession to power in 1954, and the demise of democracy in Egypt, dealt a fatal blow to the unionist cause. The breaking point came in early 1954, when Nasser executed leaders of the Muslim Brotherhood for opposing his rule. Few Sudanese wanted to join such a regime, and the case for independence was made, even though the unionist camp won a landslide victory in the 1953 parliamentary elections. The August 1955 mutiny in the South made this definitive, since Southerners also opposed any Egyptian link (El-Affendi, 1991).

Mamdani dwelt on the Sudanese case in two of his most recent works (*Define and Rule* and *Saviors and Survivors*) to illustrate further some of the points he had made earlier regarding the constructed nature of the "native" identity and the institutions connected with it (Mamdani, 2009, 2012). In the latter, he also touched on neoliberal imperialism and its ramifications, which are of relevance to the current debate. However, as in the earlier work, too much focus on the role of colonialism in creating native identities neglects a number of crucial issues. This includes, first, the fact that colonialism also "created" the "national" identities of which opponents of tribalism are so enamored. Second, the identities concerned were not just "created" by outside powers but have their own history and inner dynamics. They were often aspects of political struggles that have preceded colonialism and survived it. Third, and more to the point, these identities kept evolving with time. In the case of Darfur, for example, sectarian and tribal identities played competing as well as mutually reinforcing roles. "Sectarian" identities encompassed in fact complex coalitions of tribal, regional, and "modern" identities. Attempts by both left-wing and Islamist radicals to reshape these identities contributed to the current crises in both Darfur and South Sudan.

Violence and Ethical Disarmament

The perpetuation of colonial rule thus depended primarily on superior military force, assisted by techniques of sociopolitical management of the subjected societies. No less important, however, were narratives of "ethical supremacism," embedded around claims of "civilizing missions." In Sudan's case, this was enhanced by one of the earliest claims of "humanitarian intervention," as the Mahdist revolution had been depicted as a barbaric brutal regime as well as a dangerous and radical one. British media went to town with these claims, especially against the background of the murder of the popular Charles Gordon, the last "Egyptian" governor-general of Sudan in 1885. (There are interesting parallels between American and British media coverage of the Mahdist rebellion and the coverage of the Iranian revolution a century later.) Later, the writings of Rudolf Slatin (the Austrian former governor of Darfur, who became a captive of the Mahdists before escaping in 1895) and others also fed the propaganda calling for intervention in Sudan. The campaigners against the slave trade, missionaries, and others were also enthusiastic advocates of the "reconquest" of Sudan.

The points raised earlier about the interconnection between the claims of liberalism and the justifications of colonialism are also relevant here. The pretenses of early European expansionism (from the Crusades to the Reconquista and early excursions into Africa and the "New World") were at first religious: infidels needed to be saved or punished. Later, arguments from "natural law" theories modified those claims: natives needed to be educated and civilized. According to these arguments, "natives" could not be dispossessed or enslaved without just cause. However, "just cause" was usually readily found. Natives were deemed barbaric, indolent, or just possessing too much land.

Indeed the "ethical" pretentions were so overpowering that those who later rose against colonial rule were not only advocates of such narratives; they were in fact their creatures. The first generations of nationalist leaders, educated in the culture and language of the colonial masters, bought into the narratives of "civilizing" and "modernizing" their communities. Many even spoke no language other than that of the colonial "motherland"; some were converts to its religion. In most countries, the postcolonial order evolved into an *Animal Farm* scenario where those who prided themselves in ridding the nation of the colonial yoke became more ardent promoters of colonial norms of governance, administration, and acculturation than their former masters. Even in countries that have never been colonized, such as Turkey, the elite were happy to impose foreign norms and cultural practices (including the alphabet, dress, and laws) with brute force.

This raises a central question about why the disproportionate violence deployed was even necessary, given this efficacy of "soft power"? Part of the answer was the one given by my Sudanese tribal interlocutor quoted earlier: the colonial violence provided the "pacified" space in which soft power could be exercised. Educational institutions produced intellectuals such as the venerable Egyptian literary figure Taha Husain who could, in 1938, argue that Egypt has no future unless it decided to integrate itself into Europe and copy European culture and norms indiscriminately, "the sweet and the bitter, the good and the bad, what is praiseworthy and what is condemnable" (Hussein, 2012: 43).

Earlier anti-colonial activists, such as Sayyid Jamal ad-Din al-Afghani (1838–1897), were not that accommodating. Alarmed at colonial techniques of violent subjugation precisely because they appeared to work, Afghani saw a threat of dehumanization, even species-changing eventuality: making the subjugated into a subhuman race, herded like cattle by their "human" overlords. On this rendering, the colonial venture would not be a "civilizing mission" but a "domestication mission." Afghani deplored the acquiescence of the colonized into their subjugation and wondered why the millions of Indians did not use their numerical advantage to throw off the colonial yoke (Keddie, 1983: 60–4).

Part of the answer to this question might be that the acquiescence so deplored had been partially the outcome of failed revolts. The repeated failure and high cost of successive revolutions forced the victims of colonialism to act more cautiously, aiming first to restore some balance in military, economic, and political (one should add ethical) terms, before launching the resistance.

This raises another key question: why had Western military superiority persisted for so long? At one point at the turn of the nineteenth century, hope arose that non-Western peoples could soon attain parity with the West. In particular, Japan's victory over Russia in 1905 was celebrated in the Middle East as a great victory for "Oriental" peoples. During that period, even African Americans felt solidarity with the Japanese and hoped that the non-white majority around the world would come back into play (Maeda, 2005: 1085). However, we all know how disastrously the Japanese experiment went. It had thus contributed to the "moral disarmament" of the victims of imperialism, recasting the leading Western nations (through the United Nations and the postwar world order) in the position of ethical leadership in the name of new humanitarian principles.

This remains a recurring theme in the West's relations with the "rest." The violence and repression of colonialism had often been justified as necessary precisely because it was needed to curb the "barbarism" of the "uncivilized," and bring about a "more humane" world. It was a "humanitarian intervention." The effectiveness and minimalism of Western violence, from "surgical bombing" to "smart" missiles, continues to be contrasted to the crude barbarism of primitively armed rebels or the car bombs of insurgents.

This gap becomes structurally ingrained in the world order and self-reinforcing in its dynamics. Thus, the fact that the major powers and their sociopolitical systems are more or less impermeable to external threat enables them to be "magnanimous" and able to (only just) afford human rights. In contrast, the oppressed are left with few options other than submit to the will of the dominant power. For if they resort to crudely brutal tactics, this will only contribute to their moral disarmament and enhance their vulnerability. They would be portrayed as "terrorists," and their oppression would be regarded as "humanitarian." Major powers can, and *do*, also "act barbaric" when threatened, as can be observed in recent years. But again, they can afford to.

As in the economic arena, where the poor face more demands on their limited resources, and have less access to credit, in the politico-moral sphere, the have-nots are required to be more ethically blameless when demanding redress. The slightest transgression of the existing laws and norms that underwrite the very injustice they are subject to can bring dire consequences. They have to protest "peacefully" and wait patiently for justice, even if it never came. They have to forgive their oppressors when the latter agree to stop their oppression. In contrast, the haves in terms of power can afford to be nasty and brutal much longer, and with fewer consequences.

The Submissive Road to (Partial) Freedom?

We can therefore summarize the colonial problem thus: the colonial situation (notwithstanding objections by Partha Chatterjee and others) is an extension of the rise and global expansion of the modern European state's "modernizing" capacities, which included subjugation of recalcitrant populations internally. The unique power of this formation rests on what David Scott (basing himself on Foucault's concept of "governmentality" or governmental rationality) refers to as a specific "political rationality." It rests on the twin processes of leaving control of the economy to Adam Smith's mythical "hidden hand" and constructing the Hambermasian "public sphere" of communicative rationality (Scott, 1995). In this manner, DIY governance (or the "conduct of conduct") becomes the instrument of governance. Both within civil society and the economy, the presumed pursuit of private interests and agendas not only yields public goods, as the myth has it, but also delivers self-induced obedience. As the bulk of the population are conditioned into conformity through subtle and complex mechanisms of education, "discipline," and socialization, "hegemony" becomes self-generating.

The "problem of colonialism," Scott thus argues, is also the "problem of modern power" as it emerged in Europe, in particular its "point of application" in civil society. That problem is summed up as

[t]he emergence of a new—that is, modern—political rationality in which power works not in spite of but through the construction of the space of free social exchange, and through the construction of a subjectivity normatively experienced as the source of free will and rational, autonomous agency. (Scott, 1995: 201)

The essence of the colonial endeavor can then be seen as the application of this type of governmental rationality to the colonial sphere in such a way as to transform the very condition of existence in the colonial arena so as to channel the conduct of colonial subjects into a certain direction. "Colonial modernity" would thus consist in

> [t]he emergence of a distinctive political rationality—that is, a colonial governmentality—in which power comes to be directed at the destruction and reconstruction of colonial space so as to produce not so much extractive effects on colonial bodies as governing effects on colonial conduct. (Scott, 1995: 205)

Scott here provides a differently theorized version of the point we have made earlier about "indirect rule" being the essence of the colonial endeavor, even in the arena of "civil society," posited by Mamdani as qualitatively different from the "customary" world of indirect rule. The much-discussed logic of globalization has shifted this process to the global arena. Nowadays, even major powers (not to mention former recalcitrant powers like China and Russia) submit, however reluctantly, to the logic of world governmentality.

However, this analysis omits several major differences between European and colonial modernization. To start with, whether intentionally or not, European modernization has resulted in a progressive inclusion of excluded categories. (It has often been argued, not without justification, that it was imperialism which facilitated this inclusion, especially class inclusion. But this is another issue.) In contrast, colonialism was inherently exclusivist, even when it raised the banner of "civilizing" or "republican" missions, or when, as in Algeria, the "mother country" annexed the territory. Here, as Chatterjee argues, the "rule of colonial difference" (or racial difference) constantly operated (Chatterjee, 1993: 14–34). Related to this is the objective exclusion of the colonies from effective modernization, also with "race" as a factor. However, the colonial populations, in spite of "centuries" of partial modernization in some cases, were still unable to build up sufficient capacity to stand up to their oppressors. In the few cases where the military option was taken to fight for independence, as in Algeria, Vietnam, Angola, Afghanistan, and so on, the price was exorbitantly high in terms of casualties and social brutalization. In the end, it was still negotiations and international dynamics (in addition to internal shifts in the colonial power), which resolved the issue.

Related to this is the persistent gap of "underdevelopment" that continues to plague former colonial societies (or even some that had never been colonized, such as Afghanistan or Yemen). Part of this was the result of imperialist exclusion. Egypt, for example, was on the threshold of becoming a major world power, but it was forcibly "de-developed" under European threats (Marsot, 1984: 242–9). However, it could be argued that Germany has been "de-developed" a couple of times during the last century. France was also "downsized" and occupied a few times over the past two centuries. That was how the "balance of power" system functioned.

What is of interest is the enduring failure of "decolonization." Specifically, the failure of radical regimes on the continent and elsewhere to defy global capitalism. That struggle looked like desperate wriggling within the quagmire or a quicksand pit:

the more you struggled, the deeper you sank. Part of the problem was combining the anti-colonial struggle with embracing the colonial state and its apparatus of control and using it against "internal enemies." This in turn enhanced the colonial "divide-and-rule" advantage.

As mentioned earlier, the asymmetric nature of the conflict makes violent anti-colonial struggle costly even in ethical terms, due to the use of relatively primitive tactics that are habitually condemned as "barbaric." The mismanagement of difference by anti-colonial forces has also generated instances of barbaric conduct in the course of internal conflicts. It was a supreme irony that the involvement of marginalized groups in internal conflicts over power in postcolonial settings has contributed to this escalation of barbarism. On the African continent, this happened in Chad, the Democratic Republic of the Congo (DRC), Liberia, Sierra Leone, Sudan, Angola, Rwanda, Mozambique, Ethiopia, and so on. This puts into focus the question of "civility," both in regards to the role of civil society in contrast to "native authority" and also in terms of the acquisition of levels of "civility" through socialization in the colonially constructed political system. For when complete outsiders get engaged violently into a system that has completely excluded them, the result is what we have seen from the Lord's Resistance Army (LRA), Janjawid, the Islamic State of Iraq and Syria (ISIS), and similar groups.

At the same time, conceding too much to the dominant structures, as the "conservatives" had done, does not appear to have yielded more favorable outcomes. It is true that countries that had adopted market economies and maintained friendly relations with the West had fared much better economically, at least in the first phase. Later, some of these countries, such as the so-called "Asian Tigers," made considerable progress through sustained liberalization and rapid economic development. However, even here, these "tigers" had to pay some form of "tribute" to be tolerated. In fact, as is the case with some Gulf countries, such as the United Arab Emirates (UAE) and Saudi Arabia, you have to pay to be colonized. Here, it is not only DIY colonialism; it is "pay-as-you-go" colonialism as well!

Conclusion: Rethinking Decolonization

If I were to sum up the central questions of this inquiry, they would be: Do we have a viable theory of colonialism? And do we have a science of decolonization? My answer for both would be negative. In spite of heroic efforts, including from Mamdani, Chatterjee, and others, we still do not have a proper theoretical "manual" for decolonization.

Our ancestors responded instinctively to colonialism. First they extended the habitual hospitality to traders and "guests" in the early phases of the intrusion. When they finally discovered the treacherous nature of these "guests," they fought them, waging various types of struggles and jihads. In the face of the "shock and awe" tactics of the intruders, they were forced to submit and reconsider their options. Colonialism partially entrenched itself by being judicious in its subjugation and governance techniques, using a calibrated combination of sheer terror, inducements, and enlisting collaboration. Indirect rule was its tool from the start. The British, in particular, made ample use of it, permitting the locals relative freedoms in cultural and religious domains and some economic leeway.

At a later stage, new anti-colonial movements emerged, this time as a consequence of the dynamics of colonialism itself. From the beginning, the struggle was faced with stark options of confronting colonialism directly and violently, or working with the colonial powers and seeking gradual amelioration of the situation. The latter was usually the most successful course of action, but it was ironically parasitical on the former. Kenneth Kaunda illustrated this most convincingly when he recalled in his memoirs how his call for nonviolent resistance was largely ignored, both by the Zambian people and by the colonialists. This changed when, one day, an armed attack was launched against a British military camp. The next day, the British began courting him and treating him as a leader (Kaunda, 1977). Similar processes occurred in other struggles. In particular, the Palestinian struggle was ignored in its peaceful phases, until it erupted into violence and wars. The Palestine Liberation Organization (PLO), when it emerged in the 1960s, was demonized as a terrorist outfit until the more deadly Hamas emerged. Then it was actively courted. In the African American struggle for recognition, the peaceful and inclusive approach of Martin Luther King Jr only gained attention due to the radical approaches by followers of Malcolm X or the Black Panther movement, among others.

The First World War and the Cold War also helped. We owe our (partial and limited) freedom largely to Hitler and Stalin. During the Second World War, the colonialists were on their knees begging their colonial subjects to come to their aid, making all sort of promises, most of which were not kept once the war was won. But then Stalin had the bomb, and the courting of "hearts and minds" started again. Anti-colonial pressure groups (the left, humanitarians, etc.) and some trends within metropolitan centers also helped the decolonization.

Partly due to these external factors, most countries obtained their independence without a substantial shift in the internal balance of power with the former colonial masters. In almost all cases, direct colonialism was only replaced with indirect control, more blatant in the case of the French, characteristically subtle in the case of the British. With globalization, most countries started competing with each other and begging to be exploited by international big business. I could not help smiling, as I walked through Cape Town Airport on my first visit, as I read the entreaties for big business to accept the hospitality of this lovely city.

There is no point deploring this situation and expressing anger, without fully comprehending it. Quixotic anti-globalization struggles (which have now, in an extreme irony, shifted to Washington, London, and Paris) could destroy one's country, as happened in Mugabe's Zimbabwe, Chavez's Venezuela, El-Bashir's Sudan, and, before that, in Mengisto's Ethiopia, Gaddafi's Libya, and so on. Recently, we have listened to some hot heads entertaining the idea of civil war in South Africa as a kind of solution to persistent inequalities. I can assure anyone who cares to listen that civil wars do not bring prosperity or a fairer sharing of resources.

On the other hand, the passive acquiescence into capitalist hegemony or colonial overlordship is no solution either. What is needed is a smart strategy toward comprehensive decolonization. Hitherto, only a few former colonies managed to make patience and the skilled navigation of the world system work in their favor. The so-called Asian Tigers now enjoy some leeway of action. Turkey, before its recent serious setbacks due to its being sucked into the Syrian crisis, was a good example of "enlightened neo-liberalism," with a development strategy focused on small business and poverty reduction. It also combined political independence and economic self-reliance with good relations with major world actors.

Most other actors had to do with some form of DIY colonialism. One can see that an illustration of the failure of both approaches is most graphically illustrated in the Palestinian case, where both the rejectionist Hamas and the submissive PLO are performing the function of DIY colonialism, relieving the colonial power of the tasks of keeping the peace, providing services, and administering the "subjects," free of charge. Many other states, we know, have made a craft of collaborating with multinationals. This trend suffered a reversal when the Arab oil embargo and the rise of the Organization of the Petroleum Exporting Countries (OPEC) shifted the balance of power to oil-producing countries. However, differences among them, and bowing to pressures, reversed the trend in the 1980s. More recently, the "oil curse" took a new meaning, when some very wealthy Arab Gulf countries adopted a pay-to-be-colonized policy, offering US president Trump billions of dollars in "protection money." The alliance of the same Gulf plutocracies with Israel is even more interesting from our current perspective, since it combines DIY colonialism with assisting one of the last ongoing direct settler-colonial projects in the world.

The challenge today is to develop intelligent strategies of decolonization that eschew the proven futility of counterproductive tactics more helpful to hegemonic interests, contributing as they do to the moral disarmament of victims of colonialism. But they must also eschew the abject submissive acquiescence into DIY colonialism as destiny. Smart anticolonialism must act creatively to develop new strategies that do not repeat the errors of either approach.

The South African experience suggests one viable method of resolving this problem. While it has partially adopted "DIY colonialism," it has done so from a vantage position of a viable and realistic decolonization agenda. What went wrong, I believe, as has happened with many "moderate" or "realist" regimes, was getting too comfortable with the first stage of accommodation with hegemonic interests.

References

Benlahcene, B. (2011). "Malek Bennabi's concept and interdisciplinary approach to civilisation." *International Journal of Arab Culture, Management and Sustainable Development*, 2(1): 55–71. https://doi.org/10.1504/IJACMSD.2011.044896.

Beshir, M. O. (1974). *Revolution and Nationalism in the Sudan*. London: Collings.

Chatterjee, P. (1993). *The Nation and its Fragments: Colonial and Postcolonial Histories*. Princeton: Princeton University Press.

Cole, J. R. (1999). *Colonialism and Revolution in the Middle East: Social and Cultural Origins of Egypt's Urabi Movement*. Cairo: American University in Cairo Press.

Collins, R. O. (2008). *A History of Modern Sudan*. Cambridge and New York: Cambridge University Press.

Cooper, F. (2005). *Colonialism in Question: Theory, Knowledge, History*. Berkeley: University of California Press.

Daly, M. W. (1983). "The development of the governor-generalship of the Sudan, 1899–1934." *Journal of African History*, 24(1): 77–96. https://doi.org/10.1017/S0021853700021538.

Daly, M. W. (1991). *Imperial Sudan: The Anglo-Egyptian Condominium 1934–1956*. Cambridge: Cambridge University Press. https://doi.org/10.1017/S0020743800022765.

Daly, M. W. (2004). *Empire on the Nile: The Anglo-Egyptian Sudan, 1898–1934*. Cambridge: Cambridge University Press.

Deng, F. M. and Daly, M. W. (1990). *Bonds of Silk: Human Factor in the British Administration of the Sudan*. East Lansing: Michigan State University Press.

El-Affendi, A. (1991). *Turabi's Revolution: Islam and Power in Sudan*. London: Grey Seal Books.

El-Affendi, A. (2010). "Political culture and the crisis of democracy in the Arab world," in I. Elbadawi and S. Makdisi (eds.), *Democracy in the Arab World: Explaining the Deficit*. London: Routledge, pp. 12–40.

Goldschmidt, A. (1993). "The Butrus Ghali Family." *Journal of the American Research Center in Egypt*, 30: 183–8. https://doi.org/10.2307/40000236.

Hussein, T. (2012) [1938]. *Mustaqbal al-Thaqafa fi Misr [The Future of Culture in Egypt]*. Cairo: Hindawi Foundation.

Kaunda, K. D. (1977). *Zambia Shall be Free*. London: Heinemann.

Keddie, N. R. (1983). *An Islamic Response to Imperialism: Political and Religious Writings of Sayyid Jamal ad-Din "al-Afghani,"* Vol. 586. Near Eastern Center: University of California Press.

Maeda, D. J. (2005). "Black panthers, red guards, and Chinamen: Constructing Asian American identity through performing blackness, 1969–1972." *American Quarterly*, 57(4): 1079–103.

Mahmud, T. (1997). "Migration, identity and the colonial encounter." *Oregon Law Review*, 76: 633–90.

Mamdani, M. (1996). *Citizen and Subject: Contemporary Africa and the Legacy of Late Colonialism*. Princeton: Princeton University Press.

Mamdani, M. (2009). *Saviors and Survivors: Darfur, Politics, and the War on Terror*. London: Verso.

Mamdani, M. (2012). *Define and Rule: Native as Political Identity*. Cambridge: Harvard University Press.

Marsot, A. L. A. S. (1984). *Egypt in the Reign of Muhammad Ali*. Cambridge: Cambridge University Press.

Pakenham, T. (2015). *The Scramble for Africa*. London: Hachette.

Pitts, J. (2010). "Political theory of empire and imperialism." *Annual Review of Political Science*, 13: 211–35. https://doi.org/10.1146/annurev.polisci.051508.214538.

Roberts, H. and Roberts, M. H. P. (2003). *The Battlefield Algeria, 1988–2002: Studies in a Broken Polity*. London: Verso.

Scott, D. (1995). "Colonial governmentality." *Social Text*, 43: 191–220. https://doi.org/10.2307/466631.

Tignor, R. L. (2015). *Modernization and British Colonial Rule in Egypt, 1882–1914*. Princeton: Princeton University Press.

Tocqueville, A. (2001). *Writings on Empire and Slavery*. Translated and edited by J. Pitts. Baltimore: Johns Hopkins University Press.

Von Trotha, T. (2006). "Colonialism," in S. Berger (ed.), *A Companion to Nineteenth-Century Europe*. Hoboken: Blackwell Publishing, pp. 432–47. https://doi.org/10.1002/9780470996263.

Ypi, L. (2013). "What's wrong with colonialism?" *Philosophy and Public Affairs*, 41(2): 158–91. https://doi.org/10.1111/papa.12014.

6

The Contemporary Challenge of Citizenship in Ethiopia and the Role of Empire in the Making of Subject Populations

Namhla Thando Matshanda

Introduction

The expansion and ascendancy of the Amhara national identity during the period 1950–90 laid the foundation for the competing national narratives that currently threaten to unravel the unity of the Ethiopian state. Ethiopia is in the midst of a power struggle between those who espouse a centralized and narrow definition of national identity that is reminiscent of the pre-1991 period and those who seek a decentralized view of national identity that promotes ethnic nationalism. This tension has been in the making since the formation of the modern Ethiopian state in the late nineteenth century. However, this chapter locates its most recent foundations to the time following Italian occupation, namely during the period of the imperial and military regimes.

Mamdani's *Citizen and Subject* grapples with the form of politics that dominates postcolonial Africa and the inherent violence that accompanies it. For many, an image or definition of such a postcolonial reality may not immediately invoke the image of Ethiopia. Yet, Ethiopia's imperial past and its entanglements with foreign powers, before and during the Cold War, led to a political history that is characterized by both similarities and differences with other African countries that experienced the full extent of European colonialism. For instance, Mamdani's (1996) urban/rural divide that draws a contrast between citizens and subjects appears in the center/periphery or highland/lowland divide in Ethiopia. However, in Ethiopia this divide takes on additional nuances that are unique to that country, such as the much longer history of forging both nation and state. The challenge of citizenship in Ethiopia since 1991 needs to be contextualized and historicized. The rest of this chapter does this by tracing the historical foundations of the national identity that dominated the state for over half a century. This resulted in an authoritarian and top-down approach to national identity where large sections of the population were regarded as subjects and those who fully or partially embraced the Amhara identity were largely regarded as citizens. The long-term survival and dominance of this national identity, the chapter argues, was aided by the role of empire. This was a product of the Cold War but began much earlier when Ethiopia was liberated from the Italian occupation during the latter stages of the Second World War. Following the Italian occupation, Ethiopia came under British Military Administration (BMA) for approximately a decade. During this period, the imperial state of Haile Selassie fought to reinstate Ethiopian sovereignty. As part of the campaign to retain the territorial integrity of the preoccupation state, Ethiopia's imperial rulers promoted the Amhara identity as national identity. The context required a discourse that glorified the past as an attempt to navigate a period of great vulnerability. Amhara became the social indicator of inclusion and exclusion, even though "Amhara" does not symbolize a particular ethnic group. There is general consensus that Amhara as an ethnic unit has never existed in Ethiopia prior to ethnic federalism. It is also agreed that Amhara is best defined as a social category that refers to the possession of power and that it is most useful as a cultural reference (Teka, 1998: 117). In imperial Ethiopia, Barth's boundaries were defined and maintained according to Amhara culture, with limited interconnection except for assimilation (Barth, 1969: 10–12). This is because of the historical roots of this culture, which date back to the ancient Ethiopian empire—Abyssinia. The absence of a unifying national discourse in imperial and socialist Ethiopia is responsible for the contemporary challenge of establishing equal citizenship for all. Keller (1981) notes that Haile Selassie's social policy paid no attention to "the national question," in spite of the fact that a large part of the empire consisted of culturally subordinated ethnic groups. Yet, as Tronvoll (2009: 46) notes, the existence of an "Amharised Ethiopian state" and the process of *Amharization* were very real.

This chapter argues and demonstrates that the promotion and entrenchment of Amhara national identity at the expense of the majority of the people who inhabited the Ethiopian territory was sustained by imperial powers during the period from 1950 to the late 1980s. The alliance of the Ethiopian state with the United States following the Italian occupation played a major role in violently silencing opposing national discourses, most notably in Eritrea. Similarly, after 1974, the Derg—the military junta that came into power following the overthrow of the imperial regime—continued to centralize state power and to promote the Amhara national identity in the face of a revolution that purported to eradicate the ethnic chauvinism that characterized the *ancien régime*. The Derg received significant support from the Soviet Union in silencing emerging Somali nationalism in eastern Ethiopia during the 1977–8 war with Somalia. The argument presented here aims to locate the specific political experience of Ethiopia within a larger context of the global political economy in which Ethiopia and many other African countries were bound to from the late colonial period to the present. The argument deploys a constructivist understanding of nation-making and draws from Anderson's (1991) concept of "imagined communities."

This argument is developed by first outlining the present context of citizenship in Ethiopia, which is characterized by ethnic federalism. The challenge faced by the present construction of national citizenship is explored in this section; this includes the legacy of an authoritarian past that undermines current attempts to democratize and decentralize the state. Next, the modern Ethiopian history of conquest where highland kingdoms ventured to the south at the turn of the nineteenth century is outlined. This is a necessary background that foregrounds the emergence of the Amhara national identity. This section offers a brief history of boundary-making within the context of the expanding empire. The chapter then considers the period after the Italian occupation where assimilation and a centralized bureaucracy were used to entrench the Amhara identity; this section explores this development, particularly as it relates to Eritrea and the Somali region of Ethiopia. During this period, a decentralized despotism emerged where, unable to reach the lowlands, the imperial state made use of "chiefs," who were called *balaabat* in Amharic (Mamdani, 1996). The next section demonstrates the role of imperial powers in violently silencing opposing articulations of nationalism before and during the Cold War. The section reveals the role of the United States in the annexation of Eritrea in 1962 and the role of the Soviet Union in the 1978 Ethiopian victory in the war with Somalia. Finally, the chapter presents concluding remarks, bringing together the key elements of the chapter.

The Contemporary Challenge of Citizenship in Ethiopia

The idea of citizenship and its lived experience are currently in a state of crisis in Ethiopia. This crisis is rooted in the history of the Amhara-dominated nation and state that emerged in the late nineteenth century. This history is dominated by the exploits of the highland societies that laid the foundations of the contemporary state. What we presently know as "Ethiopia" is based on a narrowly constructed narrative that centers on the Amhara national identity. Ethnic federalism seemingly challenges this narrative and demands an inclusive interpretation of the notion of citizenship and belonging in Ethiopia. The federal experiment is a crucial test of the ideals and conceptions of Ethiopian statehood, of which the retention and control of the peripheries are a fundamental part (Matshanda, 2015: 19). The decision made by the Tigrayan People's Liberation Front (TPLF) as leader of the Ethiopian People's Revolutionary Democratic Front (EPRDF) to adopt ethnic federalism in 1991 is arguably the boldest attempt yet to address the "national question" in Ethiopia.

The adoption of ethnic federalism suggests that the TPLF espoused a radically different interpretation of the Ethiopian nation. Although the Tigrayans are historically part of the political "core," they experienced systematic exclusion from political power under the imperial rule of Haile Selassie and during the period of the Derg military regime. Clapham (2002) notes that as far as the TPLF was concerned, "national unity" was no more than a pretext for suppression. It was thus with relative ease that the TPLF redefined citizenship by dismantling the hegemony of the Amhara identity. This was not an entirely selfless decision by the TPLF. It had a profound awareness of what was at stake—the state could disintegrate if the numerous ethno-nationalist struggles within were not addressed. In addition, the Tigrayans are a minority, and they needed other groups in order to take full control of the country (Samatar, 2004: 1134). Furthermore, in being seen as taking seriously the nationalist ambitions of oppressed sections of the population, including the Eritreans, the TPLF sought to reinforce its legitimacy (Tronvoll, 2009: 199).

Mamdani (2002) notes that the understanding of citizenship is often dominated by the civic dimension. Yet, citizenship exists on a continuum that ranges from its most basic form—civic—and also encompasses political and social dimensions (Marshall, 1950). Tilley (1995: 6) summarizes existing literature and suggests a relational, cultural, historical, and contingent view of the identity of citizenship that results from a "set of mutual, contested claims between agents of states and members of socially constructed categories." This is a fitting conceptualization for understanding the emergence of ethnic-based citizenship in Ethiopia and its challenges. In particular, the interplay between civic and ethnic citizenship has been a source of tension between the regions and the central state. Ethnic identities have been used as the basis for citizenship in Ethiopia since 1991 within a context of democratization and decentralization. This experiment has been characterized by fundamental challenges that threaten its continued existence.

The conflict that erupted in November 2020 between the government of Prime Minister Abiy Ahmed and the former dominant party within the ruling coalition—the TPLF—demonstrates the inherent challenge of arriving at a mutually agreeable understanding of an Ethiopian identity. For Samatar (2020), this latest conflict is a reflection of the country's political history that has been dominated by minority ethnic elites. These elites, the Amhara and Tigrayans, stand accused of concentrating power among themselves and suppressing minority rights and political expression. This challenge is evident in the relationship between the center and the Somali region and with Eritrea since 1991.

The post-1991 political context in Ethiopia's Somali region reflects the consequences of a fragmented indigenous system of authority among the Somali people. Sharp divisions among the different clans demonstrate the loss of a broad Somali national identity; they also symbolize the struggles of the Somali people in relation to the central state, a struggle which dates back to the nineteenth century (Samatar, 2005). Markakis (2011) aptly notes that it is in the Somali region that the success of Ethiopia's ethnic federalism will be determined. Samatar (2005) points out that the initial decision of the majority of Somalis in Ethiopia to adhere to EPRDF rules was a wise one, given an alternative that would have thrust the region into war with the new rulers. However, the struggle for political positions in the region threatened the reappearance of an age-old rivalry between two major clans, the Ogadeen and Isaq. From the outset in 1991, the Ogadeen clan appeared ready to (re)claim the region with the Ogaden National Liberation Front (ONLF) participating in the national conference that was convened by the TPLF (Samatar, 2004). This was of course problematic since the vast Somali region occupies a diverse terrain with five distinct localities that are occupied by different Somali clans and subclans (Markakis, 2011: 53). Subsequently, the region has been characterized by political disorder as regional elites engaged in power struggles, and with Somalis having to reckon with their transformation from subjects to citizens (Hagmann, 2005; Hagmann and Khalif, 2006).

With regards to Eritrea, the TPLF has a long history with that country's liberation movements, most notably with the Eritrean People's Liberation Front (EPLF), an alliance that emerged out of their mutual struggle against the Derg. When the TPLF came into power in 1991 they were ardent advocates of a reconstructed Ethiopian national identity, which later gave way to the full expression of Eritrean national identity in 1993 (Matshanda, 2020). The 1998–2000 war between Ethiopia and Eritrea demonstrates conflicting understandings of national and territorial statehood by the two countries. The Eritrean state challenged the hegemonic claims of both the imperial and Derg regimes of Ethiopia, where they demonstrated an opposing narrative of their national identity (Iyob, 2000). The secession and independence of Eritrea in 1993 generated widespread resentment in Ethiopia, despite clear evidence that points to a separate Eritrean national identity, or because of it. The wrath of the Ethiopians was evident in the determination with which they fought in the 1998–2000 war, where the war was perceived as a "second Adwa" (Triulzi, 2006: 128). This war raised a number of questions regarding post-1991 politics of national identity in Ethiopia, with many struggling to make sense of the popular support of this war in a context that recognizes and promotes ethnic identities. Tronvoll (2009: 203) posits that the near-unanimous support of the war in Ethiopia can be explained by "historical conceptions of state and power in Ethiopia," which stem from the unitary Amhara nation-state of the past. This suggests that the founding principles of Amhara nationalism continue to linger in the present and that they provide motivation for the ongoing opposition to ethnic federalism.

The next section explores the emergence of the imperial state and how this process gave birth to a narrowly constructed imagination of an Ethiopian nation that was based on the culture of the ruling class. These twin processes set Ethiopia apart from much of sub-Saharan Africa, yet there are notable similarities which are rooted in ethnic diversity and interactions with imperial powers.

Becoming an Empire State and the Emergence of an Ethiopian National Imaginary

At the inception of the modern Ethiopian state toward the end of the nineteenth century, there was sufficient evidence to suggest that the new nation was to be modeled on a very specific imagination of who belongs in it. This corresponds with global trends in the development of the modern state where the state has an explicit connection to a particular cultural group (Mamdani, 2002: 495). As Anderson (1991) demonstrates and argues in *Imagined Communities*, there were clear emotional and cultural forces at play when the idea of modern Ethiopia emerged. These emotions carried with them myths and images of a distant and idealized past (Prunier and Ficquet, 2015). This is illustrated by the narrative of *Greater Ethiopia*, wherein the Christian northern highlands are viewed as the center of civilization and authority (Levine, 1974). This narrative recalls the ancient kingdom of Abyssinia, which was seen as a precursor to the modern Ethiopian state that emerged in the nineteenth century. The legitimacy of the latter rested on its mythological connection to Abyssinia. Mythmaking has been at the center of the Ethiopian national imaginary for centuries. This is evident in the story of the Ark of the Covenant, Queen of Sheba, and King Solomon—a story that often prefaces discussions about Ethiopia and its people (Prunier and Ficquet, 2015: 1).

This founding myth was used for centuries by various Ethiopian rulers and ruling elite to legitimize their authority over many others whose origins did not fit the image of this myth. Anderson (1991) demonstrates that the emergence of nations is predicated upon a number of things and events that may lead groups of people to imagine themselves as a community. In addition to mythmaking and the memorialization of the ancient civilization, in Ethiopia there was also the advent of European capitalism and colonialism in the nineteenth century. These are the cultural and material conditions that gave rise to the imagination of an Ethiopian nation during the course of the nineteenth century. According to Ethiopian historian Bahru Zewde, the Italian territorial ambitions on Ethiopia began around 1869 when they acquired the port of Assab on the Red Sea south of Massawa, with British assistance (Zewde, 1991: 56). At the same time, France and Britain had made significant advances in delineating what would be their spheres of influence in northeast Africa, resulting in Ethiopia fighting for its independence (Rubenson, 1976). Holcomb and Ibssa (1990) argue that competing British and French interests in the region contributed to the "invention" of the Ethiopian empire in the late 1800s. The authors are skeptical about the extent to which Ethiopian rulers independently secured their independence but rather suggest that this outcome was part of the European colonial contest in the Horn of Africa.

Following initial Italian attempts on Ethiopian territory, there unfolded a series of events that expanded the territorial limits of the Ethiopian empire and the political dominance of the Kingdom of Shoa. King Menelik of Shoa ventured south of his kingdom, conquering neighboring peoples and incorporating them into his expanding empire. Also, quite significantly, the kings of Tigre and Gojjam, two of the most important provinces of the empire, both renewed their loyalty to Menelik, thus creating a unified and strong political center (Rubenson, 1976: 396–7). Touval (1963) notes that the Scramble for Africa coincided with the resurgence and extension of central authority in Ethiopia. However, this period is surrounded by controversy. The main contention is how Ethiopia managed to gain its independence. Building on their initial argument on the "invention" of Ethiopia, Holcomb and Ibssa (1990: 2) argue that the emergent Ethiopian nation-state became a "dependent colonial empire." The authors are making two fundamental points: the first one is that Ethiopia became a colonial empire; the second point is that the maintenance of this colonialism depended on the vagaries of the international world order—of which European colonialism was its embodiment. Not only did the territorial expansions give shape to the geographical limits of the modern state, they also laid the foundations for the enduring nature of political power and authority that defined the Ethiopian state and nation. King Menelik's exploits and the victory against the Italian forces at Adwa in 1896 sealed the fate of modern Ethiopia (Zewde, 1991). The events at Adwa brought significant changes to the political landscape in the Horn of Africa. Following Adwa, Britain and France sought to define their colonial interests in the Horn of Africa. Legal international agreements were entered into by Ethiopia, Britain, France, and Italy—compelling Ethiopia to participate in the colonial partition of Africa.

Consequently, the Ethiopian polity reached a particular stage of state formation that made boundary-making a necessary process. Ethiopia was catapulted onto an international system of states that functioned according to specific norms and rules. Biersteker and Weber (1996) note that territory, population, and authority, in addition to recognition, are important aspects of state sovereignty. However, they argue that each of these elements or a combination of them is socially constructed and has specific historicity. Ethiopia qualified in at least two of these requirements, with authority and recognition still under construction. By 1896 Ethiopia was undergoing extensive territorial expansion under the leadership of Menelik II—incorporating into the empire, peoples and territories to the south, east, and west of the highland core. However, the acquired territory was not guaranteed and the boundaries of the expanding polity were not yet determined. The only certainty was who the conquered populations were and to whom they owed allegiance.

The Making of International Boundaries

Following the victory at Adwa, Ethiopia closely resembled the classic definitions of the state, including what Max Weber termed a "political community" (Weber, 1968: 902). Yet, the way in which Ethiopia resembled these classic definitions of statehood was temporary and could not be sustained due to a number of external factors. Most pressing after Adwa for both Menelik and his European neighbors was the determination of their respective frontiers (Government of the UK, 1897). Representatives of European colonial powers made their way to Menelik's court in Addis Ababa where they expressed their recognition of Ethiopian sovereignty. The boundary between Ethiopia and the various Somali territories was formally decided by Ethiopia and the three colonial powers that administered French Somaliland, Italian Somaliland, and the British Somaliland Protectorate, between March and May of 1897 (Florida State University, 2008). The boundary with French Somaliland did not give rise to any major disagreements. The International Boundary Study (IBS), a database containing the histories of African boundary treaties and agreements, states that the Anglo-Ethiopian Treaty of 1897 modified the limits of British Somaliland by excluding most of the Haud grazing pasture (Florida State University, 2008). A large part of the grazing lands fell into Ethiopian jurisdiction. The annexes of the 1897 Treaty contain special arrangements that afforded the right of movement of adjacent peoples across the boundary for grazing and other purposes (Government of the UK, 1897). The Anglo-Ethiopian boundary agreement was never contested. Yet, it was only demarcated between 1933 and 1935, thirty years after it was delimited (Government of the UK, 1957).

The Italian Somaliland boundary with Ethiopia was contested from the beginning and has had a different historical trajectory when compared to the Anglo-Ethiopian boundary. The IBS database (Florida State University, 2008) states that in September 1897 the Italian government sent a telegram accepting the proposed boundary line— however, official texts of the delimitation were never exchanged and copies of the map cannot be found to this day. The database further notes that it was clear that different terms of reference had been used by Ethiopia and Italy to determine their mutual boundary and that a large triangular area broadening northeastward was of questionable sovereignty. Tension mounted between Ethiopia and Italy following the failure to agree on the initial boundary line. Emperor Menelik made a request to the Italians to reopen negotiations for the 1897 boundary (Wolde-Mariam, 1964: 202). The result of the renewed negotiations was, according to Wolde-Mariam (1964: 202), a "master piece of ambiguity." Wolde-Mariam argues that the agreement of 1908 failed to eliminate the ambiguous line that separated Italian Somaliland and Ethiopia because it was not specific enough on the route to be taken when delimiting the boundary.

During the course of these state-making processes, Ethiopian national identity was defined according to the history outlined earlier—that of the Christian and Semitic cultures of the central highlands. Imperial rulers were concerned with safeguarding recently acquired territories and ensuring that the acquired sovereign status is incontrovertible. Yet, in 1936 the Ethiopian state found itself defending its independence from Italian aggression (Marcus, 1994: 138). The Ethiopians put up a formidable resistance for nearly eight months, but this proved insufficient when a battle fought near Maichew in southern Tigray saw the Italian forces moving dangerously close to the capital (Henze, 2000: 218). On 3 May 1936 Emperor Haile Selassie and his family boarded a ship from Djibouti bound for England, and the following day Marshal Pietro Badoglio's forces entered the capital, Addis Ababa (Marcus, 1994: 146).

What happened next has two fundamental implications for the argument that is pursued in this chapter: the first one relates to locating the modern foundations of Ethiopian national identity; the second relates to how foreign imperial powers would later play a role in entrenching this national identity. These are important developments because the Italian occupation presents an important disruption in the articulation and imagination of Ethiopian national identity. The occupation forced the imperial state to articulate more forcefully the Amhara national identity as part of redefining the state.

The next section explores the post-occupation period by highlighting the proliferation of the Amhara national identity and the emergence of *Amharization* as state policy. The section demonstrates that during the period of the BMA, in particular, there emerged a decentralized despotism that sought to entrench Amhara national identity in the peripheries of the imperial state. This process was facilitated by centralized state bureaucracy.

The Rise of Amhara National Identity after the Italian Occupation

The struggle to liberate Ethiopia from Italian occupation was carried out on two fronts. In the first instance, Haile Selassie carried out the diplomatic negotiations on the international stage. His appearance at the League of Nations in 1936 arguably promoted him to the international community (Hess, 1970; Zewde, 1991). In the second instance, the struggle was fought on home soil. Zewde (1991) notes that the Italian occupation was denied legitimacy in part due to the efforts of the patriots who put up a brave fight. The more the Italians unleashed violence on the population, the more the patriotic resistance gathered strength and became more widespread (Miller, 1999). However, when Emperor Haile Selassie entered Addis Ababa in May

1941, he was doing so under very different circumstances. The world was at war and his own country was regarded as an Occupied Enemy Territory. On his return, Emperor Selassie capitalized on the prevailing sentiment of national pride and used the moment to gain support in the fight to reclaim Ethiopian sovereignty.

Reid (2011) notes that at the time of liberation, the internal situation in Ethiopia was far from stable and was dangerously volatile. The instability was due to the amount of weapons in circulation, uncertainty about the loyalty of key regional nobles, and doubt over the sovereign status of the Ethiopian polity. This background prompted a debate about the strength and resilience of the nation in the face of such uncertainty. This was certainly the case in relation to the territorial changes that were attempted by the BMA. The latter promised to unravel the tentative imagining of both the state and nation that existed prior to the Italian occupation. These threats were most apparent in eastern Ethiopia, where dual administration emerged between the BMA and the Ethiopian authority (Matshanda, 2019: 665). This and other developments sowed feelings of doubt regarding British motives in eastern Ethiopia. British attempts to modify the boundary and its support for Somali nationalism gave credence to these suspicions (Matshanda, 2019: 670). This played a role in provoking Emperor Selassie to pursue a rigorous process of centralizing and modernizing state bureaucracy in order to promote the Amhara national image and to suppress emerging national consciousness in the peripheries.

The Italian occupation temporarily transformed the borders of the Horn of Africa, where Mussolini forged ahead with his vision to establish his *Africa Orientale Italiana* (Henze, 2000: 223). The consequences proved dire for Ethiopia's future relations with its northern and eastern peripheries as Eritrea was enlarged to include the Ethiopian northern province of Tigray, whereas Italian Somaliland absorbed the Ogaden region of Ethiopia (Reid, 2011: 143). It was primarily to reverse these mergers that in the period following the occupation, the imperial state focused on consolidating its territory and restoring its sovereignty.

Centralized Bureaucracy and the Emergence of the Provinces of Hararge and Eritrea

One of the key initiatives of the Ethiopian government after the occupation was to redraw provincial boundaries. In the course of these changes emerged Hararge province, a fief of the imperial family that became the largest province of the empire (Markakis, 1974: 289). It is important to note that in the process of provincial restructuring, the demarcation of lowland provinces tended not to have cultural or ethnic considerations. Markakis (1974) notes that the criteria for homogeneity and historical identity gave way to considerations of political and administrative convenience. Hararge province was home to Somali, Oromo, Harari, and other ethnic groups. The ethnic and cultural composition of the new provinces reflected significant heterogeneity, which indicates that imperial authorities perceived these populations as imperial subjects more than separate ethnic groups.

In 1962 Eritrea was controversially annexed into Ethiopia following a United Nations mandate for a federation (Lyons, 1986). This moment marks one of the earliest examples of the suppression of the national ambitions of those who were forcibly included into the Ethiopian territory. The key foundations of Eritrean nationalism can be located first in the colonial experience with Italy and subsequently in the contentious federation with Ethiopia (Negash, 1997; Dirar, 2007). Negash (1997) notes that the Italian colonial experience of racial policies, wage labor, and participation on the Italian side in the conquering and pacification of Ethiopia contributed to the development of an Eritrean national identity or consciousness. On the other hand, Ethiopian claims to Eritrea are founded on the belief that the ancient kingdom of Abyssinia ruled over much of the Horn of Africa, an area that includes parts of present-day Eritrea—the Greater Ethiopia narrative (Levine, 1974).

The social stratification of society that emanated from the political center has arguably been the main driving force for the form of social organization that emerged in Ethiopia in the twentieth century. Tradition and hierarchy formed the basis of social organization leading to the emergence of a specific type of political culture—one that embraced centralized and authoritarian bureaucracy. There are several explanations for why this structure was pervasive in Ethiopia's political development. Some accounts take into consideration religion and the type of social and political ethos that were embedded at the center. For instance, the economic basis of political power in Ethiopia has always been tribute and surplus labor (Zewde, 1991: 87). The essays in the seminal work by Donham and James (2002) on imperial Ethiopia—*The Southern Marches of Imperial Ethiopia*—underscore the importance of the imperial expansions to the south. They note that these were facilitated and supported by the cultural, political, and economic underpinnings of Abyssinian society (Donham, 2002: 3–13). In summing up this structure, Markakis (1974) notes that the core (Amhara-Tigre) society presented the classic trinity of noble, priest, and peasant. This hierarchy, according to Markakis, was maintained by a range of practices that included the division of labor, distinct social categories, and a clear awareness of these distinctions. The emerging "modern" institutions within this structure thus sought to entrench the economic and political ideology and objectives of the ruling classes, which were dominated by Amhara culture.

An outline of the organizational underpinnings of power and authority in imperial Ethiopia is fundamental for understanding how the nation came to be defined at the height of imperial rule. The attainment of sovereignty by the modern state was the defining moment that led to a particular imagination of the nation that was modeled on the cultures of those who held political power and excluded those who were conquered. Territorial sovereignty in particular and the determination of boundaries led to the categorization of the people within the said territory. Administrative changes found expression in the 1942 provincial administrative decree and two imperial orders of 1943 that reconstituted the functioning of the central state. Decree No. 1 of 1942 on administrative regulations established the roles of provincial directors general, governors, courts, and provincial secretariats; the decree also created structures such as the provincial council (FDRE, 1942). The Orders of 1943 laid out the powers and functions of the ministers, with the Minister of Interior holding preponderant power and the ministry mandated with supervising security throughout the empire (FDRE, 1943). The importance of these legal codes is noted by Zewde when he states that "it was with these legislative measures that the provincial administration and the central bureaucracy of our age were laid" (Zewde, 1991: 34). These measures transformed the structures of provincial authority by establishing a form of indirect rule. For instance, Amhara military personnel from the center were often appointed to positions of governor-general and deputy governor-general in Hararge province, whereas locals were appointed to the positions of "adviser" and "adviser-general" (FDRE, 1962).

Assimilation: Amharization as State Policy

Amhara national identity is a contested past and present reality in Ethiopia. Discussions on the construction of Amhara identity within the Ethiopian state evoke different emotions from Ethiopians. We see this tension in how, for the duration of the nineteenth and twentieth centuries, being "Ethiopian" was experienced in vastly different ways by people who inhabited the same geographic territory called Ethiopia. For instance, this can be observed between Amhara or *Amharized*[1] Ethiopians and those from the Eritrean territory or from the Somali regions of Ethiopia.

Pankhurst (1998) notes that the Amharic language began to replace Geʿez, the ancient court language, sometime during the nineteenth century. Most significantly, during the latter parts of the nineteenth century and into the twentieth century, prominent schools began using Amharic as the main language and thus integrated many non-Amhara speakers into the language and culture (Pankhurst, 1998: 84). These schools served an important purpose—that of preparing future civil servants, which was a very important category in the period after the Italian occupation. Civil servants were tasked with modernizing state bureaucracy and they were responsible for shaping the Amhara national identity, especially in the peripheries.

The decade from 1950 to 1960 represents the apex of state centralization in imperial Ethiopia. The decade saw the acquisition of Eritrea and what Reid calls "the steady erosion of that territory's federal autonomy" (Reid, 2011: 154). The same decade witnessed the return to Ethiopia of the Ogaden and other territories that were previously under BMA. The 1950s were a decade of determined state centralization and territorial consolidation by Emperor Haile Selassie. These processes were closely accompanied by an uncompromising project of entrenching Amhara as the dominant all-encompassing national identity. Ethiopia's ruling classes had no interest in promoting an Amhara ethnic group identity. Instead, nation-building followed a categorical process of imposing Amhara national identity on the entire population of the empire because the ruling Amhara and *Amharized* elite felt that they were the embodiment of the state (Teka, 1998: 121).

Pankhurst (1998) introduces us to the figure of Tedla Haile who wrote a thesis in the 1920s on ethnic integration and assimilation in Ethiopia. Haile was of noble Shoan background and thus very much believed in the superiority of the Amhara identity. Haile's ideas are important as they provide a glimpse of the general thinking on assimilation in policy circles at the time. It is also noteworthy that upon his return from overseas, Haile was briefly in charge of the Ministry of Education (Oumer, 2020).

---

[1] This refers to those who had assimilated to this culture, in the processes eschewing their previous ethnic origins.

Haile's assimilationist vision was mainly aimed at the Oromo, but it can be argued that the sentiment was intended to have a much wider reach that included other ethnic groups that were incorporated into the Amhara state. His ideas for enacting assimilation included settling Amharas in predominantly Oromo areas, where they would teach Amharic, Ethiopian history, and geography, among other things (Pankhurst, 1998: 89).

The history and culture of the historic "core" regions of Ethiopia are in stark contrast to those of the lowland peripheries. The political histories of the latter are characterized by Islam, resistance to northern advances, conquest, and subordination (Markakis, 2011). Since official incorporation into the Ethiopian empire, people in these peripheries have been confronted with a hegemonic national identity that is in stark contrast to their own. Because Amharic was the official national language, the inhabitants of the lowlands were compelled to learn the language. Those who opted not to learn Amharic were guaranteed political, social, and economic exclusion and marginalization. Many others did not learn Amharic; they survived on the margins of the state, with very little connecting them to the state. However, the history of the various people who inhabit Ethiopian peripheries, such as the Somalis, is nuanced and cannot be reduced to assimilation or resistance (Matshanda, 2015). For instance, the relationship between Ogadeen Somali and the Ethiopian state from 1960 to 1991 is characterized by two overlapping phases. These can be loosely termed as phases of cautious engagement with the Ethiopian state and open revolt against the state (Matshanda, 2015: 201). Known Ogadeen revolt against the Ethiopian state has existed since the region was officially incorporated into the Ethiopian empire (Lewis, 1980: 234). Since then, uprisings have occurred intermittently. The history of cautious engagement by Ogadeen Somali with the state helps us to better understand some of the origins of the contemporary challenge of citizenship in Ethiopia as it relates to the Somali region.

Emperor Selassie instituted a system akin to a decentralized despotism in Hararge province where he courted Ogadeen "chiefs." However, the "chiefs" and their Ogadeen clansmen sometimes demonstrated that their loyalties cannot be guaranteed. Their engagement with imperial authority reveals political and economic expediency. They were often interested in securing grazing pasture for their livestock, as seen in a May 1960 *Ethiopian Herald* newspaper article that reports on an Ogadeni delegation that sought the emperor's intervention on the issue of the Haud grazing area (*Ethiopian Herald*, 1960).

With the Somalis, the Ethiopians faced different challenges before and after 1960. Prior to Somali independence in 1960, the Ethiopians were interacting with Somali pastoralists mainly to ensure the extraction of tribute. They were less interested in absorbing the Somalis into the Ethiopian nation. However, following Somali independence in 1960, the Ethiopian state had to contend with the emergence of Somali nationalism in the eastern lowlands. To deal with the first challenge, the Ethiopian imperial state instituted a system similar to the "Native Authority" (Mamdani, 1996: 52). The state established a tribal organization that carried out certain duties on behalf of the imperial state (Matshanda, 2019: 671). It appointed chiefs, known as the *balabbat* in the Amharic language. Many of these Somali chiefs had to learn the language. Drysdale (1964) outlines the functions of the *balabbat* as that of mediating between the various clans and the Ethiopian state. The attempts of the latter to fully integrate the Ogadeen and Somalis in general came under strain upon Somali independence in 1960.

Following Somali independence and the unification of former colonial territories in 1960, the new government in Mogadishu sought the loyalties of clans. The foreign policy objectives of the new Somali Republic came to rest on the level of influence it enjoyed in the Somali-inhabited regions of its neighbors, including Ethiopia. Conversely, the emergence, development, and dissolution of notions of self-identification in these other Somali-inhabited regions were also largely influenced by the extent of their contact with the Somali Republic. The most notable impact of the formation of the Republic on the Ethiopian state was the potential threat of Somali nationalism. Having previously gone to great lengths to discourage any form of Somali unity, the Ethiopian state was now confronted with suggestions of Somali nationalism on its eastern periphery. The Ethiopians were decidedly unnerved by the independent Republic of Somalia. The next decade would see the Ethiopian state, with the aid of imperial superpowers, suppress the emergence and expression of ethno-national movements.

The Role of Imperial Powers in Ethiopia's Response to Somali and Eritrean Nationalism

The various states in the Horn of Africa were inevitably thrust into the Cold War rivalry between the East and the West where regional conflicts became internationalized (Schwab, 1978: 6). In addition, internal politics were heightened and given impetus by the role of the superpowers within the respective states. The military alliance between the United States and Ethiopia dates back to 1953 when the two countries signed the Mutual Defence Assistance Agreement (Baissa, 1989: 51). On the other hand, in 1963 the Republic of Somalia formally accepted $30 million in military aid from the Soviet Union (Lefebvre, 1998: 612). This section aims to demonstrate that the imperial state and the Derg regime accelerated the process of entrenching the Amhara national identity mainly through military aid that was provided by imperial superpowers.

US military assistance to Ethiopia is especially important as it relates to Eritrea. In the context of the Second World War, in the 1940s the United States established a military communications facility outside Asmara and it wanted to continue using it after the end of the war. Lyons (1986) notes that the Kagnew station was ideally situated for US global communication purposes. Thus, to protect this strategic interest, they gave full support to the United Nations-sanctioned federation of Eritrea to Ethiopia in 1952. Lefebvre (1998: 616) summarizes the converging interests of the United States and Ethiopia, stating that "Eritrea's future would be determined by US strategic interests and Ethiopia's geopolitical designs." The federation of Eritrea to Ethiopia in 1952 paved the way for the unilateral abrogation of the federal arrangement by Ethiopia in 1962, a decision that ended hopes of Eritrean autonomy. It can be argued that such a bold move by Ethiopia was possible because the country was emboldened by the political, military, and economic support that was afforded by its alliance with the United

States. The development and proliferation of Eritrean nationalism began with Italian colonialism but evolved and culminated in a new national identity based on common experience (Sorenson, 1991: 309). Subsequently, Eritrean nationalism had to contend with an Ethiopian state that enjoyed immense support by imperial superpowers. Various liberation movements waged a struggle for independence against Ethiopia, most notably the EPLF that emerged as the leader of the movement (Young, 1996: 113). Prior to the EPLF taking center stage in the Eritrean struggle, its predecessor, the Eritrean Liberation Front (ELF), had initiated the struggle for independence. The ELF pursued a secessionist agenda shortly after the annexation of Eritrea in 1962 to which the Ethiopian state responded by sending armed forces (Schwab, 1978: 14). Ultimately, the fate of the Eritrean struggle for independence lay in its alliance with the TPLF, a cooperation that emerged following the Ethiopian Revolution in 1974. Young (1996) notes that EPLF support for the Tigrayans of Ethiopia rested on acceptance of the view that Eritrea was a colony and had a right to self-determination. This objective, as we know, was fulfilled by the TPLF in 1993 when together with the Eritreans, they overthrew the Derg and assumed political power.

US assistance was also crucial for silencing Somali nationalism in eastern Ethiopia. In 1963, shortly after Somali independence in 1960, Somalia and Ethiopia went to war over a rebellion in the Somali-inhabited regions of Ethiopia. The timing of the rebellion coincided with what was gradually becoming the overriding foreign policy objective of the new government in Mogadishu—the pursuit of a Somali nation-state. In the latter part of 1963, a guerrilla movement that opposed imperial rule emerged from southeastern Ethiopia. The Western Somali Liberation Front (WSLF) was a force conceived entirely from within Ethiopia but had the sympathies of the Somali Republic. Early in 1964, the Republic was drawn into the internal conflict that was raging in eastern Ethiopia. The Republic gave military support to the WSLF. Because the latter materialized at the same time as a tax rebellion, their activities were viewed by the Ethiopians as an attack on the territorial integrity and authority of the state. The Ethiopian state retaliated by launching ground and air attacks on Somali border posts and towns (Markakis, 2011: 146–8). The efficiency and haste with which the rebellion was put down by the imperial Ethiopian government was undoubtedly owed to the military power of the Ethiopian army at the time, which was a direct outcome of US military assistance. Emperor Haile Selassie is known to have put immense pressure on the United States to increase military assistance and to ensure the timely delivery of armaments (Schwab, 1978; Lyons, 1986). The support given by imperial powers to Ethiopia manifested in the militarization of the state. Following the 1963 conflict in the Ogaden, and the emergence of the WSLF, the imperial state militarized the region. Gilkes (1975: 221) notes that, by the early 1970s, the Ethiopian army's third division was permanently based in the Ogaden district, where it "spends a substantial amount of time collecting tax." The "modernization" of the state, which included increased revenue collection and establishing an elaborate bureaucracy, provided both the context and pretext for the militarization of the Somali-inhabited region.

The Soviet Union also features significantly in the Ethiopian quest to amass military power in order to silence emerging nationalist voices inside the country from 1960 onward. Initially, Emperor Selassie flirted with the Soviet Union, in part to expand potential sources of military aid but also to force the United States to increase its military assistance to Ethiopia (Lyons, 1986; Baissa, 1989). The emperor visited Moscow in 1959, on the eve of Somali independence when Britain was preparing to grant the Somali territories independence, a move that received tacit support from the United States (Brind, 1983: 79). However, it was only in the late 1970s, after the imperial government was overthrown in a revolution, that the Soviet Union gained a firm foothold in Ethiopia. The military junta, known as the Derg, radicalized and militarized the state and further exacerbated the suppression of opposing national identities that existed in the peripheries. According to Clapham (2002: 14), "the Dergue represented the centre-periphery conceptualization of Ethiopia in its most intense form." By 1977, the Ethiopian state was involved in a military confrontation with the Eritreans in the north and at the same time faced increasing threats from Somalia on the eastern frontier.

Following the Ethiopian Revolution in 1974, Ethiopia shifted alliances from the United States to the Soviet Union. At this time, the Eritrean Liberation Movement (ELM) and other Marxist formations believed that the new Marxist regime in Addis Ababa would be more sympathetic to their plight. Furthermore, Somalia was in a solid alliance with the Soviet Union. With these seemingly aligning interests, and what appeared to be a major political rupture in Ethiopia, why then was there so much continuity in the conceptualization of the nation by the Marxist regime? Schwab (1978) suggests that there are multiple reasons for this, but most importantly, there was no single dominant ideology among the officers of the Derg. There were fundamental policy differences among the officers. We can argue that these differences extended to how the new nation was to be imagined by the military junta. In this regard, a significant number of officers within the Derg, many of whom were Amhara or *Amharized*, held the belief that the Amhara national identity remains relevant and that the territorial integrity of the Amhara state should not be compromised. The 1977–8 war with Somalia took on a nationalist tone when it was branded as a case of Ogadeni secession and Somali irredentism, and the Eritreans were branded as separatists. The military junta drew on the strong Amhara identity of the imperial state in order to galvanize national support for the wars with Somali secessionists and the Eritrean freedom fighters.

The change in alliances in the Horn of Africa was as a result of the US retreat from Ethiopia as it believed that it no longer had significant influence there. This immediately led the Soviet Union to fill the military aid vacuum (Schwab, 1978: 17). The Soviet Union gambled and hoped to secure the interests of both Somalia and Ethiopia, but the superpower was forced to choose sides when they were expelled from Somalia in November 1977 (Schwab, 1978; Brind, 1983). This meant that Soviet military support was solely focused on Ethiopia during the course of the war, where Moscow was able to throw its weight fully behind the Ethiopians. Tareke (2000) notes that Soviet aid ranged from military hardware to military advisers and technicians. With Cuban and Soviet assistance, the Derg claimed victory in 1978. The strength of the Ethiopian army was a result of decades of US military aid and recent Soviet support. The support of the superpowers ensured that by 1978, Mengistu Haile-Mariam, the chairman of the Derg and head of state, had "defeated the Somalis, the Eritreans, civilian dissidents, and opposition within the Dergue" (Marcus, 2002: 195).

Conclusion

This chapter argues that the roots of the contemporary challenge of citizenship in Ethiopia can be traced back to the construction of the Amhara national identity, whose long-term dominance can be attributed to the role of imperial superpowers that provided military and other forms of material support to the state. The chapter locates the beginning of this support in the aftermath of the Italian occupation. This was a critical time for Ethiopian statehood as the BMA was preparing to administer large parts of Ethiopia. The US-Ethiopia alliance began on a mutually beneficial basis when the United States realized the strategic significance of Ethiopia and the latter was in need of a powerful ally to help restore its sovereignty. The alliance with the Soviet Union on the other hand was purely a product of the Cold War. In making this argument, this chapter seeks to connect the violent form of politics that took root during the nineteenth and twentieth centuries in Ethiopia to the global political economy of the same period, which very few African countries could escape. This helps us to broaden our understanding of the colonial legacy and not limit it to direct colonization but also to the role of empire during the postcolonial era. The emergence and dominance of the Amhara national identity unfolded with a context of the violent suppression of opposing ethnic national identities in Ethiopia.

In locating Ethiopia within discourses on the postcolonial state in Africa, this chapter seeks to expand the lenses through which we understand the central thesis of *Citizen and Subject*. The explanatory power of the notion of a decentralized despotism helps us to unpack the crisis of citizenship that we have witnessed in Ethiopia since 1991. The key features of this crisis include an enduring legacy of centralized authoritarian rule that was predicated on a narrowly constructed national identity. The consequences of this legacy are the inability of the state to initiate a complete break with the past when thinking about inclusive citizenship and belonging. This challenge poses a threat to current and future plans for democratization in Ethiopia.

Ethiopia is currently at a crossroads regarding the long-term survival of the state in its current form. Many different actors are jostling for state power. These actors are first and foremost driven by their ethnic identities and affiliations, and one of their priorities is to redefine the national identity of the state. Renowned scholar of Ethiopian studies John Markakis warns that "the project of state building is far from completion and its end cannot be predicted . . . the analysis of succeeding crises along the route highlights the structural faults in its design, which is the centre's monopoly of power" (Markakis, 2011: 355). Markakis rightly foresees another political rupture in the center, based on how ethnic federalism has been implemented, particularly in the historic lowland peripheries.

References

Anderson, B. (1991). *Imagined Communities: Reflections on the Origins and Spread of Nationalism*. London: Verso.

Baissa, L. (1989). "United States military assistance to Ethiopia 1953–1974: A reappraisal of a difficult client-patron relationship." *Northeast African Studies*, 11(3): 51–70.

Barth, F. (1969). *Ethnic Groups and Boundaries: The Social Organisation of Culture Difference*. Boston: Little, Brown and Company.

Biersteker, T. and Weber, C. (1996). "The social construction of state sovereignty," in J. Biersteker and C. Weber (eds.), *State Sovereignty as Social Construct*. Cambridge: Cambridge University Press, pp. 1–21.

Brind, H. (1983). "Soviet policy in the Horn of Africa." *International Affairs*, 60(1): 75–95. https://doi.org/10.2307/2618931.

Clapham, C. (2002). "Controlling space in Ethiopia," in W. James (ed.), *Remapping Ethiopia: Socialism and After*. Oxford: James Currey, pp. 9–32.

Dirar, U. (2007). "Colonialism and the construction of national identities: The case of Eritrea." *Journal of Eastern African Studies*, 1(2): 256–76. https://doi.org/10.1080/17531050701452556.

Donham, D. (2002). "Introduction," in W. James and D. Donham (eds.), *Remapping Ethiopia: Socialism and After*. Athens: Ohio University Press, pp. 1–9.

Donham, D. and James, W. (eds.). (2002). *The Southern Marches of Imperial Ethiopia: Essays in History and Social Anthropology*, 2nd ed. Oxford: James Currey.

Drysdale, J. (1964). *The Somali Dispute*. London: Pall Mall Press.

Ethiopian Herald. (1960). "Ogaden notables petition emperor." *Staff Writer*, May 21.

Federal Democratic Republic of Ethiopia (FDRE). (1942). "National decrees and orders." Negarit Gazeta, FDRE, Addis Ababa.

Federal Democratic Republic of Ethiopia (FDRE). (1943). "National administrative regulations." Negarit Gazeta, FDRE, Addis Ababa.

Federal Democratic Republic of Ethiopia (FDRE). (1962). "National provincial appointments." Negarit Gazeta, FDRE, Addis Ababa.

Florida State University. (2008). "Ethiopia-Somalia boundary," International Boundary Study No. 153, College of Law, Florida State University. https://fall.fsulawrc.com/collection/LimitsinSeas/IBS153.pdf.

Gilkes, P. (1975). *The Dying Lion, Feudalism and Modernization in Ethiopia*. London: Julian Friedmann Publishers.

Government of the United Kingdom. (1897). "Anglo-Ethiopian treaty," Foreign Office, 881/6943. Public Records Office, the National Archives, London.

Government of the United Kingdom. (1957). "Ethiopian agreement, retention of reserved area," Foreign Office 1015/57. Public Records Office, the National Archives, London.

Hagmann, T. (2005). "Beyond clannishness and colonialism: Understanding political disorder in Ethiopia's Somali Region, 1991–2004." *The Journal of Modern African Studies*, 43(4): 509–36. https://doi.org/10.1017/S0022278X05001205.

Hagmann, T. and Mohamud, K. (2006). "State and politics in Ethiopia's Somali region since 1991." *Bildhaan: An International Journal of Somali Studies*, 6(2): 25–49. http://digitalcommons.macalester.edu/bildhaan/vol6/iss1/6/.html.

Henze, P. (2000). *Layers of Time: A History of Ethiopia*. London: Hurst and Company.

Hess, R. (1970). *Ethiopia: The Modernization of Autocracy*. Ithaca: Cornell University Press.

Holcomb, B. and Ibssa, S. (1990). *The Invention of Ethiopia: The Making of a Dependent Colonial State in Northeast Africa*. Trenton: The Red Sea Press.

Iyob, R. (2000). "The Ethiopia-Eritrea conflict: Diasporic vs. hegemonic states in the Horn of Africa, 1991–2000." *The Journal of Modern African Studies*, 38(4): 659–82. https://doi .org/10.1017/S0022278X00003499.

Keller, E. (1981). "Ethiopia: Revolution, class, and the national question." *African Affairs*, 80(321): 519–59. https://doi.org/10.1093/oxfordjournals.afraf.a097365.

Lefebvre, J. (1998). "The United States, Ethiopia and the 1963 Somali-Soviet arms deal: Containment and the balance of power dilemma in the Horn of Africa." *The Journal of Modern African Studies*, 36(4): 611–43. https://doi.org/10.1017/S0022278X98002870.

Levine, D. (1974). *Greater Ethiopia: The Evolution of a Multi-Ethnic Society*. Chicago: University of Chicago Press.

Lewis, I. (1980). *A Modern History of Somalia: Nation and State in the Horn of Africa*. London: Longman Group.

Lyons, T. (1986). "The United States and Ethiopia: The politics of a client-patron relationship." *Northeast African Studies*, 8(2/3): 53–75.

Mamdani, M. (1996). *Citizen and Subject: Contemporary Africa and the Legacy of Late Colonialism*. Princeton: Princeton University Press.

Mamdani, M. (2002). "African states, citizenship and war: A case-study." *International Affairs*, 78(3): 493–506. https://doi.org/10.1111/1468-2346.00263.

Marcus, H. (1994). *A History of Ethiopia*. Berkeley: University of California Press.

Marcus, H. (2002). *A History of Ethiopia*, 2nd ed. Berkeley: University of California Press.

Markakis, J. (1974). *Ethiopia: Anatomy of a Traditional Polity*. Oxford: Clarendon Press.

Markakis, J. (2011). *Ethiopia: The Last Two Frontiers*. Suffolk: James Currey.

Marshall, T. (1950). *Citizenship and Social Class*. Cambridge: Cambridge University Press.

Matshanda, N. (2015). "Centres in the periphery: Negotiating territoriality and identification in Harar and Jijiga from 1942," Unpublished PhD thesis, University of Edinburgh, Scotland.

Matshanda, N. (2019). "Constructing citizens and subjects in eastern Ethiopia: Identity formation during the British Military Administration." *Journal of Eastern African Studies*, 13(4): 661–77. https://www.tandfonline.com/doi/full/10.1080/17531055.2019 .1678927.

Matshanda, N. (2020). "Ethiopian reforms and the resolution of uncertainty in the Horn of Africa state system." *South African Journal of International Affairs*, 27(1): 25–42. https://www.tandfonline.com/doi/full/10.1080/10220461.2020.1736139.

Miller, D. (1999) "'Raising the tribes': British policy in Italian East Africa, 1938–41." *Journal of Strategic Studies*, 22(1): 96–123. https://doi.org/10.1080/01402399908437745.

Negash, T. (1997). *Ethiopia and Eritrea: The Federal Experience*. Piscataway: Transaction Publishers.

Oumer, B. (2020). "Ethiopia's diversity challenge and the politicization of identity." *Awash Post*, December 15. https://www.awashpost.com/2020/12/15/ethiopias-diversity -challenge-and-the-politicization-of-identity/.

Pankhurst, R. (1998). "Tedla Haile, and the problem of multi-ethnicity in Ethiopia." *Northeast African Studies*, 5(3): 81–96.

Prunier, G. and Ficquet, E. (2015). "Introduction," in G. Prunier and E. Ficquet (eds.), *Understanding Contemporary Ethiopia: Monarchy, Revolution and the Legacy of Meles Zenawi*. London: Hurst and Company, pp. 1–14.

Reid, R. (2011). *Frontiers of Violence in North-east Africa: Genealogies of Conflict since C.1800*. Oxford: Oxford University Press.

Rubenson, S. (1976). *The Survival of Ethiopian Independence*. London: Heinemann Educational Books.

Samatar, A. (2004). "Ethiopian federalism: Autonomy versus control in the Somali region." *Third World Quarterly*, 25(6): 1131–54. https://doi.org/10.1080/0143659042000256931.

Samatar, A. (2005). "Ethiopian ethnic federalism and regional autonomy: The Somali test." *Bildhaan: An International Journal of Somali Studies* 5(9): 44–76. http://digitalcommons.macalester.edu/bildhaan/vol5/iss1/9/.html.

Samatar, A. (2020). "Ethiopia's war: The last gasp of minority ethnic chauvinism and pseudo-democracy." *Daily Maverick*, November 19. https://www.dailymaverick.co.za/article/2020-11-19-ethiopias-war-the-last-gasp-of-minority-ethnic-chauvinism-and-pseudo-democracy/.

Schwab, P. (1978). "Cold war on the Horn of Africa." *African Affairs*, 77(306): 6–20. https://doi.org/10.1093/oxfordjournals.afraf.a096955.

Sorenson, J. (1991). "Discourses on Eritrean nationalism and identity." *The Journal of Modern African Studies*, 29(2): 301–17. https://doi.org/10.1017/S0022278X00002767.

Tareke, G. (2000). "The Ethiopia-Somalia war of 1977 revisited." *The International Journal of African Historical Studies*, 33(3): 635–67.

Teka, T. (1998). "Amhara ethnicity in the making," in M. Salih and J. Markakis (eds.), *Ethnicity and the State in Eastern Africa*. Uppsala: Nordiska Afrikainstitutet, pp. 116–26.

Tilley, C. (1995). "Citizenship, identity and social history." *International Review of Social History*, 40(3): 1–17.

Touval, S. (1963). *Somali Nationalism, International Politics and the Drive for Unity in the Horn of Africa*. Cambridge: Harvard University Press.

Triulzi, A. (2006). "The past as contested terrain—commemorating new sites of memory in war-torn Ethiopia," in P. Kaarsholm (ed.), *Violence, Political Culture and Development in Africa*. Oxford: James Currey, pp. 123–37.

Tronvoll, K. (2009). *War and the Politics of Identity in Ethiopia: The Making of Enemies and Allies in the Horn of Africa*. Suffolk: James Currey.

Weber, M. (1968). *Economy and Society: An Outline of Interpretive Sociology, Vols 2 and 3*, translated by R. Guenther and K. Wittich. New York: Bedminster Press.

Wolde-Mariam, M. (1964). "The background of the Ethio-Somalian boundary dispute." *The Journal of Modern African Studies*, 2(2): 189–219. https://doi.org/10.1017/S0022278X00003992.

Young, J. (1996). "The Tigray and Eritrean people's liberation fronts: A history of tensions and pragmatism." *The Journal of Modern African Studies*, 34(1): 105–20. https://doi.org/10.1017/S0022278X00055221.

Zewde, B. (1991). *A History of Modern Ethiopia, 1855–1974*. Athens: Ohio University Press.

7

Political Identity and Postcolonial Democracy

Karuna Mantena

Introduction

Mahmood Mamdani's landmark intervention, *Citizen and Subject: Contemporary Africa and the Legacy of Late Colonialism*, scrutinized the construction of identity, custom, and tradition and positioned it within an ambitious and provocative theory of colonial and postcolonial state formation. In so doing, Mamdani redefined the stakes and scope of postcolonial critical scholarship. *Citizen and Subject* moved away from both Marxist analyses that focused on the dynamics of underdevelopment and economic dependency as well as nationalist and postcolonial cultural critique which highlighted sociocultural and epistemic domination and exclusion, as the chief legacies of colonialism to be reckoned with, contested, and overturned. In contrast, *Citizen and Subject* enabled a critique and analysis of colonialism that was primarily *political* and *institutional* by making visible an enduring set of inheritances given in colonial state formation.

Mamdani defined colonialism in terms of the emergence of a distinctive form of rule and state form, a bifurcated state that institutionalized power and identity along the axes of indigeneity, race, and ethnicity. These axes in turn came to delineate major fault lines of postcolonial politics. On the one hand, by focusing on the colonial moment as a key moment in the institutionalization of identity, Mamdani sought to undo the persistent temptation to view the prominence of tribal or ethnic categories to post-independence African politics as simply the resurgence of precolonial or primordial forces. On the other hand, *Citizen and Subject* also proposed a powerful frame from which to rethink the limits of anti-colonial nationalism. It suggested that in some crucial respects the project of decolonization had been left radically unfulfilled. In Mamdani's striking terms, official decolonization ended in "deracialization without democratization" (Mamdani, 1996: 8).

In *Citizen and Subject*, the bifurcated state, the distinctive state form of late colonialism, was shown to be divided between a directly ruled civic sphere where power was marked by racial exclusion and an indirectly ruled customary sphere comprised of native authorities differentiated on tribal lines. Both in different ways worked to privilege and politicize claims of indigeneity. Racial polarization divided settlers and natives, colonizers and colonized; while the sphere of the native was further demarcated into territorialized ethnic regimes. Colonialism invested racial and ethnic identities with status, power, and authority and therefore acute political consequences. After independence, conflicts along these lines would lead to some of the worst forms of extreme violence and genocide and hence Mamdani's provocative suggestion that the politicization of indigeneity was colonialism's greatest crime (see Mamdani, 2002: 14).

Anti-colonial struggles were organized for, and largely successful at, the deracialization of civil society. Independence erased racial exclusion and the subordination of the colonized native in the legal and political spheres. But only in rare cases was tribalization of the rural sphere challenged, leaving untouched underlying institutions that in the competition for resources and power pitted ethnicities against one another. The realizability of universal citizenship, as promised by deracialization itself, would be contaminated and destabilized by these contradictions and conflicts. In this sense, the achievement of deracialization—independence from alien rule and the assumption of national popular sovereignty—did not resolve but rather escalated underlying dilemmas of representation and differentiated citizenship.

The problem of incomplete decolonization is an important and characteristic concern of postcolonial critique and analysis. In political terms, it often involves claims about the persistence of some key and troubling features of the colonial state into the formal structure of its postcolonial avatars—for example, tendencies toward authoritarianism and despotism (see, for instance, Chatterjee, 1986; Guha, 1998; Hussain, 2003). Mamdani also highlights this inheritance in relation to the fused and unchecked power of unreformed native authorities. But, to my mind, Mamdani's distinctive achievement and provocation lies elsewhere. It is to keep front and center the problem of *political identity* as the paramount and persistent dilemma of postcolonial politics. Mamdani challenges us to take identity seriously without either reifying it or undervaluing its durability and appeal. His strategy for avoiding both pitfalls involves, firstly, an insistence that the politicization of identity is irreducibly political. Though the terminology is tautological, it suggests that identity formation has a distinct political logic of its own, which cannot be fully explained by ideological, cultural, or economic factors. Secondly, Mamdani takes politicization to be a dynamic process marked by conjunctures that can escalate, dampen, or reposition tendencies toward collision and competition. Attentiveness to such key moments makes Mamdani's analyses granular and nondeterministic. For all the concern given to the legacies of colonialism, this inheritance is never taken to preordain or necessitate violent conflict.

In *When Victims Become Killers* (2002), Mamdani's analysis of genocide in Rwanda, the centrality of political identity becomes even sharper, with a focus on the historical construction of settler and native, ruling and subject races, and the conditions for their extreme polarization. Here, Mamdani makes novel use of *race* and *ethnicity* as analytical categories. Building on the edifice of *Citizen and Subject*, race and ethnicity become less terms that name or describe particular identities in and of themselves. Rather, they mark two different logics of opposition, exclusion, and incorporation. Race is a relation of hard exclusion, which often implies subordination but most importantly carries with it the potential for such acute polarization that secession, expulsion, and genocide become politically possible. The colonial imagination and investment of the Tutsi in Rwanda and Arabs in Sudan as racially distinct ruling groups laid the groundwork of this kind of extreme polarization, whose history and contemporary implications Mamdani has skillfully traced (2002, 2009, 2012, 2020). Ethnicity is a form of incorporation that fragments and differentiates native and subject populations. When ethnic competition and conflict become sharper and polarized, it has the potential to mutate into racial opposition.

These different relations of opposition reveal that not all identities and communal affiliations are equivalent in their political implications. In this sense, the terms *race* and *ethnicity* might usefully capture variation in identity assertion and vulnerability in numerous postcolonial settings. For instance, race and ethnicity could illuminate why democratic incorporation and empowerment of marginalized groups have followed very different trajectories and with differing results that do not map onto differential resources alone. In India, for example, this would allow for a nuanced accounting and comparison of the unexpected post-independence political trajectories of Dalits, Muslims, and Adivasis along these lines. Likewise, this lens can help historicize and diagnose the differing dynamics of so-called religious and sectarian conflicts, of why some differences become more inflected with divisive and violent implications. Though the terms *race*, *tribe*, and *native* acquire a density of signification in the African colonial experience and in important respects are tied to that historical experience, they nevertheless might have a more general relevance to understanding contemporary conflict in the wider postcolonial world.

I suspect that something akin to this generalizability is what Mamdani had in mind when he challenged us to think: "What can the study of Africa teach us about late modern life?" (Mamdani, 2002: xv). In his most recent work, *Neither Settler nor Native* (2020), Mamdani has broached this question by showing how the logic of colonial statecraft—the practices of indirect rule—was part and parcel of state-building as such and thus a general feature of political modernity. In this sense, both the crisis of extreme violence in the postcolonial world and the struggle over race and immigration in the west are byproducts of the continuous manufacture of naturalized majorities and minorities necessitated by the idea of nation-state itself.

In this chapter, I take up Mamdani's challenge in a similar spirit and explore what political theory can be generated from the post-independence African experience. I do so by recasting what Mamdani points to as the limits of decolonization—the dynamics of deracialization without democratization—in terms of a theory of postcolonial democracy. Instead of focusing on the logic of nationalism and postcolonial state-building, I turn to what decolonization and the struggles of postcolonial democracy reveal about the contradictory workings of democracy and democratization. Akin to how Mamdani sees majority and minority, native and settler, as coincident with nation-state formation, I argue that democracy as such is centrally implicated in the politicization of identity. Such a connection is not an occasional or accidental implication of democracy, given, for example, by the brute sociological fact of cultural pluralism. Rather, it stems from and illuminates central paradoxes of modern democratic politics.

An endemic source of conflict in modern democracy lay in rival and multiple senses of how majority rule is to be authorized, institutionalized, and enacted. The *how* of democracy and the procedures and practices of majority rule are often confounded with some concrete claim of *who* should constitute that majority. This is the core conundrum I will highlight, namely the continual slippage and conflation between the *who* and *how* of ruling, between the formal structures of democratic authorization, competition, and decision-making and the demographic group or majority that stakes a claim to sovereignty and attempts to fix the demos in their image. This conflation is also played out in the slippage between democracy as a principle of legitimacy (the who and how of authorization) and democracy as a form of rule (the who and how of governing democratically). This is akin to the distinction between democratic sovereignty and democratic government emphasized by Richard Tuck in his account of the origins of modern democracy (Tuck, 2016).

For Tuck, modern democracy begins with the institutionalization of majority rule as a mode of popular authorization, that is, of establishing democratic sovereignty, not government. Yet Mamdani, most sharply in *Neither Settler nor Native* (2020), and Richard Bourke, in his incisive analysis of the conflict in Northern Ireland as a dispute borne of modern democracy, have argued that it is precisely the assumption that majorities are the grounds of democratic legitimacy and thereby set the terms of inclusion, which fuels extreme conflict and violence (Bourke, 2003; Mamdani, 2020). Political majorities should be properly viewed as temporary and conjunctural outcomes of democratic procedures, not as preexisting demographic groupings that prescribe membership in a democratic state. In the latter case, according to Bourke, we have a *majority state* and not a legitimate democratic state; in Mamdani's terms, it is a nation-state built on manufactured majorities and not a true democracy (Bourke, 2003; Mamdani, 2020).

Anti-colonial revolt was successful at deracialization, at throwing off alien rule and asserting self-determination. Indeed, decolonization was the key moment in which democracy as a principle of popular sovereignty became effectively globalized. But with independence, popular sovereignty had to be given a governing structure. And as soon as democracy is institutionalized as a kind of rule, various crises of representation and citizenship become visible. In a democracy, any constitutional settlement and governing structure will privilege some groups—that is, numerically dominant groups—and render vulnerable others. At its most intense and immediate, when demographic majorities were explicitly privileged as the source of legitimacy, decolonization was concomitant with partition, secession, and the violent redrawing of political boundaries. Beyond such founding moments, nativist and majoritarian democratic imaginaries were generated through the procedures of democratic competition, which likewise play on the ambiguity between the who and how of democratic rule.

Popular discussions of democracy, identity, and violence—especially as they relate to so-called ethnic conflict in the postcolonial world—abound with references to tribal loyalties, sectarian intolerance, and ancient hatreds. Subtler scholarly attempts to conceptualize the democratic nature of communal identity formation still tend to portray these phenomena as aberrational, as stemming from deviant forms of nationalism and populism. In assessing the imbrication of democracy and violence in the twentieth century, Michael Mann's *Dark Side of Democracy*, for instance, differentiates civic or "good" democracy from ethnic or "bad" democracy (Mann, 2004). In segregating the two, as Richard Bourke (2007) argues in a pointed critique, Mann merely names and classifies what in fact needs to be explained, namely the practices and processes by which something called *ethnic democracy* emerges (see also, Bourke, 2003, 2016). Moreover, studies of nationalist violence—as well as more recent work on populism and its connection to democracy and violence—tend to analyze democracy as an ideological and normative project and worry most about how the demos is symbolically defined and demarcated. I try to move away from the implicit privilege given to symbolic conceptualization to how the collective is mobilized via democratic practice. That is, I try to tether ideological and symbolic work to practice by focusing on how democratic imaginaries—of majorities and minorities—are constituted and sustained via the material structures, processes, and dynamics of electoral competition.[1]

Decolonizing Political Theory

Mamdani's pointed question—"What can the study of Africa teach us about late modern life?"—also gestures toward another space of incomplete decolonization, namely the intellectual world of social science and how it figures the politics and history of modern Africa. Mamdani here joins a number of postcolonial critics who have in different ways questioned the unilinearity and universality of social science. I take this to be a key thread in Partha Chatterjee's work (1986, 1993, 2006, 2011) as well as Suren Pillay's *Decolonizing the University* (2015).

The categories of modern political thought and modern social science have so closely tracked the particular historical development of modernity in the West that that trajectory and experience have been deemed normative. Other histories are judged in comparison to these models and narratives, and difference is taken as a sign of failure, deviance, or exoticism. I take the task of postcolonial theory to build on the recognition that is always already implicit, that the majority of the world experiences and practices politics in ways that do not conform to the models inherited from Western social and political thought. The alternative strategy that Mamdani has recommended and pursued is to attend to the historical specificity of African, Asian, and Latin American political histories, by locating and defining the predicaments and sequences that make up their distinct political histories and trajectories. The concept of the bifurcated state emerged from Mamdani's explicit attempt to think of Africa as a coherent unit of analysis.

But in moving away from the "abstract universalism" of Western social science, the call for historicization and specificity also has to avoid the opposite pitfall, what Mamdani has called "intimate particularism" (Mamdani, 1996: 9–11). Emphasizing difference and specificity risks sliding into claims of exceptionalism, idiosyncrasy,

---

[1] On the move to practice, see Frank (2010, forthcoming). See also Rosanvallon (2008: 17), on the need to focus on "democratic activity" in order to move beyond dichotomous characterizations of direct/indirect or real/ideal democracy.

or exoticism, confirming the language of deviation and pathology so prevalent in discussions of non-Western politics. This is what makes Mamdani's call for reimagining and reinvigorating the project of comparison so compelling. Whereas *Citizen and Subject* employed comparison to produce a unifying account of African state formation, the call for comparison beyond Africa comes in the Preface to *When Victims Become Killers* (2002). Comparison can break the barriers of area studies as traditionally defined and place the overlapping histories of non-Western politics into direct conversation. Thinking together political experience across the South would, in turn, occasion new theory. Mamdani's concept of the bifurcated state and Partha Chatterjee's idea of political society are exemplars of this form of theory generation; they speak to the need to innovate new ideas and forms of analysis that better capture the complexity of political life in the postcolonial world.

In *Neither Settler nor Native* (2020), Mamdani pushes the project of comparison onto a fully global terrain and uses his unique perspective on colonial statecraft and post-independence African politics to rethink and criticize core elements of political modernity. Indirect rule in different guises is discerned and analyzed in state projects from the United States to Israel. For Mamdani, it provides the template and key to understanding the foundations, limits, and legacy of the modern nation-state. In this chapter I pursue a different but complementary strategy for decolonizing social science and generating postcolonial political theory. In addition to inaugurating and creatively testing new and original concepts, the comparative study of postcolonial politics can also lead to a rethinking and revision of some of the central concepts of political theory.[2] This would begin by taking a concept like democracy that comes overlaid with a whole series of ideological, normative, and sociological assumptions and attempt to disinter the concept from these accretions through careful consideration of how democracy has come to be practiced and adopted across the postcolonial world.

Exploring the dynamics of democracy in new and diverse contexts, contexts that fall far outside democracy's supposedly original or ideal typical spaces, might reveal to us some more durable truths about the nature of democratic politics. My wager is that the postcolonial experience of democracy has made visible fundamental features of democratic politics and processes that have remained hidden or less conspicuous in their Euro-American incarnations. This strategy in effect reverses what is usually taken as the norm and the exception of democratic practice. If what is happening in postcolonial society might in fact track a more universal trajectory of democracy, then our task is to clarify in theoretical terms why that might be the case.

Here are two quick examples to illustrate the possibility of this kind of reversal and what it might open up in terms of democratic theory. Take for instance the enormous and unexpected variation in the rate of voter turnout across the world. As we know, prior to the 2020 presidential elections, the United States had one of the lowest voter turnout rates, and it was especially bleak in municipal elections where in off-season cycles it plummeted as low as 20 percent even in major urban centers. On the other hand, voter turnout in municipal elections in South Africa has ranged

---

[2] Adom Getachew and I have more recently elaborated these two modes of decolonizing political theory in terms of *innovating* new concepts and *reanimating* inherited ones (2021).

between 48 percent and 58 percent. These figures lag far behind South Africa's parliamentary elections turnout rate which averages around 75 percent but are still significantly higher than US presidential elections. In India, the reversal of expected trends is even starker. Not only do voters from marginalized groups consistently vote at higher rates than their urban, richer, male, upper-caste compatriots, but the more local the election the higher the turnout becomes, averaging above 98 percent in panchayat elections (see Banerjee, 2014).

No doubt myriad factors come into play to make real sense of these numbers. But the idea that people would be invested in those elections that are most intimate to them and have the deepest impact on their daily lives seems eminently plausible. If so, we might want to take higher voter turnout at the local level to be the normal expectation and treat the trend toward low turnout as a deep and striking anomaly that needs to be explained. Political scientists who treat the United States as an exemplary model of a "mature" democracy sometimes recognize this problem, but they tend to see it as a "gap" between democratic theory and practice. In doing so, they are blind to the potential theoretical relevance of the gap. They do not allow it to trouble basic assumptions of the theory. The price for such blindness is that democratic theory seems more and more ideological and out of sync with the realities of democratic life. By contrast, we can use the diversity of experience across the globe to cast into radical doubt what is normal and what is pathological and rethink what we take to be given in the nature of democracy.

Consider a second example concerning the relationship between universal suffrage and wealth redistribution. Democrats and socialists often argued for the expansion of suffrage in the hope and expectation that enfranchising the poor would lead to radical demands for redistribution. Liberals, for their part, shared this expectation but worried that such demands would be deeply destabilizing. Evidence from the last two and a half centuries of democracy has not borne out this expectation. Indeed, one could argue that the more common trend points to the opposite conclusion. It seems it is only under rare and highly conjunctural moments that electoral democracy becomes the catalyst for radically egalitarian outcomes. More alarmingly, modern democracy sometimes seems compatible with extreme inequality.

India provides a troubling example in this respect. As suggested earlier, the poorest classes in India seem to be genuinely enfranchised and make up a significant share of the voting electorate. And yet, large-scale voting has not resulted in radical or even consistent calls for redistribution. These trends should provoke serious questioning of very common and long-standing presumptions of democratic politics. In the case of redistribution, we know that economic power thwarts campaigns and programs of and for economic reform, and that there are many externally imposed pressures from having to function within a system of global capitalism. But the seeming compatibility between democracy and inequality should also provoke us to consider what obstacles to redistribution are thrown up from *within* the logic of democratic politics. What aspects of the logic and procedures of democratic politics make elite capture possible, invisible, and/or compatible with democracy?

This is the kind of fundamental rethinking that the project of comparison can offer to political theory. Only when democracy travels into very different historical and sociological settings can we discern its general features.[3] By exposing democracy's constraints, challenges, and possibilities, the study of postcolonial democracy can clarify endemic features of democracy. It can thereby revitalize a form of democratic theory whose universality comes closely tethered to actual democratic practice.

Defining Democracy

Democracy is a particularly apt term to attempt this critical appropriation and retheorization. For a start, democracy has become the dominant (albeit amorphous) political norm the world over and seems likely to remain so for the foreseeable future. Not only has it become institutionalized and adopted in diverse contexts but democratic imaginaries have become truly popular, shaping the terms of political contestation from below.

Moreover, it is a concept that has never been contained by a single origin story or national narrative; the history of democracy has been a history of appropriation and reinvention. A key moment in that history was the moment of its modern reinvention, where an ambivalence between democracy as a principle of legitimacy and as a form of government became essential to its functioning and a source of permanent tension. In both registers, questions of who authorizes and governs and how that rule is structured are continually confounded in ways that make the politicization of identity an internal and ever-present effect of democratic politics.

Prior to its modern reinvention, democracy was most often understood not as a principle of legitimacy but rather as a form of rule, a regime, a distinctive way of arranging political offices. Democracy meant the practice of direct, popular participation in ruling. Selection by lot and short terms made rotation and not representation the central mechanism to ensure accountability and egalitarian share in ruling (in turns).[4] Democratic forms of rule also implied some substantive sense of who would rule. Democracy was the rule of the poor, the plebian majority, the common man; in this sense, it was popular and anti-elite in orientation. Studies of classical Athenian democracy have also shown how this radical egalitarianism was itself made possible by hereditary status restrictions in citizenship along the lines of gender, native birthright, and slavery.

The modern idea of democracy, by contrast, is closely tied to ideas of popular sovereignty and self-determination, of democracy as a principle of legitimation and authorization. Perhaps the most puzzling fact about democracy's recovery and rehabilitation is that it emerged historically alongside the self-conscious rejection of the actual institutional forms of participatory democracy. Dunn writes that for most of its history, democracy was a term of abuse; the consensus among political thinkers

---

[3] John Dunn (2013) suggests and pursues something along these lines in his analysis of Indian democracy. Likewise, Rosanvallon (2008: 26–7) suggests a broad comparative scope as a way to "de-Westernize" democratic theory.

[4] For arguments that emphasize the contrast between ancient and modern democracy in these terms (and for polemical effect), see especially Finlay (1985), and Manin (1997).

from Plato to John Stuart Mill was that democracy as a form of government, and specifically Athenian democracy, was a "disorderly, unstable and intensely dangerous" form of politics (2005: 61).

Modern liberal democracy emerged as a critique of direct democracy of the Athenian kind and favored more elite and indirect forms of representative democracy. In representative democracy, participation is usually limited to voting in mediated and infrequent elections, which means at best a minute percentage of the citizenry actually share in the practice of ruling. And this limitation was intended: representative government is a form of popular government in which the people as such do not and are not meant to rule. In *Federalist* 63, James Madison famously argued that the novelty of representative government—why it was an advance upon ancient democracy—was that it was built upon "*the total exclusion of the people in their collective capacity* from any share in" governing (Hamilton et al., 2008: 364). Institutions that mediate, disperse, and check legislative sovereignty were regarded as more stable and better suited for securing individual liberty within the context of diverse, large-scale commercial societies.

Why then do we refer to this form of government as democratic or popular? What role do the people play in such a regime? To be sure, periodic elections offer some form of democratic accountability (Rosanvallon, 2008). But the democratic credentials of representation seem most closely tied to its function as a mode of popular authorization and legitimation. Representative government can be called a democracy because in principle the people authorize who can rule in the form of elections. In this formulation, however, a great deal of ambiguity exists about the nature of popular authorization and its intended consequences.

Dunn suggests that in the twentieth century there was a purposeful conflation between democracy and representative government—for example, in the hybrid term "liberal democracy." Indeed, for Dunn, liberal democracy is a kind of bait and switch. Liberal critics of democracy successfully hijacked the term democracy and its moral force while instituting a form of rule that thwarts democracy's egalitarian and revolutionary potential. What most concerns Dunn about this conflation is that it fundamentally confuses our expectations. We work under a severe mismatch between the utopian scale of our aspirations for democracy—that it can deliver freedom, equality, prosperity, peace—and the harsh realities that none of these ideals may be intrinsically connected to democratic politics (Dunn, 2000, 2005, 2013; Bourke, 2003). Aspirations to democratic control, equality, and unity constantly run up against the exercise of democratic power. In Bourke's view, we need to accept the fact that democratic "procedures are competitive, and so potentially exclusive." Hence, "actual politics within a democracy" will always and necessarily carry risks of "disunity and inequality" (2003: xi).

In an alternative account of what made the modern reinvention of democracy possible, Tuck (2016) places emphasis on the conceptual distinction between democratic sovereignty and democratic government, which he argues was most fully worked out and defended by Jean-Jacques Rousseau. Partially in line with the skepticism toward ancient democracy, modern democracy—in the form of majority-rule voting—was defended as a mechanism for popular authorization but rejected as a way to govern and administer modern societies. Defining democracy in terms of procedures of and for popular sovereignty makes liberal democracy intelligible and not quite a deception. At the same time, Tuck is critical of liberal attempts to thwart the radical potential of majority rule by limiting the role of popular referenda or plebiscites, and more generally working against institutionalizing forms for the enactment of popular sovereignty.

The history of democratic thought shows why the experience of modern democracy is necessarily riddled with contradictory tendencies. Questions about the relationship between the who and how of rule, and of sovereignty to government, point to fundamental dilemmas that democratic practice does not resolve but rather takes shape around. Although Tuck (2016) is right to emphasize the conceptual distinction between democratic sovereignty and democratic government, I want to suggest that in practice the line between them is not easy to sustain and open to contestation. Despite liberal attempts to question and contain spaces of direct participation, the moral appeal of democracy will push up and resist these limitations.

An important source of resistance to the mediating features of representative democracy is given in a third definition of democracy. This is the idea of democracy as more of a social process than a set of institutional arrangements. Alexis de Tocqueville (2010) refers to democracy as both a theory of government—the theory of popular sovereignty—and a social state. As a social state, democracy was defined by the equality of conditions, leveling processes that render all forms of hierarchy and authority suspect. This is a key element of the democratic social imaginary, linked to sociological transformations in how societies are structured and how individuals are (dis)connected. But it also signals elements of a distinctively democratic moral psychology (see Kaviraj, 2014), attitudes about equality and hierarchy, for instance, that contain important political implications. These elements of the democratic imaginary embolden plebian upsurges as well as populist majoritarianism—orientations that shape, infiltrate, and sometimes destabilize democratic institutions from within.

Democracy, Identity, Violence

Building on these broad understandings of the dilemmas of democracy, I take up three dynamics—founding, electoral, and moral-psychological—and briefly sketch how we might situate the politicization of identity as an inherent or endemic feature of democratic politics. As I suggested earlier, it might be useful to think of politicization as emanating from the continual conflation of the *who* and *how* of ruling. In the ideal and formal sense, democracy aspires to self-determination and political equality in which all citizens partake. The notion of a self-ruling people in concrete terms often takes the form of mobilized communities making a claim to rule, to the legitimate exercise of that power, or more generally the moral right to rule. In democracy, this moral right to rule has been powerfully tied to a specific kind of demographic imagination, where the claim to rule is tied to the constitution of a numerical majority.

Studies of colonial censuses have made visible how dramatic and consequential the effects of enumeration can be. The census rigidified myriad linguistic, cultural, and religious affiliations by transforming them into exclusive, ascriptive ethnic and racial identities. More mobile aspects of social identity subject to processes of individual and collective acculturation and conversion, for example, became fixed and distributed into racial categories. Such identities became especially entrenched wherever they were inflected with political meaning, that is, when they defined access to power.

Bernard Cohn characterized the transformation of identity induced by the colonial census as a process of objectification, whereby individuals begin to see themselves as a part of (imagined) abstract, nonlocal communities (Cohn, 1998). In the case of caste—which was Cohn's focus—objectification was linked to the publicity of the census and the open contest about the relative rank of caste groups. But objectification also made one conscious of the size of one's community vis-à-vis others. Enumeration of this kind made visible a different sense of relative position and power, one that tracked and catalyzed democratic imaginaries (see especially, Scott, 1999; Kaviraj, 2010). Consciousness of size is directly felt as relative strength and power or weakness and vulnerability, a moral-psychological and cognitive revelation that can be hard to restrain and hence politically divisive.

In founding or constitutional moments, when democratic sovereignty is enacted and instituted, the dangers of conflating the who/how of ruling are especially acute. Where a democratic, demographic imaginary around ascriptivized groups has emerged prior to or in tandem with decolonization, independence was shot through with escalating conflict over how power will be devolved and/or shared between these enumerated groups. It is not surprising that in British colonies where religion was an important category of managing and defining populations and some minimal forms of representation were introduced—for example, in India, Ireland, and mandate Palestine—the crisis of decolonization occasioned partition, war, and violent transfer of populations. These crisis moments have been variously described and analyzed as problems of competing exclusive or sectarian nationalisms. But here we can see that they embody ever-present dilemmas of democracy, of who constitutes the demos that has the right to self-rule and how that rule is institutionalized (Bourke, 2003).

A second dynamic of the demographic-democratic imaginary comes into play most clearly when we consider the central mechanisms and procedures of democratic politics, namely competitive elections and their attendant techniques of organization and mobilization. What the experience of postcolonial democracy has confirmed is how responsive collective identities—of caste, ethnicity, and religion—have been to the logic of electoral democracy. Caste and tribe not only survive but also seem to thrive. This no longer surprises us. But Western democratic theorists assume kinship and birthright to be premodern and/or apolitical categories and therefore have paid little analytical attention to them (except as remnants of distorted, ethnic, and nativistic nationalisms). But in the paradigmatic case of ancient Athens, as Demetra Kasimis (2018) has vividly shown, autochthony and native birthright shaped core practices of Athenian democracy, from stabilizing democratic equality to grounding imperial citizenship. In this view, nativism and the scrutiny and politicization of identity are concomitant with and constitutive effects of democracy. This suggests some promising and hitherto untapped overlap with studies of postcolonial democracy, making possible novel accounts of the imbrication of kinship and democracy and its theoretical relevance.

Identities need not have a deep colonial past and/or prior legal institutionalization to become activated in and through democratic politics. In the case of caste, there are myriad reasons why caste has become so central to the functioning of Indian democracy. To be sure, many stem from legal and administrative categorization inherited from the colonial regime—from the size and demarcation of castes, their relation to Hinduism and Hindu personal law, to the delineation of which castes and tribes are provided special state support and allocated reserved seats in political bodies, the civil service, and educational institutions. But the politicization of castes was also thrown up inadvertently and unexpectedly by the dynamics of electoral competition, for example, the wave of agricultural castes that rose to regional political dominance by leveraging numerical majorities. For example, the state of Andhra Pradesh has gone through successive bifurcations (from Madras Presidency in 1952 and from Telangana in 2014) and amalgamations (with Telangana in 1956), and each phase reconfigured demographic majorities. The original call for amalgamation was spearheaded by the communist-led Andhra Mahasaba. Rivals such as the political organizations led by the Reddy caste resisted amalgamation on those grounds. And yet, the first decade of regional elections thrust the Reddys—a dispersed but numerically large caste in the newly enlarged state—almost unexpectedly into political dominance. The Reddys and the Kammas, the two largest caste groups, have since dominated Andhra politics and have leveraged that political power into economic power.[5] As democratic politics in India continues to entrench caste into its very core, the dynamics of imbrication continue to transform the meaning and experience of caste. In the broadest sense, the rise of caste as a political identity seems coincident with the secular decline of caste as the organizing principle of social structure. Moreover, traditionally caste was a social form that tended toward segmentation and division. But the logic of democracy has stopped that process and reoriented it toward aggregation, horizontal ethnicization, and even inverse hierarchization.

Elections paradoxically drive tendencies toward majoritarian aggregation as well as factionalization and polarization. The building of coalitions and large, creative, plural majorities is also undercut by the forms of intimidation, competition, and antagonism. The democratic logic of numbers imbues collective protest with a similar double logic of enacting democratic sovereignty—the greater the crowds, the closer you concretize popular will—as well as of asserting sheer power. When numbers are mobilized to function as a demonstration of power, on the street or via the ballot box, democracy, in Gandhi's terms, becomes (and is resented as) a species of might over right, jeopardizing its claim to legitimacy (Mantena, 2022).

Lastly, democracy as social state signals a fundamental shift in values—the suspicion of hierarchy and authority and the championing of egalitarian values—which seem part and parcel of the working out of the implications of universal franchise. I am not sure to what extent this is a sociological process as much as a shift in the social imaginary,

---

[5]   On this latter point, see Damodaran (2008).

a moral-psychological shift that internalizes a presumption toward egalitarianism and a suspicion of authority (Kaviraj, 2014). In the Indian case, this process is sometimes called the plebianization or vernacularization of democracy. Yogendra Yadav (1999) characterizes it as a democratic upsurge made possible via universal suffrage. If we take, for example, India, Turkey, and South Africa, iterative elections have occasioned the downward shift in political power in the strict sense of ordinary people being able and willing to shape political outcomes. This gives rise to more populist forms and languages of doing democracy as well as assertions that in democracy rulers should be from and look like the majority. Here, pressures for more descriptive representation recur and are viewed as one kind of fulfillment of self-rule.

In India and Turkey plebian upsurges involve newly incorporated populations working out an equalizing process and expressing varying degrees of anti-elite sentiment. It is sometimes accompanied with open disdain for and conflict with secular ideology, seen as the rhetoric of a Western-oriented paternalistic elite. Politicization here can be both egalitarian and at the same time an expression of a newly felt popular power. Indeed, the braiding of moral-ethical claims to legitimacy and egalitarianism with claims to power makes democratic majoritarianism an ever-present possibility, and one that is especially hard to temper and restrain. When politicization and anti-elite sentiment are accompanied by violence against vulnerable minorities—as it has been in Turkey and India—the threat of majoritarianism and authoritarian populism becomes concrete.

In ideal models of democratic voting, majorities and minorities are temporary and conjunctural, always shifting in makeup with every political decision. Majoritarian claims, however, collapse the logic of voting with the logic of power and seek to endow a descriptive majority with a permanent right to rule. I have tried to suggest that this logic and possibility flows from tendencies and dilemmas internal to democratic politics and is not a feature of a deviant or distorted democratization. Ultimately, the purpose of such a reorientation is to be able to confront more squarely the real constraints and possibilities of democratic politics as well as to think more creatively about various forms of remedies that might further the egalitarian logic of democracy while mitigating its coercive and violent tendencies.

Coda

One of *Citizen and Subject*'s most original claims was the provocation that decolonization had remained radically incomplete. Mamdani characterized this predicament as one of achieving "deracialization without democratization" and showed why self-determination and anti-racism were neither equivalent to nor automatically entailed democracy. Mamdani was in effect redefining the meaning and horizon of political decolonization. In Africa, democratization required challenging the legacies of colonial indirect rule, the authority granted to tribes, and the political investment in ethnic identities. In *Neither Settler nor Native* (2020) Mamdani returns to the dilemmas of decolonization and further clarifies its task and purpose today. If colonialism's greatest crime was the politicization of identity—a claim pressed even more radically in *Neither Settler nor Native* where this politicization is taken to be an inherent feature of the modern nation-state—then decolonization requires the decoupling of identity from political status. Ultimately this would involve nothing less than the decoupling of state from nation. Colonial statecraft and state formation—whether in the United States, South Africa, or India—maintained rule by differentiating populations along racial and ethnic lines, which resulted in naturalized and permanent-seeming majorities and minorities. In undoing this inheritance, political decolonization aims at the *depoliticization* of such identities and the restructuring of political community in nonnational terms.

Mamdani envisions decolonization not as a singular revolutionary event but a conjoined process of political imagination, inventive reform, and hard negotiation, which together work to unsettle inherited identities—to convert perpetrators and victims into survivors, natives and settlers into citizens, nation-states into inclusive democracies. In decolonized democracies governing majorities would not mirror or track demographic or cultural majorities. Rather, they would be the product of democratic action, where shifting coalitions of interest, constructed through persuasion, come to power through political competition. Democratic majorities would be the outcome of the democratic process and not identified with pre-political, already existing dominant groups.

This chapter is very much aligned with Mamdani's attempt to rethink the political horizon of decolonization as well as his call for more inventive thinking and experimentation to overcome identity investments of colonial categorization and exclusivist nationalism. But in this endeavor, I suggest that democracy, both as a claim to sovereignty and as a set of procedures that determine rule, has to be critically interrogated, for democracy also carries within it endemic processes that contribute to the politicization of identity along majoritarian lines. Decoupling demographic majorities from political majorities, like the hoped-for decoupling of state from nation, will require imagination and institutional innovation.

Traditionally, the problem of majoritarianism or the so-called tyranny of the majority has been treated with various counter-majoritarian tactics and institutions. In the case of the US constitution, these include checks on uniform legislative sovereignty via conjoined powers, judicial review, and the executive veto. Some mechanisms were explicitly designed to break and moderate electoral waves, such as rolling elections and the electoral college, while others rely on unelected institutions. In the latter case, legal institutions and instruments, such as constitutional courts practicing judicial review of legislation and enforcing rights, are especially prominent. Another strategy institutionalized in the United States was to empower differently elected bodies—an upper house or senate or president—to compete with, check, and constrain legislative sovereignty. All of these measures were partly meant to prevent the formation of powerful majorities through the purposive fragmentation of sovereignty.

Mill and Tocqueville, in different ways, were skeptical that such institutional engineering on its own could stop the potential tyranny of the majority, which could insinuate itself into all governing institutions in a democratic society. On the other hand, Schwartzberg (2005, 2013) and Tuck (2016) worry that counter-majoritarian procedures and institutions necessarily dampen the radical potential of democratic sovereignty understood in terms of its aspirations to egalitarianism as well as institutional experimentation. While such mechanisms may protect some vulnerable minorities, they also make it much easier for a whole series of powerful minorities (economic elites, for example) to check legislation that might undermine privilege (see Schwartzberg, 2013). There is a further problem that arises from explicit counter-majoritarian arguments and tactics. Simply put, they tend to engender political backlash and fuel democratic resentment. This kind of resentment—and the sense of being excluded or wronged by a conspiracy of elites—is at the core of majoritarianism and populism.

In this context, we ought to think more imaginatively about mechanisms that might fragment majoritarianism and mitigate polarization but in a manner that genuinely feels consistent with the deepening of democracy. Here are some very tentative provocations of what these mechanisms might look like and aim for. Scaling up has been a recurrent response to what people regard as the deficiencies of national popular sovereignty. Various forms of empire, federation, and global governance have been used to fragment majoritarianism. But these are exactly the kinds of configurations that provoke backlash, especially in our contemporary context. Perhaps experimenting with the opposite tool is worth considering, namely a push toward radical localization. There is evidence that certain forms of communal or ethnic conflict have tended to be much more virulent in cities than in rural settings, and this fact might be worth reflecting on more closely.

A second tactic might be an orientation toward radical individuation. The preference for voting and majority rule in Rousseau (and perhaps in Hobbes too) over the deliberative assembly as the model for democratic activity lies in its individuating function. In its ideal form, Rousseau imagined voting to be free from deliberation and the immediate pressure of partial associations (political parties) and other corporate authorities that might deform moral judgment through informal modes of coercion and domination. Though we take parties to be essential to the electoral process, this would question that assumption and opens up experiments with other kinds of voting. In this vein, following Tuck's reading of Rousseau, we might consider voting not in terms of selecting candidates but as plebiscites on issues.

Finally, and more generally, we might consider expanding participation with a view toward increasing the conjunctural quality of democracy. Voting and other forms of decision-making would be more short-term, less entrenched, and subject to rotation and revision. This lessens some of the stakes of voting and might enable something of experimentalism that democracy as a form of rule promises.

References

Banerjee, M. (2014). *Why India Votes?* New Delhi: Routledge Press.

Bourke, R. (2003). *Peace in Ireland: The War of Ideas.* London: Penguin Random House.

Bourke, R. (2007). "Modern massacres." *The Political Quarterly*, 78(1): 182.

Bourke, R. (2016). "Introduction," in R. Bourke and Q. Skinner (eds.), *Popular Sovereignty in Historical Perspective*. Cambridge: Cambridge University Press, pp. 1–14.

Chatterjee, P. (1986). *Nationalist Thought and the Colonial World.* London: Zed Books.

Chatterjee, P. (1993). *The Nation and its Fragments: Colonial and Postcolonial Histories.* Princeton: Princeton University Press.

Chatterjee, P. (2006). *The Politics of the Governed: Reflections on Popular Politics in Most of the World.* New York: Columbia University Press.

Chatterjee, P. (2011). *Lineages of Political Society: Studies in Postcolonial Democracy.* New York: Columbia University Press.

Cohn, B. (1998). *An Anthropologist Among the Historians and Other Essays.* Oxford; New York: Oxford University Press.

Damodaran, H. (2008). *India's New Capitalists: Caste, Business, and Industry in a Modern Nation.* Hampshire: Palgrave Macmillan.

Dunn, J. (2000). *The Cunning of Unreason: Making Sense of Politics.* New York: Basic Books.

Dunn, J. (2005). *Settling the People Free: The Story of Democracy.* London: Atlantic Publishers.

Dunn, J. (2013). *Breaking Democracy's Spell.* New Haven: Yale University Press.

Finlay, M. (1985). *Democracy Ancient and Modern.* New Brunswick: Rutgers University Press.

Frank, J. (2010). *Constituent Moments: Enacting the People in Postrevolutionary America.* Durham: Duke University Press.

Frank, J. (forthcoming). "Populism and practice: Between the electorate and the multitude," in K. Mantena (ed.), *Means and Ends: Rethinking Realism in Comparative Perspective.* Philadelphia: University of Pennsylvania.

Getachew, A. and Mantena, K. (2021). "Anticolonialism and the decolonization of political theory." *Critical Times,* 4(3). https://doi.org/10/1215/26410478-9355193.

Guha, R. (1998). *Dominance without Hegemony: History and Power in Colonial India.* New Delhi: Harvard University Press.

Hamilton, A., Madison, J. and Jay, J. (2008). *The Federalist Papers,* edited by L. Goldman. Oxford: Oxford University Press. https://global.oup.com/academic/product/the -federalist-papers-9780192805928?cc=us&lang=en&.

Hussain, N. (2003). *The Jurisprudence of Emergency: Colonialism and the Rule of Law.* Ann Arbor: University of Michigan Press. https://doi.org/10.3998/mpub.17774.

Kasimis, D. (2018). *Classical Greek Theory and the Politics of Immigration.* Cambridge: Cambridge University Press.

Kaviraj, S. (2010). *The Imaginary Institution of India: Politics and Ideas.* New York: Columbia University Press.

Kaviraj, S. (2014). "The empire of democracy," in P. Chatterjee and I. Katznelson (eds.), *Anxieties of Democracy: Tocquevillian Reflections on India and the United States.* Oxford and New York: Oxford University Press. https://doi.org/10.1093/acprof:oso /9780198077473.001.0001.

Mamdani, M. (1996). *Citizen and Subject: Contemporary Africa and the Legacy of Late Colonialism.* Princeton: Princeton University Press.

Mamdani, M. (2002). *When Victims Become Killers: Colonialism, Nativism and Genocide in Rwanda.* Princeton: Princeton University Press.

Mamdani, M. (2009). *Saviors and Survivors: Darfur, Politics, and the War on Terror.* New York: Doubleday Books.

Mamdani, M. (2012). *Define and Rule: Native as Political Identity.* Cambridge: Harvard University Press.

Mamdani, M. (2020). *Neither Settler nor Native: The Making and Unmaking of Permanent Minorities.* Cambridge: Harvard University Press.

Manin, B. (1997). *The Principle of Representative Government*. Cambridge: Cambridge University Press.

Mann, M. (2004). *The Dark Side of Democracy: Explaining Ethnic Cleansing*. New York: Cambridge University Press.

Mantena, K. (2022). "Mass satyagraha and the problem of collective power," in M. Goswami and M. Sinha (eds.), *Political Imaginaries in Twentieth-Century India*. London: Bloomsbury, pp. 51–71.

Pillay, S. (2015). "Decolonizing the university," Transcript of a talk at UCT. http://africasacountry.com/2015/06/decolonizingAtheAuniversity/.

Rosanvallon, P. (2008). *Counter-Democracy: Politics in an Age of Distrust*. Cambridge: Cambridge University Press.

Schwartzberg, M. (2005). *Democracy and Legal Change*. Cambridge: Cambridge University Press.

Schwartzberg, M. (2013). *Counting the Many: The Origins and Limits of Supramajority Rule*. Cambridge: Cambridge University Press.

Scott, D. (1999). "Community, number, and the ethos of democracy," in *Refashioning Futures: Criticism after Postcoloniality*. Princeton: Princeton University Press. http://www.jstor.org/stable/j.ctt7rkms.10.

Tocqueville, A. (2010). *Democracy in America: Historical-Critical Edition of* De la démocratie en Amerique, edited by E. Nolla, translated by J. T. Schleifer. Indianapolis: Liberty Fund.

Tuck, R. (2016). *The Sleeping Sovereign: The Invention of Modern Democracy*. Cambridge: Cambridge University Press.

Yadav, Y. (1999). "Politics," in M. Bouton and P. Oldenburg (eds.), *India Briefing: A Transformative Fifty Years*. Armonk: M.E. Sharpe, pp. 3–38.

8

Colonial Legacies of Ethnicized Violence, Gendered Subjectivity, and Feminist Emancipatory Politics

Lyn Ossome

Introduction

Postcolonial feminisms are faced with the political problem of locating gender power within colonial histories that have tended to subordinate gendered difference to ethnic and racial difference, the latter two which constitute the presumed domain of "politics proper." Mamdani (1996) preempts this problem in this conclusion that with the inevitable deracialization that follows independence from colonial rule, the major problem facing democratizing states would be the de-ethnicization of the state. Race and ethnicity had been central to the logics of native control through indirect rule. Yet, the condition of possibility of the stabilization of colonial rule on the basis of ethnicity and race had been a deeply entrenched gendering of both ethnicity and race. Women—through the control of their productive and reproductive labor (Brownhill, 2009), sexuality (Santoru, 1996; Thomas, 2003), kinship land and resources (Amadiume, 1987; Brownhill, 2009), and ultimately, their gender and generational power—had been the basis upon which colonists could stabilize the colonial state. Mamdani's various works (1996, 2001, 2012) are instrumental in laying out the political foundations of this project of stabilization on the basis of ethnicization and racialization of native populations.

In the postcolonial/post-independence state, however, it is the liberal apparatus such as elections and representative democracy that sought to accommodate women in the state. In the colonial state, the link between gender and politics or women and *state* politics was a more tenuous one. This is because women had not been the primary subject of colonial rule: they did not constitute the core of the native question, and neither were they ever granted any serious consideration for political responsibilities at the twilight of colonial rule as colonists and nationalists negotiated the constitution of post-independence states. Women's political significance would have to be found elsewhere: in the *political economy* of colonial rule. That is, in relation to the colonial accumulation project that was deeply intertwined with and dependent upon the political stabilization of the state. Women played significant roles in this structural edifice, as evidenced by the gendered coding of customary laws through the repugnancy laws, the gendering of race through, for instance, the anti-miscegenation laws, and the gendering of ethnicity through the redefinition by colonists of the roles that women and men could play in the customary domain of decentralized rule, and so on.

This chapter offers preliminary reflections on these concerns by engaging Mamdani's ideas through a gendered critique of the political economy of the colonial state, and the implications of these insights for postcolonial feminist politics. In this initial critique, the aim is to pose the gender question of colonial rule as a problem for feminist politics in the postcolonial democratizing state. The question of democracy— or rather its limits, given the legacies of politicized ethnicity—is a major concern that constitutes much of Mamdani's work. This chapter engages these legacies of ethnicity and extends beyond them through an examination of the legacies of the gendered constitution of the colonial state, enquiring into the analytical implications which both of these legacies portend for feminist emancipatory politics in the postcolonial state.

Colonialism and Challenges to Identitarian Politics

What emancipatory potential do liberal human rights hold out for groups such as women, whose construction outside of the parameters of politicized ethnicity has historically silenced their claims within the liberalizing postcolonial state with its attendant language of rights? Beginning in the late 1980s, Africa's democratization projects catalyzed around diverse contestations, which rather than articulate transformative agendas as struggles for social justice, were often more concerned about the mere competition for political power articulated through/as the national question. In the postcolonial moment of ostensible liberation, feminist critiques turned their gaze on inequalities that were being simultaneously perpetrated and silenced by ethnic, class, racial, gender, ecological, and contested queer identities. Such critiques sat uneasily within postcolonial studies, which some feminists saw as reinstating the national question at the expense of democratic pluralism. More recent critiques from within and outside of the feminist tradition have sought to understand what a focus on the structures, conditions, and institutions that circumscribe freedom would highlight in relation to the individual constituted under liberalism as being formally "free" and "equal," a status ascribed through a set of rights and liberties.

Those, however, concerned with emancipatory political practices confront a set of paradoxes, the central one being that the question of the liberatory or egalitarian force of rights is always historically and culturally circumscribed; that is, rights have no inherent political semiotic, no innate capacity either to advance or impede radical democratic ideals (Brown, 1995). Through the objectivist pursuit of a liberal discourse of universality, rights (necessarily) undermine particular histories and legacies of slavery, colonialism, imperialism, and neocolonialism (Ossome, 2014). A further set of questions are here, rendered apparent: do human rights ever become even normatively available to oppressed communities as a mechanism for defining and actualizing disparate justice claims? Can human rights function other than as instruments for reinforcing a world view that seeks emancipation in a transcendent ideology of equality (Marx, 1977), in order to reflect a historically situated critique of the subjugation to which nations, groups, and individuals are confined in the normative ordering of colonial and postcolonial dispossession?

Post-structuralist thinkers like Mouffe (1992), in asking whether one can imagine a non-capitalist liberal democracy, insist that the problem lies not as much in the assertion of "really existing" liberal democratic capitalism as the "end of history," but rather in the pursuit of "a more radical democracy" (1992: 1). This, she insists, does not imply the rejection of liberal democracy and its replacement by a completely new political form of society, as the traditional idea of revolution entailed, but rather a radicalization of the modern democratic tradition. This would be attained by employing the symbolic resources of that very tradition:

> Liberalism has generally been identified with the defence of private property and the capitalist economy. However, this identification is not a necessary one. . . . Rather, it is the result of an articulatory practice, and as such can therefore be broken. Political liberalism and economic liberalism need to be distinguished and then separated from each other. Defending and valuing the political form of society specific to liberal democracy does not commit us to the capitalist economic system. (Mouffe, 1992: 2–3)

Mouffe's insistence is, in other words, to extend democracy "within the framework of a liberal-democratic regime" (1992: 3), a formulation that does not interrogate *who* is included within, and who is excluded from its ambit. Such a formulation is problematic because while it can be feasibly argued that political liberalism and economic liberalism need not necessarily enact a mutual inclusivity, in social contexts where scarcity, marginalization, and deprivation summon, within the boundaries of the nation-state, a liberal politics of (human) rights claims as the discursive language of liberty and justice, there invariably emerge multiple and collective claims that reinstate the centrality of both the economic and the political to which liberal individualism has no response. This is certainly true for those women emerging from the colonial context, who unlike some African men, had historically been excluded from the colonial lexicon of political rights, and whose rights claims in the postcolonial state could, therefore, not be a choice between political and socioeconomic rights.

The intertwining of the economic and political is itself productive of the relentless affirmation in theory as well as in practice of the notion of state sovereignty, whose contradictions (ever-deepening conditions of subalternity and statelessness) place a critique of the state as a necessary prerequisite of any serious pursuit of emancipatory politics. Sovereignty is in this sense, wrenched away from its attachment to the liberal tradition of freedom.

The fallacy underlying the definition of state sovereignty—as that which must be relinquished by individuals to the state in order that freedoms may be better protected—is unmasked as entirely dependent on the insider status of the individuals in question. Being "nothing but human beings" (Arendt, 1958: 295) then is not enough to ensure the visibility that participation in a political community takes for granted.

What ought to be the most concrete instantiation of one's being turns out to be the most elusive and abstract. Yet, the processes by which human beings are categorized as visible or not, concrete or abstract, remain at their core, material in the wake of colonial dispossession. This fact leads to a much more complex formulation of what a project aimed at the pursuit of a more egalitarian postcolonial society might entail.

Stated differently, it is through a critique of the exclusionary, oppressive, racist histories of slavery, colonialism, neocolonialism, and imperialism that the possibility emerges of embarking on a trajectory of freedom and emancipation that exceeds those defined (within liberalism) by the pursuit of rights—which necessarily never transcend the identities upon which they are constructed. In the liberal tradition, women can only ever be freed as women, Black people only ever as Black, queer communities only ever as queer, and so on. The ressentiment of injury and subjectivity as the necessary condition of the survival of the individual or group so defined appears in this regard, as obvious.

Colonial Legacies: Ethnicization and the Gendered Bifurcation of the State

While violence in the post-colony has been theorized as the profound legacy of the mode of colonial rule, a residual question for feminists remains why it is that colonial/ postcolonial forms of violence manifested in particularly gendered forms: why and how did the gendering of the native become central to the colonial project? The insights which Mamdani (1996) provides on the question of the emancipatory potential of rights in the postcolonial moment expose the peril inherent in a pursuit of justice within a domain of politics that had not—and could not at the exact postcolonial moment—shed its racist, anti-humanist, and ethnicized character. Under direct rule— what Mamdani terms as "centralized despotism" that demanded native conformity to European laws—rights were accessible only to the "civilized" who occupied civil society, equated with colonial, white society.

The rationale of this preoccupation with the "civilized" was culturally rather than racially determined: the privilege of citizenship would, under direct rule, become the preserve of those deemed as "civilized." The epistemological determinism concealed within this formulation presented contradictions that both threatened to undermine the racist colonial imperialist project and, in colonies where the native question also carried with it a majoritarian dilemma—that is, how a small minority of whites could wrestle control of the labor and resources of the majority—the limitations of direct rule soon became apparent: the idea of "civilization" could not be preceded by its material imperatives. In other words, the very boundaries of possibility asserted by a realm between the "civilized" and "uncivilized" had to be realized through the creation of a desiring subject. The subjective invention of Europe's "others" necessitated a different form of rule, which Mamdani (1996) articulates as an indirect form of control.

Indirect rule ushered in a colonizing structure that functioned on the basis of a legal dualism—entrenching both political inequality and civil inequality. The coexistence of direct and indirect rule, then, was the resolution to the limitations of the former. The urban civil power and native exclusion from civil society found its balance in the rural tribal authority that incorporated natives into a state-enforced customary order under indirect rule. The result, Mamdani shows, was a bifurcation of the state—urban power spoke the language of civil society and civil rights (i.e., focused on the protection of rights), while the language of rural power was based on community and culture (i.e., charged with enforcing tradition). What survived the fabrication of the nation-state was the negation of tradition and its subsumption under a rights regime of people who hitherto had not been the subject of rights. The rights regime itself stood above question—its failings were placed squarely on "problem people" (Du Bois, 1898),[1] for whom the impossibility of a liberal emancipatory trajectory stood circumscribed by the alter-identities that constitute them in opposition to the false internal coherence of liberal individualism.

Actually, existing civil society, Mamdani (1996, 2001, 2012) argues, was imbued with a history of racism and was an offshoot of the colonial state. The state in this sense could not be abstracted from the society out of which it sprung—and in dialectal terms, its ideological and political indebtedness to the racist society it mirrored could be expected to define the terms of the postcolonial state's relationship to its urbanized, racialized citizens. The very rules of governance that liberated the urban native—free association, public participation, and political representation—alienated him from the tribalized native, who was governed by extra-economic coercion and an administratively driven mode of justice, rather than the rule of law and a regime of rights. The language of coercion on the one hand, and that of rights on the other, maintained the urban native strata in limbo, an outcome of the development of civil society which Mamdani traces through four historical moments.

The first, he argues, was the colonial state's presentation as protector of the society of colons. The second moment, the anti-colonial struggle, was a struggle against the colonial state, and was decisive in shaping the relationship between state and civil society as it was also in essence a struggle of the embryonic middle- and working classes for entry into civil society. Out of that emerged an indigenous civil society of limited significance: it was neither independent nor autonomous, and emerged as a reflection of the colonial state's bifurcated logic and exclusionary characteristics. The deracialization of the state, Mamdani argues, had to form part and parcel of the democratization of society. This possibility of the formulation of society from below is a critical one in relation to how it is that people become legible to the state at various times, and the set of conditions, often political, that manifest in the process. The predicament then was that identities (white, male, Christian) that had externally

---

[1]   Du Bois posed this question in his study of the so-called "Negro problem" thus: "If a Negro discusses the question, he is apt to discuss simply the problem of race prejudice; if a Southern white man writes on the subject, he is apt to discuss problems of ignorance, crime and social degradation; and yet each calls the problem he discusses the Negro problem, leaving in the dark background the really crucial question as to the relative importance of the many problems involved" (1898: 9). For Du Bois, the problem lay not with the people but with the structures to which they were being forced to conform. Compelling racially oppressed groups to seek justice within a racist system would only affirm the validity of the racist system and place the problem of injustice at the doorstep of the oppressed.

delimited the form of the colonial state, could no longer act as discursive and material embodiments of what the state was *not,* and so remained constituted as such within the racialized civil society.

The third moment was national independence and birth of a deracialized state but not civil society, the realm to which the defense of racial privilege shifted. The state's attempts at deracializing civil society followed a path of affirmative action and Africanization. While these varied processes managed to unify people on the question of race, they at the same time engendered fragmentation on the question of redistribution, which became articulated to identitarianism—regional, ethnic, familial, religious—a mode of rule perfected under colonialism. With deracialization of the state, Mamdani (1996) argues, the language of defense of racial privilege could no longer be racial: racial privilege receded into civil society but defended itself in the language of civil rights, individual rights, and institutional autonomy. The domain of civil society, therefore, retained its fundamentally racialized characteristic.

To victims of racism, the language of rights rang hollow. The postcolonial subjects rather formulated their demands in the language of social justice and nationalism (Mamdani, 1996). The former followed a liberal logic that disarticulated questions of justice from the historical imperatives for justice; the latter, a reflection of the national bourgeoisie, was thoroughly patriarchal, masculinist, and disarticulated from the demands which women were making beyond the bounded nation-state in making. Consider Kenyan nationalist and Justice Minister Tom Mboya's vision for women in post-independence Kenya:

> There is room for a mass movement of women, not as a separate political entity, but as an enormous pressure-group for advancement in a certain field. . . . I found the tales of Mary Mukasa, the schoolteacher's wife, who looked after four young children, kept her house spotless and put on a clean dress before her husband returned home, and who pleaded with him at budget sessions for an increase in the milk vote, both charming and worthwhile. I would agree with the description of her, coined by her husband Augustine—"Flower in the Home." If there were many such Flowers in East Africa, we would revolutionize the homes of twenty-five million people. I hope it may still be possible to form a mass movement of women, who will challenge the government and the men in each district to give them greater facilities, and who will seek out every woman in a gigantic campaign for literacy and self-improvement. That will be the best preparation of all for consolidating independence. (Mboya, 1963: 161–2)[2]

Mboya hoped for millions of "housewifized" "flowers."[3] There was no room for women's right to access what they needed directly. Rather, they were expected to access

---

[2] Tom Mboya was a conservative unionist who was to become a high-level government official under Jomo Kenyatta's presidency from 1963.

[3] Brownhill (2009) shows in her work that as with many women worldwide in the 1950s, women in Kenya were exposed to propaganda and state-sponsored social welfare programs aimed at producing good housewives. The housewife was to be a woman with no land or other independent means of production. She was wageless and depended for money on a husband. "Housewifization,"

the resources they needed through the generosity of men. The government seemed content to deny women's land rights, to prejudice them in inheritance and divorce and to construct necessary facilities only when women had organized enough pressure to make the cost of not providing those facilities greater than the cost of providing them. While the government allocated land to men, women were left to their own devices, to organize and pressure the government and their husbands for what was rightfully theirs (Brownhill, 2009: 223). The state, as represented through its officials, sought to demarcate this private *apolitical* space within the home, out of which women could continue to produce and reproduce for the state and capital, and also as the only sphere within which women were guaranteed an exchange, being the main site of "giving"[4]— of protection and security which they could only access through the male head and the state. This mode of access meant that for women, the very structures through which they sought an emancipatory politics paradoxically also facilitated the means through which identitarian access to the state and resources (ethnic in our case) would map onto their bodies, with violent manifestations and expression in the terrain of politics.

The fourth moment in this trajectory was the collapse of the embryonic indigenous civil society, trade unions, autonomous civil organizations, their absorption into political society, and the resultant proliferation of state nationalism, which accompanied the demobilization of civil society and statization of political movements. Two factors were critical here: first, it exposed the limits of deracialization of civil society, given that the objective of enforcing custom on tribes-people had driven the organization of the local state along ethnic rather than racial lines. The reform imperative of the local state would need to be detribalization, not deracialization as had been the case. The failure to democratize the local state took its toll on post-independence generations, and the unreformed Native Authority meant that the more that civil society was deracialized, the more it took on a tribal form (Mamdani, 1996). This colonial legacy had, as I argue in the next section, far-reaching implications for the ways in which subjecthood would come to violently articulate to feminist emancipatory politics in the postcolonial state. The deracinated but ethnicized gendered subject presents the contemporary limits of an emancipatory politics that seeks among other things, to transcend the identitarian perils inherited from colonialism. Such a politics is, however, delimited by the hegemonic, neoclassical idea of rights as the language of freedom.

The liberal democratic ideology within which rights are presently embedded subverts the discourse on freedom, and in the contemporary context, attains an

---

then, was the process through which women lost access to self-directed and organized subsistence livelihoods and were encouraged to submit to often unwaged work under the control of a man who, in turn, was incorporated into relations of commodified exploitation (Brownhill, 2009: 185).

[4] Marcel Mauss in his essay on the "gift" argues that the giver does not merely give an object but also part of himself, for the object is indissolubly tied to the giver: the objects are never completely separated from the men who exchange them (1966: 31). Because of this bond between the giver and the gift, the act of giving creates a social bond with an obligation to reciprocate on the part of the recipient. To not reciprocate means to lose honor and status. Because gifts are inalienable, they must be returned: the act of giving creates a gift-debt that has to be repaid. Because of this, the notion of an expected return of the gift creates a relationship over time between two individuals. In other words, through gift-giving a social bond evolves that is assumed to continue through space and time until the future moment of exchange. Gift exchange, therefore, leads to a mutual interdependence between giver and receiver.

almost mystical quality. This point is related to what Roesch (2013) views as the constitutive dimensions of the neoliberal capitalist project and the backlash against women which, she argues, can shape our understanding of rape, sexual assault, and, in general, gender-based violence in the context of political contestations like elections. Two of these dimensions are particularly relevant in light of the preceding discussion: (1) the notion of liberation delinked from any project of social equality; and (2) the destruction of social protections and the concomitant importance of the privatized nuclear family—both signifying a material increase in the oppression of women and also an intensification of the ideological assault on women. The delinking of liberation from projects of social equality functions through the notions of "freedom" under neoliberalism, and the idea of "choice" (Roesch, 2013). The backlash is generated from notions of women's "autonomy," whose narrative broadly says that "if only women could discard their victim mentality and take control of our own sexual choices, then women could stop themselves from being raped" or violated (Roesch, 2013). Both these claims conceal the deeply gendered ways of being in the world, which in the following section I draw out through a historicized reading of the construction of ethnicized subjects and their proximity to violence.

Reproduction of Ethnicized, Gendered Subjects of Violence

The thinking here, through an interrogation of the question of politicized ethnicity (the ethnicization of politics and the violence that has accompanied such investment in the post-colony), is an attempt to highlight the relationship and continuities between the gendered and ethnicized subject of colonization—who in the post-colony is recuperated as the subject of violence. Because ethnicization is the radicalization of the *nation*-state model, which demands a conception of "nation" premised on vulgar authenticity, ultimately appealing to a form of mythic purity and, given the specific historic model of Euro-modernity in the colonies, it means also a *radicalized masculinity* (Gordon, 2008).

Holden (2008), for instance, shows the vital role that autobiographies of key nationalist independence leaders such as Gandhi, Nkrumah, Nehru, Lee Kuan Yew, and Mandela played in nation-building—in the construction of national identity and in the conception of what constituted the emergent nation. One of the most significant features these texts shared, Holden argues, is the emphasis on masculinity as reflected in frequent references to the masculinity of the independence leader, and in the subtle ways notions of masculinity pervaded these different autobiographies. The image which these autobiographies projected, of the nationalist leader as a strong, determined, self-controlled, and dependable man, emphasized the masculinity of the leader and was in turn extrapolated to the emerging notion of the new nation as strong, forward-looking, resolute, and responsible. Foundational to these notions had been the imperial project, which had been thoroughly imbued with notions of masculinity and patriarchy.

While the problem of tribalization articulates to a methodological concern (the mechanism of colonial rule, following Mamdani), that of *detribalization* in the postcolonial period presents an ontological question that renders unresolved the radical masculinization of the nation-state. What then does it mean to confront the racializing/tribalizing system that renders Black persons and natives in turn, as "problem-people"? And what does it mean to confront such a system if its mechanisms violently exclude those whose grammar does not articulate to its rationalizations and logics of rule? Put differently, if colonialism did not offer the possibility of thinking through its subject as other than an inverted version of European man, where, if any, does the possibility lie of a female/feminist articulation of the question of freedom against the persistent violence that the ethnicization of politics, of the political itself produces? The masculinization of rational thought itself exceeds the scope of this chapter, but suffice to say that the ways in which it functions in the political system are thoroughly modern, and in near recent history may be traced to eugenicist notions of purity that pervaded the construction of the colonial subject—the male European "other"—slave, the migrant laborer, the chiefs, collaborators. In the postcolonial transition that sought to deracialize the tribalized realms of society, legibility based on an ethnic identity was also one imbued with a masculinized identity. As illustrated, for instance, through *Mau Mau* historiography, the British colonialist project of divide and rule deeply penetrated the nation and concretized, through a rigid sex/gender system, notions of what it meant to be "male" and "female" in the colonies.

For women, politically rehabilitated and bounded within a private/domestic sphere of activity, the "political" itself became an act of transgression. If the brush of tribalization marked the nation in general, it is women who marked its internal boundaries: as ethnic identity, through its politicization, developed an internal coherence—quite distinct and separate from the "civilized" coherence claimed by the colonizer—so did its stabilization and regimentation become a question of *native self-rule*. Far from the claim that asserts native complicity in colonial rule, the argument here is a dialectical one: the domestic sphere of reproduction to which women were being pushed was articulated to the colonial political economy in two ways that were fundamental to the accumulation project. First, women's early political activism and acts of resistance against the destruction and appropriation of commons' lands had presented an immediate challenge to the ways in which labor could be organized in the colonies. The terracing strikes in 1939 colonial Kenya (see MacKenzie, 1998; Turner and Brownhill, 2001) and the generational cycle of domestic labor for Black South African women under apartheid signified such instances of the consolidation of this gendered dichotomy. The predicament posed to the colonial authorities in both instances was how to ensure the reproduction of the colonies as a whole (both native and civil society) at the same time as it was appropriating the natives' labor. The authorities sought to settle the question of labor segregation.

Second, internally, the organization of traditional sex/gender system lent itself to the broader project of labor segmentation and regimentation. Authority normatively shifted away from the patriarchal unit into the patrimonial ambit of colonial rule—individual masculine agency gave way to a collective masculinized authority that acted on behalf of whole communities. The alienation that accompanied labor appropriation legitimated claims based on the clan/community/ethnic unit (which were legible to colonial authorities), to which the domestic unit became subjugated. The *subject* of colonial rule had not been the gendered subject who was confined to the reproduction of the colony: rather, the gendered subject *constituted the possibility of indirect rule.* The violent interpellation of the gendered subject into the mode of indirect rule thus defined the parameters which feminist emancipatory politics needed necessarily to exceed in the postcolonial moment.

The primary argument here is that the question regarding the mechanisms of colonial rule needs to be understood not only in relation to the bifurcation of the colonial state (Mamdani) but with regard also to the structural dynamics which facilitated the stabilization of the bifurcated domains of rule. The foregoing discussion suggests that whereas the raison d'être for the tribalization of Native Authority had been to stabilize colonial rule (a response to the native question), this was a process highly articulated to the productive and reproductive roles to which women in the colonies were confined. Women's legibility as subjects (their subjectivity) could not be understood outside of their roles within the tribalized nation. This process, through which the mapping of ethnicity onto the bodies of women proceeded, I argue, was not only articulated to the cultural dynamics of colonized society but was also highly politicized—a precursor to the ways in which women would experience political life in the post-independence state. The question that emerges out of this is whether, in a democratizing context where the politicization of ethnicity continues to function as the means of accessing the state, gendered and ethnicized subjects could escape the violence mobilized and orchestrated on the basis of identity. In other words, if violence accompanies the expression of political power itself, should not (contra Arendt, 1958) the relationship between the formation of political community and violence be rethought?

The arguments put forward so far seek to historically situate (gendered, ethnicized, and sexualized) violence within a larger politics and political economy of colonial dispossession and rule. The persistence of violence in the era of democratization asserts the political as a crucial dimension of this critique. Understanding these forms of violence necessitates a critique, not of the liberal democratic state per se but of *liberal democracy in the post-colony.* The question in this regard might then be posed as such: How does the postcolonial state govern women? What is the relationship between ethnicity and democracy? Should not the focus, as Mamdani provocatively enquires, rather be on how to problematize this (ethnicized) mode of mobilization, which is a response to the mode of rule itself? Should violence necessarily be thought of as a wholly negative force?[5] If violence, in the Fanonian sense, guarantees the only realm through which colonized subjects can encounter the possibility of freedom (violence as power), should we not read the violence that has been productive of liberal democratic politics in postcolonial states, differently—as holding out an emancipatory possibility? How does this formulation call on us to make sense of the violence that has accompanied women as gendered and ethnicized subjects? How does this colonial legacy and agency differ in the democratizing state? And what are the implications for a feminist emancipatory politics? I attempt an abstracted response to this set of questions in the concluding section.

---

[5]   I draw this formulation from comments to an earlier draft of this chapter presented at the Makerere Institute of Social Research (MISR) Seminar Series in March 2016.

Liberalism's Challenges for Feminist Emancipatory Politics

The questions posed earlier present the difficulties of exceeding the subjective limits of the state—that is, the ethnic paradigm of organizing power and resources. The feminist predicament here is generated by a number of contradictions raised in the preceding discussion: (1) that the popular democracy inaugurated through multiparty politics runs the risk, in seeking to include everybody, of actually universalizing identities so much as to invisibilize differentiations among them; (2) that *particular* injuries suffered by individuals and groups based on their class, race, gender, or ethnicity are no longer transparent when examined within the very structures (of liberal human rights discourses) that reproduce them as injuries; and (3) that lacking logic of the ways in which class, gender, race, or ethnicity function to subordinate women, women's rights that historically originate from within this liberal discourse of human rights, therefore, function normatively to maintain women within these same oppressive structures. The point here is not to dismiss the pursuit of human rights as a feminist emancipatory concern. Rather, it is to expose certain limitations inherent in the liberal construction of rights, and show how these limitations structure *violent* power—or power *as* violence—within "democratic" institutions of the neoliberal state.

The ways in which the liberal rights discourse interacts with politicized identities raise important questions regarding the ability of human/women's rights to tackle historical oppressions that are the result of political, economic, and social exclusion of women. For example, on the potential of women's rights, Brown (1995) poses a set of critical questions that are worthy of serious reflection: when does identity articulated through rights become production and regulation of identity through law and bureaucracy? When does legal recognition become an instrument of regulation, and political recognition become an instrument of subordination?[6] Further, in reflecting on what it means for women to turn to the state for emancipation, Brown poses the following questions: "How does the nature of the political state transform one's social identity when one turns to the state for political resolution of one's subordination, exclusion, or suffering? What kind of subject is being held out to the state, for what kind of redress or redemption?" (1995: 101).

In other words, do women implicitly accept their subordinate status, and in fact reinscribe it, by turning to the state for redress? How much fairness can women expect from a capitalist, patriarchal, masculinist, and ethnicized state? How do feminist demands couched in the language of rights reinscribe class, gender, and ethnic marginality to the extent that rights are ontologically constructed by assumptions regarding the inferiority/ superiority of one class over another, of one gender over another, of one ethnic community over another? Who is to decide the point at which equality is deemed to have been achieved, and *whose* conception of equality prevails? And if, as the preceding discussion argues, rights tend to universalize difference, then does it not invariably become the case that the identity politics engendered under the rubric of women's rights might surface a new kind of subordinate position for women that is based solely upon their gender—

---

[6] The law is, for example, able to construct sexual violence as being an act of "barbarism" while ignoring the violent political/economic conditions that give rise to such violence.

an identity politics that claims women are oppressed *because* they are women—thus eschewing analysis of the ways in which gender intersects with oppressions based on women's varying identities of class, ethnicity, race, or sexual orientation?

The violent legacies of colonialism witnessed in the context of democratization require not only a return to the source of the exclusionary identitarian politics that reproduced gendered and ethnicized subjecthood under colonial rule. Critical to this project is also a continuation of the thinking around what citizenship portends when its stabilization is premised on liberal forms of accommodation, a contradictory view to the kinds of radical raptures (imbued with possibilities of violence) through which formerly colonized subjects have sought an emancipatory path. For women so constituted, this means not only exceeding the limits of the nation-state but also interrogating the very limitations inherent in its formation and continued reproduction in the colonial, paternalistic register.

References

Amadiume, I. (1987). *Male Daughters, Female Husbands: Gender and Sex in an African Society*. London: Zed Books.

Arendt, H. (1958). *The Origins of Totalitarianism*. New York: Harvest.

Brown, W. (1995). *States of Injury: Power and Freedom in Late Modernity*. Princeton: Princeton University Press.

Brownhill, L. (2009). *Land, Food, Freedom: Struggles for the Gendered Commons in Kenya −1870 to 2007*. Trenton: Africa World Press.

Du Bois, W. E. B. (1898). "The study of the Negro problems." *The Annals of the American Academy of Political and Social Science*, 11: 1–23.

Gordon, L. (2008). *An Introduction to Africana Philosophy*. Cambridge: Cambridge University Press.

Holden, P. (2008). *Autobiography and Decolonization: Modernity, Masculinity and the Nation-State*. Madison: University of Wisconsin Press.

MacKenzie, D. F. (1998). *Land, Ecology and Resistance in Kenya: 1880–1952*. London: Heinemann.

Mamdani, M. (1996). *Citizen and Subject: Contemporary Africa and the Legacy of Late Colonialism*. Princeton: Princeton University Press.

Mamdani, M. (2001). *When Victims Become Killers: Colonialism, Nativism and Genocide in Rwanda*. Princeton: Princeton University Press.

Mamdani, M. (2012). *Define and Rule: Native as Political Identity*. Cambridge: Harvard University Press.

Marx, K. (1977). "On the Jewish question," in D. McLellan (ed.), *Karl Marx: Selected Writings*. Oxford: Oxford University Press, pp. 46–70.

Mauss, M. (1966), *The Gift: Forms and Functions of Exchange in Archaic Societies*. London: Cohen and West.

Mboya, T. (1963). *Freedom and After*. Nairobi: Heinemann.

Mouffe, C. (ed.). (1992). *Dimensions of Radical Democracy*. London: Verso Books.

Ossome, L. (2014). "Can the law secure women's rights to land in Africa? Revisiting tensions between culture and land commercialization." *Feminist Economics*, 1(20): 155–77.

Roesch, J. (2013). "Talk presented at the Historical Materialism Conference, New York, April." http://www.youtube.com/watch?v=1NdYu4P_PJM.

Santoru, M.E. (1996). "The colonial idea of women and direct intervention: The Mau Mau case." *African Affairs*, 95: 253–67.

Thomas, L. M. (2003). *Politics of the Womb: Women, Reproduction and the State in Kenya*. Kampala: Fountain Publishers.

Turner, E. T. and Brownhill, L. S. (2001). "African jubilee: Mau Mau resurgence and the fight for fertility in Kenya, 1986–2002." *Canadian Journal of Development Studies*, 22: 1037–88.

9

The Bifurcated Society

Citizen and Subject in Contemporary South Africa

Steven Friedman

Introduction

Is the distinction between citizen and subject a consequence of the form of state or society? Mahmood Mamdani's *Citizen and Subject* (Mamdani, 1995) seems to describe in uncanny detail the contours of contemporary South Africa. It insists that the present is shaped by the past, that an essential feature of that continuity is a differential citizenship, that "civil society" is a domain from which many are excluded, and that post-independence elites could perpetuate the divide between urban and rural, which was a core feature of colonization, and these are all realities in South Africa today. The book's relevance to the issues facing the society is confirmed by the daily headlines.

But, while this testifies to the work's prescience, it does not necessarily confirm its central thesis. For Mamdani, the continuity was a consequence of the "bifurcated state" (Mamdani, 1995: 3–33) which rested on a "dualism of power"—direct rule in the urban areas, "decentralized despotism" in the countryside. At independence, rule was deracialized but the despotism continued to reduce most putative citizens to subjects. In this view, the patterns in today's South Africa are a consequence of the survival of this form of state which has been formally deracialized but whose central features are unchanged. The resonances with Mamdani's work are clear enough for one commentator to claim that the society is paying the price for not heeding *Citizen and Subject*'s warning. Johnny Steinberg, reflecting on attempts by the South African state to "distort" rural land ownership patterns, writes,

> Here is the warning Mamdani issued in 1996: in their struggle to deracialise the civilised laws of Europe in the cities, South Africans will be blindsided to the continuation of despotic rule in the countryside. And the consequences will not be confined to out-of-sight rural ghettos but will come to shape SA's collective fate. (Steinberg, 2015)

As we will see shortly, Mamdani's warning was far more conditional than Steinberg claims. But the inaccuracy is perhaps understandable, given the degree to which events in South Africa seem to confirm his diagnosis of a potential divide between urban and rural and between citizenship and subjection. But important similarities between the argument of *Citizen and Subject* and current reality do not necessarily mean that one of Mamdani's key arguments—that the source of the malaise is a particular form of the state—is accurate. Nor does it necessarily mean that the urban-rural divide of which Steinberg writes is a cause rather than a symptom of patterns which generate differential citizenship.

This chapter analyzes trends in South African society which appear to confirm the prognosis of *Citizen and Subject*. It argues that, while Mamdani was prescient in insisting that formal democracy and deracialization would not necessarily close the divide between the included and excluded, the source of the problem is not the continuation of a form of state which uses "extra-economic" coercion (Mamdani, 1995: 26) to exclude some from citizenship. It is, rather, the survival of patterns of domination and power which the state reflects but does not shape. This chapter also argues that, while a growing urban-rural divide is a key feature of current South African politics and society, it is a consequence of a particular economic and social trajectory rather than the form of the state. Before discussing the nature of bifurcation in contemporary South Africa, a discussion of *Citizen and Subject's* argument as it relates to South Africa is necessary.

The Endurance of Despotism: Mamdani's Warning

It is perhaps inevitable that a work as influential as *Citizen and Subject* will often be oversimplified and misinterpreted. It is, therefore, important to summarize its argument, particularly as it relates to South Africa.

The book's chief concern is to challenge accounts of post-independence Africa which imply that governance failures and democratic deficits are consequences of the cultural proclivities of African elites and citizens. Mamdani seeks to show, therefore, that these patterns are not breaks with the colonial past but are its products—African elites are not discarding the Weberian bureaucratic rationality of the colonial regimes but continuing their despotic rule. The colonial state, Mamdani argues, relied on direct rule in the cities, and indirect rule in the countryside. On independence, "The bifurcated state that was created with colonialism was deracialized but it was not democratized" (Mamdani, 1995: 26). Whether states retained the ethnically divided "Native administrations" or rejected them, the despotism of the colonial state survived. The gulf between town and countryside was maintained either by supposed reverence for tradition or the coercion of a supposedly modernizing center in the cities (Mamdani, 1995: 26). Mamdani also proposed a way forward for African democrats who, at the time *Citizen and Subject* was written, were pressing for a "second independence," not from the despotic rule of the colonizer but from that of the elites who replaced it. He warned that unless democratic reform of the national state was accompanied by democratization of the local state, the bifurcation and despotism would continue (Mamdani, 1995: 25). Reformers needed to break with the assumption that the urban, where individual citizens enjoyed rights and activity in civil society, was superior to the rural (Mamdani, 1995: 34).

A key theme of *Citizen and Subject* is that this analysis applies to South Africa under apartheid too, despite the attempts of much scholarship to suggest otherwise. Mamdani acknowledges differences between South Africa and the other states he analyzes—the labor movement is far more substantial and, more generally, "the specificity of the South African experience lies in the strength of its civil society" (Mamdani, 1995: 28). Both were products of urbanization and a much larger formal economy. But apartheid, he argued, was not unique: it sought to forestall the threat of urban revolt which urbanization brought by imposing ethnicity and rural despotism on Africans (Mamdani, 1995: 31). A key pillar of this system was migrant labor, but even the abolition of influx control in 1986 was designed to achieve the same end—it was as if "the government hoped that, by allowing rural people to flood into the cities, it would drown the urban revolt" (Mamdani, 1995: 27). Looking only at labor and urbanization might demonstrate South African uniqueness—but if the focus shifts from "the labor question to the native question," apartheid becomes a bifurcated form of colonial rule like all others. For Mamdani, explanations of apartheid which see it purely as a form of economic domination, cannot fully explain it as a form of state: "Its accent is on the mode of exploitation, not of rule" (Mamdani, 1995: 27).

Mamdani acknowledges that, despite apartheid's attempt to stem the tide of urbanization, the "center of gravity" of the fight against the system was urban township authorities. But he insists that the trajectory of the "struggle" underlines his point that a division between the rural and urban is bound to hamper democratization, even in an urbanizing society. He argues that the labor movement's "social base" rested on migrant labor. But hostel-based migrants became marginal to the urban revolt and then actively blocked it, prompting violence between city dwellers fighting apartheid and migrants seeking to protect the rural order. This conflict was a product of the failure of urban movements to develop "an agenda for democratizing customary power" (Mamdani, 1995: 29).

It is this failure which causes Mamdani to warn of the dangers of preserving the bifurcated state in a post-apartheid order (which was very young when *Citizen and Subject* appeared). Contrary to Steinberg's claim, the book does not predict this will happen—it warns of the need to avoid it. If the post-apartheid state left indirect-rule intact, South Africa would not escape the trajectory of other post-independence African countries:

> With free movement between town and country, but with Native Authorities in charge of an ethnically governed rural population, it will reproduce one legacy of apartheid but in a non-racial form. If that happens, this deracialization without democratization will have been a uniquely African outcome! (Mamdani, 1995: 32)

Either the gulf between urban and rural, between democracy in the cities and despotism in the countryside, would be closed or the democratic project would be hobbled, presumably by similar conflicts between countryside and city to those which plagued the fight against apartheid.

The Contours of Bifurcation: Key Features
of South African Society

Have Mamdani's fears been realized, as Steinberg insists, by developments since 1994? In two articles, one discussing social and economic patterns (Friedman, 2015c), the other the content of citizenship (Friedman, 2015a), I have tried to develop an analysis of contemporary South Africa which implicitly addresses this question.

The first, general analysis locates current realities in Douglass North's notion of "path dependence" (North, 1990) which holds that institutions—"behavioral routines, social connections, or cognitive structures" (Page, 2006: 89)—established under one political order do not disappear simply because a new one is established. North was interested in patterns which impeded or supported growth, not in the distribution of power and privilege; he, therefore, did not discuss the persistence of power relations from one political order to another. But if he is correct that behaviors, social relations, and ways of seeing the world may well survive a change in political order, then it follows that the power relations which sustain these also endure. This, it argues, accurately describes the contours of post-1994 South Africa.

This analysis does not support the oft-heard view that formal democracy has not changed the lives of South Africans. Since 1994, the extension of nonracial citizenship has offered citizens both protection against arbitrary power and, more important, the means to act in support of their interests. While the electoral dominance of the African National Congress (ANC) has not enabled citizens at the grassroots to wield power by playing political parties off against each other—as the slum dwellers in Kolkata described by Partha Chatterjee (2004) do—the vote and the extension of civil liberties have enabled people living with HIV and AIDS to secure treatment which has possibly saved over three million people from an early death (Friedman and Mottiar, 2005; Friedman, 2010; Thom, 2013). Democracy has stimulated the growth of a Black middle class and may also, contrary to oft-made claims, have reduced poverty (Meth, 2014) and extended social services in a way which has increased access to assets (Bhorat et al., 2014). Social grants now reach over sixteen million people, providing them with a lever into the economy as well as protection against destitution (Van der Berg and Siebrits, 2010). What has not changed is the power of the social and economic hierarchies which prevailed before 1994. In the economy, the partial deracialization of the market has preserved the exclusion of many—the view of an International Monetary Fund (IMF) official that one-third of working-age adults are excluded (Lipton, 2016) is in all probability an underestimation. According to the last census, income inequality has not reduced since 1994 despite the extension of services (Manuel, 2012). So, the economy is still divided between insiders and outsiders although the composition of the insiders has changed.

The second analysis teases out how this divide manifests in relationships between citizens and the state and in political behavior. It argues that, contrary to a strain of scholarship which sees South Africa as a "dominant party" polity in which, despite regular elections, the ANC monopolizes power, it is more accurate to see it as a country in which "archipelagos of dominance" shape political life. In the suburbs of the major metropolitan areas, the ANC is neither socially nor politically dominant. It wins only a fraction of the vote—and it only attracts this support because it wins the votes of domestic workers; owners and renters of property vote overwhelmingly for the official opposition, the Democratic Alliance (DA).[1] Its influence over the lives of suburban residents is often restricted to its role as a butt of suburban anger—it has little sway over the daily lives of residents who are reliant on the market economy and who are often able to access private education, health care, and security. While suburban residents see the ANC as a threat to their freedoms and livelihoods,[2] they enjoy unfettered freedom of speech, which they use to denounce the "tyranny" of the governing party. They also, despite frequent complaints, enjoy much better levels of service than residents of the urban townships where the Black poor live, let alone dwellers in rural areas.

In the townships and shack settlements, freedom of expression is often constrained by local power holders (usually but not exclusively ANC office-bearers) who are used to dominating the area and tend not to tolerate independent centers of power. In many cases, they work with local police to suppress social movements and other expressions of popular politics (Vally, 2003: 24; Pithouse, 2011; Newham and Tamukamoyo, 2013). Here, the ANC is dominant—it is often the sole political vehicle. At first glance, this claim would seem to be contradicted by the high levels of protest in these areas directed at local government, but these disputes are usually channeled through the ANC. It is common for ANC activists to organize protests against ANC mayors or councilors or for aspirant ANC councilors to do the same to force their way onto party lists and thus into positions in local government, which are tickets into the middle class (Von Holdt et al., 2011). The local elites' relationship with the ANC is often complex—in their quest for resources and power, elites will often use ANC membership when it suits their purpose and move out of its orbit when it does not (Von Holdt et al., 2011). But they assume that it is impossible to accumulate wealth or power without using the ANC. Because residents in townships and shack settlements do not command the resources or leverage available in the suburbs, the quality of public services and the responsiveness of local government is substantially inferior to that in the suburbs.

In Mamdani's terms, suburban residents are clearly citizens. Despite the fact that they do not vote for the governing party, they enjoy substantive as well as formal political rights, which they use to ensure a higher standard of service and more responsive government than the townships, shack settlements, and rural areas enjoy. People who live in townships and shack settlements cannot be neatly slotted into either category. Certainly, their citizenship is attenuated by local power holders and by poverty—often they are forced into the streets in protest because they insist that this is the only way to persuade the authorities to listen to them (Von Holdt et al., 2011). But they are not always subjects either—some do exercise their citizenship rights in social movements, local civic associations, or ANC branches. Some do challenge local authority—they may at times be organized by a local political aspirant but would not be available for protest if they had no grievances—and, despite the ANC's electoral

[1]   See calculations in Friedman's "Archipelagos of Dominance" (2015a).
[2]   "Our houses are mortgaged and we're in debt to our eyeballs trying to avoid catastrophic state schools and hospitals and paying outrageous prices for the things the state . . . administers." (Bruce, 2011: 8)

dominance, they do use their vote to send a signal to the governing party. After police shot striking platinum miners at Marikana, the ANC lost a by-election in the area (Stone, 2012); after media reports revealed that large sums of public money had been spent on a presidential homestead in Nkandla, KwaZulu-Natal province, the ANC lost a by-election in the area to the Inkatha Freedom Party (IFP) (*News24*, 2012). But this does not alter the reality that many are excluded from full citizenship and that the patterns of apartheid persist into the present—a reality in which suburban residents enjoy substantive political rights, high living standards, and adequate services, while just about everyone else receives none of the above, should be familiar to students of South Africa because it, of course, mirrors the reality under white rule even if, once again, the racial identity of those at the top has changed to some degree while that of those at the bottom has not.

What is clear is that there is a significant gulf between those who derive employment and income from the market and those who do not. The insiders' control over the national debate is so profound that it renders the outsiders invisible—the contest between "left" and "right" which appears in this conversation is often, in reality, a debate between insiders about outsiders who remain mute (Friedman, 2011). An anecdotal example conveys some of its flavor: a leader of the Economic Freedom Fighters (EFF), often assumed to be the voice of the poor and dispossessed, was asked how he came to own two houses. He responded that "like every young South African," he had used his first salary check to buy a home (SAFM, 2008). Most young South Africans do not receive a salary check; the vast majority of those who do cannot afford to buy a house. That the speaker who portrayed the experience of the insiders as that of all, was not the head of a pro-business think tank but the putative representative of the dispossessed, illustrates the degree to which the insiders have relegated the world of everyone else to invisibility.

From Town to Countryside

This bifurcation is also reflected, as Mamdani expected, in a contrast between town and countryside. A key feature of apartheid was the replacement of traditional rulers who were unwilling to do the bidding of the white state, with those who were, and the elevation of the latter to positions of authority in ethnic "homelands," some of which were afforded notional "independence." This "Bantustan" system was accurately identified by the ANC and other "liberation" organizations as a key resource for white power and those who occupied positions of authority in it were widely regarded as agents of the apartheid state. The constitution which ended apartheid, therefore, abolished Bantustans and extended equal citizenship rights to their residents (Ntsebeza, 2004: 72). After 1994, the government's response to traditional authority was initially ambivalent—it did not strengthen it and at times sought to democratize it; it was largely stripped of its formal political authority. But many of its features persist (Tipe, 2014). Traditional leadership is thus recognized by the constitution. The Traditional Leadership and Governance Framework Act (TLGFA) of 2003 renamed tribal authorities "traditional councils," requiring one-third of council members to be women and 40 percent elected. These partial reforms were resisted—the law was amended in 2011 to deal with the reality that most authorities had not complied (Centre for Law and Society, 2013). Thus, an analysis of the law concluded that,

> although the draft legislation presents serious critiques of colonial and apartheid legislation on traditional leadership and governance, by maintaining the tribal authority boundaries the TLGFA reproduces many of the violences and material inequalities . . . that its predecessors set in place. (Tipe, 2014)

Another analysis is more emphatic: "If you look at a map of traditional councils in terms of (the act), that's basically spaces of tribal governance reproducing almost, as it were, the apartheid homeland maps" (Jara, 2014).

Land rights, identified by Mamdani as the most important source of traditional authority's power (Mamdani, 1995: 17), received similar treatment: repeated efforts to democratize access to rural land did not remove this prerogative from traditional authorities. Whether rural-dwellers enjoy access to land, which does not depend on traditional authorities, decides "whether (they) . . . continue to be subjects under the political rule of unelected traditional authorities or will enjoy the citizenship rights, including the right to choose leaders and representatives, that the South African Constitution confers on all South Africans" (Ntsebeza, 2004: 73). The key vehicle for addressing land was the Communal Land Rights Act (CLRA) of 2004. While it did offer people living under tribal authority a greater say in land decisions, it was widely criticized for vesting continued control in traditional authorities:

> Some critiques . . . suggest that the Act entrenches particular versions of "customary" land tenure that resulted from colonial and apartheid policies, and that this will have the effect of undermining rather than securing land rights . . . (The Act) shifts the balance of power away from individuals and households towards the group and its authority structures, on the one hand and towards the Minister (as advised by officials), on the other. Ownership at the level of the traditional council/ chieftaincy will "trump" the rights that exist at lower levels. (Cousins, 2007: 290)

Claassens (2014) suggests that the law was skewed toward traditional authorities to defuse a rebellion by traditional leaders, who "threatened in 2003 to boycott the forthcoming national elections because the new Traditional Leadership and Governance Framework Bill did not give them enough power." The government

> backed down when the Communal Land Rights Bill (CLRB) was amended at the eleventh hour to give traditional councils the power to represent rural communities as the "owner of the land." The amendment sparked an immediate outcry from rural women and land rights organisations. (Claassens, 2014)

But, if the government was willing to concede to the demands of traditional leaders, the courts, another arm of the state, were not—in 2009, this law was ruled to be unconstitutional (Cousins, 2009). The pattern of the post-1994 period, in which the government signaled a commitment to rural democratization but sought not to offend traditional authorities, continued: despite promises, no new measure replaced it and so the reform of communal land tenure was halted.

Forward to the Past: Revitalizing Traditional Authority

One view of this trajectory is to see it as a capitulation to, or endorsement of, traditional authority—the response against which Mamdani warned. Cousins (2009) agrees: "Since 2003 . . . law and policy have come down squarely in favour of transferring title of communal land to traditional leaders and institutions, as opposed to the people who live on and work it."

But it would be more accurate to see it as an unsuccessful attempt to balance "the nature of customary land tenure and democratic rights" (Cousins, 2007: 291). Ntsebeza sums up the process:

> The Department of Land Affairs intended to subject traditional authorities to a system that would make them more representative and accountable to their communities. However, . . . establishing democratic and accountable structures while recognising an undemocratic and unaccountable institution of traditional leadership, especially in the form that has been inherited from the apartheid past, is a fundamental contradiction. (Ntsebeza, 2004: 81)

The reality was not that the control of traditional authority was bolstered by the new state, but that attempts to erode or democratize it were half-hearted and ineffectual: "After fifteen years of debate, law making and legal action, post-apartheid South Africa is no nearer to addressing the key issue of the uncertain legal status of the land rights of millions of people living under communal tenure, mostly in the former reserves" (Cousins, 2009).

If law and policy really had entrenched traditional leadership, there would be no need for attempts by a faction of the governing party, led by then president Jacob Zuma, to strengthen the power of traditional authorities at the expense of their subjects. Traditional authorities' lack of formal power did not prevent them, in some areas at least, from delivering the votes of their "subjects" to political parties. The ANC's initial failure to achieve an electoral majority in KwaZulu-Natal was a consequence of the hold of the IFP on traditional leaders and, through them, their subjects. In the period before the 2009 general election, Zuma, who is steeped in the politics of the province's "traditional" areas, persuaded traditional leaders to cross to the ANC—this probably won it the province. To ensure that the ANC remained attractive to traditional leaders, a law boosting their power, namely the Traditional Courts Bill (TCB), was introduced in 2008. In 2014, when the ANC largely lost the support of the urban Black middle class, its factions reacted in two ways, dependent on their location in the political economy. The urban insiders sought to regain middle-class support while a patronage faction based in the rural provinces, assuming that these voters were lost to the ANC forever, sought to ensure a block rural vote—with Zuma drawing on the KwaZulu-Natal experience, they hoped to do this by strengthening traditional authority.

Their first vehicle was the TCB, which sought to respond to demands by traditional authorities for an enhanced role for these courts, which enforce their power, as well as "the removal of provisions for people to opt in or out of the system" (Gasa, 2015). These demands "exactly mirrored apartheid-era legislation and the official customary law defined under colonialism," which traditional leadership now wanted "formalised and protected in law." The Bill, tabled in 2008, was the result: "By its own admission, the Department of Justice consulted only traditional leaders and a few stakeholders" (Gasa, 2015). The Bill was opposed by activist campaigns and urban ANC politicians.

The strategy of the governing party faction which then sought to strengthen traditional authority turned to a stress on their role in land restitution. It encouraged traditional leaders to engage actively in the process, which is meant to restore land to people deprived of it by apartheid. This would enable them to control the land and those who live on it. A "last-minute" addition to a Traditional and Khoi-San Leadership Bill gave traditional councils "unfettered power to transact on community land without consulting the people living on (it)" (Boyle, 2016: 7). In an address to the House of Traditional Leaders in early 2016, Zuma exhorted them to play a key role in land restitution (Makinana, 2016). As a result, traditional leaders "launched restitution claims to vast swathes of 'historical tribal land' in response to the . . . enactment of the Restitution of Land Rights Amendment Act, and President Zuma's encouragement to do so" (Claassens, 2014). The strategy was, predictably, justified not as an attempt to shore up traditional power but as an anti-colonial campaign to return land to indigenous people. One consequence was a rural conflict in which an alliance between traditional leaders, provincial governments, and private companies sought to wrest land from farmers organized into communal property associations. The Constitutional Court came to the aid of the communal farmers (Evans, 2015) but the attempt to dispossess them continued.

These trends show why *Citizen and Subject* seems to describe contemporary South African reality. Steinberg (2015), on these attempts to strengthen traditional authority's power, wrote:

> The government is dressing an apartheid legacy as a claim to be erasing apartheid legacies. After all, the degradation of citizenship is happening under the aegis of land restitution. And so, opponents of the government's project are caught in a bind; the moment they voice their protest they are accused of being against people retrieving stolen land. They have to explain that they are in fact the ones in favour of restitution—the restitution of the rights of ordinary people.

For him, the link to the book's thesis is clear:

> Apartheid thinking had so deeply infected South African thinking, Mamdani worried, that we would not understand the implications of what was happening. Caught up in the quest to deracialise the cities, we would not understand the significance of the countryside. He was quite right. Urban politics in SA is suffused with

anger . . . the call for apartheid legacies to go is deafening. And yet this urban movement is quite oblivious to what is happening in the countryside, an obliviousness it shares, ironically enough, with white people who live in cities. (Steinberg, 2015)

This judgment seems to have been vindicated by later developments. In late 2017, Zuma's faction, which sought to boost traditional authority, lost the ANC presidency to Cyril Ramaphosa—some "insider" members of the Ramaphosa faction in the ANC had opposed the TCB. This suggested that, since their political priorities centered on the market, laws imposing the power of traditional authorities on their "subjects" would be dropped after Ramaphosa became president. But the Ramaphosa-led ANC did what Zuma's faction could not—it passed the Bill, complete with the clauses forcing citizens (subjects?) in traditional areas to use these courts (RSA, 2019). This was not as surprising as it seemed, since Ramaphosa had, since his election as ANC president, assiduously courted traditional leaders (Eye Witness News, 2019). The ANC seemed, in 2019, to have followed Mamdani's conservative path, passing a law reducing millions of rural citizens to subjects.

All this seems to show clearly that, with one exception, South Africa, after more than two decades of democracy is bifurcated in the way Mamdani feared that it might be. That exception is the tenacity of racial hierarchies in the economy and society, arguably, the one aspect of contemporary South African reality which does not fit *Citizen and Subject*'s prognosis. While the polity has been deracialized, poverty and inequality remain racialized—the values of the racial minority still dominate the society's intellectual and cultural elite, prompting the political commentator Aubrey Matshiqi's observation that "White people remain a cultural majority. And it is their world view that continues to dominate the shaping of social and economic relations" (Matshiqi, 2011). While the book discusses the postcolonial order's deracialization of the state, not of society, the continuation of patterns of racial domination is not one of its core concerns—understandably, since settler colonialism was a reality in only a few African countries and the problem of race was largely settled when the colonizers went home. In former settler colonies, the presence of a formerly dominant racial minority introduces a dynamic which is exclusive to them. In South Africa, whose white minority is the most numerous and most influential on the continent, the legacy of race remains a source of differential citizenship which has distinctive features.

But this does not necessarily mean that this is a consequence of the persistence of the apartheid-era state form. The remainder of this chapter argues that the patterns discussed here are the product not of the form of the post-1994 state but of continuities between apartheid society and current social reality.

The All-Conquering State?: Urban-Rural Conflict in Late Apartheid

To examine *Citizen and Subject*'s applicability to current realities, it is necessary to begin with its understanding of apartheid. Mamdani's complaint that urban-based resistance failed to develop a strategy for democratizing customary power is well-founded. While in the 1950s rural-dwellers in Pondoland did rebel against traditional leaders (Mbeki, 1964), this did not prompt a sustained attempt by the ANC to organize rural people. The holders of that power were judged by the resistance movement not by the degree to which their relationship with those subject to their authority was democratic but by whether they were for or against "the struggle." While many were more inclined to defend a status quo which was the source of their authority, some—in the Eastern Cape and in Sekhukhuneland—sided with the resistance movement (Mandela, 1994: 31). If they did, no questions were asked about the nature of their rule. During the transition period and after, politicians who had participated in Bantustan governments, as well as traditional leaders who supported the ANC, were welcomed into its ranks. Despite the role of the Bantustans in shoring up apartheid, the fault line was where traditional power stood on the "national question"—deracialization—rather than on the nature of governance or its role under apartheid. Ramaphosa's embrace of traditional leaders continues, therefore, a long-standing ANC tradition. The lack of a coherent response to the rural was also partly responsible for a failure to win the support of migrant workers who, as Mamdani points out, were seen as premodern obstacles rather than products of a particular social reality. The divide between town and countryside was evident in the strategies and the contours of anti-apartheid resistance.

But was this divide created or sustained by "decentralized despots"? The migrant labor system was largely responsible for the urban-rural divide and the tensions it produced. Migrant labor was not necessarily a feature of societies in which chiefs ruled in the countryside: many countries had chiefly power but no system of labor migrancy. Nor did migrancy in South Africa need traditional authority. It was at times helped by it—as in the 1950s when chiefs were expected to force women to carry passes (and were replaced by "chiefs" who would do this if they refused) (Manson and Mbenga, 2012). Some used force to recruit labor for the mines and factories. But it was, in the main, enforced directly by the apartheid state's agencies and could have survived if there were no chiefs. Since migrant labor is not a necessary product of the colonial state, and traditional authority was not essential to its maintenance in South Africa, we must look beyond the nature of the state for explanations. The most credible accounts of migrancy see it as a product of what Mamdani calls the "mode of exploitation," not the "mode of rule," as the way in which white colonizers extracted cheap labor from Black people rather than a strategy to quell political resistance (Wolpe, 1987; Friedman, 2015b). In 1973, when migrants formed the core of the Durban strikes, "decentralized despotism" was on their side: a minister in the KwaZulu administration, Barney Dladla, provided invaluable support to the strikers (Hemson, 2009). Chiefly rule was not necessarily bound to control people on apartheid's behalf—it was sometimes a source of resistance (which is why the ANC could see some chiefs as allies). By supporting wage increases, Dladla was also undermining the apartheid state's strategy of making life as uncomfortable for Black city dwellers as possible to induce them to depart for the Bantustans.

Citizen and Subject's analysis of migrancy imputes exaggerated power to the state. It suggests that the end of influx control was a product of state strategy designed to weaken urban revolt by flooding the cities with migrants from the countryside. But how can the state defuse urban protest both by restricting Black access to cities and by allowing Black people to "swamp" them? In reality, the system was abolished not because the state found a new way of suppressing revolt, but because it was left with no option by the resistance of Black people who refused to comply either as an act of defiance or as an individual response to economic necessity (Cole, 1987). To convey some of the flavor of this clash between the will of the state and the agency of those it sought to dominate, a government official, when asked why the state did not crush the resistance to influx control by force, responded, with some anguish, that it had spent years trying, including using floodlights to demolish shacks by day and by night, "but they kept coming back like black ants." The system collapsed not because the state was powerful enough to end it, but because it was powerless, in the face of social reality, to maintain it. This particular attempt to keep apart that which social reality brought together was a failure because society proved stronger than the state. This is not an isolated example—almost from its inception, apartheid's attempt to stem the tide of social change was in retreat, forced repeatedly to change tack in the face of social pressures. What *Citizen and Subject* sees as the works of the state is a product, rather, of its limited ability to shape the nature of society.

A similar point can be made about Mamdani's perceptive warning that rebellion against control over the movement of Black people by migrants tended to descend into authoritarianism. He remarks, famously, that many shack settlements established by people denied housing, "began with an emphasis on participation and ended up with a shacklord" (Mamdani, 1995: 295), a despot who used force to lord it over residents. The most notorious example was the fate of the action which began the end of influx control—the movement of residents of men's migrant hostels into shacks in the Crossroads camp in the Western Cape. This protest descended into internecine war as vigilantes controlled by "shacklords" imposed their will violently, attacking urban activists fighting apartheid (Cole, 1987). The framework proposed in *Citizen and Subject* explains this as a sign of the tenacity of the rural state form when it constitutes itself in the cities—shack leaders become shacklords because the despotism of the countryside from whence they come shapes the way they rule the shack settlement. But while the migrants who opposed urban protesters in Soweto were linked to a rural state structure—KwaZulu-Natal—the Crossroads vigilantes were not and so it could not be credibly argued that they were operating within the parameters of a rural authority structure. Since authoritarian power structures in areas occupied by land invasions are not a purely South African or African phenomenon, it seems more appropriate to see it as a symptom of the constraints to democratic organization where residents depend for their continued residence not on a guaranteed right but on the power of a local leader, than of the form of state. Given the origins of Crossroads, it is more appropriate to see it as a symptom of the breakdown of state control than as its product.

Citizen and Subject teaches us much about the clash between urban organization on the one hand, and migrant laborers and people living in informal housing on the other—at the time it appeared, the triumphalism of a successful fight against apartheid often obscured these realities. But it does not show that the distinction between those who are permanently in the cities and those on their peripheries is the product of a form of state, rather than a consequence of the failure of state policy in the face of social reality. The same can be said of the post-apartheid realities discussed here.

Victim or Villain?: The State and Economy after Apartheid

The social bifurcation analyzed here is consistent with the ethos of *Citizen and Subject* but diverges in important ways from its reliance on state form as an explanatory category. The separation of South African society into "insiders" and "outsiders" is not a neat urban-rural division. The divide between suburbs and townships is much more significant than that between town and country. Within the urban economy the key divide is between core and periphery. While migrancy is certainly a reality for some outsiders (Webster, 2013) and exclusion has a spatial dimension (Beall et al., 2000), the divide is manifest within cities rather than between them and the countryside. It is also significant that patterns of politics in towns which were once part of the Bantustans and governed by decentralized despots are much the same as those in urban townships—the division is less between urban and rural but between inclusion in and exclusion from mainstream economic and social institutions.

This is crucial since the urban insiders and outsiders are not products of different forms of state. In the cities, Black people were, under apartheid, ostensibly governed by Black Local Authorities which were intended as instruments of indirect rule. But they never achieved that status in practice since the central government, in keeping with *Citizen and Subject*'s hypothesis, relied on direct rule in the cities and was, therefore, unwilling to extend to them the powers which would have allowed them to play their intended role—they were far more liable to be labeled "toothless toy telephones" than instruments of effective control. They were never a distinctive state form since it was always clear that the white government controlled the townships. But much the same could be said of the Bantustans—while despotism was decentralized in principle, in practice the white government remained in control. So, the divide between township and suburb is not between products of different forms of state but between social groups within a common form of state. Since 1994, as in urban townships, the politics of exclusion and inclusion in former Bantustan towns has far more to do with relationships to local power structures than with the traditional authority structures created by apartheid. Whether we see the contours of inclusion and exclusion as economic, political, or cultural—or all three—they are products of patterns in society, not of differing forms of state.

Nor should it be assumed that the divide between citizen and subject is as clear-cut as Mamdani assumes. A critique of *Citizen and Subject* by Steven Robins argues that,

> with its urban/rural and citizen/subject dichotomies, (it) does not engage with the complex, hybrid and situated subjectivities of post-colonial citizen-subjects. In its quest for symmetry and conceptual clarity, (it) sacrifices the more ambiguous and "messy" forms of everyday life in the post-colony. . . . Most people in South Africa

act as both citizens and subjects, and they strategically and situationally engage with "rights talk" and the political discourses of liberal democracy. (2008: 11)

Evidence of this may be the 2016 local elections in which voting patterns in rural provinces largely mirrored those in the major metropolitan areas.[3] The complex nature of citizenship and subjection in contemporary South Africa means that there are convergences as well as divergences between town and country which we would not expect to find if they were products of the bifurcated state.

None of this, of course, means that the bifurcation identified by Mamdani does not live on in contemporary South Africa—the evidence presented here shows that it does. But it does show that the form of state is not its cause. Mamdani's view that the "native question" has greater explanatory power than the "labor question" is apposite. However, "the native question" is not a product of a particular form of state—it stems, rather, from the complex ways in which racial power reproduces itself in a society whose law has seemingly abolished it and in the distinctly racial flavor of social and economic exclusion. The racial hierarchies of the past endure, but because social power is stronger than that of the state, not because the state continues to impose them on society. Again, it is not the form of state, but the state's limited capacity to change social power relations, which is decisive.

The attempt, for over a decade, to impose traditional authorities on rural areas, which has culminated in the passage of a law which enables despotism, may seem at first glance to refute this but in reality, it strengthens the argument. There would, of course, be no need to try to ensure rural vote banks by strengthening traditional despotism if this reality already existed. It is precisely because apartheid-style control over rural areas has eroded, that laws are now considered necessary to revive it. Before apartheid ended, the links between rural residents and the urban economy frustrated an attempt by Mangosuthu Buthelezi, then head of KwaZulu, to maintain the apartheid form of state by seceding. One constraint was the response of migrant workers, many of them supporters of Buthelezi's IFP, who feared this would cut them off from work outside the province.

The 2016 local elections also raise doubts about the assumption that traditional authorities are strong enough to shape the voting patterns of their putative subjects. The role of KwaZulu-Natal traditional authorities described earlier may have been an exception rather than the rule. In 2016, the ANC lost between 9 and 18 percentage points in rural provinces, a bigger percentage drop than in the cities. This is not necessarily a new development:

The 1994 election results are probably the best indicator of the danger of relying on traditional leaders to deliver the rural vote. In that year, the ANC won more than 90% of the votes in Limpopo and more than 80% in the North West, Mpumalanga and the Eastern Cape—all rural provinces that had been intensely involved in anti-bantustan and anti-chief rebellions during the build-up to the elections. (Claassens, 2016)

---

[3]   See official election data: Independent Electoral Commission, www.elections.org.za

The attempt to build a rural power base which will counteract the political influence of the cities does not seek to entrench current power relations in the rural areas—it hopes to recreate them precisely because they are now not nearly strong enough to be relied upon.

But what if the passage of the TCB does now empower chiefs in the way *Citizen and Subject* feared? Would that not create a form of rural state which would hamstring democracy? It remains unlikely that the Bill will stand. As noted earlier, the courts are also part of the state and they have shown no enthusiasm for rural despotism. It seems almost inevitable that the Bill will be challenged in court and highly likely that it will be overturned. Until and unless the courts somehow endorse the view that it is constitutional to subject millions of people to a judicial process which allows none of the safeguards for citizens' rights that the constitution entrenches, then the form of state has not changed to permit rural despotism. It is also important to stress that, as harsh and authoritarian as the law is, it does not deny rural citizens the right to vote, which they used in 2016 to undermine despotic rural authority, or the civil liberties that enable them to resist despotism. The law is oppressive but it does not change the form of state.

If chiefly control over rural citizens is exaggerated, then so too is the power which control of the state is said to bestow on the ANC. One flaw in *Citizen and Subject*'s analysis is that, by implication, it imputes more power to African post-independence political elites than they really enjoy. For decades, these governments may often have been able to dominate their own citizens but they were always subject to the economic power of the Global North. Similarly, the ANC, as the earlier discussion of "archipelagos of dominance" argued, has limited power over the economic elites which apartheid created or indeed over society: the township dynamics discussed earlier suggest that it is often more a symptom of social reality than their shaper. While its pre-1994 program called for a "national democratic revolution" in which control by a racial minority would be defeated, racial domination in the economy remains a feature of current reality—this is the result not of the form of state but of the governing party's unwillingness or inability to negotiate changes to social reality. In the townships and shack settlements, the ANC dominance discussed earlier reflects not the continuation of a particular form of state, but power relationships which emerged during the fight against apartheid, and continued economic exclusion, which ensures that local politics is often a way of extracting resources rather than representing citizens. The state is open to the charge that it has not changed these patterns, but it did not cause them.

The post-1994 reality is arguably not the strength of the state and its influence over society, but the intractability of some of the social patterns of the apartheid period despite a change in the nature of the state. An appropriate theoretical framework for understanding the limits of the state's role is proposed by Bob Jessop (1990), who, from a Marxist perspective, argues against "crude instrumentalism"—the idea that the state simply does the bidding of the ruling class. For our purposes, the importance of his argument lies in his view that states are not independent actors: they are rooted in social interests and processes. Marxism's view that the state-advanced class interests were not automatic—it could only do this if a "national popular project" united society. Without this, the state might be able to perform only its narrow control function (Jessop,

1990: 8–9). The state is not necessarily doomed to reflect social reality—it can place its imprint on society. But this is not assured: it would require it to initiate conscious action that recognized social realities—and, therefore, the limits of the state—and sought to change them within the limits of the possible. The state cannot simply impose itself on society: it can influence it and perhaps even reshape it, but it is always forced to negotiate a relationship with society and so is never able to shape it as it pleases.

In post-1994 South Africa, the form of state has changed significantly—it provides opportunities for citizens to exercise power which did not exist before 1994 (Friedman and Mottiar, 2005). But the state's role in changing social reality has been limited and the power relationships established by apartheid remain stubbornly resistant to the change in state form. It is South African society that remains bifurcated, a reality which its altered, and no longer bifurcated, form of state has thus far been unable to change.

References

Beall, J., Crankshaw, O. and Parnell, S. (2000). "Victims, villains and fixers: The urban environment and Johannesburg's poor." *Journal of Southern African Studies*, 26(4): 833–55. http://doi.org/10.1080/713683609.

Bhorat, H., Van der Westhuizen, C. and Yu, D. (2014). "The silent success: Delivery of public assets since democracy," DPRU Working Paper 201403, July. Development Policy Research Unit, University of Cape Town.

Boyle, B. (2016). "Foxes left to guard the hens that lay community nest eggs." *Business Day*, August 10.

Bruce, P. (2011). "The thick end of the wedge." *Business Day*, September 5.

Centre for Law and Society (CLS). (2013). "Questioning the legal status of traditional councils in South Africa," Fact Sheet, Rural Women's Action Research Programme, University of Cape Town, August. http://www.cls.uct.ac.za/usr/lrg/downloads/CLS_TCStatus_Factsheet_Aug2013.pdf.

Chatterjee, P. (2004). *The Politics of the Governed: Reflections on Popular Politics in Most of the World*. New York: Columbia University Press.

Claassens, A. (2014). "Communal land, property rights and traditional leadership," Wits Institute for Social and Economic Research (WISER), University of the Witwatersrand. http://wiser.wits.ac.za/system/files/documents/Claassens2014.pdf.

Claassens, A. (2016). "Rural vote notions." *Letters, Business Day*, August 12.

Cole, J. (1987). *Crossroads: The Politics of Reform and Repression, 1976–1986*. Johannesburg: Ravan Press.

Cousins, B. (2007). "More than socially embedded: The distinctive character of 'communal tenure' regimes in South Africa and its implications for land policy." *Journal of Agrarian Change*, 7(3): 281–315. https://doi.org/10.1111/j.1471-0366.2007.00147.x.

Cousins, B. (2009). "Key provisions of the Communal Land Rights Act are declared unconstitutional. Where to now?" Blog—Another Countryside, November 10. Institute for Poverty, Land and Agrarian Studies (PLAAS), University of the Western Cape. http://www.plaas.org.za/blog/key-provisions-communal-land-rights-act-are-declared-unconstitutional-where-to-now/.

Evans, S. (2015). "ConCourt hands land back to North West community." *Mail and Guardian*, August 20.

Eye Witness News (EWN). (2019). "Ramaphosa praises house of traditional leaders as essential part of society." February 18. https://www.msn.com/en-za/news/national/ramaphosa-praises-house-of-traditional-leaders-as-essential-part-of-society/ar-BBTOTfb.

Friedman, S. (2010). "Gaining comprehensive AIDS treatment in South Africa: The extraordinary 'ordinary,'" in J. Gaventa and R. McGee (eds.), *Citizen Action and National Policy Reform*. London and New York: Zed Books, pp. 44–68.

Friedman, S. (2011). "Whose freedom? South Africa's press, middle class bias and the threat of control." *Ecquid Novi: African Journalism Studies*, 32(2): 106–21. https://doi.org/10.1080/02560054.2011.578887.

Friedman, S. (2015a). "Archipelagos of dominance: Party fiefdoms and South African democracy." *Zeitschrift für Vergleichende Politikwissenschaft (Journal of Comparative Politics)*, 9(3): 139–59. https://doi.org/10.1007/s12286-015-0246-9.

Friedman, S. (2015b). *Class, Race and Power: Harold Wolpe and the Radical Critique of Apartheid*. Scottsville: University of KwaZulu-Natal Press.

Friedman, S. (2015c) "The Janus face of the past: Preserving and resisting South African path dependence," in X. Mangcu (ed.), *The Colour of Our Future: Does Race Matter in Post-Apartheid South Africa?* Johannesburg: Wits University Press, pp. 45–63.

Friedman, S. and Mottiar, S. (2005). "A rewarding engagement? The treatment action campaign and the politics of HIV/AIDS." *Politics & Society*, 33(4): 511–65. https://doi.org/10.1177/0032329205280928.

Gasa, N. (2015). "State repeats mistakes in third attempt at Courts Bill." *Business Day*, June 22.

Hemson, D. (2009). "So long to a fiery spirit." *Mail and Guardian*, November 27. https://mg.co.za/article/2009-11-27-so-long-to-a-fiery-spirit.

Jara, M. (2014). "Beyond social compacting: A power matrix in flux in post-Mandela South Africa," in B. Gilder (ed.), *20 Years of South African Democracy: So Where to Now?*. Johannesburg: MISTRA, pp. 82–8. https://doi.org/10.2307/j.ctv13qfwd0.14.

Jessop, B. (1990). *State Theory: Putting the Capitalist State in its Place*. University Park: Pennsylvania State University Press.

Lipton, D. (2016). "Bridging South Africa's economic divide," International Monetary Fund (IMF), July 19. http://www.imf.org/en/News/Articles/2016/07/18/20/15/SP071916-Bridging-South-Africas-Economic-Divide.

Makinana, A. (2016). "Zuma questions 'lopsided' land reform law, calls for radical action." *City Press*, March 3.

Mamdani, M. (1995). *Citizen and Subject: Contemporary Africa and the Politics of Late Colonialism*. Kampala: Fountain.

Mandela, N. (1994). *Long Walk to Freedom*. London: Little Brown.

Manson, A. and Mbenga, B. (2012). "Bophutatswana and the North West Province: From pan-Tswanaism to mineral-based ethnic assertiveness." *South African Historical Journal*, 6(1): 96–116.

Manuel, T. (2012). "Proof of how much we have done—And must still do." *Business Day*, October 21.

Matshiqi, A. (2011). "Why Manuel is right and wrong about Manyi's 'racism.'" *Business Day*, March 8. http://www.businessday.co.za/articles/Content.aspx?id=136509.

Mbeki, G. (1964). *South Africa: The Peasants' Revolt*. Harmondsworth: Penguin.

Meth, C. (2014). "Ending can only be bad for SA's 'good story' on statistics." *Business Day*, April 11.

Newham, G. and Tamukamoyo, H. (2013). "The Tatane case raises hard questions for South Africa's national prosecuting authority," ISS Today, April 11, Institute for Security Studies (ISS). http://www.issafrica.org/iss-today/the-tatane-case-raises-hard -questions-for-south-africas-national-prosecuting-authority.

News24. (2012). "ANC loses Nkandla by-election." December 6. http://www.news24.com/ SouthAfrica/Politics/ANC-loses-Nkandla-by-election-20121206-4.

North, D. C. (1990). *Institutions, Institutional Change, and Economic Performance.* New York: Cambridge University Press.

Ntsebeza, L. (2004). "Democratic decentralisation and traditional authority: Dilemmas of land administration in rural South Africa." *The European Journal of Development Research*, 16(1): 71–89. https://doi.org/10.1080/09578810410001688743.

Page, S. E. (2006). "Path dependence." *Quarterly Journal of Political Science*, 1(1): 87–115. http://dx.doi.org/10.1561/100.00000006.

Pithouse, R. (2011). "The case of the Kennedy 12: No easy path through the embers." *Counterpunch*, August 1. https://www.counterpunch.org/2011/08/01/no-easy-path -through-the-embers/.

Republic of South Africa (RSA). (2019). "National assembly agrees to traditional Courts Bill," Parliament of the Republic of South Africa, March 12. https://www.parliament .gov.za/press-releases/national-assembly-agrees-traditional-courts-bill.

Robins, S. (2008). *From Revolution to Rights in South Africa: Social Movements, NGOs and Popular Politics After Apartheid.* London: James Currey; Scottsville: KwaZulu-Natal Press.

SAFM Radio. (2008). *Morning Live*, with Tshepiso Makwetla, April.

Steinberg, J. (2015). "We should've heeded Mahmoud Mamdani's warning." *Business Day*, October 2.

Stone, S. (2012). "ANC loses ward near Marikana in by-election." *Business Day*, November 8.

Thom, A. (2013). "Motsoaledi happy with HIV response." *NSP Review*, December 11. http://www.nspreview.org/2013/12/11/motsoaledi-happy-with-hiv-response/.

Tipe, T. (2014). "The boundaries of tradition: An examination of the traditional leadership and governance framework act." *Harvard Human Rights Journal*, November 4. http://harvardhrj.com/2014/11/the-boundaries-of-tradition-an-examination-of-the -traditional-leadership-and-governance-framework-act/.

Vally, S. (2003). "The iron fist and the velvet glove." *Mail and Guardian*, December 20.

Van der Berg, S. and Siebrits, K. (2010). "Social assistance reform during a period of fiscal stress," Working Paper 17/2010, Department of Economics, Stellenbosch University.

Von Holdt, K., Langa, M., Molapo, S., Mogapi, N., Ngubeni, K., Dlamini, J. and Kirsten, A. (2011). "The smoke that calls: Insurgent citizenship, collective violence and the search for a place in the new South Africa," July. Centre for the Study of Violence and Reconciliation (CSVR); Society, Work and Development Institute, Johannesburg.

Webster, E. (2013). "The promise and the possibility: South Africa's contested industrial relations path." *Transformation*, 81(82): 208–35.

Wolpe, H. (1987). *Race, Class and the Apartheid State.* London: James Currey.

10

Predicaments of the Colonized

Being Coloured, Indian, and Free after Apartheid

Suren Pillay

Introduction

A recent history of violence has brought to the attention of many—who pay attention to post-apartheid South Africa—a politics often submerged by the imperatives of national unity. Events at Siqalo in Mitchells Plain in the Western Cape pitted new residents in temporary housing against an adjacent older working-class community in permanent housing (Eyewitness News, 2018), reminded us of the intensity of the racialized language that circulates between "Coloured"[1] and African populations in the Cape. More recently—during July 2021—large-scale dramatic violence was triggered across large swathes of the province of KwaZulu-Natal by a judicial order that sent the country's former president Jacob Zuma to prison for contempt of court, in the wake of his refusal to testify in a government commission on state corruption. This violence became most acute in the Phoenix settlement in KwaZulu-Natal. An inquiry of the South African Human Rights Commission (SAHRC) currently underway has been hearing testimonies that describe the violence in ways that pits South Africans of Indian descent against black Africans (Mkhize, 2021).

Responses to these events so far tend to be divided along different lines. On the one hand, there is a group—among them former anti-apartheid activists, well-known journalists and bloggers, and educated elites—denouncing the politics that might be explicit or lying-in wait, in references to being Coloured or Indian. For this group, the references to being Coloured or the new incarnation of "first nations" or "Khoi" conceal a racism toward Africans at best, and at worst are identities being instrumentally mobilized by charlatans, chauvinists, and political entrepreneurs masking opportunistic interests in the language of justice. On the other hand, a more "popular" view considers these expressions as the articulations of legitimate political problems, that is, that Coloured populations are being marginalized in post-apartheid

---

[1] I have used "Coloured" in quotation marks, following a convention in South African political discourse, in order to indicate that it is used with circumspection. For ease of reading, I refer to it without these conventions in the rest of the chapter.

South Africa; or alternatively, that Coloured is an identity that should be replaced by more affirming precolonial cultural self-descriptions, such as Khoi or Griqua.[2] In the case of the Indian question, there is a popular view that insists that there is a legitimate truth in claiming that Indian South Africans—and the more recent South Asian migrants—are racist toward black Africans. My aim here is not necessarily to argue for, nor refute any one side of these responses. Rather, drawing on a conceptual formulation developed by Mahmood Mamdani (2001), of the "subject races," my aim here is to put these sentiments in an historical context so that we illuminate where they emanate from.

By de-exceptionalizing this violence, I wish to argue that what we are witnessing are the predicaments of postcolonial political justice that have confronted certain population groups grappling with what it means to be free after decolonization, particularly in Africa. One of the truisms of colonial rule, particularly in the British colonies, and particularly after certain experiences of revolt that they faced in India and parts of Africa, was the lesson that a united native population was an extremely threatening proposition (Akpan, 1956; Chatterjee, 1993; Dirks, 2001; Silverstein, 2019). The result was a policy pioneered first in West Africa, then East Africa, and then Southern Africa, of first dividing the local population in order to better rule them, and second, to implement a policy of co-opting local political leaders and refashioning local customs, so that these leaders become the indirect rulers of the colonial state. If local populations had different cultural identities, these were now transformed into tribal identities. Tribes were ascribed to certain territories that would be their "homelands," where they would live under customary law administered by chiefs anointed by the colonial administrator. Cultural identity was now turned into political identity (Mamdani, 2013). Europeans, on the other hand, were not a tribe but were defined by their racial identity, while black Africans were defined by their ethnic or tribal identities. To be a "native," classified as "indigenous," meant that one had to be defined as an ethnic subject of a particular territorial-administrative unit.

But some states went even further. As the Zimbabwean historian James Muzondidya has noted, colonial Rhodesia further distinguished between an "aboriginal native" and a "colonial native" (2007). An "aboriginal native" was an ethnic subject defined as belonging to that particular territory and, therefore, having certain rights of access to land and other benefits. However, "colonial natives" were different: they lived on the land but did not belong there. They were "ethnic strangers." In Rhodesia, this often meant they were descendants of refugees who fled political conflict in eighteenth-century South Africa, or they were migrant workers. As the Government Notice No. 223 of 1898 expressed it, colonial natives were "all members of the Zulu, Bechuana and Zambesi tribes, all kaffir tribes of the Cape Colony, and any native not being a descendent of an aboriginal of Rhodesia" (Muzondidya, 2007: 328). Natives "belonged"

---

[2]   As an example, a movement called "Gatvol Capetonians" addresses this sentiment, placing the emphasis on the perceived economic marginalization of Coloured communities. See: https://www.thesouthafrican.com/news/what-is-gatvol-capetonian. The other growing trajectory is the rejection of "Coloured" as an apartheid racial classification in favour of what is regarded as a precolonial identity of being Khoi and San. See: https://www.citizen.co.za/news/south-africa/1983352/chief-khoisan-wants-the-word-coloured-abolished/

in these ethnic reserves, while the city or the town "belonged" to the racial subjects: the Europeans. Hence, the Vagrancy Act of 1893 and the Registration of Natives Regulations of 1895 in Rhodesia made it compulsory for Africans to carry a pass in any urban area. A native found in a town, and who was not there for the purpose of work, was guilty of loitering without intent, and regarded as a vagrant. These pass laws regulating the movement of Africans between town and countryside became a feature of this mode of rule by the colonial state across British Africa, and were not specific to South Africa.

This experience of the colonial world, therefore, comprised two main identities: the settler—who was racialized as European or white, and the native—who was ethnicized as a tribal subject. But across the continent there were also categories of populations who did not fit neatly into the division of white settler and Black native. Among those who did not fit the racialized account of white settler and Black native were, for example, those settlers who were either freed or free-born descendants of African slaves in the United States, who, supported by the American Colonization Society, created the present-day West African states of Liberia and Sierra Leone (Abdullah, 2004). These new settlers, such as those who became known as Americo-Liberians, were defined more by culture and geography than by being a distinct race. They differentiated themselves from the populations they found there by ironically recreating hierarchies and styles of rule—including architectural styles—they had experienced or recalled from the slave plantations—then as slaves, now as masters. While Americo-Liberians were rulers from 1822 onward, the franchise was only given to indigenous Liberians in 1904. As a group, they evolved into an endogenous cultural, political, and economic elite minority, and regarded the local population as being in need of upliftment through Christian missionary eyes. This history culminated, after more than a century, in the revolt that saw the military officer who was of local genealogy, Samuel Doe, seize power in 1980 and the summary executions and exile of the Americo-Liberian descendants, starting with the then president, Tubman, those in his inner circle, and his family (Adebajo, 2007; Moran, 2013). Subsequently, a series of armed groups in turn all set their eyes on the political capital, Monrovia. In the bloody and gruesome civil wars that ensued, a descendant of Americo-Liberians, Charles Taylor, seized power and the conflict took on a regional dimension, including Sierra Leone, which is more widely known in the contemporary history of African political violence.[3]

It is the other groups to whom the binary between a white settler and a Black native refers that is the main preoccupation here. There were categories of populations internal to the African continent in origin, but who were not defined as ethnic, such as the Europeans, who were classified as races under colonial law. Like the Europeans, colonial thinking insisted that they came from elsewhere, and were, therefore, not indigenous. In northern Nigeria, this ascription was given to those classified as Fulani. In Rwanda, the Tutsi were defined as a nonindigenous race, while the Hutu were defined as ethnic natives. In East Africa and Southern Africa, the Indians were defined

---

[3] This war has mostly become known through the political economy of "blood diamonds"— the resources mobilized to fuel civil war in Sierra Leone (Hoffman, 2011), or accounts of the grotesqueness of the violence, and a more scholarly literature focused on the role of the generational question of the youth involved (Abdullah, 2004).

as a race. In Southern Africa, more broadly, the descendants of slaves and mixed populations were defined as "Coloureds," mestizos, or creoles. These groups have been theorized as "subject races" by Mamdani:

> The colonial state made a distinction in law between "race" and "ethnicity." This is the question I would like to begin with. What is the difference in law between a race and an ethnicity? Is it the difference between biology and culture, between biological race and cultural ethnicity? Not really, if you take a closer look. In indirect-rule Africa, only natives were said to belong to ethnic groups; nonnatives had no ethnicity. Nonnatives were identified racially, not ethnically. There was in fact an entire racial hierarchy, with Europeans—meaning whites— at the top, followed by "Coloureds," then Asians, then Arabs, and then Hamites (the Tutsi). Races were considered a civilizing influence, even if in different degrees, while ethnicities were considered to be in dire need of being civilized. The colonial state divided the population into two: races and ethnicities. Each lived in a different legal universe. Races were governed through civil law. They were considered as members, actually or potentially, of civil society. Civil society excluded ethnicities. (2001: 654)

Subject races became intermediaries between the Europeans and those regarded as "indigenous" tribes; they were elevated above the "native," but kept well below the European. The result was to produce a double contempt that was to confront these population groups when the question of justice posed itself in the wake of colonial rule: they were held in contempt by those who ruled over them, and held in contempt by those over whom they held petty authority.

To refine the point, Mamdani differentiated between colonizer and colonized on the one hand, and races and ethnicities, on the other, rather than collapse these categories into each other:

> [T]he distinction between races and ethnicities was not the same as the distinction between colonizers and colonized. The hierarchy of races included both colonizers and colonized. Similarly, the colonized were divided into those indigenous and those not; in other words, whereas all natives were colonized, not all nonnatives were colonizers. The hierarchy of race included master races and subject races. Who were the subject races of indirect-rule Africa? They were the Indians of East, Central and Southern Africa, the Arabs of Zanzibar, the Tutsi of Rwanda and Burundi, and the "Coloureds" of Southern Africa. The distinction between subject races and subject ethnicities is worth grasping. While both were colonized, the former were a fraction of the latter. Subject races were either non-indigenous immigrants, like the Indians of East, Central and Southern Africa, or they were constructed as nonindigenous by the colonial powers, such as, for example, the Tutsi of Rwanda and Burundi. In contrast, subject ethnicities were indigenous. Finally, subject races usually performed a middleman function, in either the state or the market, and their position was marked by petty privilege economically and preferential treatment legally. (Mamdani, 2001: 656–7)

By historicizing race and ethnicity as differentiated legal-political identities, Mamdani drew attention to the fundamental political charge that was invested in this distinction—races came from elsewhere and ethnicities were cast as indigenous to territory. Here Mamdani drew substantively on a seminal article by Edith Sanders (1969) on what is known as the Hamitic hypothesis. In short, this hypothesis relies on an Enlightenment account of race as the coincidence of biology and culture in which some are more advanced than others because of where they are at, in this time line of progress. Europeans in this account are the most advanced race, and any sign or symbol of culture or civilization of any complexity that was recognizable to Europeans as such would have to be explained by the presence or absence, and degree of mixing or otherwise, of European blood. Sanders described with considerable alacrity how this particular discursive account of race became the organizing framework for how colonial knowledge—first in an imperial and, later, colonial imperative—was entwined. Sanders traces how an early version of the Hamitic hypothesis—in which the descendants of Ham are considered cursed and savage in a theological story—becomes recast after the Napoleonic expedition to Egypt in 1798, as the European-inflected descendants responsible for what might be considered signs of a civilized culture.

As Sanders (1969: 521) noted, the Hamitic hypothesis "states that everything of value ever found in Africa was brought there by the Hamites, allegedly a branch of the Caucasian race." To sum up the thesis, she recalled the influential textbook of Charles Seligman first published in 1930, *The Races of Africa*, and republished as a canonical text until 1966—in which the Hamitic hypothesis was formulated as follows:

> Apart from relatively late Semitic influence . . . the civilizations of Africa are the civilizations of the Hamites, its history the record of these peoples and of their interaction with the two other African stocks, the Negro and the Bushman, whether this influence was exerted by highly civilized Egyptians or by such wider pastoralists as are represented at the present day by the Beja and Somali. . . . The incoming Hamites were pastoral "Europeans"—arriving wave after wave—better armed as well as quicker witted than the dark agricultural Negroes. (Sanders, 1969: 521)

The Hamitic hypothesis was put to work across the continent to provide a classificatory "grid of intelligibility," as the French philosopher Michel Foucault (1990: 93) would say, to account for difference, and, on the basis of that, to ethnographically interpret this difference on a sociocultural scale. It is central to the historiography of East Africa, recalled through the figure of John Speke (1827–64), the colonial explorer who went in search of the source of the Nile. Speke became an ardent proponent of the Hamitic hypothesis in his writings, notably on the Buganda kingdom (Burton and Speke, 1859). The novelty of Mamdani's reading of Sanders's account of the Hamitic hypothesis lies in the connection he develops between colonial knowledge—the classificatory episteme that is her preoccupation—and the modes of colonial and postcolonial rule—that are his preoccupation. If Sanders provides the epistemic account, it is to Frederick Lugard's

Dual Mandate (1922) that Mamdani turns for a theorization of colonial administration, in particular, the theory of indirect rule.

It is worth reading Lugard's text in the way that the British intellectual historian Quentin Skinner encourages a reading of the canon of Western political theory, from Machiavelli through to Hobbes and Locke. By that I mean less as philosophical abstractions or as answers to the proverbial major questions of Man eternal to the ages, but rather as "interventions," as answers to a particular historical political problem.[4] Along that grain, it is worth thinking of the texts of colonial adventurer-administrators—the empire's proverbial men on the ground—just as much as expressions of Western political theory, rather than as somehow lesser knowledge immersed in the technical elaborations that describe administration. Nor are they texts marked by the quaintness of their time or as ethnological and, therefore, belonging to an epistemic world outside of the biography of Western political theory. Skinner's interest in Hobbes's *Leviathan*, for example, illustrates his regard for it as the answer to a political problem which requires a theory of obligation (2002: 264–86)—and to that extent, Lugard's *Dual Mandate* is concerned too with a theory of obligation. In this case, it is not the question so much of how natural rights-bearing free and autonomous beings submit themselves willingly to a power which may take their lives, but how a foreign minority might rule over a numerally larger majority that has been subjugated through the conquest of defeat. But crucially, a majority that has to be ruled in an efficiently ordered and frugal way without continually resorting to the violence of conquest which recreates the chaos of colonial war.

More to the point, Lugard developed a theory of colonial rule and obligation that exemplified the account of the Hamitic hypothesis outlined earlier, that is, that those defined as ethnicities were indigenous and those defined as races were external to Africa but were the civilizing forces of history. The notion of an alien race was explicitly described by Lugard in his account of the role of the Fulani:

> The Fulani of Northern Nigeria are, as I have said, more capable of rule than the indigenous races, but in proportion as we consider them an alien race, we are denying self-government to the people over whom they rule, and supporting an alien caste—albeit closer and more akin to the native races than a European can be. Yet capable as they are, it requires the ceaseless vigilance of the British staff to maintain a high standard of administrative integrity, and to prevent oppression of the peasantry. (1922: 197)

As Lugard would go on to say,

> [T]here can be no doubt that such races form an invaluable medium between the British staff and the native peasantry. Nor can the difficulty of finding any one capable of taking their place, or the danger they would constitute to the State if ousted from their positions, be ignored. Their traditions of rule, their monotheistic

---

[4] Skinner outlines his method in a number of texts, but this wide-ranging interview is also useful: https://booksandideas.net/Theories-as-Social-Action.html

religion, and their intelligence enable them to appreciate more readily than the negro population, the wider objects of British policy . . . while their close touch with the masses with whom they live in daily intercourse, mark them out as destined to play an important part in the future, as they have done in the past, in the development of the tropics. (1922: 199)

This assessment of the role of the alien, more civilized race—akin to the European but closer to the native—set the blueprint for the model of indirect rule that could find a place for the subject races in a theory of colonial obligation.

Law—The Key to Institutionalizing the Episteme

For Mamdani, the link between the episteme and its institutionalization is law. It is the endowment of these epistemic categories with juridical force, through institutions, that shapes both rule and the revolt. Enforced as legal identities, political calibrations are made about the distribution of hierarchies of rule and subjection, and distribution of material benefits.

The centrality of law and the political identities it has bequeathed a postcolonial present have been put into question by some recent scholarship on political violence in Africa. For example, in his study of youth in the aftermaths of the Liberian and Sierra Leonian civil wars, the anthropologist Danny Hoffman (2011) suggests that the focus on identity in studies of violence in Africa is increasingly misplaced and anachronistic. Hoffman acknowledges that the focus on "culture and the everyday," and on "identity formation," has been useful as forms of critique that challenged primordialist stereotypes in discussions of violence in African conflicts. But after the American 9/11 events, this kind of thinking, he argues, obscures more than it illuminates:

The "tribalism" narratives of Rwanda have been replaced by the Islamization fantasies of the world media and Euro-American governments. That the identities of young people are up for grabs and are constructed by the worlds around them is integral to the logic of anti-Islamic "hearts and minds" campaigns. The United States military's Africa Command is only one of a host of new security apparatuses intent on understanding identity formation as a form of military intelligence. An anthropology too wedded to the language of belonging, autochthony, and ethnicity risks reproducing a very conservative mode of identity politics, a politics put to pernicious effects by African elites, transnational business interests, and international security forces. Moreover, work on "African identities" often occludes one of the most important and fascinating aspects of the lives of youth in the postmodern postcolony: an ability to live productively through the fractured, experimental, and decidedly unfixed nature of what it means to be African in the world today. (Hoffman, 2011: xi)

Hoffman turns to a revised genealogy of political economy to put the emphasis on "survival" and modes of work as central to the choices and conditions within which youth are making decisions. This turn allows him to de-exceptionalize the account of agency he wishes to advance, and to situate this violence in a more universal set of predicaments that are not peculiar to Africa: those being the universals of capitalist forms of work and labor. What Hoffman misses, though, in his dismissal of thinking about identity formation in Mamdani's work is twofold. First, Mamdani's account is not simply motivated by a desire to "humanize" the story, as Hoffman puts it. Rather, it is more concerned, I would argue, with a will to historicize political identities.[5] Second, it does not conceive of identity as a straightjacket without an account of agency. Hoffman's approach wants to free identity from a supposedly static overdetermining account of identity by recognizing in Africa "an ability to live productively through the fractured, experimental, and decidedly unfixed nature of what it means to be African in the word today" (Hoffman, 2011: xv). In my view, there is a troubling aspect in this way of thinking about agency. In a different context, the "house negro" could, as Malcolm X might say, be fulfilled serving the master—a version of what Plato would call the happy slave. But does that make the institutional context of plantation slavery less important to think about, than the violently structuring predicament that shapes the happy slave's agency in the first place? (Depelchin, 2005).

One would venture to say that even the accounts of "survival" offered by Hoffman as a way in which youth reject "tribalized" accounts of identity in the turn to Islamization, one would have to consider, happens in the context of an impulse to disavow dominant political and historical cultural-political identities. After all, a turn *toward* one path is always a turn *away* from other paths—and what it may be a turn away from is the profoundly political-historical question that cannot dispense with the politics of identity formation. The "unfixed" and fluid nature of identities that scholars like Hoffman tend to valorize cannot be disentangled from the "fixed"; the one is the condition of possibility for the other and they have to be thought in relation to each other. The question remains whether this fluidity that survivalist studies venerate "dares to invent" a new postcolonial freedom in the way that Fanon might have desired. By turning away from the politicization of culture, the politicization of tribe, territory, and indigeneity, this kind of scholarship turns away from the indispensability of the state, of law, and of institutions in the making and remaking of political futures. Not because the state is a priori normatively something we should want to have or preserve or encourage, but because it is the legitimating language of power in our times and, therefore, cannot be a priori disavowed by critical scholarship. Survivalist studies in this kind of anthropology tend to put the novelty of their approach on taking subjectivity seriously. But they do so by delinking subjectivity from subject formation. Why is it that subjectivity can be "fluid" but subject formation—the world of law and institutions— can be rendered as static? The point, analytically, should be to think the two together as an instability that law and order is always seeking to fix and stabilize *in* law as political identity that can be presented or narrated as stable. The notion of ancient histories of stable tribal custom and traditions belonging to a specific territory is, for example, one such attempt to produce an ancient past for the purposes of a present political claim of

---

[5]   For an elaboration of the debate on agency in Mamdani's work, see Mamdani (2019) and Michael Neocosmos (2020).

autochthonous belonging, as described in the important work of the anthropologists Peter Geschiere and Francis Nyamnjoh (1998). It is, therefore, not given but produced within a constellation of historically dynamic forces coming together in a moment; something to be thought of as a conjuncture of "articulations," as Stuart Hall argued (2017). A critical scholarship should, therefore, be interested in how these moments of articulation or fixity come together to produce a hegemonic political identity, which in turn produces both major and minor terms of action, reaction, and resistance in the political field.

As we see in Lugard's articulation of the strategy, it was a deliberate policy that drew on racial conceptions of who was said to have some European blood in them, and was motivated by a political calculation aimed at dividing an opposition to the colonial state. The decision, for example, to co-opt the Coloured population in the Cape evolved along these lines. An attorney general of the Cape in the early 1900s remarked: "I would rather meet the Hottentot at the hustings voting for his representative than meet the Hottentot in the wilds with a gun on his shoulder" (Walker, 1968: 151). Prime Minister Hertzog's policy on voting for the Coloured population in the Cape in the Pact government of 1924 was motivated by his observation that, "It would be very foolish to drive the Coloured people to the enemies of the Europeans—and that will happen if we expel him—to allow him eventually to come to rest in the arms of the native" (Hertzog, 1925: 14, as cited in Paterson, 1957).

This thinking would crystalize most forcefully in the mind of Secretary of Native Affairs, and close ally of Prime Minister Hendrik Verwoerd, the anthropologist Dr. W. M. Eiselen, who explained the vision in 1955: "Briefly and concisely put, our Native policy regarding the Western Province aims at the ultimate elimination of the Natives from this region" (Eiselen, 1955: n.p.). By "natives" he meant, of course, black Africans, who would be defined as belonging to a tribe, and therefore belonging in a homeland elsewhere. In the Cape, a deliberate policy of social engineering designed to co-opt the Coloured population was put in motion through Influx Control laws: the Coloured Labour Preference Area Policy. The policy was systematically implemented over the next few decades. In the first phase, as Dr. Eiselen pointed out, there would be "the removal of foreign Africans and freezing of the number of African families, coupled with the limited importation of single migrant workers to meet the most urgent needs" (Eiselen, 1955: n.p.). In December 1965, Black Labour Regulations were introduced, designed to end long-term contracts for black African laborers in the Cape so that they would not get passes to work in the city (Goldin, 1984). In 1966, an official freeze on building family housing for Africans was declared, with no state housing built for the next ten years thereafter. The new labor law stipulated that, "if an employer wishes to employ an African, he is required to obtain a Coloured labour preference clearance certificate from the Department of Manpower stating that no suitable Coloured person is available to fill the position" (Buchanan and Hurwitz, 1950: 399).

This does not imply that these policies were implemented with the full support of those classified as Coloured, nor without often successful resistance (Haines, 1978; Nolutshungu, 1982; Naidoo, 1988). But, as waves of successive laws forcefully implemented by the state, they fundamentally reshaped, and remapped the demographic and spatial present of the Cape into what was inherited in 1994.

The predicament for Coloured and Indian populations navigating post-apartheid freedom is not dissimilar then to the predicament that subject races like the Fulani, the Omani Arabs or the Tutsi faced across the continent after independence: during colonialism they were the beneficiaries of certain policies designed to co-opt them and prevent a united opposition emerging among the colonized, but they were also victims of colonial segregation and subjugation. Because the colonial state treated some a little better than others, those who were treated a little better tended to internalize their relative superiority. Tutsi nationalists regarded themselves as naturally superior to Hutu (Uvin, 1997). Indians over time tended to think of themselves as better than Africans and Coloureds (Nyar, 2012); while Coloureds considered themselves better than Africans, but not better than whites (Adhikari, 2013). It is a tragic reality that the designs of the colonial state have become accepted as the natural order of things by many, today still.

Writing in the midst of the land reforms in Zimbabwe over a decade ago, Muzondidya (2007: 335) noted:

> Coloureds and Indians [in Zimbabwe] faced an even more complicated situation. Specifically constructed by the state as an alien, urban people without rural ancestral homes (kumusha), they could neither acquire nor settle on land in Native Reserves and all other designated African areas, including Native Purchase Areas and African townships in urban areas.

When land reform finally came around in Zimbabwe, designed to undo the legacy of white settler monopoly on land, these "subject minorities" found themselves ineligible to make land claims. To access that land, one had to belong to an ethnic or tribal authority. Coloureds and Indians had no ethnic identity, since they were defined as a race, and now find themselves betwixt and between. Under colonialism, to have a racial identity was an identity of privilege, while having an ethnic identity condemned one to severe marginalization as a rural subject. After colonialism, in the name of justice, states tended to reverse the order in the name of Africanization and redistributive justice: ethnic subjects are now the most eligible for redress, and racial subjects would be last in the line. This is called "fair discrimination" in our current law (RSA, 2000), and it is on a sound footing from the vantage point of justice. But it might also activate certain political demands, such as changing from the racial identity of being "Coloured" to the ethnic identity of being "Khoi" or "Griqua." This moves one into a different category of eligibility and puts one on a more secure footing if indigeneity is a marker of belonging in the future. No wonder also that some Indians in Kenya and Uganda campaigned to be classified as a tribe; in the case of Kenya, they succeeded in 2018 in becoming recognized as the "forty-fourth" officially recognized tribe in Kenya (Warah, 2018). After the Asian expulsions of 1972 in Uganda, many realized that races continued to be seen as foreign, but ethnicities were seen to be indigenous. To be classified as an ethnicity would, therefore, be to put the right to belong beyond question; a colonial logic reproduced by the postcolonial state, and grounds of activism in its civil society.

The greater social and political challenges lay in reshaping how the descendants come to think about each other and those constituted as "other": the extent to which colonial constructions have come to be embodied and lived in our dispositions toward each other, and our discourses about others. These are amplified by the extent to which market-based inequalities breathe new life into racial and ethnic stereotypes and prejudices. That many can be found in the Coloured areas of the Western Cape who think it natural that there should be a Coloured or Khoi majority in the Cape, reflects perhaps on a post-apartheid education that has not done more to show how the Coloured Labour Preference Act worked to expel Africans from the Cape, and what its intentions were.

An instance of how indirect rule was deployed can be found in the institutionalization in the apartheid-era military of a battalion that came to be known as the South African Cape Corps, a unit specifically designed to co-opt Coloured men. The first formations of this unit date all the way back to 1781, under the name *Corps Bastaard Hottentotten*. It went through various phases of disbandment and reconstitution under different colonial administrations from the Dutch through to the British (De Villiers, 1975). The last incarnation of the unit was disbanded in 1994 when all army battalions were deracialized and integrated into a single national defense force. A prominent role played by one version of the Cape Corps was in the form of 31 Battalion, that was to accompany the notorious white South African counterinsurgency army unit known as 32 Battalion. Here they acted as highly regarded trackers in the "bush wars" on the South African border with Angola, and inside of South Africa-administered South West Africa against the liberation movements seeking to wage armed struggles there and in South Africa. The Coloured Corp members would be deployed in a support function to track guerilla fighters coming across the borders characterized by vast rural semi-desert expanses. In a 2018 *Foreign Policy* magazine article on the politics unfolding around being Coloured, Khoi, and the restitution of land after apartheid, the case of a newly established Khoi Party is described by the journalist Laura Secorum (2018) in which she narrates how these members turned their post-apartheid dilemmas into a political campaign:

> Each self-proclaimed Khoisan leader has a different solution to the land problem. January wants to take the government to court, while another king has chosen to secede and start a new country. Williams is trying to lobby Parliament, but the First Nation Liberation Alliance, a tiny Khoisan political party, is busy setting up a parallel government. Larry Fazel Varrie, one of the party's leaders, says freedom may require violence and claims to have an army at the ready. "South Africa's black colonial government does not represent the Khoisan," he said. "If they won't give us our land back, we are ready to take it by force."
>
> What Varrie calls his "army" is actually a volunteer group of retired Khoisan servicemen. Most members served in the South African Cape Corps—a battalion of coloured soldiers inside the South African Army, which existed intermittently from the late 18th century until the early 1990s. After apartheid ended, coloured soldiers were meant to reintegrate [into] the South African National Defence Force, but most ex-Cape Corps [soldiers] were dismissed during this transition. Jobless and frustrated, a few hundred of these middle-aged veterans formed what

they call the Khoisan Nation Self Defence Unit. Now, some threaten to use their military training to recover their ancestral land.

Similarly, it may be that significant numbers of South Africans of Indian descent may consider themselves as superior to Africans, reflecting a colonial policy of divide and rule, of creating hierarchies among the colonized, and spatially segregating them so that difference enabled their domination. Undoing these logics could draw succor from a history of continuous resistance by those few who mobilized others against attempts by apartheid colonial administrators to design citizenship laws which would seek to co-opt the Coloured and Indian subject races—the 1933 Hertzog Bills; later the 1978 Koornhoff Bills; and later still, against the co-option strategies of the Tricameral Parliament in 1983 (Karis and Gerhart, 1997). Each of these moments of resistance enabled the internal opposition to apartheid to foster new ways of thinking about political identity in inclusive and deracialized ways—such as the ideological articulation of Black unity as the designation of a political rather than a racial identity of shared oppression and discrimination that would include Coloureds, Indians and Africans in a subversive unity (Biko, 1996; Badat, 2009; Magaziner, 2010). So too, the concept of "non-racialism" developed by a major apartheid political tradition enabled the strategic rejection of apartheid attempts to fracture black Africans from subject races (Soske, 2011; Pillay, 2015).

But there is a key difference that many who come from those activist traditions might have to wrestle with in order to find a politics more appropriate to our moment. Under apartheid, resistance movements eventually emphasized sameness over differences—unity as uniformity in the face of diversity as another code for apartheid. Schooled in a tradition of non-racialism as resistance to the categories of difference of apartheid has left many erstwhile activists with a deep anxiety toward acknowledging difference of any kind (Everatt, 2009; Suttner, 2012; Pillay, 2015; Rassool, 2019).[6] The reaction is almost immediate among many to denounce those who wish to see themselves in anything but the race-blindness that a certain variant of non-racialism holds onto, regardless of changing political context (Sosibo, 2014). Or the reaction is to denounce those who draw attention to histories or current manifestations of Coloured or Indian racism toward black Africans (Maharaj, 2014). Whatever the motivations are of those political elites who are naming this problem, these are legacies that might need to be contended with, more so because their effects are not just symbolic but they are also material.

By opening a public debate on the problem, rather than legislating it out of the public discourse, political interventions could emerge that both recognize the legitimate grievances and challenge the stereotypes and the prejudices. As both victims and beneficiaries of apartheid's policies of divide and rule, the predicament of those classified as Coloured or Indian subject races needs to be historically located within a colonial practice and seen as a legacy of the past. Manifestations of Coloured or Indian racism are less the originary causes of a problem than they are consequences of a colonial past. Political interventions may need to attend to making more popular

---

[6]   I discuss this in greater detail in Pillay (2015).

and public how that past has brought the terms of contention to where they are, and how history has been written to produce a past that has shaped how many think about themselves and about others. Colonial history produced an understanding of the past that suited settler logics, that politicized the question of indigeneity, and also politicized cultural difference by attaching land and resources to it.

The African continental experience suggests that political discourse might need both a new concept of justice, and a new concept of difference. A concept of justice that is not simply about reversing the logic of colonialism but *refusing* the logic of colonialism. Returning to the fate of subject races—it is worth underscoring that Mamdani is significantly located within a Fanonian genealogy that itself turns on a Hegelian dialectic: there can be no master without a slave; there can be no Black without white; there can be no native without settler. Fanon diagnosed the native's response as one of violence, because it is the exemplary language of power given to the native by the colonizing settler.

Even if the violence of the settler produces the impulse to counterviolence in the native, it is not an overdetermining relationship; Fanon himself hints that *a different way is possible*. In the last chapter of the *Wretched of the Earth* (1963), Fanon lays out the challenge for the native if decolonization is a break out of the terms inherited from the colonial episteme: the native must dare to invent. A truly decolonized freedom will have to refuse the terms of colonial rule as the form of an anti-colonial revolt. Violence may beget violence, but it need not be so:

> When I search for Man in the technique and the style of Europe, I see only a succession of negations of man, and an avalanche of murders. The human condition, plans for mankind, and collaboration between men in those tasks which increase the sum total of humanity are new problems, which demand true inventions. Let us decide not to imitate Europe; let us combine our muscles and our brains in a new direction. Let us try to create the whole man, whom Europe has been incapable of bringing to triumphant birth. (Fanon, 1963: 312–13)

Freedom as invention, and the making of new discoveries imply breaking with the reactive logic that the last shall be first, and the first shall be last. And we need a concept of difference that does not use one's past to decide if one belongs and has a political future. One that allows an embrace of the multiple historical routes through which peoples find themselves in particular settler-colonial societies—as locals, as descendants of slaves, as indentured laborers, as traders, exiles, and refugees or those who came looking to make a better life, and a pan-African concept of difference that remains open to inviting new migrants to becoming citizens as well. The challenge is to dare to invent a future with difference, with economic justice, but without racism.

References

Abdullah, I. (ed.). (2004). *Between Democracy and Terror: The Sierra Leone Civil War*. Dakar: Council for the Development of Social Science Research in Africa (CODESRIA).

Adebajo, A. (2007). *Liberia's Civil War: Nigeria, ECOMOG, and Regional Security in West Africa*. Boulder: Lynne Rienner Publishers.

Adhikari, M. (2013). *Burdened by Race: Coloured Identities in Southern Africa*. Cape Town: UCT Press.

Akpan, N. U. (1956). *Epitaph to Indirect Rule: A Discourse of Local Government in Africa*. London: Cassel.

Badat, S. (2009). *Black Man, You Are on Your Own*. Braamfontein: Steve Biko Foundation.

Biko, S. (1996). *I Write what I Like*. Randburg: Ravan Press.

Buchanan, K. and Hurwitz, N. (1950). "The 'Coloured' community in the Union of South Africa." *Geographical Review*, 40(3): 397–414. https://doi.org/10.2307/211217.

Burton, R. F. and Speke, J. H. (1859). "Explorations in Eastern Africa." *Proceedings of the Royal Geographical Society of London*, 3(6): 348–58. https://doi.org/10.2307/1799169.

Chatterjee, P. (1993). *The Nation and its Fragments: Colonial and Postcolonial Histories*. Princeton: Princeton University Press.

Depelchin, J. (2005). *Silences in African History: Between the Syndromes of Discovery and Abolition*. Dar es Salaam: Mkuki Na Nyota Publishers.

De Villiers, J. (1975). "The Pandour Corps at the Cape during the rule of the Dutch East India Company." *Military History Journal*, 3(3). http://samilitaryhistory.org/vol033jv .html.

Dirks, N. B. (2001). *Castes of Mind: Colonialism and the Making of Modern India*. Princeton: Princeton University Press.

Eiselen, W. (1955). "The native in the Western Cape, 1955." *ICS microfilm* M897 (l), item 10.

Everatt, D. (2009). *The Origins of Non-Racialism: White Opposition to Apartheid in the 1950s*. Johannesburg: Wits University Press.

Eyewitness News. (2018). "Police monitoring Siqalo settlement after protest sees road shut." May 2. https://ewn.co.za/2019/05/07/police-monitoring-siqalo-settlement-after -protest-sees-road-shut.

Fanon, F. (1963). *The Wretched of the Earth*. New York: Grove Press.

Foucault, M. (1990). *The History of Sexuality: An Introduction*. New York: Vintage Books.

Geschiere, P. and Nyamnjoh, F. (1998). "Witchcraft as an issue in the 'politics of belonging': Democratization and urban migrants' involvement with the home village." *African Studies Review*, 41(3): 69–91. https://doi.org/10.2307/525354.

Goldin, I. (1984). "The coloured labour preference policy: Co-option and contradiction." *mimeo*. https://sas-space.sas.ac.uk/4125/1/Ian_Goldin_-_The_coloured_labour _preference_policy%2C_co-option_and_contradiction.pdf.

Haines, J. (1978). "The opposition to general J.B.M. Hertzog's Segregation Bills, 1925– 1936: A study in extra-parliamentary protest," Unpublished MA thesis, University of Natal.

Hall, S. (2017). *Gramsci and Us*. Verso Press Blog. https://www.versobooks.com/blogs /2448-stuart-hall-gramsci-and-us.

Hoffman, D. (2011). *The War Machines: Young Men and Violence in Sierra Leone and Liberia*. Durham: Duke University Press.

Karis, T. and Gerhart, G. M. (1997). *From Protest to Challenge: A Documentary History of African Politics in South Africa, 1882–1990. Vol. 5: Nadir and Resurgence, 1964–1979*. Bloomington: Indiana University Press.

Lugard, F. (1922). *The Dual Mandate in British Tropical Africa*. Edinburgh: W. Blackwood and Sons.

Magaziner, D. R. (2010). *The Law and the Prophets: Black Consciousness in South Africa, 1968–1977*. Athens: Ohio University Press.

Maharaj, B. (2014). "Hambakhaya! Hambauyee Bombay! (Go home! Go to Bombay!): Challenges facing South African Indians in the post-apartheid era," in O. P. Dwivedi (ed.), *Tracing the New Indian Diaspora*. Leiden: Brill. https://doi.org/10.1163/9789401211710_003.

Mamdani, M. (2001). "Beyond settler and native as political identities: Overcoming the political legacy of colonialism." *Comparative Studies in Society and History*, 43(4): 651–64.

Mamdani, M. (2013). *Define and Rule: Native as Political Identity*. Johannesburg: Wits University Press.

Mamdani, M. (2019). "Place, interest and political agency: Some questions for Michael Neocosmos." *Social Dynamics*, 45(3): 442–54. https://doi.org/10.1080/02533952.2019.1690755.

Mkhize, M. (2021). "Phoenix residents tell SAHRC hearing of racial tension, abuse during July unrest." *Times Live*, November 17. https://www.timeslive.co.za/news/south-africa/2021-11-17-phoenix-residents-tell-sahrc-hearing-of-racial-tension-abuse-during-july-unrest/.

Moran, M. H. (2013). *Liberia: The Violence of Democracy*. Philadelphia: University of Pennsylvania Press.

Muzondidya, J. (2007). "Jambanja: Ideological ambiguities in the politics of land and resource ownership in Zimbabwe." *Journal of Southern African Studies*, 33(2): 325–41. http://www.jstor.org/stable/25065199.

Naidoo, K. (1988). "Internal resistance in South Africa: The political movements," in S. Johnson (ed.), *South Africa: No Turning Back*. London: Palgrave Macmillan. https://doi.org/10.1007/978-1-349-19499-5.

Neocosmos, M. (2020). "The academic intellectual as knowing subject and the reason of the excluded: A response to Mahmood Mamdani." *Social Dynamics*, 46(1): 164–78. https://doi.org/10.1080/02533952.2020.1749434.

Nolutshungu, S. C. (1982). *Changing South Africa: Political Considerations*. Manchester: Manchester University Press; New York: Africana Publishing Company.

Nyar, A. (2012). "Some new perspectives on South African Indians and 'non-racialism': Findings from the AKF non-racialism focus group data." *Politikon*, 39(1): 89–112.

Paterson, S. (1957). *Colour and Culture in South Africa: A Study of the Status of the Cape Coloured People within the Social Structure of the Union if South Africa*. London: Routledge & Kegan Paul.

Pillay, S. (2015). "Why I am no longer a non-racialist: Identity and difference," in X. Mangcu (ed.), *The Colour of our Future: Does Race Matter in Post-Apartheid South Africa?* Johannesburg: Wits University Press, pp. 133–52.

Rassool, C. (2019). "The politics of non-racialism in South Africa." *Public Culture*, 31(2): 343–71. https://doi.org/10.1215/08992363-7286861.

Republic of South Africa (RSA). (2000). "Promotion of equality and prevention of unfair discrimination act, no 4 of 2000," Department of Justice. https://www.justice.gov.za/legislation/acts/2000-004.pdf.

Sanders, E. R. (1969). "The Hamitic hypothesis: Its origin and functions in time perspective." *The Journal of African History*, 10(4): 521–32. http://www.jstor.org/stable/179896.

Secorum, L. (2018). "South Africa's first nations are being forgotten." *Foreign Affairs*, June. https://foreignpolicy.com/2018/10/19/south-africas-first-nations-have-been-forgotten-apartheid-khoisan-indigenous-rights-land-reform/.

Silverstein, B. (2019). *Governing Natives: Indirect Rule and Settler Colonialism in Australia's North*. Manchester: Manchester University Press.

Skinner, Q. (2002). "The context of Hobbes's theory of political obligation," in Q. Skinner (ed.), *Visions of Politics*. Cambridge: Cambridge University Press, pp. 264–86. https://doi.org/10.1017/CBO9780511613784.012.

Sosibo, K. (2014). "Anti-Indian lyrics sow seeds of hatred." *Mail and Guardian*. https://mg.co.za/article/2014-08-21-anti-indian-lyrics-sow-seeds-of-hatred/.

Soske, J. (2011). "Review of: *The Origins of Non-Racialism: White Opposition to Apartheid in the 1950s*, by David Everatt, Johannesburg: Wits University Press, 2009." *Transformation: Critical Perspectives on Southern Africa*, 76: 150–5. https://doi.org/10.1353/trn.2011.0026.

Suttner, R. (2012). "Understanding non-racialism as an emancipatory concept in South Africa." *Theoria: A Journal of Social and Political Theory*, 59(130): 22–41. http://www.jstor.org/stable/42705231.

Uvin, P. (1997). "Prejudice, crisis, and genocide in Rwanda." *African Studies Review*, 40(2): 91–115. https://doi.org/10.2307/525158.

Walker, E. (1968). *A History of South Africa*. London: Longman.

Warah, R. (2018). "The 44th tribe, the Asian question and the politics of exclusion." *The Elephant*, March 5. https://www.theelephant.info/features/2018/03/05/the-44th-tribe-the-asian-question-and-the-politics-of-exclusion/.

11

The Legacy of Bandung

Partha Chatterjee

Introduction

In 1996, Mahmood Mamdani had demonstrated with consummate analytical elegance the general form of political power in colonial Africa—a bifurcated state consisting of a racialized civil society in the cities and a traditionalized rural society ruled by customary native authorities. *Citizen and Subject* ended by showing how mainstream nationalism, pursuing the politics of deracialization at home and anti-imperialism abroad, successfully ended racial segregation in civil society without, however, democratizing the tribal order in the countryside (Mamdani, 1996). More recently, participating in a symposium on Siba Grovogui's *Beyond Eurocentrism and Anarchy*, Mamdani has observed how the struggle against colonialism and racism has now been superseded by a new international doctrine that imposes on nation-states the "responsibility to protect" the rights of individuals (Mamdani, 2016). Reviewing the history of the African university, he has also observed how the first wave of Africanization was followed by the more recent spell of institutional reform which has pitted the supposedly universalist standard of excellence against local and contextual concerns of relevance (Mamdani, 2015).

In this chapter, I revisit some of these questions by looking at the emergence of the contemporary international order from the standpoint of the peoples of Asia and Africa. A key event in my story is the 1955 Bandung Conference of Afro-Asian nations.

It has been alleged recently that just as the Treaty of Westphalia was reinterpreted in the nineteenth century as the mythical source of a law of nations based on state sovereignty, so is the Bandung Conference being recreated now by a group of postcolonial scholars as the mythical foundation of global anti-imperialist politics. Both sides of this analogy are vastly overstated. While the nineteenth century was doubtless an important period when positive international law based on the formal acts of sovereign states was compiled in standard and widely accessible scholarly volumes, it is not true that the significance of Westphalia in the emergence of state sovereignty was not noticed earlier. Emerich de Vattel's work, composed in the middle of the eighteenth century and enjoying general acceptance well into the nineteenth, could be said to have explicitly formalized a set of practices that were acknowledged as having been largely inaugurated at Westphalia (De Vattel, 1916). As for Bandung, its significance lies, as I argue later, in the explicit assertion that state sovereignty everywhere must be legitimately based in the will of the people and that the sovereignty of every state must be recognized as formally equal. These were goals that were set before the peoples of the world. Those goals are yet to be achieved. Hence, our invocation of Bandung today is not the regurgitation of a mythical story but the declaration of a contemporary set of demands of global politics.

To understand the point, we need to think a little more about what the leaders at Bandung were fighting against.

The Law of Nations in the East

The practices of modern empire in the nineteenth century emerged within a new conceptual frame developed by Jeremy Bentham and the utilitarians who proposed that governments everywhere, in every part of the world, could be compared and ranked according to a common set of measures (see Chatterjee, 2012). Hence, certain universal norms could be fixed against which each country could be measured and its deviation from the norm identified. Suitable policies could then be devised for bringing the governments of those countries closer to the universally desirable norm. Empire thus came to be thought of as a new educational project of normalization, that is, disciplining. The techniques ranged between two types—a *pedagogy of violence* and a *pedagogy of culture*. While culture increasingly became the preferred method, including legal reform, reform of social and economic institutions and the spread of Western-style education, it was asserted at the same time that the proper conditions for cultural pedagogy may often have to be ensured by the use of imperial force. The history of imperialism since the nineteenth century is fundamentally characterized by debates over the degree, sequence, combination, and points of application of the pedagogical techniques of violence and culture.

The normative considerations involved questions of both morality and law. Occupying a central place in these debates over imperial policy was the concept of sovereignty. In each case where the issue came up of whether or how much to intervene, the application of moral as well as legal norms required a determination of the existence and quality of sovereignty. The striking fact, even though largely unacknowledged until quite recently, is that the evolving practices of imperial power in the Americas, Asia, and Africa had a profound effect in shaping the so-called law of nations and defining the place within it of the modern sovereign nation-state.

Looking at the debates that took place in the sixteenth and seventeenth centuries about the moral and legal propriety of the European conquest of the Americas and those in the eighteenth century about the British territorial acquisitions in India, one notices a significant shift in the discursive conditions. The debates between the scholastics and the humanists over the legitimacy of the early conquests of America were framed within Roman law concepts such as *dominium* and *imperium* (Armitage, 2000; Pagden, 2000). By the time of the acquisition of territory in India in the eighteenth century, the dominant philosophical framework was that of natural law: the legal arguments were now those of Grotius, while the moral-political arguments tended to come largely out of Montesquieu (Tuck, 1999). In the nineteenth century, alongside the emergence of utilitarian reasoning in political affairs, the legal domain was marked by the rise of positivism, of which John Austin was the foremost proponent, his ideas becoming posthumously influential in the latter half of the century.

The shift from natural law to legal positivism was marked by the devaluing of universal natural law assumptions, which were taken to be principles of morality rather than of law, and an emphasis on the empirical evidence of legal acts executed by sovereign state authorities. In domestic society, only the positive law made by a sovereign state could qualify as proper law. In the field of international law, this definition raised a problem, voiced by Austin himself: in the absence of a globally sovereign state, there could not be, properly speaking, any international *law*. However, this fundamentalist objection was circumvented by the argument that the body of extant international law consisted of specific acts, such as treaties, conventions, and agreements entered into by sovereign states.

But who were these sovereign states whose legal transactions with other sovereign states could produce a body of positive international law? The argument was made that the mutual treaties and agreements between these sovereign states were based on certain shared premises and had, over the years, produced a set of mutually recognized and accepted principles of international transaction. In other words, what might be otherwise called customary had been actually incorporated into a body of positive international law because, in fact, those sovereign states constituted an international society, or perhaps a "family" of nations.

In his landmark study on the subject, C. H. Alexandrowicz has argued that before the nineteenth century, legal relations between European powers and states in India and Southeast Asia existed "on a footing of equality" (Alexandrowicz, 1967). The former acknowledged the sovereignty of the latter and even adopted, or at least tried to fit into, the legal practices that prevailed in interstate relations in the region. The Europeans were aware that there were different classes of sovereigns in the East, ranging from suzerains, such as the Emperor of China or the Mughal Emperor, to minor sovereigns who were otherwise vassals of a suzerain, to vassals on the borderline of sovereignty and non-sovereign feudal status. Some of the treaties between Europeans and Indian rulers were declared to be transactions between sovereigns, even when they were only concluded between their local representatives, such as, for instance, the treaty of 1547 between the kings of Portugal and Vijayanagara. Even when Indian rulers effectively surrendered territory to the East India Company in the eighteenth century, as in Bengal or the Carnatic, or in the Maratha territories, they did so as sovereign powers through treaties. The situation changed drastically in the nineteenth century when, with the adoption of legal positivism in place of natural law theories, the sovereign status of Eastern rulers came to be doubted and the family of nations comprising the proper subjects of international law restricted only to the countries of Europe and the new republics of the Americas. Paradoxically, therefore, as Alexandrowicz points out, the domain of the law of nations in the nineteenth century "shrank to regional dimensions though it still carried the label of universality" (Alexandrowicz, 1967: 2).

While this argument might seem persuasive from a legal point of view, the change in legal regimes makes better sense if one places it within the changing political context of relations between European powers and Eastern rulers in the nineteenth century. The world in the nineteenth century as seen from Europe was quite different from the way it looked in the eighteenth. The attraction of Asian, and later African, territories as sources of raw material for European industry, land for European commercial agriculture and markets for European industrial manufactures had become overwhelming.

Added to this was the expansion through the nineteenth century of the balance of power system of Europe to include within its scope the territories of virtually the entire globe. The classical balance of power system had developed a mechanism, through territorial transfers and shifting alliances, to prevent the emergence of a single dominant power or coalition in Europe. Thus, the relative strengths of the core players of the system—Britain, France, Austria, Russia, and Holland (replaced by Prussia after 1815)—were frequently adjusted by territorial acquisitions at the expense of minor powers (the partitions of Poland in the late eighteenth century being the most notorious example) and, in the case of the maritime powers, by overseas territories. Overseas territories, in fact, became the chief means for maintaining the European balance in the nineteenth century, reaching egregious limits in the partition of Africa at the Berlin Colonial Conference of 1884–5 (Chatterjee, 1975;[1] Poulose, 1976). Further, with the rising tide of democratic and nationalist movements in Central and Eastern Europe, resonating with the threatening revolutionary rhetoric of the natural rights of peoples and nations to self-government, the discursive shift in the legal domain from natural law to positivism made good conservative sense. This was the political background to the changing significance of the law of nations in the nineteenth century. The European powers became the only proper subjects of the purportedly universal law of nations because the entire globe was now properly the object of European power.

The effect of this change on the Indian subcontinent becomes dramatically clear from a chart prepared by Michael Fisher showing the annexation of territory by the East India Company (Fisher, 1993; Chatterjee, 1995). Until 1799, the bulk of the territory effectively held by the company, mostly in Bengal and the Carnatic, was not quite annexed since de jure sovereignty still lay with various Indian rulers. With Wellesley's term as governor-general began a new aggressive policy, not always endorsed by the British government or the company's directors in London, of annexing Indian territory. From 1799 to 1806, the company annexed in Mysore, Awadh, and the Maratha country some 135,000 square miles of land—the size, Fisher points out, of reunited Germany today. Indeed, during Wellesley's period in office, the company annexed some 30,000 square miles of territory every year (Fisher, 1993: 18). Annexations continued through the early nineteenth century. Lord Hastings, governor-general from 1813 to 1823, proclaimed the legal doctrine of paramountcy by which the authority of the company as the paramount power superseded that of all Indian rulers and bestowed on it the right to annex their territories if, in its view, there were sufficient grounds to do so.

From the 1830s, however, despite acknowledging the material benefits of territorial expansion in the form of increased revenue and commerce, the principal justification for annexation became the plea that the people living under various Indian rulers

---

[1] I have discussed the transformation of the classical balance of power system in an early work (see Chatterjee, 1975: 75).

needed to be protected from misgovernment. The consideration that the people wanted and deserved better government, it would be asserted, could trump all prior legal provisions of treaties and override the objections of the rulers whose presumed rights of sovereignty had been superseded by the paramount power assumed by the British. Two influential bodies of opinion in Britain led this new campaign—radical Benthamite reformers who demanded better government for the welfare of the people and Evangelicals keen to extend their successful anti-slavery movement to an effort to Christianize and civilize India.

It is here that the history of European territorial acquisitions in Asia, and later in the nineteenth century, Africa, would pose conceptual problems for the law of nations. Even though in the course of their imperial advance, European powers such as Britain had entered into various treaties and agreements with Oriental rulers and chieftains, were the latter really to be regarded as sovereign entities? To admit this would be to acknowledge that the family of sovereign nations that was the source of international law included such non-European members. On the other hand, to deny them any sovereign authority would imply that the treaties they had entered into with European powers had no legal standing. The problem dogged imperial policy in India in the nineteenth century.

The solution was devised, once again, by reference to the new comparative scheme of normalization of governmental attributes. It allowed European jurists to make a basic distinction between civilized and uncivilized nations. By virtue of this distinction, the family of nations that constituted the proper subject of international law could be restricted to only the civilized nations of Europe and the white settler nations of the Americas. John Westlake, the doyen of British scholarship on international law in the nineteenth century, defined this "society of states" as the Europe that was born in classical Greece and Rome, consolidated at Westphalia, and which now included European and American states plus "a few Christian nations such as the Hawaiian Islands, Liberia and the Orange Free State" (Westlake, 1894: 81).

As for the uncivilized peoples of the rest of the world, some had no state formations or legal regimes at all, while others had rulers who were arbitrary and whose laws were shaped by religions and cultures that did not value the underlying principles that had produced the law of civilized nations. The uncivilized nations could not be regarded as proper subjects of international law. Westlake, writing at the end of the nineteenth century, was clear on this point. Sovereignty was a purely European concept and a native chief in Africa could not be said to have transferred something of which he had no concept. "International law has to treat natives as uncivilized. It regulates, for the mutual benefit of the civilized states, the claims which they make to sovereignty over the region and leaves the treatment of the natives to the conscience of the state to which sovereignty is awarded" (Westlake, 1894: 143). By the nineteenth century, then, the proper subjects of international law had become restricted to the "civilized nations": it was for *their* mutual benefit that international law was supposed to regulate the transactions between nations.

Was this then a shift that had been brought about by a discursive change from universalist natural law doctrines to legal positivism? Martti Koskenniemi, who does not give much credence to the theory of change in legal regimes, argues that appeals to universalist values did not disappear in the nineteenth century. Nor indeed was the universalist humanism of the natural law doctrines of Grotius and Vattel "a secular variant of the Christian view of a single god," an impediment to excluding the non-European subject by emphasizing its radical difference according to some purely European standard (Koskenniemi, 2001: 131). Even when non-European nations were regarded as capable of engaging in acts of sovereignty, the proper subjects of the law of nations were always the European states. If there was a change in the discursive practices of law, it took place entirely *within* a purely European discourse (Liu, 2004: 70–139).[2]

But the distinction between civilized and uncivilized nations still left unanswered the question of whether the treaties entered into by the former with the latter were legally valid. One response was to resort to the flexibility afforded by the normalized scheme of comparison between nations and suggest that there were different degrees of sovereign-ness among uncivilized states. These degrees translated into different kinds of treaties between European and non-European states, ranging from trade agreements to cession of territory. Each of these transactions implied a certain degree of capacity by the uncivilized state to engage in international transactions. The acquisition of territory by European powers could take place by cession of territory by treaty, or by annexation, or by conquest. There would also emerge in the nineteenth century the concept of the protectorate by which a backward state would, through its legal consent, be brought under the control of an imperial power without the latter taking on the burden of administration. Imperial practices in Asia, and later, Africa, thus imparted the quality of variation and complexity to the positivist concept of state sovereignty. This enabled, for instance, in 1856, the inclusion of Ottoman Turkey in an international peace conference, and later in the century the recognition of Japan, Siam, Persia, and China as occasional members of the "family" of sovereign nations. Not only that, these imperial practices brought out the conceptual obverse of the idea of sovereignty: it was necessary for an entity, that is, an uncivilized nation, to first possess sovereignty precisely in order to be able to give it up through a valid legal agreement with a civilized European power. Lassa Oppenheim, writing his canonical text in the early twentieth century, revealed some bewilderment when he observed: "cession of territory made to a member of the family of nations by a State as yet outside that family is real cession and a concern of the Law of Nations, since such State becomes through the treaty of cession in some respects a member of that family" (1912: 86).[3] Antony Anghie (2005: 105) correctly concludes: "the development of the idea of sovereignty in relation to the non-European world occurs in terms of dispossession, its ability to alienate its lands and rights."

---

[2] For an interesting discussion on the ambiguities of international law in the context of Imperial China in the nineteenth century, see Liu (2004:70–139).

[3] In the eighth edition of the book, edited by Hersch Lauterpacht, the passage was changed to "cession of territory made to an independent State by a State not yet recognised as such is... a real cession and a concern of the Law of Nations, since such State becomes through the treaty of cession in some respects a State enjoying a certain position in international law." Clearly, in the age of the United Nations, the idea of some states being excluded from "the family of nations" was no longer legitimate (Oppenheim, 1955: 547–8; Briggs and Lauterpacht, 1960).

Further, these earlier treaties could not be discarded all of a sudden, not because of any consideration for the sensibilities of Oriental or African rulers but because of the restraint of legal practice they placed on mutual relations *between* the European powers. To allow the validity of these treaties to lapse would introduce a dangerous instability into the relations and practices that had been established among the various European powers themselves in Asia and Africa. Anghie (2005: 71) notes: "It was precisely the fear of disputes over title to colonial territories among European powers that inspired the Conference of Berlin in 1884–1885. Consequently, the non-European world had to be located in the positivist system, not merely for purposes of control and suppression, but to prevent its ambiguous status from undermining European solidarity." Not surprisingly, this feature once more confirmed the virtually exclusive centrality of the European powers to the "family of nations" that made international law in the nineteenth century.

By the middle of the nineteenth century, the legal concept of the protectorate had emerged so that "one state could acquire complete control over another . . . without necessarily assuming the burden of its administration . . . it was this feature of the protectorate which favoured its extensive adoption by European Powers in the spread of their dominion" (Lindley, 1926: 182). But although control of internal affairs was left to the native ruler, that function could be taken over by the protecting power either because of a provision in the treaty or because the native ruler was incapable of providing good government. The grounds for such intervention were, however, left vague and undefined, affording the paramount power a considerable range of strategic flexibility in framing its policies toward the so-called protected states. Even within the ostensibly positivist framework defined by the concept of undivided sovereignty, the law of nations in the East had to proceed by keeping sovereignty flexible and undefined, and thus subject to policy rather than fixed legal principle. Lauren Benton calls this "quasi-sovereignty" and recognizes it as a pervasive feature of colonial empires (Benton, 2010: 222–78; see also Benton, 2009, 2014; Ross, 2010; Cagle, 2011; Peters, 2011; Williams, 2011; Ogborn, 2012; Purcell, 2012; Nordman, 2013).

The history of European imperialism in Asia and Africa thus reveals a general feature of the history of international law itself. It would be said in the latter half of the twentieth century that with the rivalry between the two superpowers, the United States and the Soviet Union, in extending their control and dominance over every part of the globe, the field of international law was taken over by policy in place of law: the so-called diplomatic school which preferred flexible principles and case-by-case negotiated settlements won over the legal school which demanded firm principles of law and permanent international institutions of adjudication. The superpowers began to use the language of law to justify their political acts of foreign policy (see Koskenniemi, 2001: 413–509). A deeply committed universalist liberal jurist, Koskenniemi (2001) argues that international law was dead by the 1960s (see also Mullerson, 2002; Simpson and Koskenniemi, 2002; Carty, 2003; Emberland, 2003; Hueck, 2003; Mettraux, 2003; Neff, 2003; Topulos and Johnston, 2003; Tsagourias, 2003; Simons, 2006).

The history of the law of nations in the Indian subcontinent in the nineteenth century almost exactly prefigures the history of international law in the second half of the twentieth century. Until the eighteenth century, relations between the European powers and Oriental states appear to have largely conformed to the restraints imposed by the concept of sovereignty enshrined in Europe since the Peace of Westphalia in 1648 and theorized in the eighteenth century by Vattel. This was because the European presence in India was either distinctly inferior in terms of power compared to the Indian states or because, as in the eighteenth century, they dealt with the Indian states within a certain balance of power framework. The law of nations as developed in Europe was quite reasonably suited to such a framework. By the early nineteenth century, the British power began to be projected in India as a hegemonic power. Other powers, whether European or Indian, were no longer serious competitors in the region. There was no reason left to abide by the constraints imposed by a law of nations designed to maintain the balance of power. Law was now mobilized to further the policy objectives of the paramount power.

Indeed, our discussion of the legal and policy debates over British relations with the Indian states in the nineteenth century, and our survey of the technical instruments they produced for a dominant power to exercise control over other putatively sovereign entities, allows us to offer a general definition of modern empire that covers most examples of imperial power in the world in the last two centuries. *The imperial prerogative*, we could say, *lies in the claim to declare the colonial exception*. It is, of course, a claim whose effectiveness and legitimacy were open to negotiation. In the nineteenth century, the principal site where such claims were negotiated, and sometimes challenged, was that of the so-called family of civilized nations, mainly consisting of the major European powers. In a related sense, the claim also had to be negotiated with domestic political formations in the imperial countries. Only in a peripheral and utterly subsidiary sense were they negotiated with the people of subordinated states. Besides, the privilege of declaring the colonial exception here applies to relations between a sovereign power and other political entities whose sovereignty has to be recognized even if only for them to surrender that sovereignty, whether wholly or partially. There are, of course, a variety of techniques that are developed, but all involve a determination that the universal principles that apply to relations between sovereign states cannot apply in this exceptional case because, for one reason or another, the entity does not deserve the full status of, or has lost its legitimacy as, a proper sovereign state. This is the definition of modern empire that emerges from its history over the last two hundred years.

In the nineteenth century, therefore, "empire's law" was made to replace the law of nations in the Indian subcontinent, as indeed in other parts of the colonial world. Carl Schmitt, who railed against the supersession after the Second World War of the public international law of Europe by the claims of both the United States and the Soviet Union to wage war on behalf of humanity, would not have flinched if he heard our account, since he did not believe that the Indian states were ever the proper subjects of the law of nations. It was legitimate and rational, he would have said, for the stability of the European states system that Britain should bring under its domain the control of that part of the world. But in order not to succumb to nationalist sentiments of outrage or nostalgia, we should also remind ourselves that the effective erasure in the nineteenth century, under British imperial auspices, of the law of nations from the territorial space of the Indian subcontinent was an essential step for the imagining of undivided national sovereignty in the twentieth century. Indeed, the second half of the nineteenth century was when, as Manu Goswami (2004: xi, 401) has shown, the territory of subcontinental India, *including* the princely states, now effectively consolidated under British paramountcy, began to be geographically imagined as a national space, with a map, with borders, and with physical and human resources that could be claimed for economic and political assertion by an Indian nation (see also Bhattacharya, 2005; Prakash, 2005). When in 1947, Vallabhbhai Patel, the home minister of newly independent India, proceeded to cajole and sometimes coerce the hundreds of Indian princes, hitherto under the "protection" of the British, to integrate their territories with those of the Indian state through treaties of accession, his acts were, from the formal point of view of the law of nations, no less imperialist (see Menon, 1956; Rushbrook-Williams, 1957). But such, invariably, is the tangled story of the sovereignty of most modern nations on earth.

The Normalization of the Nation-State

In the years following the First World War, however, a crucial restructuring took place in the international order. A wide spectrum of opinion now came to accept the nation-state as the universally normal and legitimate form of the modern state. This was indicated by the espousal of the right of self-determination of nations by two leaders holding entirely opposed ideological views on most things. Both Woodrow Wilson and Vladimir Ilyich Lenin argued from their own political forums that this was a right that legitimately belonged to all peoples that had formed themselves as nations. Wilson, of course, was thinking of the nationalities that had been part of the Austrian and Ottoman Empires, and believed that the so-called backward peoples of Asian and African colonies still needed to go through a period of tutelage under Western supervision. But he played a leading role in incorporating these ideas into the structure of the League of Nations. Recent historians have argued that "self-determination" became a slogan in the early decades of the twentieth century to justify the creation of new nation-states in Eastern Europe while providing a seemingly democratic ground for continued European domination over colonized people in Asia and Africa. Timothy Mitchell (2011: 66–85) has shown how the idea of "self-determination" emerged, especially in the writings of the liberal J. A. Hobson and the soldier-administrator Jan Smuts, as a sophisticated justification of continued rule by white settlers in South Africa. This was an idea that was generalized in the Mandates regime of the League of Nations. But the very fact that such a slogan had become necessary suggests the degree to which the idea of self-governing nation-states had acquired widespread legitimacy.

There are two dimensions along which the nation-state came to be normalized in the era of the League. One was that of sovereignty. There was a general presumption that the locus of sovereignty everywhere in the modern world was the nation-state. Among the members of the League were countries such as Albania, Bulgaria, Czechoslovakia, and Hungary, which were until recently parts of the Ottoman and Austrian Empires, and Ireland, which was a British colony until the Irish Free State was created in 1922. There were League members such as Canada, Australia, New Zealand,

and South Africa, which were within the British dominions, and India which was still a British colony. Thus, despite the fact that their sovereign status was ambiguous, they qualified as members because they were seen to be actual or potential nation-states.

Most interesting was the status of the so-called mandated territories. These were the Arab provinces of the Ottoman Empire and the former colonial possessions surrendered by Germany. These territories were mandated to individual member-states, under the supervision of a Permanent Mandates Commission, in order to facilitate their transition to self-governing states. Article 22 of the League Covenant noted that these territories were "inhabited by peoples not yet able to stand by themselves under the strenuous conditions of the modern world" and declared that "the tutelage of such peoples should be entrusted to advanced nations who, by reason of their resources, their experience or their geographical position, can best undertake this responsibility . . . as Mandatories on behalf of the League."[4] It was the old liberal colonial project now brought under the management of an international organization and hence subjected to a single juridical order that classified different types of mandates according to degrees of social development.

Who had sovereignty over the mandated territories? Not the mandatory powers because they were only given the task of administering the territories. Rather, sovereignty was, as it were, held in abeyance until such time that the people of the territory acquired the capability to govern themselves. Until then, sovereignty remained latent in the potential nation-state (see Anghie, 2005: 147–9). The goal of independent national sovereignty was explicitly declared for the so-called A Mandates, that is, the British mandates of Palestine and Mesopotamia (which, in fact, became the independent Republic of Iraq in 1932) and the French mandate of Syria (including Lebanon), while self-government was left ambiguous for the B and C mandates, that is, the former German colonies of Africa and the Pacific, because the mandatory powers, namely, South Africa, Australia, and New Zealand (which wanted to annex those territories), refused to accept ultimate independence as the objective of their mandates. The recognition by the League of Nations of national sovereignty as the goal of what was in effect colonial trusteeship was a major step in the global normalization of the nation-state. What the mandatory powers were asked to do was nothing less than *create* the conditions of sovereignty that would turn the mandated territories into normal nation-states. Not only that, by grading the mandates into A, B, and C types according to the level of social development, the League suggested, as Antony Anghie has pointed out, "that sovereignty existed in something like a linear continuum, and that every society could be placed at some point in the continuum, based on its approximation to the ideal of the European nation-state . . . the Mandate System . . . acquired the form of a fantastic universalizing apparatus that, when applied to any mandated territory . . . would be directed to the same ideal of self-government and, in some cases, transformed sufficiently to ensure the emergence of a sovereign state" (2005: 148).

Besides sovereignty, the other dimension along which the national form of the state was normalized was that of governmental practice. Here the Permanent Mandates

---

[4]   Covenant of the League of Nations, Article 22, paras 1–2 (US Dept of State, 1919).

Commission tried to initiate a major effort to devise, by using comparative empirical methods, a general administrative science that could help in framing suitable governmental policies according to the level of social and economic development of a people. The classification of mandates acknowledged the qualitative difference between the social formations of Mesopotamia, Syria, Lebanon, and Palestine, governed for centuries within a sophisticated bureaucratic empire, and the predominantly tribal African societies of Cameroon, Togoland, Ruanda-Urundi, and Tanganyika and, even more so, the "primitive" societies of New Guinea or Samoa. But by organizing the production of massive sets of standardized information on the economic and social institutions of the mandated populations, the League brought them within a single comprehensive conceptual scheme in which they could all be described comparatively as having different degrees of "state-ness." Indeed, the production and classification of information and the devising of manuals of administration for the mandated territories suggest the image of a great Benthamite legislative factory devising "the best possible laws" for the peoples of the world, according to the particular abilities and needs of each but all tending toward the same universally desirable norm.

The standardization of governmental procedures across the world was also greatly accelerated in the League era by the new international organizations it created, namely, the International Labour Organization, the Health Organization, and the Commission for Refugees. With varying degrees of effectiveness, these bodies tried to put in place governmental technologies of caring for the basic needs of safety, health, and habitation of populations in all member countries and making it the normal responsibility of modern states. By doing this, it inaugurated a major process of international supervision of standard governmental practices across the world—something that would become a feature of biopolitical practices in the late twentieth century. In addition, by creating the Permanent Court of International Justice, the League also introduced the first institutional step in erecting a judicial framework for the legal monitoring of the activities of sovereign nation-states.

Much has been said of the ineffectiveness, and indeed the failure, of most of these efforts of the League of Nations. But it is important to grasp the significance of the changes that were brought about by the League system in the very structure of the international order. Until the First World War, the international system effectively meant only the major powers of Europe and, by extension, the European settler colonies of the Americas. Only those countries were members of the so-called family of nations, both in diplomacy as well as in international law. This changed with the League system. Although the colonial possessions of Britain, France, Holland, Belgium, and Portugal remained intact, the space of the international order was significantly expanded to include the nations formerly within the Austro-Hungarian and Ottoman Empires and declared as potential nation-states those that still colonies. Even more significant was the technical apparatus that was created, through international agencies, information systems, and administrative practices, for the normalized regulation of all nation-states everywhere. As Susan Pedersen (2015) has shown in her magisterial study of the mandates system, many of the consequences of these institutional innovations were not what their architects had intended, because they were far more interested in the continuation of imperial control. But the very internationalization of the imperial project undermined its legitimacy (see also: McKenzie, 2016; Riemens, 2016; Yearwood, 2016; Goldstein, 2017; Palen, 2017; Payk, 2017; Janik, 2018; Marcus, 2018). Further, despite the shortcomings in realizing their goals, the normative strength of the technical practices introduced by the League was shown by the fact that most of them were taken up once more after the Second World War under the rubric of the United Nations. This time, the formal end of colonial rule and the actual universalization of the nation-state form were near at hand. The anti-imperial struggles had by then scored major victories in many parts of the colonial world. A new world order grounded on the universal principle of non-interference in national sovereignty was about to be founded.

Through the middle decades of the twentieth century, there were, of course, scattered proposals aimed at avoiding the logic of national self-determination and popular sovereignty. These proposals were made by unrepentant imperialists as well as by anxious liberals among the colonized people terrified by the prospect of aggressive majorities riding roughshod over the privileges of the propertied and the rights of minorities. Liberal politicians in West Africa, the Caribbean, and India, for instance, were keen to slow down the process of transfer of power from the British and the French, provide constitutional safeguards for property and minority rights, and delay the inauguration of universal suffrage. Particularly interesting was an elaborate proposal by the Aga Khan at the end of the First World War to create a South Asiatic Federation extending from Aden, Mesopotamia, and the shores of the Persian Gulf to India, Burma, and Ceylon all the way to the Malay Peninsula (see discussions in Devji, 2013; Malik, 2014). These fantastic imaginings testify to the continued attraction of empire for privileged minorities among the colonized. In West Africa, where nationalist mass mobilization was weaker, the idea of some sort of continued partnership between the imperial power and the colonized elite was sometimes prominent, even in the 1950s and 1960s. To think of these moves as potential alternative forms of the modern state, as recent historians such as Frederick Cooper (see in particular Cooper, 2014; as well as Chafer, 2015; Warson, 2015) and Gary Wilder (see in particular Wilder, 2015; as well as Berliner, 2016; el-Malik, 2017) have attempted to do, seems to deny not merely the overwhelming structural logic of the new global order as it was unfolding in the period but also, as we will see next, the most powerful ideas of collective justice sweeping through the colonial world.

The Internationalism of the Non-Aligned

The years after the Second World War are well known for the emergence of two rival international blocs led by two new superpowers. The Western bloc was consolidated around the economic power of the United States over global capitalism, a series of military alliances across the world, and the gradual decolonization of the European empires. The Eastern bloc was dominated by the Soviet Union, bolstered by the revolution in China and the establishment of a communist regime in North Korea. Continuing the tradition of communist internationalism, the Soviet Union supported both militarily and diplomatically the struggles of national liberation in Asia and

Africa. This was countered, both militarily and diplomatically, by the Western alliance. But within this polarized world, a new space of internationalism was created by the so-called non-aligned movement.

The point of origin here is usually seen to be the Bandung Conference of twenty-nine Afro-Asian nations in 1955 attended by such leading lights of the postcolonial world as Zhou Enlai, Jawaharlal Nehru, Gamal Abdel Nasser, Ahmed Sukarno, and U Nu. As newly independent nations, the participants held national sovereignty to be of supreme importance in ensuring their rights in the global community of nations. Several countries had launched programs of independent economic development. The Bandung Conference also included delegates from countries such as Turkey, the Philippines, and Pakistan who had just concluded defense pacts with the United States. Nevertheless, the conference affirmed the five principles of promotion of world peace, namely, mutual respect of all nations for sovereignty and territorial integrity, non-aggression, non-interference in internal affairs, equality and mutual benefit, and peaceful coexistence. Amplifying on these principles, the conference affirmed the right of each nation to defend itself singly or collectively, but warned that arrangements for collective defense must not be used to serve the particular interests of the big powers.

On the political side, the main discussion at the conference was on the subject of human rights. It is particularly interesting to re-read these discussions today because they show how radically the context as well as the framework of debate on this subject has changed. In 1955, at Bandung, no one had any doubt about the principal problem of human rights in the world: it was the continued existence of colonialism and racial discrimination. There was little doubt either about the chief instrument by which human rights were to be established: it was the principle of self-determination of peoples and nations. Affirming liberty and equality, the postcolonial peoples were demanding that those principles be applied to the collective right to autonomy of each nation founded on popular sovereignty. That was the principle the United Nations had enshrined. The leaders assembled at Bandung asserted that the UN charter and declarations had created "a common standard of achievement for all peoples and nations" (Appadorai, 1955: 8). Accordingly, the conference supported the rights of the Arab people of Palestine. It called for the end to racial segregation and discrimination in Africa. It supported the rights of the peoples of Algeria, Morocco, and Tunisia to self-determination. It called for the admission to the United Nations of Japan, Ceylon, Nepal, Jordan, Libya, Laos, Cambodia, and a united Vietnam. These sentiments from Bandung were later invoked quite often when the movement of non-aligned nations was formally launched in Belgrade in 1962.

Needless to say, the discourse on human rights has now shifted completely, especially since the 1980s, with several postcolonial regimes in Africa and Asia having become the principal targets of accusations of human rights violations, the accusers being governments and organized opinion in the erstwhile imperial countries. Whereas at Bandung, it was the newly independent nations that were asserting the primacy of universal principles of equality and national self-determination in a world dominated by the cynical and strategic pursuit of power by the rival Cold War alliances, now we see the universal claims of humanity being asserted by Western governments against the privileges of national sovereignty claimed by allegedly oppressive rulers in Asia and Africa.

On the economic side, the Bandung Conference stressed the principle of unfettered sovereign rights over the economic and intellectual resources of the formerly colonized countries, something that had not been automatically guaranteed by formal decolonization. As Sukarno said in his inaugural speech,

> Colonialism has also its modern dress, in the form of economic control, intellectual control, actual physical control by a small but alien community within a nation. It is a skillful and determined enemy, and it appears in many guises. It does not give up its loot easily. Wherever, whenever and however it appears, colonialism is an evil thing, and one which must be eradicated from the earth. (Indonesian Ministry of Foreign Affairs, 1955: 19–29)

The conference resolutions show that most countries in the region saw themselves as exporters of primary commodities and importers of industrial products. They were particularly keen to explore the possibilities of collective action to stabilize the international prices of primary commodities. Many were also attracted by the idea of state-led industrialization through planning and regulatory regimes.

In this respect too, the world has changed radically since Bandung. The countries of East and Southeast Asia as well as India have transformed their economies into dynamic and diversified industrial powers while large parts of Africa remain poor and stagnant. No one talks of an Afro-Asian economic world any more.

Conclusion

What then is the legacy of Bandung? The formal equality of sovereign nation-states has been normatively established today on a global scale and is embodied in international organizations such as the General Assembly of the United Nations. The old practices of imperial power, involving conquest and annexation of colonial territories, are no longer legitimate. But the imperial privilege to declare the colonial exception, hinted at by Sukarno at Bandung, continues in many guises. As I have indicated earlier, formal equality of status among nation-states merely establishes a norm on the basis of which real inequalities can be measured as deviations, just as formal equality of citizenship does not abolish but merely sets the standard for comparison of real inequalities. The colonial exception is declared when the universal claims of equal sovereignty are suspended in the case of a particular nation-state on grounds of misgovernment, mistreatment of citizens because of cultural prejudices, or danger to global security. These are exactly the same grounds on which the legal obligations of existing treaties were set aside by the British in India in the nineteenth century. The imperial privilege still exists in a world without colonies.

Examples are plentiful. The UN Security Council has five permanent members with veto power, on the realist justification that no collective security measure would succeed unless all the major powers were in agreement. This is perfectly in line with many realist justifications in history of the imperial privilege that claims more than what is entailed by the equal right of sovereignty. Again, a plethora of exceptional practices surround the place of Israel as the most recent European settler colony in Asia and the corresponding denial of the political rights of sovereign nationhood promised to Palestinians by the League of Nations mandate (every other mandated territory is now an independent nation-state and UN member). To cite another example, everyone agrees that nuclear proliferation is dangerous and should be stopped. Yet who decides that India may be allowed to have nuclear weapons, and also Israel, and maybe even Pakistan, but not North Korea or Iran? US drones may be sent in to strike terror targets in Pakistan or Yemen without the willing approval of those states, but such action would be inconceivable if the terrorist targets were in, say, Russia or Spain. Public outrage over an oil spill in the Gulf of Mexico will induce the United States to demand that BP pay several billions of dollars to clean up the mess, while it would use diplomatic pressure, with the covert connivance of those in power in India, to ensure that Union Carbide pay no more than $2,000 for each of some 20,000 persons killed in Bhopal in 1984 in the worst industrial disaster in history. Many countries have run up unsustainable public debts in recent times, but why was it Greece that was made the exemplary case where, in blatant violation of the sovereign will of the people of that country, its newly elected government was forced to swallow a bailout package it did not want? Those who claim to decide on the exception do indeed arrogate to themselves the imperial prerogative.

The demands made at Bandung still remain the unfulfilled promises of a global order founded on the freedom and equality of nations and peoples. That is why the memory of 1955 still refuses to go away, even though the world has changed so much in the past sixty-seven years.

References

Alexandrowicz, C. H. (1967). *An Introduction to the History of the Law of Nations in the East Indies*. Oxford: Oxford University Press.

Anghie, A. (2005). *Imperialism, Sovereignty and the Making of International Law*. Cambridge: Cambridge University Press. https://doi.org/10.1017/CBO9780511614262.

Appadorai, A. (1955). *The Bandung Conference*. New Delhi: Indian Council of World Affairs.

Armitage, D. (2000). *The Ideological Origins of the British Empire*. Cambridge: Cambridge University Press.

Benton, L. (2009). *A Search for Sovereignty: Law and Geography in European Empires, 1400–1900*. Cambridge: Cambridge University Press. https://doi.org/10.1017/cbo9780511988905.

Benton, L. (2010). *A Search for Sovereignty: Law and Geography in European Empires, 1400–1900*. Cambridge: Cambridge University Press.

Benton, L. (2014). *A Search for Sovereignty: Law and Geography in European Empires, 1400–1900*. https://doi.org/10.1017/CBO9780511988905.

Berliner, B. A. (2016). "Review of: *Freedom Time: Negritude, Decolonization, and the Future of the World*, by Gary Wilder. Durham: Duke UP, 2015." *Callaloo*, 39(1): 229–32. https://doi.org/10.1353/cal.2016.0007.

Bhattacharya, T. (2005). "Review of: *Producing India: From Colonial Economy to National Space*, by Manu Goswami. Chicago: University of Chicago Press, 2004." *The Journal of Asian Studies*, 64(1): 223–5. https://doi.org/10.1017/s0021911805000525.

Briggs, H. W. (1960). "Review of: *International Law Reports, 1955, 1956*, by Hersch Lauterpacht. London: Butterworth & Co., 1958." *The American Journal of International Law*, 54(4): 905–6. https://doi.org/10.2307/2195156.

Cagle, H. G. (2011). "Review of: *A Search for Sovereignty: Law and Geography in European Empires, 1400–1900*, by Lauren Benton. New York: Cambridge University Press, 2010." *Itinerario*, 35(2): 104–6. https://doi.org/10.1017/s0165115311000349.

Carty, A. (2003). "Review of: *The Gentle Civilizer of Nations: The Rise and Fall of International Law 1870–1960*, by Martti Koskenniemi. Cambridge: Cambridge University Press, 2001." *Rechtsgeschichte—Legal History*, Rg2: 207–9. https://doi.org/10.12946/rg02/207-209.

Chafer, T. (2015). "Review of: *Citizenship Between Empire and Nation: Remaking France and French Africa, 1945–1960*, by Frederick Cooper. Princeton and Oxford: Princeton University Press, 2014." *French History*, 29(3): 404–5. https://doi.org/10.1093/fh/crv048.

Chatterjee, K. (1995). "Review of: *The Politics of the British Annexation of India 1757–1857*, by Michael H. Fisher. Oxford in India Readings. Delhi: Oxford University Press, 1993." *The Journal of Asian Studies*, 54(3): 871–3. https://doi.org/10.2307/2059486.

Chatterjee, P. (1975). *Arms, Alliances and Stability: The Development of the Structure of International Politics*. Delhi: Macmillan; New York: John Wiley.

Chatterjee, P. (2012). *The Black Hole of Empire: History of a Global Practice of Power*. Princeton: Princeton University Press.

Cooper, F. (2014). *Citizenship Between Empire and Nation: Remaking France and French Africa, 1945–1960*. Princeton: Princeton University Press. https://doi.org/10.23943/princeton/9780691161310.001.0001.

De Vattel, E. (1916). *The Law of Nations or the Principles of Natural Law*, 3 vols., translated by C.G. Fenwick. Washington: Carnegie Institutions.

Devji, F. (2013). *Muslim Zion: Pakistan as a Political Idea*. Cambridge: Harvard University Press.

el-Malik, S. S. (2017). "Review of: *Freedom Time: Negritude, Decolonization and the Future of the World*, by Gary Wilder. Durham: Duke UP, 2015." *African and Black Diaspora: An International Journal*, 10(1): 104–6. https://doi.org/10.1080/17528631.2016.1179832.

Emberland, M. (2003). "Review of: *The Gentle Civilizer of Nations: The Rise and Fall of International Law 1870–1960*, by Martti Koskenniemi. Cambridge: Cambridge University Press, 2001." *International and Comparative Law Quarterly*, 52(1): 272–4. https://doi.org/10.1093/iclq/52.1.272.

Fisher, M. (ed). (1993). *The Politics of British Annexation of India, 1757–1857*. New Delhi: Oxford University Press.

Goldstein, E. (2017). "Review of: *The Guardians: The League of Nations and the Crisis of Empire*, by Susan Pedersen. Oxford: Oxford University Press, 2015." *The Journal of Modern History*, 89(1): 166–7. https://doi.org/10.1086/690131.

Goswami, M. (2004). *Producing India: From Colonial Economy to National Space*. (Chicago Studies in Practices of Meaning.) Chicago: University of Chicago Press. https://doi.org/10.1086/ahr/110.2.457.

Grovogui, S. (2006). *Beyond Eurocentrism and Anarchy: Memories of International Order and Institutions*. New York: Palgrave Macmillan.

Hueck, I. (2003). "Review of: *The Gentle Civilizer of Nations: The Rise and Fall of International Law 1870–1960*, by Martti Koskenniemi. Cambridge: Cambridge University Press, 2001." *German History*, 21(3): 425–7. https://doi.org/10.1093/026635540302100315.

Indonesian Ministry of Foreign Affairs. (1955). *Africa-Asia Speaks from Bandong*. Djakarta: Indonesian Ministry of Foreign Affairs.

Janik, R. (2018). "Review of: *The Guardians: The League of Nations and the Crisis of Empire*, by Susan Pedersen. Oxford: Oxford University Press, 2015." *Austrian Review of International and European Law Online*, 20(1): 450–2. https://doi.org/10.1163/15736512-00000018.

Koskenniemi, M. (2001). *The Gentle Civilizer of Nations: The Rise and Fall of International Law, 1870–1960*. Cambridge: Cambridge University Press. https://doi.org/10.1017/cbo9780511494222.

Lindley, M. F. (1926). *The Acquisition and Government of Backward Territory in International Law*. London: Longman, Green.

Liu, L. H. (2004). *The Clash of Empires: The Invention of China in Modern World Making*. Cambridge: Harvard University Press.

Malik, I. H. (2014). "Review of: *Muslim Zion: Pakistan as a Political Idea*, by Faisal Devji. Cambridge: Harvard University Press, 2013." *Contemporary South Asia*, 22(4): 422–4. https://doi.org/10.1080/09584935.2014.965492.

Mamdani, M. (1996). *Citizen and Subject: Contemporary Africa and the Legacy of Late Colonialism*. Princeton: Princeton University Press.

Mamdani, M. (2015). "Between the public intellectual and the scholar: Decolonization and the African academy," Paper presented at the forum Commemorating the Sixtieth Anniversary of the Bandung Conference, Hangzhou, China, April.

Mamdani, M. (2016). "A critique of Eurocentrism: Then and now." *Comparative Study of South Asia, Africa and the Middle East*, 36(1): 174–7.

Marcus, N. (2018). "Review of: *The Guardians: The League of Nations and the Crisis of Empire*, by Susan Pedersen. Oxford: Oxford University Press, 2015." *Journal of Contemporary History*, 53(4): 890–2. https://doi.org/10.1177/0022009418786695c.

McKenzie, F. (2016). "Review of: *The Guardians: The League of Nations and the Crisis of Empire*, by Susan Pedersen. Oxford: Oxford University Press, 2015." *Diplomacy & Statecraft*, 27(3): 578–9.

Menon, V. P. (1956). *The Story of the Integration of the Indian States*. Calcutta: Orient Longmans.

Mettraux, G. (2003). "Review of: *The Gentle Civilizer of Nations: The Rise and Fall of International Law 1870–1960*, by Martti Koskenniemi. Cambridge: Cambridge University Press, 2001." *International Criminal Law Review*, 3(1): 79–85. https://doi.org/10.1163/156753603767877110.

Mitchell, T. (2011). *Carbon Democracy: Political Power in the Age of Oil*. London: Verso.

Mullerson, R. (2002). "Review of: *The Gentle Civilizer of Nations: The Rise and Fall of International Law 1870–1960*, by Martti Koskenniemi. Cambridge: Cambridge University Press, 2001." *European Journal of International Law*, 13(3): 727–35. https://doi.org/10.1093/ejil/13.3.727.

Neff, S. C. (2003). "Review of: *The Gentle Civilizer of Nations: The Rise and Fall of International Law 1870–1960*, by Martti Koskenniemi. Cambridge: Cambridge University Press, 2001." *British Yearbook of International Law*, 73(1): 370–2. https://doi.org/10.1093/bybil/73.1.370.

Nordman, D. (2013). "Review of: *A Search for Sovereignty: Law and Geography in European Empires, 1400–1900*, by Lauren Benton. New York: Cambridge University Press, 2010." *Revue D'histoire Moderne et Contemporaine*, 60–1(1): 210–11. https://doi.org/10.3917/rhmc.601.0210.

Ogborn, M. (2012). "Review of: *A Search for Sovereignty: Law and Geography in European Empires, 1400–1900*, by Lauren Benton. New York: Cambridge University Press, 2010." *The American Historical Review*, 117(3): 814–16. https://doi.org/10.1086/ahr.117.3 .814.

Oppenheim, L. (1912). *International Law: A Treatise*. London: Longmans, Green.

Oppenheim, L. (1955). *International Law*, edited by H. Lauterpacht. London: Longman, Green.

Pagden, A. (2000). *Lords of All the World: Ideologies of Empire in Spain, Britain and France, c.1500–c.1800*. New Haven: Yale University Press.

Palen, M.-W. (2017). "Review of: *The Guardians: The League of Nations and the Crisis of Empire*, by Susan Pedersen. Oxford: Oxford University Press, 2015." *The English Historical Review*, 132(559): 1638–9. https://doi.org/10.1093/ehr/cex324.

Payk, M. M. (2017). "Review of: *The Guardians: The League of Nations and the Crisis of Empire*, by Susan Pedersen. Oxford: Oxford University Press, 2015." *Verfassung in Recht und Übersee*, 50(1): 85–6. https://doi.org/10.5771/0506-7286-2017-1-85.

Pedersen, S. (2015). *The Guardians: The League of Nations and the Crisis of Empire*. New York: Oxford University Press.

Peters, K. (2011). "Review of: *A Search for Sovereignty: Law and Geography in European Empires, 1400–1900*, by Lauren Benton. New York: Cambridge University Press, 2010." *Geografiska Annaler: Series B, Human Geography*, 93(4): 344–6. https://doi.org/10.1111 /j.1468-0467.2011.00391.x.

Poulose, T. T. (1976). "Review of: *Arms, Alliances and Stability: The Development of the Structure of International Politics*, by Partha Chatterjee. Delhi: Macmillan; New York: John Wiley, 1975." *International Studies*, 15(3): 443–4. https://doi.org/10.1177 /002088177601500308.

Prakash, G. (2005). "Review of: *Producing India: From Colonial Economy to National Space*, by Manu Goswami, 2004. Chicago: University of Chicago Press." *American Historical Review*, 110(2): 457. https://doi.org/10.1086/ahr/110.2.457.

Purcell, K. (2012). "Review of: *A Search for Sovereignty: Law and Geography in European Empires, 1400–1900*, by Lauren Benton. New York: Cambridge University Press, 2010." *British Yearbook of International Law*, 82(1): 495–500. https://doi.org/10.1093/bybil/ brs014.

Riemens, M. (2016). "Review of: *The Guardians: The League of Nations and the Crisis of Empire*, by Susan Pedersen. Oxford: Oxford University Press, 2015." *Journal of Global History*, 11(3): 488–90. https://doi.org/10.1017/s1740022816000279.

Ross, R. J. (2010). "Review of: *A Search for Sovereignty: Law and Geography in European Empires, 1400–1900*, by Lauren Benton. New York: Cambridge University Press, 2010." *Law and History Review*, 28(4): 1113–16. https://doi.org/10.1017/s0738248010001008.

Rushbrook-Williams, L. F. (1957). "Review of: *The Story of the Integration of the Indian States*, by V. P. Menon. London and New York: Longmans, Green, 1956." *International Affairs*, 33(2): 251. https://doi.org/10.2307/2608947.

Simons, P. (2006). "Review of: *The Gentle Civilizer of Nations: The Rise and Fall of International Law 1870–1960*, by Martti Koskenniemi. Cambridge: Cambridge University Press, 2001." *Journal of the History of International Law/Revue d'histoire du droit international*, 8(1): 125–9. https://doi.org/10.1163/157180506777834399.

Simpson, A. W. B. and Koskenniemi, M. (2002). "Review of: *The Gentle Civilizer of Nations: The Rise and Fall of International Law 1870–1960*, by Martti Koskenniemi. Cambridge: Cambridge University Press, 2001." *The American Journal of International Law*, 96(4): 995–1000. https://doi.org/10.2307/3070707.

Topulos, K. and Johnston, D. M. (2003). "Review of: *The Gentle Civilizer of Nations: The Rise and Fall of International Law 1870–1960*, by Martti Koskenniemi. Cambridge: Cambridge University Press, 2001." *International Journal of Legal Information*, 31(3): 539–41. https://doi.org/10.1017/s0731126500003784.

Tsagourias, N. (2003). "Review of: *The Gentle Civilizer of Nations: The Rise and Fall of International Law 1870–1960*, by Martti Koskenniemi. Cambridge: Cambridge University Press, 2001." *Leiden Journal of International Law*, 16(2): 397–9. https://doi.org/10.1017/s0922156503211225.

Tuck, R. (1999). *The Rights of War and Peace: Political Thought and the International Order from Grotius to Kant*. Oxford: Oxford University Press.

United States Department of State. (1919). *Covenant of the League of Nations, Articles 1–26*. Office of the Historian. https://history.state.gov/historicaldocuments/frus1919Parisv13/ch10subch1.

Warson, J. (2015). "Review of: *Citizenship Between Empire and Nation: Remaking France and French Africa, 1945–1960*, by Frederick Cooper. Princeton and Oxford: Princeton University Press, 2014." *Africa*, 85(3): 554–5. https://doi.org/10.1017/s0001972015000418.

Westlake, J. (1894). *Chapters on the Principles of International Law*. Cambridge: Cambridge University Press.

Wilder, G. (2015). *Freedom Time: Negritude, Decolonization and the Future of the World*. Durham: Duke University Press.

Williams, M. (2011). "Review of: *A Search for Sovereignty: Law and Geography in European Empires, 1400–1900*, by Lauren Benton. New York: Cambridge University Press, 2010." *Tijdschrift voor Geschiedenis*, 124(1): 113–14. https://doi.org/10.5117/tvgesch2011.1.b1.

Yearwood, P. (2016). "Review of: *The Guardians: The League of Nations and the Crisis of Empire*, by Susan Pedersen. Oxford: Oxford University Press, 2015." *Reviews in History*. https://doi.org/10.14296/rih/2014/1900.

12

Looking Back, Looking Forward

Mahmood Mamdani

Introduction

Citizen and Subject was the result of ten years of reflection, study, writing, and rewriting. Its prehistory began in 1974, when I completed my PhD. Published two years later as *Politics and Class Formation in Uganda* (1976), this book understood the process of class formation as exclusively a consequence of the development of the market. At the heart of the book was a lacuna in the understanding of the agrarian and peasant question. Except for an analysis of landlord-tenant relations in the Buganda countryside in the aftermath of the 1900 Agreement, the book showed little understanding of those parts of Uganda where access to land was a "communal" rights and colonial rule was experienced through the network of power relations known as "customary." This had wider consequences. Without an understanding of the dynamics driving nonmarket relations in the countryside, it was not possible to provide a political explanation of practices described as "tribalism" in mainstream literature.

Armed with a PhD, I got my first full-time academic job at the University of Dar es Salaam (1973–9). There, I honed my skills in political economy through intense involvement in as many as six study groups a week. Much of the discussion on the Hill in those years focused on two issues: one, the nature of class formation after the Arusha Declaration, in particular the effect of nationalization on the development of a managerial alongside an administrative bureaucracy in the state, and two, the possibility of capitalist development in the era of imperialism. Issa Shivji wrote *The Silent Class Struggle* (1973) and *The Class Struggle Continues* (1976), calling attention to the specificity of class formation in the context of state-centered accumulation. His major critic was the Ugandan lawyer Dani Wadada Nabudere, who wrote several books—among them *The Political Economy of Imperialism* (1980) and *Imperialism and Revolution in Uganda* (1981)—defending a classical understanding of class formation as exclusively an effect of market formation, alongside a claim that no independent (national) bourgeoisie could develop in the era of imperialism. In raising the question of the political (the state) with reference to class formation, Issa Shivji had moved away from the narrow understanding of political economy as focused on market formation.

I returned to Uganda in 1979 after Idi Amin had been ousted by Tanzanian troops, and began teaching at Makerere University the following year. For the next six years (1980–6), I did research in the countryside (Buganda in central Uganda, Lango in northern Uganda, Kisoro and the Ruwenzori mountains in western Uganda, parts of Karamoja in northeastern Uganda, and Busia in eastern Uganda). The research familiarized me with the nature of social differentiation where land was not a scarce factor. My focus, however, was on objective constraints on choices faced by peasant households. I had yet to explore questions related to peasant subjectivity.

That changed in 1986, the year the National Resistance Army (NRA) came to power and appointed the National Commission of Inquiry into Local Government, which I chaired. The NRA's coming to power was no simple change of government, and yet, it was not the revolution we had all hoped to make. It was clear that we would have to think in terms of reform, not revolution, and that reform would need a clear understanding of the relationship between the economic and the political, especially where land and social relations were shaped by the colonial framing of the "customary." The difference between Buganda and most of the country loomed large: whereas land had become a commodity in Buganda with the 1900 Agreement, land in most of the country was held as "customary." Customary right was a usufruct right; customary land could not be sold. The effect was to keep the peasant outside of the market but subject to dictates by "customary" chiefs. The countryside, I realized, was governed with an iron fist, and this hierarchy of chiefs had been crafted in the colonial period even if it was known as "customary." This arrangement seemed hardly affected by periodic multiparty elections. As the commission spent two years going around the countryside, I focused on the question of state reform and peasant subjectivity. I noticed that every time I raised the question of reforming the institution of chiefship, it inevitably generated an animated discussion among peasant audiences. I particularly remember an elder asking a question at the end of one such discussion: "Can there be a world without chiefs?" I came out of this process (1986–8) with an understanding that where land was "customary," agrarian reform would have to be thought of in political terms, that is, with reference to the coercive relationship between the chief and the peasant.

The stakes involved in a political economy only approach became apparent to me when I visited South Africa in 1993—as a visiting professor at the University of Durban (Westville). It is the political economists who had argued that the development of South Africa into a semi-industrialized and semi-urban economy had made it "exceptional" to the African story. The problem was that a political economy lens had made the nature and significance of "customary" power truly invisible. Later, I would realize that a modernist lens, as that of Foucault, also led to a similar invisibility.

When *Citizen and Subject* was published in 1996, my comrades in Dar es Salaam felt a sense of betrayal: they saw it as an abandonment of the method of political economy. From my point of view, I had not abandoned the method as I had its language, and categories, to the extent that both remained confined to the world of market-based relations. The importance of Shivji was that he had showed that the market was too restrictive to understand the nature of social change in a context where the state was acting as a structural force. To understand the peasant question, I thought it necessary to place the political (the native question) center stage. This meant shifting attention from the "dull compulsion of market forces" (Marx, 1867: chapter 28) to the centrality of extra-economic coercion—forced crops, forced labor, forced sales, forced contributions, and so on. Instead of considering this a further development of the "Dar es Salaam debate" on the relationship of the state to class formation, as an alternative to the theory of "underdevelopment," the response of my Dar colleagues was reactive. I thought they failed to see what was new in my contribution: even if I was not quite with them, I had not parted company with them.

The realization that I had to look outside the market to understand the peasant question led to new questions: How was the subject disciplined in a colonized society like Uganda? How does the nature of custom change from the premodern to the colonial modern? Custom did not exist as a governmental power in the premodern, and it could not be so, because the state was not modern. Discipline was not carried out in colonial society through forms Foucault has made us aware of in modernist society. I would later realize that custom becomes a form of governmentality under the modern colonial state. This would call for a deeper reflection on how custom, a social construct in the premodern period, was instrumentalized by the modern colonial state. Thus, the contrast between how custom varied from one locality to another in premodern society and the production of uniformity as an authoritative customary law in the colonial modern became the focus. Custom and customary turned into a form of discipline in colonized society. Like modern governmentality, customary law has elements of self-regulation.

In discussing the structural *legacy* of colonialism, *Citizen and Subject* proposed a broadening of the lens in two ways: from the labor question to the native question, and from the race question to the tribal question. At the same time, it called for a historical understanding of the customary. Scholarship on the labor question had been particularly well developed in the South African academy. When confronted by an anomaly—that the most highly developed economy on the African continent had introduced the most repressive political system—these same political economists responded with the claim that apartheid was functional to capitalism since it produced *cheap* labor. This obscured the fact that apartheid was in the main a political response to a political dilemma: the development of capitalism had moved labor from one region to another, and from the rural to the urban, making it possible for labor to organize to improve its lot. In response, the state looked for ways to tighten political control on these same laborers. Rather than free the movement of migrant labor as a key agent of market and capitalist development and thereby increase the supply of labor and reduce the price of labor power, apartheid strengthened ethnic homeland authorities, tied access to land and recognition of land and other rights to membership of these homelands—thereby disenfranchising those who moved out of the homeland while at the same time pitting them against those who remained in the homeland.

South Africa was not an anomaly. The same tendency could be observed in other parts of the continent. The new Nigerian constitution passed after the civil war celebrated its "federal character," in effect creating a confederation whose constituent units were ethnically demarcated states. Every Nigerian was recognized first and foremost as a citizen of a state within the federation, and only then as a citizen of Nigeria. When he or she competed for a position in key federal institutions—the army, the civil service, federal universities—it was as an "indigene" of a subnational state. As with natives in apartheid South Africa, those who resided outside the boundaries of their ethnic homelands risked being disenfranchised. The political did not reflect and reinforce developments in the economy, even "in the last instance"; rather, the political tried to keep these developments in check, or even to reverse them, in the interest of maintaining law and order. As we shall see, the latest development along these lines has been the introduction of "ethnic federalism" in Ethiopia.

Ethnicity and tribe are animated by opposed logics. Ethnicity was an open and inclusive category in the premodern period: whether through conquest or contact, ethnic groups expanded over time. The Baganda were a handful of clans some centuries ago; as they conquered neighboring populations, they absorbed them—the conquered became Baganda over time. The logic was assimilationist, even if aggressively so. The same can be said of Nguni groups to the south, the Swahili to the east, the Amhara to the northeast, their Arab neighbors, the Hausa to the west, and so on. Amharization, Swahilization, Arabization, Hausization—these processes summed up the practices of aggressive assimilation.

Tribe, in contrast, was exclusive. It defined identity in one-dimensional terms and fixed it permanently: in relation to a homeland, to a community defined as indigenous to that homeland, to an authority that held sway over the homeland, and to a set of privileges and discriminations tied to homeland identity and identified as "customary rights." This one-dimensional identification defined a person's life chances: access to land, belonging in a community, and preferential treatment in community-based dispute-resolution processes. It had a modern ring about it.

Tribe was more a subset of race than a corollary of ethnic identity. Just as race distributed life chances in accordance with phenotypical identification and excluded racial others, so did tribe become the basis of privilege from which tribal others were excluded. Not only were these distinctions inscribed in law, it was in the nature of modern power that they were enforced through law. The law was constitutive of these distinctions. The administrative power of the chief was constituted by the political power of the colonial state. If the premodern was informed by an assimilationist logic, the modern colonial was informed by a segregationist logic.

Whereas direct rule was based on racial discrimination only, indirect rule turned on a double discrimination: race and tribe. This politicized both race and tribe. My argument was that tribalism needed to be understood as a necessary consequence of a mode of rule that instrumentalized Africa's cultural history rather than being its organic development. Both ethnicity and tribe have meanings which are premodern and modern. In the United States, for example, the notion of ethnicity becomes salient as referring to different ethnic groups. Ethnicity does some work in the notion of an idealized liberal democracy. It both acknowledges cultural difference and is compatible with the notion of a political melting pot. Tribe in modern times is more a form of governmentality than ethnicity.

Citizen and Subject called for a historicization of custom, distinguishing between two periods in particular: the premodern and the modern. In premodern society, custom was part of community, not of political power. In the colonial modern, custom became an instrument of the law; it became "customary law." Colonialism defined a tribe as a group with its own distinctive law. Custom lost its autonomy, and customary law became subordinate to civil law. Civil authorities had the right to annul any custom deemed to be "repugnant" to morality—of which colonial (civil) power claimed to be the custodian. Several attributes distinguished customary from civil law. Excluded from civil rights, the colonized African became subjugated to customary law. The African had been containerized first as a racial being under direct rule and then also as a tribal being under indirect rule. Rather than set in motion by market-driven forces, the peasant was "protected" from market forces and pinned to the ground through the direct exercise of the administrative power of the chief. Both the position and the powers of the chief were framed as "tribal" and justified as "customary." The transition from custom as socially observed to custom enforced as law—and thus a part of colonial power—became central to the stabilization of colonialism.

Whereas the first half of *Citizen and Subject* discussed the structure of colonial power as its legacy, the second half focused on the response of the colonized. The standard argument in the literature had distinguished "nationalism" from "tribalism," embracing the former and bemoaning the latter. In the rural areas, however, "custom" was both a language of local power and the language of local protest. The argument in *Citizen and Subject* was that custom needed to be understood as contradictory: rather than embrace or distance oneself from the language of custom, one needed to acknowledge the dual use of custom—as a language of privilege by those exercising and benefiting from "customary" power and as a language calling for equal treatment, that is, rights, when used by the victims of that power.

If every resistance is shaped by the nature of power it confronts, then the central challenge of a democratic politics in contemporary Africa, argued *Citizen and Subject*, was how to connect the rural and the urban—two struggles against two very different modes of power in the indirect-rule state. The African postcolonial experience had hitherto shown two ways of linking the rural and the urban in the postcolonial era: ethnic clientelism and centralized administrative force. Neither had been equal to the task of taking on the challenge posed by the colonial legacy.

Revisiting the Critiques

Much ink has flowed since *Citizen and Subject* was published over twenty years ago. The book has been widely reviewed since it came out, and much has happened on the ground over the past two decades. My own views have also evolved in response to developments, both in the academy and in society.

The Legacy—Critique from the Historians

One group of scholars received *Citizen and Subject* as a work of history. A few lamented that it was not comprehensive, some others complained when they did not find their own cultivated garden in the patchwork they saw as *Citizen and Subject*, and yet others complained that the book focused on colonial structures to the exclusion of historical processes (see Ansprenger, 1997; Stadler, 1997; Campbell, 1998; Costa, 1998; Haynes, 1998; Idahosa, 1998).

One way of reading *Citizen and Subject* is as an account of an unfolding dialectic between structure and agency, between colonial power and response of the colonized. A thread running through the book is that the response to power is in the first instance shaped by the very organization and language of power. I once gave the following illustration to make the point: Say a man slaps a woman in Paris, another man does the same in Khartoum, and a third man does it in KwaZulu-Natal. All three women protest: the woman in Paris protests the violation of her rights, the one in Khartoum that of her dignity, and the one in KwaZulu-Natal that of custom. How does one understand the difference in responses? I suggested that in the first instance, protest mimics the language of power, questioning its claims.

Citizen and Subject is divided into two parts: "Power" and "Resistance." The two chapters on Uganda (the Ruwenzururu, the NRA) and South Africa (the politics of migrant labor) give flesh to this claim and discuss in some detail a variety of attempts to reform the structure of power. Another chapter sets the argument in a broader comparative frame. The conclusion is summed up at the outset: "No nationalist government was content to reproduce the colonial legacy uncritically. Each sought to reform the bifurcated state that institutionally crystalized a state-enforced separation of the rural from the urban and of one ethnicity from another. But in doing so each reproduced a part of that legacy, thereby creating its own variant of despotism" (Mamdani, 1996: 8). In both instances, *Citizen and Subject* argued, the result was deracialization without democratization.

Some critics claimed the book had reified structures of power, presenting them as an iron-clad and inflexible legacy: after all, argued Frederick Cooper (1997), the structures of indirect rule had solidified in the 1920s and 1930s but had loosened in the 1940s and 1950s as a consequence of citizenship struggles in those same decades. Another claimed that *Citizen and Subject* had understood by legacy nothing but passive inheritance (Schneider, 2006). Had these critics skipped over the entire second part of the book, or were they simply disappointed not to find in it a discussion of their particular nook of the African continent?

The kind of governmentality in the colonial context evolves as the state does and modes of identification and self-identification change as the political system evolves. To understand this is to acknowledge the fact of differences between and within societies. It raises questions about how we would approach these categories in different contexts and locations. Not only do tribe and ethnicity have different logic, ethnicity in Nigeria is not the same as ethnicity in Tanzania, or indeed in the United States. There is a sameness—say, connection with the state—but the connection is also different, given that emergence of the state is different in each case. This is why the second part of the book is concerned with historical reform—which suggests that people like Cooper (1997) either have not thought about it or have not read it.

The focus of the detailed case studies in Part 2 was precisely on the movements that sought to reform the indirect-rule state, either by a democratization of the Native Authority in rural areas of Uganda and Tanzania or by a demand for a more inclusive citizenship in South Africa. If *Citizen and Subject* did not seek to cover the continent comprehensively, it was not conceived as a work of history, or an area studies compendium. As some commentators acknowledged, it was a mistake to read the work as competing with the historians; rather, it needed to be read as using the work of historians to illuminate the present (Freund, 2000).

How do we approach the present? I had critiqued reasoning by analogy as a way of understanding Africa in the shadow of Europe, as if always trying to catch up, and always failing. Many agreed. Writing on Africa has been largely an exercise in explaining what has gone wrong (Clapham, 1997). To talk of Africans as having failed only makes sense in analogy with European history; it makes better sense to look at the postcolonial experience, not as an attempt to catch up with history but to come to terms with a colonial legacy (Lonsdale, 1997).

The Political Critique: Is All Rule Indirect Rule?

A second line of criticism came from political scientists who questioned whether indirect rule was specific to colonial power and thus deserving of theorization as such. Using local rulers to buttress colonial rule is not an African novelty. As early as the dawn of modernity, argued Michael Chege (1997), Machiavelli (1998: 18) had suggested three ways of running a colony: eliminate the population, send settlers to live among them, or "set up an oligarchy which will keep the state friendly to you." Abdelwahab el-Affendi (2016) went a step further, evoking Michel Foucault: indirect rule, after all, is the very essence of modern power, whether at home or in the colonies. Could one borrow a leaf from Foucault, move away from a preoccupation with sovereignty and the law, and focus on the institutional matrix—the prison, the school, the hospital, the insane asylum, and so on—and the capillaries of power to understand how modern subjectivity is shaped and the modern subject produced?

In the colonies where the rural population lived beyond the reach of these modern institutions, how and where was the subjectivity of the colonized shaped? How was the colonial subject produced? There is no engagement with Foucault in *Citizen and Subject*. Indeed, *Citizen and Subject* was written at Makerere University over the decade spanning 1987–96, when Foucault had not yet arrived in Kampala! But the real point is that even if he had arrived, the answer could not have been read in Foucault. The problem calls on us to think through the nature of power in the colonial modern. To use the language of Foucault, should we think of the customary as a form of discipline and indirect rule as a hybrid between discipline and governmentality?

Let me begin with at least one such attempt to think the colonial. For Partha Chatterjee (1993), the colonial modern revealed a split between the public and the private: if the colonial state occupied the modern sphere, nationalists established control over the private domain. *Citizen and Subject* argued that the split between the public and the private was blurred under indirect rule. The distinctive feature of indirect-rule colonialism was precisely that colonialism took command of the private domain, defining custom, thereby shaping the terms within which the subjectivity of the colonized would be produced. Herein lies the significance of the change from custom as social to custom as colonial law. In the premodern period, custom was a set of norms and conventions that regulated gender and generational relations. As such, it was a part of the community. Under colonialism, custom became customary law. More than just observed, it was enforced. The authorities in charge of enforcing custom, so-called customary authorities, were sanctioned by the state and backed up by state violence. From a multiplicity of practices, state and customary authorities produced an authoritative version of custom as law. What the asylum, the school, the prison, the hospital, and such institutions were to the modern, the customary was to the colonial modern.

The Last Two Decades

The critical response to *Citizen and Subject* largely focused on the indirect-rule state and efforts to reform it in the post-independence period. They ignored the ways in which the experience of indirect rule has become part of historical memory in Africa. If the memory of modes of precolonial governance has been dimmed and distorted—in some cases even erased—by colonial knowledge systems, it may be said that the practice of indirect rule as a mode of statecraft has been naturalized through these very processes. The attraction of indirect rule to Africa's post-independence leadership should be obvious: not only does it fragment the population into so many minorities, it also legitimates this political outcome by presenting it as a necessary consequence of cultural difference in African society and history. The politicization of cultural difference presents the ruling power with the possibility of endlessly producing new minorities, assigning each a historic homeland under the leadership of an "indigenous" leadership charged with the right to safeguard the rights of the "indigenous" population. Uganda's attempt to reintroduce indirect rule post-1995 and Ethiopia's endeavor to introduce it afresh post-1994, illustrate this tendency.

At the heart of the changes initiated by the National Resistance Movement (NRM) when it assumed power in 1986 was the reform of local government. Central to these reforms was the dismantling of the office of the chief as an institution and the election of local committees and councils. At the same time, groups which had hitherto been politically marginalized—women and youth—were guaranteed the right to elect a representative on the nine-person council. All local officials were made accountable to these committees and councils. The committee system stood as an antidote to the indirect-rule state, which had survived a quarter century into the post-independence era.

The reform of the local state stood uneasily alongside the failure to reform the central state where the NRM ruled as a single party with an election system that claimed to reward individual merit and rule out the participation of political parties. The turning point came with the constitutional reforms of the mid-1990s: these introduced multiparty elections at the center, but at the same time cordoned off urban from rural areas, bringing districts under presidentially appointed administrators and closing them to competing parties. Over the next two decades, the center actively encouraged local groups to organize as separate ethnicities and favorably looked on their demand for separate districts as an expression of a right of (ethnic) self-determination. As the number of districts doubled and tripled from the original thirty-three, the cost of governance soared. With each district electing representatives to parliament, the number of representatives exploded, and the scarcity of sitting room turned parliament into a standing-room-only gala. And yet, there was no end in sight. There was no way the state could enfranchise each ethnic group with a district of its own; at the same time, given that every part of the country was multiethnic, new minorities emerged every time a new district was created.

A corollary to the formation of new districts (in the north and the east) was the creation of new kingdoms in the historical south. Where new kingdoms were carved out of existing ones—as in the historic Ruwenzururu region—the inevitable result was tension between the old and the new, turning violent where retired army officers had been appointed kings. The political consequence of this overall process—of district and kingdom creation on the basis of ethnic group identity, expressive of a decentralization based on group rather than territorial identity—was that ethnicities without a district or without a kingdom became defined as political minorities with a second-class citizenship.

If Uganda returned to a version of the colonial indirect rule system, the new Ethiopian government introduced the system afresh in the mid-1990s with the adoption of a new constitution promising "ethnic federalism." A federal arrangement may have been an understandable antidote to the centralizing thrust of the monarchy and the Dergue that followed it. When it came to federalism, however, there were different types. *Regional (territorial) federalism* has been the characteristic form in the West: the United States, Canada, and so on. *Ethnic federalism*, in contrast, has been an African development following the Nigerian post-civil war constitution of the mid-1970s. It followed the logic of colonial indirect rule.

As an expression of self-determination, ethnic federalism acknowledges the ethnic group—and not the population of a region—as the political self with the right to self-determination. The general principle is: for each ethnic group, a homeland. And inside each homeland, customary rights for members of the ethnic group indigenous to the homeland. In Ethiopia too—as had been in colonized Africa—those residents in the homeland but ancestrally not of it were disenfranchised. This legal innovation turned ethnic difference into a source of advantage for those acknowledged in law as indigenous and discrimination against those not. The politicization of ethnicity created an enfranchised majority alongside disenfranchised minorities in each homeland. This is what *Citizen and Subject* termed tribalism, the inevitable consequence of indirect rule.

As in the late colonial period, the post-nationalist state in Africa has come to prioritize law and order. The result is a *necessary* contradiction between the economic and the political. As the developmentalist state ushers in market-friendly reforms, it moves not only products of labor but also labor itself—landless peasants, workers—beyond local boundaries. At the same time, the indirect rule state disenfranchises those who cross these boundaries as not being indigenous to other homelands. Viewed in light of these developments, the thesis that animated *Citizen and Subject* remains as relevant now as it was when first published two decades ago.

We may think of the bifurcated state as a unique form of power introduced in Africa by colonial powers between 1880 and 1940. At the same time, we need to beware of its prehistory in India after the 1857 uprising and its overspill beyond Africa. Yet, this technology was not invented hothouse fashion bifurcated state in Africa to parts of the Middle East like Iraq and Lebanon. Not surprisingly, like much of Africa, much of the Middle East too is plagued by tribalization of politics, ethnic wars, ethnic cleansing, and genocide. All these outcomes can be seen as the debris of a modernist postcolonial project—an attempt to create a centralized modern state as the bearer of Westphalian sovereignty against the background of indirect rule. To think in these terms is to think in terms of a question *Citizen and Subject* does not formulate: the relationship of group or territorial autonomy to the overall project to realize state sovereignty in the postcolonial period. This is the question raised by the current rebellion spreading through Ethiopia. What are the implications for individual citizenship of rethinking state sovereignty alongside group rather than territorial autonomy? The discussion in *Citizen and Subject* suggests that where sovereignty rests on territorial federalism, the tendency will be to extend equal constitutional protection to all citizens, but where sovereignty rests on ethnic federalism, the tendency will be to render ethnic minorities as second-class citizens in ethnic homelands identified with other ethnic majorities. Whereas the discussion in *Citizen and Subject* does reflect on different forms of federalism, it does not explore alternatives to the question of sovereignty as we have customarily thought about it. That is a project likely to take us beyond the parameters of indirect rule.

References

Ansprenger, F. (1997). "Review of: *Citizen and Subject: Contemporary Africa and the Legacy of Late Colonialism*, by Mahmood Mamdani. Princeton: Princeton University Press, 1996." *The International Journal of African Historical Studies*, 30(3): 719–20. https://doi.org/10.2307/220644.

Campbell, P. (1998). "Review of: *Citizen and Subject: Contemporary Africa and the Legacy of Late Colonialism*, by Mahmood Mamdani. Princeton: Princeton University Press, 1996." *The Historian*, 61(1): 143. https://doi.org/10.1111/j.1540-6563.1998.tb01428.x.

Chatterjee, P. (1993). *The Nation and its Fragments: Colonial and Postcolonial Histories*. Princeton: Princeton University Press.

Chege, M. (1997). "Review of: *Citizen and Subject: Contemporary Africa and the Legacy of Late Colonialism*, by Mahmood Mamdani. Princeton: Princeton University Press, 1996." *African Studies Quarterly*, 1(1): 47–51.

Clapham, C. (1997). "Review of: *Citizen and Subject: Contemporary Africa and the Legacy of Late Colonialism*, by Mahmood Mamdani. Princeton: Princeton University Press, 1996." *International Affairs*, 73(3): 605–6.

Cooper, F. (1997). "Review of: *Citizen and Subject: Contemporary Africa and the Legacy of Late Colonialism*, by Mahmood Mamdani. Princeton: Princeton University Press, 1996." *International Labor and Working-Class History*, 52: 156–60.

Costa, A. (1998). "Revisiting Citizen and Subject—Review: *Citizen and Subject: Contemporary Africa and the Legacy of Late Colonialism*, by Mahmood Mamdani. Princeton: Princeton University Press, 1996." *South African Historical Journal*, 38(1): 222–31.

El-Affendi, A. (2016). *Contribution*, Conference on citizen and subject, University of the Western Cape, South Africa, August.

Freund, B. (2000). "Democracy and the colonial heritage in Africa: Revisiting Mamdani's citizen and subject." *Left History*, 7(1), 101–8.

Haynes, J. (1998). "Review of: *Citizen and Subject: Contemporary Africa and the Legacy of Late Colonialism*, by Mahmood Mamdani. Princeton: Princeton University Press, 1996." *History*, 83: 498–9.

Idahosa, P. L. (1998). "Review of: *Citizen and Subject: Contemporary Africa and the Legacy of Late Colonialism*, by Mahmood Mamdani. Princeton: Princeton University Press, 1996." *The International History Review*, 20(2): 493–6.

Lonsdale, J. (1997). "Power and Resistance—Review: *Citizen and Subject: Contemporary Africa and the Legacy of Late Colonialism*, by Mahmood Mamdani. Princeton: Princeton University Press, 1996." *The Journal of African History*, 38(3): 520–2.

Machiavelli, N. (1998). *The Prince*, 2nd ed. Chicago: University of Chicago Press.

Mamdani, M. (1976). *Politics and Class Formation in Uganda*. London: Heinemann.

Mamdani, M. (1996). *Citizen and Subject: Contemporary Africa and the Legacy of Late Colonialism*. Princeton: Princeton University Press.

Marx, K. (1867). *Capital: A Critique of Political Economy*, Vol. 1. New York: Cosimo.

Nabudere, W. (1980). *The Political Economy of Imperialism*. London: Zed Press.

Nabudere, W. (1981). *Imperialism and Revolution in Uganda*. London: Zed Press.

Schneider, L. (2006). "Colonial legacies and postcolonial authoritarianism in Tanzania: Connects and disconnects." *African Studies Review*, 49(1): 93–118.

Shivji, I. (1976). *Class Struggles in Tanzania*. Dar es Salaam: Tanzania Publishing House.

Shivji, I. (1973). *The Silent Class Struggle*. Dar es Salaam: Tanzania Publishing House.

Stadler, A. (1997). "Review of: *Citizen and Subject: Contemporary Africa and the Legacy of Late Colonialism*, by Mahmood Mamdani. Princeton: Princeton University Press, 1996." *South African Historical Journal*, 37(1): 220–45.

Index

Page numbers followed with "n" refer to footnotes.

aboriginal native   174
abstract universalism   127
Adivasis' land rights   62–3
al-Afghani, Sayyid Jamal ad-Din   95
Afifi Pasha, Hafiz   48 n.3
Africa
    CODESRIA   10–12
    and colonialism   13
    decolonization of universities   23–4
    political system   13
    sociology in   38
African identities   179–80
Africanization of universities   23–4
African knowledge   38
African National Congress (ANC)   158–
    60, 162–5, 168, 169
Agarwal, Bina   64–5
Agnes, Flavia   70, 71
Ahmed, Abiy   106
Albright, Madeleine   78
Alexandrowicz, C. H.   191
Algeria   88
Ali, Muhammad   51, 92, 93
Althusser, Louis   29
Ambedkar, B. R.   70, 70 n.5
Americanization   22
American revolution   20
American settler colonialism   20–2
Americo-Liberians   175
Amhara identity   103–7, 110, 115, 117
    rise of   110–15
Amharic language   113, 114
Amharization as state policy   113–15
ANC. See African National Congress
    (ANC)
Anderson, B.   104, 107, 108
Andrews, Mercia   62
Anghie, Antony   194, 198
Anglo-Ethiopian boundary
    agreement   109
annexations of Indian territory   192

anti-colonial revolt   126
anti-colonial struggle   124, 145
anti-elite sentiment   135
apartheid   21, 27–8, 32, 149, 157, 160–6,
    183–4, 211–12
archipelagos of dominance   158, 169
Arendt, Hannah   3, 46
Arnold, Thomas   49 n.5
Article 22 of the League Covenant   198
Arunachal Pradesh Land Settlement
        and Records Amendment Act
        (2018)   79
Arunachal Pradesh Women's Welfare
        Society   75
Asad, Talal   4–5
"Asian Tigers"   98, 100
Assam Land and Revenue Regulation
        (1886)   74
Assam Waste Land Grant Rules
        (1838)   74
Austin, J.   191
autochthonous   181
autochthony   133, 179

balance of power system   192
Bandung Conference of 1955   189, 201–2
"Bantustan" system   160
barbarism   88–9, 95, 96, 98
Baring, Evelyn   47
Barth, F.   104
Benton, Lauren   195
"Between the public intellectual and
        the scholar: Decolonization
        and some initiatives in post-
        independent African higher
        education" (Mamdani)   22–5
"Beyond Nuremberg: The historical
        significance of the post-
        apartheid transition in South
        Africa" (Mamdani)   18–19
Bhardwaj, H. R.   66

Biersteker, T. 109
bifurcated state 7, 128, 145, 155–7, 217, 218
Birla, Ritu 66–7
black Africans 13, 14, 144, 165–7, 173, 174, 181, 184
Black Labour Regulations of 1965 181
Black native 175
BMA. *See* British Military Administration (BMA)
Bourdieu, Pierre 35, 36
Bourke, Richard 126, 127, 131
Bowler, P. 46
Braudel, Fernand 35
Britain 193, 196
British Military Administration (BMA) 6, 104, 111, 113, 118
Brown, W. 151
Burnett, Peter H. 21
Buthelezi, Mangosuthu 168

capitalism 76, 79–81
capitalization process 80
CAS. *See* Centre for African Studies (CAS)
caste in India 133–4
CBR. *See* Centre for Basic Research (CBR)
centralized bureaucracy, Ethiopia 111–13
centralized despotism 144
Centre for African Studies (CAS) 13
Centre for Basic Research (CBR) 12, 13
Chakrabarty, Dipesh 39
Chatterjee, Partha 8, 97, 127, 128, 158, 215
Chege, Michael 28, 215
Chen, Kuan-Hsing 4
Christianity 49, 49 n.5, 52, 53
Christians, women's land rights 66
Citizen and Subject: Contemporary Africa and the Legacy of Late Colonialism (Mamdani) 1–4, 7, 13–14, 16, 27–42, 45, 85, 103, 123, 124, 128, 135, 155–7, 163–7, 169, 189, 210–12
Chege on 28
critique from the historians 213–15
defying convention 30
indexation and criticism 36–8

legacy of late colonialism 39–41
metaphysics of difference 33–6
political critique 215–16
citizenship
contemporary challenge in Ethiopia 105–7
exigencies and requirements 40
civility 98
civilized nations 193, 194
civilizing mission 88–90, 94, 95
Claassens, Aninka 161, 168
Clapham, C. 105, 117
Clark, J. C. D. 54
CLRA. *See* Communal Land Rights Act (CLRA) of 2004
CLRB. *See* Communal Land Rights Bill (CLRB)
CODESA. *See* Convention for a Democratic South Africa (CODESA)
CODESRIA. *See* Council for the Development of Social Science Research in Africa (CODESRIA)
Cohen, Felix 21
Cohn, Bernard 133
collective rights 73
colonial
legacies 144–8
modernity 97
natives 174
rule 149–50
colonialism 86–9, 93–4, 97–100, 123–4, 202
in Africa 13
and challenges to identitarian politics 142–4
defined 123
Ethiopia 108
genetic mapping of 28
indirect rule 215
problem of 96
settler 20–2
structural legacy of 211
violence and repression of 95
violent legacies of 152
colonized 176
colonizers 176
Coloured Labour Preference Act 183

Coloured Labour Preference Area
  Policy 181
Coloured people/Coloureds 7, 173–4,
  173 n.1, 176, 181–4
Comaroff, Jean 3–4
Comaroff, John 3–4
Communal Land Rights Act (CLRA) of
  2004 161
Communal Land Rights Bill (CLRB) 161
community rights 79
Convention for a Democratic South Africa
  (CODESA) 19
Cooper, Frederick 85, 200, 214
Copans, J. 28
Copts 51–2
Corps Bastaard Hottentotten 183
Council for the Development of Social
  Science Research in Africa
  (CODESRIA) 10–12, 17
counter-majoritarian tactics and
  institutions 136
Cousins, Ben 78, 161, 162
creoles 176
crude instrumentalism 169
culture 37
  national 52
  politicization of 15
curriculum reform 24
customary laws 5, 13, 21, 35, 212–13,
  216
  in India 63–4, 74–6
customary rights 210, 212

DA. *See* Democratic Alliance (DA)
Dalits 62
Daly, M. W. 91
Dayabhaga school of law 65 n.2
dead capital 77
decentralized despotism 5, 6, 86–7, 114,
  155, 165, 167
decolonization 38, 90, 98–100, 126, 133,
  135–6, 185
  failure of 97
  of universities 22–5
decolonizing political theory 127–30
Define and Rule: Native as Political Identity
  (Mamdani) 17
democracy 7, 125–9, 135–7
  decolonized 136

defining 130–2
electoral competition 133–4
founding or constitutional
  moments 133–4
moral-psychological shift 135
Democratic Alliance (DA) 159
democratic government 131–2
democratic majoritarianism 6, 126–7,
  134–7
democratic politics 128–9, 131, 133–5
democratic voting 135
democratization 13, 89, 106, 118,
  123, 125, 135, 142, 145, 156,
  157
demographic-democratic
  imaginary 133–4
Deng, F. M. 91
deracialization 123, 124, 126, 135,
  145–7, 157, 158, 164, 165
Derg 104–7, 115–17
Deshmukh, G. V. 69
De Soto, Hernando 76–9
despotism
  decentralized 5, 6, 86–7, 114, 155,
    165, 167
  endurance of 156–7
De Tocqueville, Alexis 88, 132, 136
detribalization 148
direct rule 144, 145, 155, 156, 167, 212,
  213. *See also* indirect rule
discipline 55–6
  humanities 23, 30, 31
  social sciences 30, 31
divide-and-rule tactics 92, 98
DIY colonialism 86–8, 100
Dladla, Barney 165
domestication mission 95
Donham, D. 112
double consciousness 30
Drysdale, J. 114
Dual Mandate (Lugard) 178–9
Du Bois, W. E. B. 30, 145 n.1
Dunn, John 130–1, 130 n.3
Durban strikes 165
Durkheim, Emile 35, 38

East India Company 86, 87, 191–2
economic liberalism 143
egalitarianism 135, 137

Egypt 87–9
  De Soto's study on 77
  European colonial rule in 47–9, 51,
    52
Egyptian nationalism 91, 92
Eiselen, W. M. 181
El-Affendi, Abdelwahab 5, 215
electoral democracy 53
ELF. *See* Eritrean Liberation Front (ELF)
ELM. *See* Eritrean Liberation Movement
    (ELM)
emancipatory politics 142, 147
  feminist 6–7, 147, 150–2
emergence of Ethiopian nation 107–9
empire's law 196
endurance of despotism 156–7
Enlightenment 46, 50
enslavement 90, 94
Environment Protection Act (1986) 73
EPLF. *See* Eritrean People's Liberation
    Front (EPLF)
EPRDF. *See* Ethiopian People's
    Revolutionary Democratic
    Front (EPRDF)
Eritrea 106–7
  emergence of 111–13
  nationalism 112, 116
Eritrean Liberation Front (ELF) 116
Eritrean Liberation Movement
    (ELM) 117
Eritrean People's Liberation Front
    (EPLF) 106, 116
ethical disarmament 94–6
ethical supremacism 94
Ethiopia 6
  Amhara identity 103–7, 110–15, 117
  centralized bureaucracy 111–12
  contemporary challenge of
    citizenship 105–7
  emergence of Eritrea and
    Hararge 111–13
  empire state and emergence of
    nation 107–9
    international boundaries 109–10
  ethnic-based citizenship in 106
  ethnic federalism 212, 217
  history and culture of 114
  internal situation 111
  Italian occupation 110–11

national identity 103–7, 110
1942 provincial administrative
    decree 112
polity 108–9
power and authority 112
Somali region 106
Somalis and 114
sovereignty 109–12
Soviet military support 116–17
Tigrayans 106
two imperial orders of 1943 112
US military assistance to 115–17
Ethiopian People's Revolutionary
    Democratic Front
    (EPRDF) 105, 106
Ethiopian Revolution in 1974 117
ethnic
  citizenship 106
  federalism 105, 106, 212, 217
  identity 133, 149, 182
ethnicity 5, 124–5, 141, 157, 176–7, 182,
    212, 214
  politicization of 7, 150
ethnicization 144–8
ethnicized, gendered violence 148–50
Euro-America 45
Eurocentrism 31, 37
European
  imperialism 195
  modernization 97
  powers 191–5
  territorial acquisitions 193

fair discrimination 182
family of the nations 191, 193, 194,
    194 n.3, 195, 199
Fanon, Frantz 180, 185
female feticide 65
feminist emancipatory politics 6–7, 147,
    150
  liberalism's challenges for 151–2
Fisher, Michael 192
Forest Conservation Act (1980) 72
Forest Rights Act of 2006 (FRA) 72–4
forests communities, land rights to 71–4
Foucault, Michel 177, 210, 211, 215
  governmentality 45, 52–7
founding or constitutional moments 133
FRA. *See* Forest Rights Act of 2006 (FRA)

Freund, Bill 29
Friedman, Steven 7
*From Citizen to Refugee: Uganda Asians
    Come to Britain* (Mamdani) 11
Fulani of Northern Nigeria 178

Gatvol Capetonians 174 n.2
gendered bifurcation of the state 144–8
gendered violence 6–7, 144, 148–50
genocide 20–1, 124
    Rwandan 14–15
Geschiere, Peter 181
Ghali, Boutros 91
Gilkes, P. 116
*Good Muslim, Bad Muslim: America, the
    Cold War and the Roots of Terror*
    (Mamdani) 15
Gordon, Charles 94
Goswami, Manu 197
governance 96
governmentality 45, 52–7
governmental rationality 96, 97
Gram Sabhas 73
Griqua 174, 182
Grovogui, Siba N'Zatioula 4
Guha, R. 69
Gupta, Smita 62

habitus, Bourdieu's concept of 35
Haile, Tedla 113–14
Haksar, Nandita 75–6
Hall, Stuart 181
Hamas 99, 100
Hamitic hypothesis 177–8
Hararge, emergence of 111–13
Hastings, Lord 192
Hegel, G. W. F. 30, 35, 39
Hertzog, J.B.M. 181
Hindu Gains of Learning Bill (1930) 68
Hindu laws 67–70
Hindu Marriage Act (1955) 70
Hindu Married Women's Rights to
    Property Bill (1937) 69
Hindu Succession Act of 1956
    (HSA) 64–5, 68, 70
Hindu undivided family (HUF) 66–7
Hindu Women's Right to Property Act
    (1937) 70
Hobbes, T. 54, 178

Hoffman, Danny 179–80
Holcomb, B. 108
Holden, P. 148
Horn of Africa 108, 111, 112, 115, 117
"house negro" 180
"housewifization" 146 n.3
HSA. *See* Hindu Succession Act of 1956
    (HSA)
HUF. *See* Hindu undivided family (HUF)
humanitarian intervention 94, 95
humanity 23, 30, 31
human rights 142, 201
Husain, Taha 95

Ibssa, S. 108
identity
    African 179–80
    ethnic and racial 133
    politicization of 124, 125, 130, 132,
        133, 135–6
    politics 151, 152
imagined communities 104, 107
Imperialism and Fascism in Uganda
    (Mamdani) 12
imperial power 190, 194, 196
    Ethiopia 115–17
India 125
    democracy 135
    democratic politics 129, 134
    politicization of castes 134
    Sepoy Rebellion 86, 87
    voter turnout rates 129
Indian(s) 175–6, 182, 184
    racism 184
Indian land rights. *See also* women, land
        rights
    Adivasis 62–3
    community ownership 74
    customary laws 63–4, 74–6
    Dalits 62
    De Soto's program 76–8
    environmental jurisprudence 72
    Forest Rights Act of 2006 (FRA)
        72–4
    forests and tribal communities 71–4
    gender equality 64
    Hindu Succession Act 64–5, 68, 70
    Indian Forest Acts (1878) 63, 72
    Indian Forest Acts (1927) 63, 64, 72

individual rights to land   75, 78–80
land acquisition   79–80
Land Acquisition Act   69, 72
National Forest Policy (1894 &
      1952)   72
nation-state and modernizing of
      property   69–71
personal laws   63, 67, 71
title deeds (joint *pattas*)   62, 64, 75
tribes   74-6
widows' rights to their husbands'
      property   70
zamindari system   70
Indian Removal Act   20
Indian subcontinent, law of nations
      in   195, 196
indigenous   174
   races   178
   tribes   176
indirect rule   86–8, 90–3, 97, 113, 128,
      144–5, 183, 212, 215–18
individualization of populations   52–7
individual rights to land   75, 78–80
Institute for Development Studies   24
Institute for Liberty and Democracy   76
institutionalization   183
institutional segregation   45
internal conflicts   98
international boundaries, Ethiopia   109–10
internationalism of non-aligned
      movement   200–2
international law   189, 191, 193
international organizations   199
intimate particularism   127
Islamic University of Azhar   51
Islamization   179, 180
Italian occupation, Ethiopia   110–11
Italian Somaliland boundary   109–10

Jackson, Andrew   20
Jacob, M. C.   50
James, W.   112
Janu, K.   62
Janus-faced metaphysics of
      difference   33–6
Jayakar, Mukundrao Ramrao   68
Jefferson, Thomas   20
Jessop, Bob   169
justice   15, 18–19, 142–6, 182, 185

Kammas (caste)   134
Kasimis, Demetra   133
Kaunda, Kenneth   99
Keller, E.   104
Khoi   173, 174, 182, 183
Kishwar, Madhu   70, 75
Kodoth, Pravina   68
Koselleck, R.   50
Koskenniemi, Martti   193, 195
Krishnamachari, T. T.   70
Kumar, Shailendra   65
KwaZulu-Natal   160, 162, 163, 166, 168,
      173, 214

land
   acquisition   79–80
   reforms in Zimbabwe   182
Land Acquisition Act (1894)   69, 72
land rights, in India. *See* Indian land rights
land titling programs   78
law of nations
   in the East   190–7
   the Indian subcontinent   195, 196
League of Nations   197–200
Lefebvre, J.   115
legacy of late colonialism   39–41
legal positivism   191, 193
Lenin, Vladimir Ilyich   197
Leviathan (Hobbes)   178
Levien, Michael   79, 80
liberal
   Anglicanism   49 n.5
   democracy   56, 131–2, 143, 147
   human rights   151
   individualism   143
liberalism   89–90, 143
live capital   77
living customary law   77–8
Lugard, Frederick   37, 177–9, 181
Lyons, T.   115

Machiavelli, Niccolo   37, 56, 178, 215
Madison, James   131
Mahdist revolution   92–4
Mahmood, Saba   51
Mahtab, B.   65
Maine, Henry   67
majorities/majoritarianism   6, 52, 126–7,
      131–2, 134–7

Makerere Institute of Social Research
    (MISR)   17, 41
Mamdani, Mahmood   3–5, 7, 9, 85, 93,
    97, 123–6, 135–6, 141, 142, 150,
    157–68, 189
    A. C. Jordan Chair in African Studies-
        CAS, UCT   13
    "Between the public intellectual and
        the scholar"   22–5
    "Beyond Nuremberg"   18–19
    bifurcated state   128, 145, 155–7
    centralized despotism   144
    Centre for Basic Research (CBR)   12,
        13
    Citizen and Subject (*see Citizen
        and Subject: Contemporary
        Africa and the Legacy of Late
        Colonialism*)
    citizenship   12
    at CODESRIA   11–12, 17
    colonialism definition   123
    colonizers and colonized   176
    decentralized despotism   87
    decolonization and   25, 136
    *Define and Rule: Native as Political
        Identity*   17
    despotism definition   89
    educational background   9–10
    endurance of despotism   156–7
    From Citizen to Refugee   11
    Good Muslim, Bad Muslim   15
    *Imperialism and Fascism in
        Uganda*   12
    intimate particularism   127
    at Makerere Institute of Social
        Research (MISR)   17
    "Mamdani Affair"   14
    The Myth of Population Control   11
    Neither Settler nor Native   18
    political consciousness   10
    *Politics and Class Formation in
        Uganda*   11
    races and ethnicities   176–7
    racial privilege   146
    return to Uganda   12
    Saviors and Survivors   16
    Scholars in the Marketplace   17
    "Settler colonialism: Then and
        now"   20–2

style of thinking   14
subject races   7, 174, 176–7
urban/rural divide   103
vocation   37
"When does a settler become a
    native?"   14
When Victims Become Killers
    14–15
mandated territories   198–9
mandatory powers   198
Mann, M.   126–7
Mantena, Karuna   6
Markakis, J.   106, 111, 112,
    118
marriage reform   67
Marx, Karl   11, 30
Marxism   11
Matshanda, Namhla Thando   6
Matshiqi, Aubrey   164
Mbembe, Achille   4
Mboya, Tom   146
Menelik II   108–10
Menon, Nivedita   5
mestizos   176
metaphysics of difference   33–6
military junta. *See* Derg
Mill, John Stuart   131, 136
Milner, Alfred   48–9
minorities   51–2, 125, 127, 135–7
    racial   164, 169
    rights   200
    subject   182
    whites   144, 164
MISR. *See* Makerere Institute of Social
    Research (MISR)
Mitakshara school of law   65, 65 n.2
Mitchell, Timothy   76–8, 197
Mnisi, Sindiso   77–8
mode of exploitation   165
modern democracy   126, 130–2
modernizing of property   69–71
Modi, Narendra   73
moral disarmament   95, 96
moral-psychological shift   135
Mouffe, C.   143
Muslim law   67–8
Muslims   15, 51–2
    women's land rights   66
Muzondidya, James   174, 182

The Mystery of Capital (De Soto)   76
The Myth of Population Control: Family,
    Caste and Class in an Indian
    Village (Mamdani)   11

Naga Mothers' Association   75
Nair, Mira   12
Nair women's property rights   68
Nasser, Gamal Abdel   47, 93
national democratic revolution   169
National Forest Policy (1894)   72
national identity of Ethiopia   103–7
national imaginary of Ethiopia   107–10
National Resistance Army (NRA)
    210
National Resistance Movement
    (NRM)   216
nation-state   18, 22, 45, 52, 69–71, 107,
    108, 128, 145, 148
   normalization of   197–200
   radicalized masculinity of   148–9
native
   administration   18
   identities   175
   political identity of   18
   settler *vs.*   14, 20
Native policy   181
Natives Land Act   21
Negash, T.   112
Negro problem   145 n.1
Nehru, Jawaharlal   69, 70
Neither Settler nor Native: The Making
    and Unmaking of Permanent
    Minorities (Mamdani)   18, 125,
    126, 128, 135–6
neocolonialism   12, 22, 142, 144
neoliberalism   25
Newbigin, Eleanor   66–8
"new extractivism"   81
Nigam, Aditya   79
9/11 attack   15
non-aligned movement, internationalism
    of   200–2
non-racialism   184
non-Western politics   128
the North   4, 158
North, D., path dependence   158
NRA. *See* National Resistance Army
    (NRA)

NRM. *See* National Resistance Movement
    (NRM)
Ntsebeza, Lungisile   162
Nuremberg model   19–20
Nyamnjoh, Francis   181
Nyerere, Mwalimu Julius   11

Obote, Milton   12
Ogadeen   114–15
Ogaden National Liberation Front
    (ONLF)   106
ontogeny   31
Oppenheim, Lassa   194
Organisation of African Unity (OAU)   5
Ossome, Lyn   6–7
The Other Path (De Soto)   76

Pal, Rajaram   65
Palestine Liberation Organization
    (PLO)   99, 100
Pankhurst, R.   113
Parsi, women's land rights   66
partial deracialization   158
partial freedom   96–8
Patel, Vallabhbhai   197
path dependence   158
Pedersen, Susan   199
personal laws   63, 67, 71
Petras, J.   81
Pillay, Suren   7, 127
Pitts, J.   90
political
   identities   3, 124, 179–80, 184
   liberalism   143
   rationality   96–7
   violence   3
political science   40
politicization
   of castes   134
   egalitarian   135
   of ethnicity   7, 150
   of identity   124, 125, 130, 132, 133,
    135–6
Politics and Class Formation in Uganda
    (Mamdani)   11
Politics as a Vocation (Weber)   36,
    55
post-apartheid South Africa   8, 14, 19,
    157, 162, 173, 183

Coloured populations in 173–4, 181–2
state and economy 167–70
postcolonial 1, 3–6, 13
  Africa 13, 14, 17, 27–42
  democracy 132–7
  feminisms 141
  politics 128
  sovereignty 41
  violence 16
post-independence period 216
power relations 158
property titling 76–8
Provincializing Europe (Chakrabarty) 39

quasi-sovereignty 195

race 124, 125, 141, 146, 164, 176–8. *See also* ethnicity
racial
  discrimination 23, 212
  domination 164, 169
  exclusion 123, 124
  identity 133, 182
  minorities 164, 169
  polarization 123–4
  privilege 146
racial difference. *See* rule of colonial difference
radicalized masculinity 148–9
Ramaphosa, Cyril 164, 165
Ramdas, S. 73
Rao, Ramachandra 68
Reagan, Ronald 15
Reddys (caste) 134
Registration of Natives Regulations of 1895 175
Reid, R. 111, 113
religion 53
religious freedom 52
Renaissance 31
representative democracy 131, 132
representative government 131
reproduction of the colony 149–50
resistance movements 184
Restitution of Land Rights Amendment Act 163
Right to Fair Compensation and Transparency in Land

Acquisition, Rehabilitation and Resettlement Act (LARRA) 79
Robins, Steven 167–8
Roesch, J. 148
Rousseau, Jean-Jacques 131, 137
rule of colonial difference 97
rural despotism 169
Rwandan genocide 14–15

Samatar, A. 106
Sanders, Edith 177
Sangwan, Kishan Singh 65
Sarkar, Sumit 71, 72
Saroj, Tufani 65
"Save Darfur Movement" 16
Saviors and Survivors: Darfur, Politics and the War on Terror (Mamdani) 16
Scheduled Tribes Act (2006) 72
Schmitt, Carl 55, 196
Scholars in the Marketplace: The Dilemma of Neo-Liberal Reform at Makerere University, 1989-2005 (Mamdani) 17
Schwartzberg, M. 136
Scott, David 96–7
"second Adwa" 107
Secorum, Laura 183
secular citizen(ship) 46–52
Selassie, Haile 104, 105, 110–11, 113, 114, 116, 117
self-determination 40, 116, 126, 130, 197, 200, 201, 216–17
self-realization 40–1
Seligman, Charles 177
settler
  colonialism 20–2
  identities 175
  vs. native 14, 20
"Settler colonialism: Then and now" (Mamdani) 20–2
Shariat Act of 1937 66
Shariat law 67, 69
Shivji, Issa 209, 210
Singh, Manmohan 76
Sjaastad, E. 78
Skinner, Quentin 54, 178
social scientific disciplines 30
society of states 193

soft power 95
Somalis 114–15
   independence 114–15
   nationalism 104, 111, 114–16
(the) South 1, 3, 4, 69, 128
South Africa
   apartheid 21, 27–8, 32, 149, 157,
      160–6, 183–4, 211–12
   bifurcation: key features of the
      society 158–60
         revitalizing traditional
            authority 162–4
         town and countryside 160–2
   CODESA 19
   democratization 136, 142, 156, 157
   dominant party polity 158–60
   endurance of despotism 156–7
   labor and urbanization 157
   labor law 181
   land restitution 163
   land rights 161
   migrant labor 165–6
   townships and shack settlements 159
   traditional councils 160–1
   transatlantic slave trade in 13–14
   2016 local elections 168
   urban revolt 157
   urban-rural conflict 156, 164–7
   violence in 179–80
   voter turnout rates 128–9
   white minority 164
South African Cape Corps 183
South African Human Rights Commission
   (SAHRC) 173
South Asiatic Federation 200
sovereign states 191, 196
sovereignty 8, 40–1, 54–6, 55 n.10,
      109–12, 126, 130–4, 136–7,
      190–8, 200, 201, 218
   definition of 143
Soviet Union 116–17, 195, 200
Special Marriage Act (1872) 67
Speke, John 177
Stalin, Joseph 99
Steinberg, Johnny 155–8, 163–4
subject minorities 182
subject races 7–8, 174, 176, 184, 185
subjugation 85
Sudan, sources of colonial power 91–4

"Sudan for the Sudanese" 93
suicide, Durkheim's study of 38
Sukarno 202
superpowers 195, 200
superstition 46, 46 n.1
Super-Tax Act (1917) 67
"survival" 179–80

Tanzania, radical social transformation
      in 11
Tareke, G. 117
TCB. *See* Traditional Courts Bill (TCB)
Temple, Frederick 49 n.5
territorial acquisitions 193
Third World 9, 11
Tignor, Robert L. 29
Tigrayan People's Liberation Front
      (TPLF) 105, 106, 116
Tigrayans 106
Tipe, T. 161
title deeds (joint *pattas*) 62, 64, 75
titling (property) 76–8
Touval, S. 108
TPLF. *See* Tigrayan People's Liberation
      Front (TPLF)
Traditional and Khoi-San Leadership
      Bill 163
traditional authority 160–4
Traditional Courts Bill (TCB) 162–4,
      169
Traditional Leadership and Governance
      Framework Act (TLGFA) of
      2003 160–1
Treaty of Westphalia 189, 196
tribal communities
   landowning patterns 74–6
   land rights to 71–4
tribalism 21, 89, 94, 179, 209, 212
tribalization 148–50
tribes 16, 20, 134, 212
Tronvoll, K. 104, 107
Tuck, R. 131–2, 136, 137
Turkey, democracy of 135
Tutsi 182

uncivilized nations 193, 194
underdevelopment 97, 123, 211
United Nations Security Council 202
United Progressive Alliance (UPA) 79

United States   195, 200
    American settler colonialism   20–2
    legislative sovereignty   136
    military assistance to Ethiopia   115–
        17
    9/11 attack   15
    "Save Darfur Movement"   16
universal suffrage   129
universities
    curriculum reform   24
    decolonization of   22–5
    European model   22–3
    humanities, European tradition of   23
    Humboldt University of Berlin   23
    Islamic University of Azhar   51
    University of Al Azhar   23
    University of Dar es Salaam   24
UPA. *See* United Progressive Alliance
    (UPA)
urban economy, South Africa   167–8
urban-rural conflict   156
    South Africa   156, 164–7

Vagrancy Act of 1893   175
Van Griethuysen, Pascal   80
Varrie, Larry Fazel   183
Veltmeyer, H.   81
Verwoerd, Hendrik   181
violence   3, 6–7, 85, 94–6, 133, 135,
    173–4, 185
    in Africa   179–80
    ethnicized, gendered   148–50
    gendered   144
Von Trotha, T.   89–90
voter turnout rates   128–9
voting   129, 131, 135, 137

Washington, George   20
wealth redistribution   129
Weber, C.   109
Weber, Max   39, 56
    on citizenship   40
    criticism of *Citizen and Subject*   30, 35
    Politics as a Vocation   36, 55

Wellesley, Lord   192
the West   16, 31–2, 69
Western Somali Liberation Front
    (WSLF)   116
Westlake, John   193
Westphalian system   89
the West/Western political theory   178
When Victims Become Killers
    (Mamdani)   124, 128
When Victims Become Killers: Colonialism,
    Nativism, and the Genocide in
    Rwanda (Mamdani)   14–15
white settler   175
Wilder, Gary   200
Wilson, Woodrow   197
Wolde-Mariam, M.   110
women
    land rights   61, 80–1
        in Hindu laws   67–70
        Muslim/Parsi/Christian   66
        Nair women   68
        organizations for   75
        in personal laws   64–6
        in tribal societies   74–6
        widows' rights to their husbands'
          property   70
    oppression of   148, 151–2
    political activism   149
    in post-independence Kenya   146
    rights   151
    subordinate status   151
WSLF. *See* Western Somali Liberation
    Front (WSLF)

Yadav, Yogendra   135
Young, J.   116
Ypi, Lea   85
Yuzo, Mizoguchi   17

Zaghloul, Saad   93
zamindari land rights   70
Zewde, B.   108, 110, 112
Zimbabwe, land reform in   182
Zuma, Jacob   162–4, 173

www.ingramcontent.com/pod-product-compliance
Lightning Source LLC
Chambersburg PA
CBHW070405270326
41926CB00014B/2704